THE CRIMINAL PERSONALITY

The
Criminal Personality

Volume III: The Drug User

by

SAMUEL YOCHELSON, Ph.D., M.D.

and

STANTON E. SAMENOW, Ph.D.

Clinical Psychologist, Alexandria, Virginia

A JASON ARONSON BOOK

ROWMAN & LITTLEFIELD PUBLISHERS, INC.
Lanham • Boulder • New York • Toronto • Oxford

In Memory of
Dr. Samuel Yochelson

The views expressed by the authors do not necessarily reflect the opinions, official policy, or position of Saint Elizabeth's Hospital, the National Institute of Mental Health, the Alcohol, Drug Abuse, and Mental Health Administration, or the U.S. Department of Health, Education, and Welfare.

Samuel Yochelson, Ph.D., M.D.
Stanton E. Samenow, Ph.D.

A JASON ARONSON BOOK
ROWMAN & LITTLEFIELD PUBLISHERS, INC.

Published in the United States of America
by Rowman & Littlefield Publishers, Inc.
A wholly owned subsidiary of The Rowman & Littlefield Publishing Group, Inc.
4501 Forbes Boulevard, Suite 200, Lanham, Maryland 20706
www.rowmanlittlefield.com

PO Box 317
Oxford
OX2 9RU, UK

Library of Congress Cataloging-in-Publication Data

Yochelson, Samuel 1906–1976
   The criminal personality.

   Contents: v.1. A profile for change.
v.2. The change process.
v.3. Our odyssey with the drug-using criminal.
   Includes bibliographies and index.
   1. Criminal psychology—Collected works. I. Samenow, Stanton E., 1941– , joint author. II. Title. [DNLM: 1. Criminal psychology.
HV 6080 Y54c]
ISBN 0-87668-901-2 (hardcover)
ISBN 1-56821-244-5 (softcover)   75-13507

Printed in the United States of America

Contents

Preface

THIS BOOK IS the third in the series *The Criminal Personality*. The material in this volume, as in the others, is based on the research conducted by the late Dr. Samuel Yochelson. A psychiatrist, Dr. Yochelson spent the last fifteen years of his life (1961–1976) as Director of the Program for the Investigation of Criminal Behavior at Saint Elizabeths Hospital in Washington, D.C. His goal was to understand the causes of criminal behavior and, more important, to find a method by which he could help lawbreakers become responsible citizens. At Dr. Yochelson's invitation, I joined the program in 1970.

The first chapter of Volume I is titled "The Reluctant Converts." The title refers not to the criminals Dr. Yochelson studied and treated but, rather, to himself and to me. We were reluctant to abandon concepts and procedures that we had used and found effective in earlier work with responsible people who were emotionally disturbed. But abandon the familiar we did. For as Dr. Yochelson conducted what he retrospectively referred to as a "search," not a "re-search," he developed a new, detailed understanding of who the criminal is and of the necessity of adopting different methods of dealing with him. Volume I contains a detailed profile of the criminal's thinking patterns — how the criminal views himself and the world. Volume II presents the approach development by Dr. Yochelson as he helped criminals become responsible citizens.

This third volume about the drug-using criminal, outlined before Dr. Yochelson's death in 1976, also draws exclusively from his findings. The book was written between late 1976 and mid-1978, and I have recently updated sections of it. For their help in this project, I would like to thank Mr. John Lewin for his work as research assistant and Mrs. Sylvia L. Samenow for her editorial suggestions.

Since Dr. Yochelson's death, I have been in practice as a psychologist and consultant, having left Saint Elizabeths Hospital in 1978. In my clinical work, while evaluating and counseling offenders, I repeatedly have found confirmation of Dr. Yochelson's concepts and procedures. Although criminals' preferences for specific drugs have changed somewhat over time (largely based on availability of particular substances), Dr. Yochelson's insight into the role drugs play in criminals' lives remains unique and penetrating. In Volume III, I endeavor to present this remarkable man's findings in the hope that they will be useful to others.

STANTON E. SAMENOW, PH.D.

THE CRIMINAL PERSONALITY

Chapter 1

Our Odyssey with
the Drug-Using Criminal

THIS BOOK IS ABOUT criminals who are also alcohol or drug users. Their substance abuse is simply one of many manifestations of their antisocial patterns of behavior. It is important that the reader understand that the focus of this volume will be only on criminals; it does not address alcohol or illegal drug use in the general population.

In our first volume, *The Criminal Personality: A Profile for Change,* we presented a new profile of the criminal. We described in detail fifty-two features of his thinking that must be corrected in order for him to change.* In the second volume, *The Criminal Personality: The Change Process,* we presented new techniques for achieving this change. The format of this program, in which choice and will are operational, requires criminals to report their thinking daily in a phenomenological system. Our original projection was to present in two volumes the findings of a fifteen-year study of criminals. During that time, however, a vast amount of information was accumulated that provided an important addition to the understanding of the drug-using criminal. This necessitated a third volume.

The profile presented in Volume I applies both to criminals who use drugs and to those who do not. Described in Volume II is an approach to the process of helping both groups become responsible citizens. In this book, we discuss the drug-using criminal's way of life, his decisions to use drugs, effects of drugs in altering his mental states, and his tastes and preferences in selecting drugs. We delineate the special problems that were encountered in the effort to help criminals change. We also elaborate on concepts such as the *high, nod, rush, craving,* and *addiction* in terms of their cognitive components.

The present volume also contains two reviews of literature in the field. Chapter 2 highlights controversies over the causes of drug use and the effects

---

*As we indicated in our earlier volumes, we have conducted an in-depth study during which we have spent as many as 8,000 hours with individual participants. (A breakdown of the time spent is presented in Chapter 3 of Volume I.)

on the user of particular classes of drugs. Chapter 7 presents a conceptual overview of approaches that have been utilized in treating drug users.

Most behavioral patterns can be described as extending along a continuum in terms of their frequency and severity. More than a dozen years ago, the National Commission on Marihuana and Drug Abuse (1973, pp. 95–98) stated that "drug-taking behavior" (as the Commission termed it) should be considered in terms of a continuum ranging from "experimental use" to "compulsive drug use."* The Commission listed five categories of drug abuse in its delineation of the continuum: experimental use, social-recreational use, circumstantial-situational use, intensified use, compulsive use. Clearly, there is a big difference between the college student who tries marijuana just to see what it is like and the drug-dependent heroin user.

This book is not about people who experiment with drugs; neither is it about the so-called "recreational user" who lights up a marijuana cigarette on a weekend. From the beginning of our study in 1961, we worked with *criminals,* both drug users and nonusers. Each one was in crime long before he became involved with drugs. Early in our investigation, we focused on criminal patterns other than illicit drug use. Our view was that drug use was a relatively insignificant crime compared with the murders, rapes, assaults, and other felonies that our criminals had committed. In fact, at the very beginning of the study, we did not know which participants were drug users. As we took detailed histories, this information emerged.

We found no qualitative difference between the backgrounds of the drug-using criminals and those criminals who were not users. In each group, we found similar types of experiences and patterns of behavior in the family, in the community, at school, at work, in military service, in crime, and in confinement.

It turned out that we had a potpourri of drug users and of nonusers. Our sample of users included wealthy and poor, well-educated and grade school dropouts, young and middle-aged, blacks and whites. It included those from stable homes and those from broken homes, and those from diverse religious backgrounds. As was the case with the nonusers, the users in our study ranged from those who had been arrested repeatedly to those who had never been apprehended. In the latter group, we soon found that, without exception, each member had committed hundreds of serious crimes.† We found that the drug-use patterns of our criminals encompassed a broad spectrum —

---

*National Commission on Marihuana and Drug Abuse (1973). *Drug Use in America: Problem in Perspective.* Second Report of the National Commission on Marihuana and Drug Abuse. Washington, D.C.: Government Printing Office.

†For more information on the extent of arrestability of participants in our study, see Chapter 3 of Volume I.

opiates, stimulants, depressants, hallucinogens, volatile substances, marijuana, and alcohol.

We reported in Volume I that our sample consisted of 255 male criminals.
If we were to establish the use of alcohol as our minimal criterion of drug use,
we would be speaking in this volume of the entire 255. Although alcohol is a
mind-altering substance, we are including here only those criminals who have
used other substances as well. The following is the breakdown of drug use
among the 121 people who are the subjects of this volume:

Opiates (e.g., heroin)	78	Marijuana	85
Cocaine	21	Hallucinogens (e.g., LSD)	40
Stimulants other than cocaine	38	Volatile substances	4
(e.g., amphetamines)		(e.g., glue)	
Depressants	28		
(e.g., barbiturates)			

The total figure is more than 121 because most of these people were polydrug
users.

THE MENTAL MAKEUP OF THE DRUG-USING CRIMINAL

Our objectives have been the same in working with drug users and
nonusers – to understand the makeup of the criminal and to help him to
change. In the course of our early work, criminals were providing us with excuses for committing crimes. The drug-using criminals presented the very
same reasons for using drugs that they offered to justify other crimes. Because we promised all participants in our study privileged communication
and played no administrative role in their lives, we naively believed that they
would have no reason to lie to us. Accordingly, we considered their reports
valid and recorded what they said. The statements they made were totally
compatible with current theories of crime causation.

The reason for crime most frequently cited was that the drug user was beset
by intolerable burdens of life; drugs were part of his desperate attempt to
cope with stress. The sources of such stress varied from person to person.
Many drug users poignantly described their struggles to cope with poverty,
family disorganization, lack of opportunity, and racial discrimination.
Those from upper-income homes discussed family turmoil and a variety of
overwhelming pressures in the community, school, or at work. All drug users
described life as being an unrelenting series of "hassles" with parents,
teachers, employers, and sex partners. If the world was not treating them
badly at a particular time, they complained of intolerable boredom and of a

life that seemed meaningless. Invariably, the drug user and nonuser described the same phenomena. And we found their explanations credible. Drug use was simply one other way, and a relatively effortless one, to cope with disadvantage and distress. It seemed logical to us that environmental factors were directly related to drug use, just as we believed they were to other forms of crime. In fact, drug-using inmates of the hospital's forensic division convinced us that conditions at the hospital were having a corrosive effect on them, virtually driving them to use drugs to make life in confinement tolerable. Although we opposed their drug use, we were sympathetic to their plight.

Our drug users asserted that their irresponsibility and frank criminality were, in part, efforts to gain a sense of belonging and acceptance that had eluded them at home, at school, and in the community at large. Those from neighborhoods where drugs were easily available contended that the drug-using crowd offered what they were looking for. Using drugs was one way to be "in." To turn down drugs was to become an outcast. Others from different kinds of neighborhoods admitted that it was by their own choice and initiative that they traveled to other areas to seek excitement and found drugs available there. All participants in our study, drug users and nonusers alike, found companionship with those who, like themselves, were violators. From our study of criminals' thinking patterns, we believed that they all, but particularly the drug users, were easily influenced by others. After an early interview, we wrote: "He's in the role of a little boy, anxious to please, wanting to be accepted. The underlying weakness, the suggestibility, the starvation for a friend comes into play."*

Only retrospectively did we recognize our naiveté in the early days of our study when we believed what the criminal told us about his motivation for doing the things that he had done. We were looking for the *roots* of crime and in this quest spent countless hours probing for psychological conflict and unconscious motivation. It seemed obvious to us that criminality was a way in which our participants had tried to cope with intrapsychic conflict. The drug user, in particular, had found instant relief through drugs. Drugs offered an antidote to depression and relief from a sense of despair about one's own worthlessness. We described one man as follows: "Barbiturates don't make him feel big, great, or important, but they make him feel a little less acutely about his being a nothing." Drug users averred that they used drugs to cope with anxiety. Drugs had a calming influence, offering serenity and alleviation of tension. High on drugs, the criminal replaced anxiety with optimism. We noted: "It's only when you see the effect of the drug in producing calmness that you can understand the mixed up, lonely, confused state prior to drugs."

*In this chapter, all passages in quotation marks are from our early notes that were dictated and transcribed.

Drug users contended that drugs helped them to cope with a variety of other unpleasant states, including anger, disappointment, psychosomatic symptoms, and dependency. Indeed, when a man used drugs in the course of treatment, it sometimes seemed as though he did so because he was threatened by his dependence on us as therapists. In the conventional wisdom, drugs were said to offer a quick escape from painful mental states and to allow the user to function more comfortably. In fact, some claimed that drugs facilitated their acting responsibly. Again, we absorbed what the criminal told us believing that he demonstrated insight when he stated that he had acted irresponsibly by using drugs to ward off anxiety or depression. By valuing such insight, we tended to overlook the drug use itself. Of course, we did not approve of drug use, but by accepting the user's excuses, we appeared to condone it.

We believed then, as we worked with criminals, that they were ultimately defeating themselves. This was especially true of the drug user who, in addition to running all the usual risks by engaging in crime, was jeopardizing his freedom and health by drug use. The vicious circle was obvious. A man used drugs to escape a painful mental state or to remove himself from a disagreeable environment. As drugs became a more frequent solution, he developed a "habit," at least in the case of the opiate user. To support that habit, he committed more and more crimes, placing himself almost constantly in danger of arrest. The drug became a "monkey on my back." The user increased his criminal output so that he could buy more drugs, thus increasing the risk of apprehension. Furthermore, every time he obtained, possessed, or used a drug, he committed another criminal offense. Finally he was faced with staving off withdrawal symptoms and other physical difficulties consequent to drug use. To us, the whole business of using drugs appeared overwhelmingly self-defeating because it caused the criminal's life to become even more unstable and stressful than it would have been without drugs.

Because we had imposed our framework on his statements, we believed that the criminal was unconsciously defeating himself. At the time, we perceived all criminal behavior to be self-defeating and, in other ways, pathological. As stated in the first chapter of Volume I, we initially believed that the criminal was mentally ill, whether or not he used drugs. In fact, we regarded drugs as simply another manifestation of his psychopathology.

From the outset, drug use was not our focus. The criminals' rationale for drug use emerged with the rest of the material about why they committed crimes. Even when a criminal emphasized the importance of drugs in his life, we tended to overlook this because we were focusing on other issues. However, as we continued to take careful histories and to offer individual and group treatment to criminals, significant information about drug use began to accummulate. There was much to suggest that the drug user did more than escape from unpleasantness; drugs facilitated objectives that were difficult for him to achieve otherwise. Some users talked about the courage that drugs gave them to stand up to a fight. Others mentioned having greater sexual prowess with drugs. Some indicated that drugs helped them to summon the courage to commit acts that they had been afraid to commit in the past. At the time, we did not seek elaboration on such observations but simply noted them. Our interest was centered on crime patterns, not on drugs. To us, a theft was a theft and a rape was a rape; whether a criminal used drugs while committing a crime was of secondary significance.

It was our probing of criminal thinking patterns that eventually obliged us to examine more closely what drugs did for the criminal. Drug-using criminals averred that crime was a consequence of drug use. Like the nonusers, they maintained that they were decent people, not criminals. Illegal acts were committed only to support a habit to which they had hopelessly fallen victim. Users asserted that they were caught in a cycle of drugs, crime, more drugs, more crime. Indeed, some bewailed the "daily grind" that was necessary to support their habits. And another vicious cycle emerged, but this time of a different nature. They maintained that they had to commit crimes to support their habits. However, they often were afraid to commit those crimes. Drugs eliminated fear. Consequently, they used more and more drugs to commit increasingly serious crimes. "D* stated, as did the other men, that when he had to go through the daily grind, he had a lot of fear. He needed the money, but he was afraid to commit the crimes to obtain that money. Thus he needed drugs to get rid of the fear." The drug user contended furthermore that as his drug use increased, he had less control over his behavior and was totally at the mercy of his habit. That is what drug users told us, one after the other, and that is what we believed. It appeared to make sense that most crime committed by the drug user was directed solely to supporting a habit that had passed beyond the point of his control.

However, as the hours we were spending with these people accumulated, our belief that most of the drug user's crime was aimed at supporting his habit was shaken. We were finding that, *in every case,* the criminal had embarked on his life of crime very early. He was fighting, stealing, lying, and intimidating others as a child, long before he had direct experience with drugs. Our first major objection to what the criminal was telling us was based on the discovery that, although most had not been apprehended, all criminals who had used drugs had a long history of crime that antedated their use of drugs.

As already stated, material about drug use was emerging that we noted but did not pursue. One observation was that some people needed drugs to com-

---

*Throughout this volume, drug users cited in examples will be identified simply as "D."

mit crimes that others could commit without drugs.* The major break-through that facilitated our studying this phenomenon was our gradual rejection of sociologic and psychologic excuses for criminality. It was becoming increasingly apparent that we, and traditional psychiatry, were only offering criminals more excuses for their criminality. We abandoned the search for causation gradually as we saw that no condition or set of conditions could account adequately for an individual's turning to crime. We saw as crucial the role of individual choice (actually a series of choices). Disposing of sociologic and psychologic excuses permitted us to focus on the criminal's thinking, so that we could eventually evaluate how drugs affect thinking processes.

A simultaneous development in our work was the gradual alteration of our interviewing procedure. As we learned more about our subjects and increasingly were dismissing sociologic and psychologic excuses, we stopped asking open-ended questions.† Before questioning our subjects, we told them what we knew about their thinking and acting patterns. This new format of "you know that I know" helped us to probe more effectively and eliminated some of the obstructive tactics deployed by the person being interviewed. Consequently, we were in an even better position to study thinking patterns and, more specifically, thinking patterns related to drugs.

> "After he told me that he was a thief because he needed so much money for drugs, I told him that I was very interested in this, because he'd be the first one who would convince me that drugs were the cause of his stealing. Very quickly he broke down and said that he was a thief of every variety ever since he could remember."

We learned how the criminal began to use drugs after criminal patterns were firmly entrenched. As youngsters, criminals sought others like themselves and engaged in doing whatever was forbidden. Even in early adolescence, they knew of the potential dangers of drugs but disregarded this information. Some criminals, however, regarded using drugs as a sign of weakness and were reluctant to use them at all, even if legitimately prescribed. To use a drug was a putdown because it signified that they had to rely on something other than themselves, and thus they were not in control.‡ Further-

---

*In 1963 we had noted, "The effects of drugs are only to do things with less caution and more abandon."

†For example, we did not ask them to tell us about their home life or query them as to why they committed crimes. The reader is referred to Chapter 3 of Volume II for a description of our current interview format.

‡For a development of the power and control theme, see Chapter 4 of Volume I.

more, they did not need drugs to accomplish their objectives. Drugs would only impair their effectiveness in crime and render them more vulnerable to arrest. In fact, they looked down on drug users. Another group of criminals experimented with drugs but rarely used them thereafter because they did not find their effects exciting. Furthermore, they concluded, the possible physical harm and the increased risk of apprehension were not worth it. Members of a third group were sporadic users of drugs. Finally, there were those who became regular users. When the criminal decided to use drugs, it was not with naiveté or in ignorance. He was not seduced into drug use but was a willing customer.

> "Just out of high school, D was working in a numbers outfit. He heard a great deal about narcotics, pro and con, but mostly negative opinions. But he was impressed by having heard that under narcotics a man is not afraid of doing anything. D thought a great deal about drugs, although he did not use them. Finally he decided to try them. A man owed him fifty dollars and offered to repay it in drugs. D thus began a year of snorting heroin. He associated with addicts increasingly and then exclusively."

The role of choice in crime and, in particular, drug use was becoming increasingly apparent to us. However, we were still viewing many criminals from the standpoint of having a mental illness. To us, crime (including drug use) was a choice, but we called it a "sick choice."

Increasingly, drug users chose to immerse themselves deeply in the drug world. They were resourceful in obtaining drugs by purchase or theft—at school, on the street, from medical facilities, from wherever they could be found.

Because we were meeting daily with drug users and nonusers together, we were in a favorable position to compare them. Had we worked only with drug-using criminals, it would have been more difficult for us to derive information about drug use. We learned much about the drug user directly from the criminal who was a nonuser. Both were on the street together and had had many associations with one another. Having the two groups together made it possible to focus upon common features. Every feature that we found in the nonuser was even more prominent in the user. Both were suggestible, but the drug user was extremely so. Both were fearful, but the drug user was especially fear-ridden. Both had a limited concept of injury to others, but the drug user's ideas on this subject were even more concrete and narrow than the nonuser's. Meeting together with both groups enabled us to make comparisons, and gave us leads to pursue further. So it was fortunate that when we began our work, we conceived of it as a study of criminals and did not focus on drug use.

Focusing our attention on thinking patterns led us to conclude that the basic difference between the drug user and the criminal who did not use drugs lay in the cutoff of fear. This mechanism allowed a criminal to eliminate temporarily the fears that were deterring action (see Chapter 6, Volume I). To be sure, the drug user had committed many crimes without drugs. But there were other crimes that he thought of but could not bring himself to commit without drugs because he was blocked by fears of being apprehended and pangs of conscience. Having discovered this, we commented, "The drug user is the fellow who really shouldn't be in crime because he can't be comfortable with it." The nonuser was a more effective criminal in that he did not have the additional "hassle" with drugs and thus was not in as much jeopardy.

We still believed that the primary role of drugs was to offer escape from problems, environmental or intrapsychic. As we became more critical of the self-serving accounts of all criminals, we obtained a clearer understanding of the role of drugs. Drugs enhanced cutoff of deterrents, enabling the user to do what he otherwise was afraid to do. But we also noted another element. The drug user was not simply escaping from something—he was moving toward something that he wanted very much. Early in our study, one criminal had said, "On drugs, I could do anything." This aspect of drug use, overlooked at first, was coming more and more to our attention.

As we developed techniques for training the criminal to report his daily thinking,* we were in a better position to see the world as the criminal viewed it. A significant finding was that although drugs *per se* did not make a man a criminal, they facilitated criminal thinking; they permitted the criminal to elaborate his fantasies, and they increased the amount and speed of his thinking about crime and exploitative sex. The drug user who was "on the nod" while using heroin appeared to be inert and in a dreamlike state, but his mind was racing with criminal ideas. Although we were focusing mostly on opiates, other drugs had a similar impact on thinking. We were able to study this thinking firsthand as it was reported on a day-to-day basis in long meetings with people who were using drugs both on the street and in confinement.

Drug users said that they were in search of the "high." They defined the high as "feeling great," and they wanted to continue to feel that way. Initially we accepted the idea that a high was a kind of euphoria or state of elation. Only as we dissected thinking patterns did we come to understand that this was not the case. When a user was high, he regarded himself as all-powerful: he could do anything and everything. Nothing would stand in his way. One

---

*For a description of our procedure of teaching the criminal phenomenologic reporting, see Chapter 5 of Volume II.

drug user summed up the effect of drugs by saying that he felt great because "I feel ten feet tall."

We were beginning to understand more about why a person, fully cognizant of the dangers and risks, persisted in drug use. Drugs gave him "heart" or courage and facilitated exciting thought and talk, which led to actions that were criminal. "Nothing could be further from the truth than that people use drugs just to feel 'high' in the sense of comfortable, relaxed, and easy." What we had said of the criminal nonuser was true of the user. Both wanted to be "ten feet tall," but only the user needed drugs to achieve this.

When using drugs, each man believed that he would not get "hooked." Under drugs external deterrents were eliminated, and he was afraid of nothing. This was the criminal "superoptimism" (Chapter 6, Volume I), in which he was certain that he was immune from apprehension. Conscience fears also were eliminated: "When I'm craving drugs, I don't want to be bothered by my conscience."

As we traced the drug user's thinking from his flow of ideas before a crime to his thinking after its commission, we found that drugs had served several purposes. First, fear was cut off so that he could commit the crime. After the crime these fears returned, the user again resorted to drugs to diminish them. Finally, by eliminating fears for a while, the user could celebrate his success and then prolong the state of excitement by repeating the offense or committing others.

As we came to view drugs as facilitators rather than simply as a means of relieving distress, we discovered the tremendous impetus they gave to sexual fantasy, talk, and exploitative action. Without drugs the drug user, no matter how competent in the eyes of others, considered himself "half a man." With an optimal dose of certain drugs, he could maintain an erection for hours. His staying power gave him greater power over women. We observed, "Especially under drugs, his penis was a sword with which he could make others do what he wanted." It was not so much an enhancement of the sensuality of sex that the drug user sought but, rather, the admiration and buildup by his partner. As one man viewed his eight-hour sexual performance (under drugs), "I felt like Hercules." The prolonged use of a high dosage of a drug wiped out sexual interest altogether. We learned increasingly about the user's choice of a drug for sexual conquest, his sexual practices under the drug, and his regulation of dosage for optimal effects.

The user wanted drugs primarily for crime and sexual exploitation. However, there were other purposes. One man reported using drugs to summon the courage to visit his family, whom he had not seen in a long time. Another used drugs to summon the courage to tell us the truth when his marriage was at stake and depended on his revealing facts unfavorable to himself. Some sought religious experiences on drugs. Unanticipated effects were also experienced in a few cases. Drugs intensified suicidal desires or brought out psychotic features in the few with such predispositions.

We were also learning how drugs affect the user's judgment and performance when he is not in active crime. We studied his reading habits, his evaluation of his own creative work, and his and others' estimates of his job performance.

More important than the particular drug is the makeup of the person who uses it. In the course of our studies, we investigated the effects of a spectrum of drugs. It was striking that many different drugs were used for a given purpose. A man's choice of drug was determined by what he had heard and read, by his own experience, and by the availability of the drug. Very different types of drugs had the same effects, all acting to facilitate whatever the user wanted.

The psychologic determinants of "addiction" (physical dependence) were more prominent than the physiologic. We found that the process of withdrawal was not nearly as torturous as users had stated or were themselves led to believe. Indeed, physically dependent users reported the ease with which they stopped using drugs when it was required. Our observations, history taking, and experiments were eye-opening in what they revealed about the drug user's suggestibility. Just the knowledge that he was going to obtain drugs eliminated withdrawal symptoms. If he was not thinking about drugs but passed through a neighborhood where they were available, the withdrawal symptoms reappeared. With the decision to buy drugs, they vanished. Where drugs are involved, users are very suggestible. Having unknowingly injected sterile water, they reported getting high. The same was true when they pumped their blood back and forth with a syringe. We learned that "craving" referred secondarily to physical consequences, but primarily to the user's missing what he was accustomed to — not the drug itself, so much as the excitement along criminal lines that the drug offered. We dropped the term *addiction* because we found that the concept was based largely on ideas that did not withstand close scrutiny. Popular beliefs about drug use were significantly different from what we were learning from the criminal drug users whom we studied.

Retrospectively, we were surprised to see that we had continued to accept psychologic excuses for crime from the drug-using criminal longer than we had from his counterpart who did not use drugs. We were receptive to the drug user's complaints about life's adversities. We believed that if he learned to deal constructively with those adversities, he would no longer require drugs. It took more than nine years for us to realize that the drug user was searching for more than a peaceful existence. Even when things were going well (at least from the standpoint of a responsible person), the drug user was seeking drugs. Indeed, for the habitual drug user, being without a drug of some kind in his body was as unnatural as going without food. As we studied the user's thinking, it was evident that on the street he was not concerned with life's adversities. His primary quest was finding the excitement that he wanted. His desire for the excitement that drugs offered was unrelated to events in life preceding drug use. Only if he had to account to others for his use of drugs did he recite a litany of personal adversity.*

It is true that drugs did relax the user and, in some, facilitated sociability. However, what really put him at ease was criminal excitement. Like the criminal nonuser, the user is consumed by boredom, self-pity, anger, and tension when he is deprived of the excitement of irresponsibility and violation — the oxygen of his life. When he is searching for that excitement, he is not thinking of what he wants to escape. Rather, he wants to go *to* something. By pursuing what is important to him, he manages in the process to escape what is objectionable, but it is what he wants that is primary; the escape is secondary. We concluded that the escape theme that we had subscribed to for so long was only another version of the victim stance that we had long before abandoned when working with the criminal who was not a drug user. Relating all his difficulties to an examining authority or therapist was basically a deceptive tactic, designed to blame others and absolve himself of responsibility. Some drug users had employed such defenses so often with parents, teachers, employers, law enforcement authorities, and others that they half-believed their arguments themselves.

What emerged so clearly after we finally dropped our view of drugs as an escape and of the user as a victim is the fact that the drug user, even on high doses of drugs, is very much in control. Drugs do not cause him to be irresponsible. In fact, if it is worth his while, he can give the appearance of total responsibility and do an adequate job.†

We learned more about how the drug user operated by studying his functioning in drug treatment programs. We inquired into how drug users in our study had responded to such programs as those at the federal facility at Lexington, Kentucky, at Saint Elizabeths Hospital, and at community clinics. We studied methadone treatment by examining experiences of our own subjects and interviewing patients and staff members of methadone maintenance programs. We visited the pioneering methadone program at Beth Israel Medical Center in New York City. We observed abstinence treatment in the therapeutic community at Phoenix House (New York City), where we were permitted to interview staff members and patients. Visiting Fort Carson, Colorado, and interviewing drug users, we learned of the Army's attempts to deal with them at that installation.

---

*See Chapter 6 of Volume I for a discussion of accountability reasoning.

†"Bad trips," which occur with relative infrequency, are discussed briefly in Chapter 6.

For most of the fifteen years, we studied drug users and nonusers together.* In 1970, we chose to treat two drug users separately, one whom we have followed for seven years and who has achieved basic change in all areas. The other dropped out of our program and died during commission of a crime. Although we devoted little time to discussing drugs themselves, we were able to formulate more clearly some of the problems that one must contend with in the drug user — problems even more formidable than those encountered in the nonuser. Throughout the last several years of our investigation, we studied many drug users in an attempt to extend our knowledge of their inner experience, as well as to test the validity of our earlier findings. Finally, we established a group composed solely of drug users confined in maximum security at Saint Elizabeths Hospital. Our purpose was twofold: We subjected earlier findings to scrutiny by men who had used a great variety of drugs, and we spent many hours studying what drug users reported about specific drugs and their effects. This permitted us to refine concepts and to add substantive material.

ACHIEVING CHANGE IN THE DRUG-USING CRIMINAL

In working with criminals, both drug users and nonusers (who have constituted the majority of our sample), we have come to recognize that the core problem is criminal thinking patterns. The alteration of those patterns has constituted "treatment," or what we term the "change process."† Every thinking error described in Volume I and every corrective presented in Volume II apply to the drug-using criminal.

When drug users agreed to participate in our study, they wanted something for themselves. They sought treatment because they wanted to avoid confinement or get out of confinement or because they were in a transient phase of genuine self-disgust and fearful of impending serious events. In our investigation we have used the same procedures under the same circumstances for criminals who are drug users as well as for criminals who are nonusers. Only by taking them through the change process were we able to discover how drug users think. Questionnaires, projective tests, and routine examinations have not been effective in understanding their mental processes.

Initially, we believe that the drug user who was abstinent from drugs was

---

*As indicated in the Preface, Dr. Yochelson was the senior investigator from 1961 to his death in 1976. Dr. Samenow joined the study in 1970 and completed the work in 1978.

†As we explained in Chapter 1 of Volume I, we do not use the terms *therapy* and *treatment*. These terms denote a process designed to cure an illness. To the criminal who does not regard himself as mentally ill, *therapy* represents an opportunity to deceive those who are trying to change him.

more reachable than the criminal who did not use drugs at all because, without drugs, fears of the consequences of one's actions are more likely to be sustained — that is, the fears are not instantly cut off. Furthermore, we found that we could tap the abstinent user's sentimentality and activate fears of conscience more rapidly. We believed, "The ultimate target in reaching a criminal is to get to his conscience."

> "The drug user is inwardly a more wretched person. Wretched because he can't stand what he is. Wretched because he has a driving need for power, like any other criminal. Wretched because he has a built-in deterrent in his conscience. He can cut off some of this, to be sure. But not enough. . . .It is therefore easier to reach the fellows who hurt, and these are the drug users" (dictation by Dr. Yochelson).

Rather simplistically, we believed that the user who was off drugs could not cut off our influence as quickly as the nonuser could. We thought that once the user was off drugs he would be not only more reachable but also more persistent in the change process. Again, simplistically, we believed that the teaching we were conveying to the drug user (off drugs) would be more readily received and automatically implemented.

It is true that we were often able to make a more rapid initial impact on the drug user who was off drugs than we could on the nonuser. Even so, we found that the road was beset with obstacles even more formidable than those encountered with the criminal who did not use drugs. The drug user insisted that drugs were his problem. Tired of the daily grind, fearing harm to his body, and weary of taking added legal risks, he reached a point at which he said he was completely determined to stop using drugs. There were, of course, some drug users who had no intention of ceasing drug use. They agreed to participate in a change process solely to create a more positive image with authorities who had decision-making power over the time of their release from confinement.

We found that the intentions of users who were sincere about change were short-lived.* They indicated that they wanted to change, but their concept of change consisted only of stopping drug use, despite our earlier insistence that drug use was not the core problem. They believed that all their problems would vanish if they succeeded in terminating drug use. With respect to our requirement of total change, what they gave us was only "lip service." What the user really wanted was our help in getting him off drugs, but he expected to continue a way of life that was criminal. Some thought that they would be more effective as criminals if they were off drugs; being arrested for drug use

---

*In Chapter 4 of Volume I, we discussed the difference between "sincerity" and "conviction" in the criminal's life.

would no longer be a problem, so they could devote themselves more to continuing in their path of criminality.

> "We wanted to know what D really came for. He reiterated that he was here to get rid of narcotics. Then D asked us what we thought he came here for. In response to his question, we said, 'To become an honest man.' An atomic bomb might as well have hit him. D didn't understand it. He made it clear that he never wanted to be honest, and that when he thinks of it, it is impossible and hopeless. . . . How remarkable! That a man should come for 'therapy' and decide in advance that he is going to be a crook. This is precisely what he did."

We emphasized repeatedly that eliminating drugs was no solution to the basic problem. It was simply a necessary first step in the process of providing an arena for total change.

No matter how emphatic his assertion that he wanted to stop using drugs, the user had many reservations even about this. He clung to the idea that it was not necessary to be totally and permanently abstinent. He did not conceive of living without the excitement that drugs offered. He thought that so long as he was not "hooked" or "addicted," he could use drugs sporadically ("chip"). Some agreed to give up one drug or a class of drugs, genearlly the "addicting" ones but retained the belief that other ("nonaddicting") substances were acceptable. In many cases, the final recourse after discontinuing other drugs was heavy liquor use.

Every personality feature of the nonuser was present in the user but in a more intense form. His time perspective was more limited, his prejudgments in decision making more numerous and severe, his trustworthiness less, his sense of uniqueness greater, and so on. When he was on drugs, our task of communicating meaningfully was completely futile because he was harder than ever to reach. Drugs facilitated lying, so he was extremely evasive in his cat-and-mouse tactics of opening and closing the channel of communication. He was resistant to ideas that opposed what he wanted, even though he gave his assent in order to mislead us. He was complacent, not self-critical. Yet he led us to think that he was making the self-searching moral inventory that we required. With deterrents eliminated through drug use, the drug user deployed all the tactics that we encountered in the criminal who did not use drugs (see Chapter 8 of Volume I). His opposition to our concept of change was truly massive.

In the change process the drug user readily responded with a variety of "victim" and "I can't" excuses. In fact, he used an excuse that the nonuser did not have. He viewed himself as a victim of drugs and reiterated the theme of unchangeability on the grounds of "Once a junkie, always a junkie." When he persisted in blaming others for his plight and assumed an intransigent victim stance, elimination of drugs was impossible, and so was the alteration of criminal thinking patterns. Complaining about the hopelessness of the change enterprise gave him the ultimate (albeit superficial) justification for continuing drug use. This attitude emerged when he was pressed by us, for he would repeat the lie of his earlier assent to the desirability and feasibility of change.

The drug user is far more psychosomatic than the nonuser.* We have lived through his whining and complaining about any distress, whether physical or mental, genuine or fabricated. When the user actually stopped drug use and began implementing our severe program, he became bored, self-pitying, and angry. Even though he had been off drugs for weeks, sometimes months, his psychosomatic symptoms closely resembled the withdrawal pattern so familiar to him—weakness, insomnia, muscle aches, headaches, gastrointestinal distress, itching, and running eyes and nose. These symptoms justified for him relief through illicit drug use. The desire for drugs, however, was secondary to the desire for excitement. The drugs were the means of permitting him to pursue that excitement. The user had no objection to tranquilizers, but he complained that instead of relieving his distress, they only made him sleepy. "Relief" and "relaxation" of tension were achieved by violation, not by prescribed medication.

The paramount obstacle in the process of change for the drug user was drug use itself. To a disagreeable situation he had an easy answer that the nonuser eschewed. The nonuser chose either to endure the consequences of living without criminal excitement or to quit the program. But the drug user was more vacillating in his commitment. If the going became too tough and he wanted exciting thought and action, drugs afforded instant relief.

We thought that the user in our program engaged in debate with himself before actually using drugs. This was not so. As soon as he decided what he wanted, there was no room for debate, and he was on the move. The program required that he think before acting and that he call us when a desire to commit a violation was active; he did neither. Drugs were readily available (on the street and in confinement) because the user resorted to contacts who had done "business" with him. Only later when he was held accountable did he describe an agonizing debate about whether he should use drugs. This account was totally untruthful.

With the user still on drugs, our attempts to help him change criminal thinking errors were doomed to failure. First, his thinking was altered by the drug he was using. Second, he was not truly interested in what we had to teach. Finally, there was something inherently absurd about attempting to change his irresponsible thinking patterns while irresponsible thinking itself was being fostered by his continuing drug use.

*For a discussion of psychosomatic features in the criminal, see Chapter 7 of Volume I.

The user's evaluation of himself usually was determined by whether he was using drugs. However, even this criterion of what he considered change did not hold up. Some of these men were not known as drug users by others in the community. They had been able to hold jobs and satisfy employers and maintain relationships. So they were not suspected of drug use. Even when using opiates, they were skillful enough to control their behavior and escape detection. They satisfied others' requirements, even though there was a diminution in the performance of which they were capable. Because they had been so successful in getting away with drug use and other violations, they often evaluated their behavior in these terms. Thus, they told us that they were progressing in change on the grounds that they had earned a promotion at work or that someone had complimented them on their performance. Indeed, this was often the case because their abilities far exceeded the demands of those jobs or else they were skilled con men. However, when they were using drugs, their thinking was totally irresponsible and their reports were untruthful.

Our evaluation of the user was not based on what he said, but on what he did in implementing our program. Even if he were off drugs, this was not the equivalent of changing thinking errors, which, after all, was our primary objective. His being off drugs, even for a month or two, meant nothing without evidence that he was changing his thinking patterns as prescribed. Of course, it was a fundamental requirement that drugs be eliminated completely. Only then could we even start to clarify errors and teach corrections. Some users halted all drug use, including liquor, but still committed felonies. Getting rid of drugs did not get rid of criminality.

Initially, we believed that as long as the door was shut on other drugs, the criminal might be permitted an occasional alcoholic beverage. Although we did not encourage it, we tolerated "responsible drinking" in those who had not been alcoholics. We said of one man who used most classes of drugs: "Since drinking is not a problem for D in the sense that he is not an alcoholic, we can say that we don't have to strive for total elimination of drinking, but it has to be always responsible." This decision proved to be fallacious. We soon realized that one drink opened the door to irresponsibility, and undesirable consequences were always the result. Criminal fantasies were stirred up, the drug user became discontented with his newly established life, and strife ensued at home or at work. In some instances, drinking lessened restraints to other drug use and to further violation. We have had considerable difficulty in convincing the drug user that total abstinence from alcoholic beverages is as necessary as total abstinence from other drugs. Fears are reduced by alcohol as well as by other drugs, and this leads only to irresponsibility and, ultimately, violation.

We require that participants in our program be off all drugs, except those legitimately prescribed to treat medical conditions. Working with a man on methadone was not acceptable, because methadone was no different from the other drugs he had used, in that it furthered his thinking along criminal lines. Working with a man on high doses of tranquilizers was also unacceptable, because his thinking was too sluggish to grasp new concepts adequately and implement them.

The problems that we were facing led to a gradual alteration in our view of the drug user's changeability. Although he was easier to reach initially, he was much more difficult to deal with than was the criminal who did not use drugs. We learned that if there were fifty-two patterns of thinking to alter in the nonuser, the same was true of the drug user, and to a greater extent. That is, one could say that we found the user more "hardcore" than the "hardcore" criminal nonuser. (On a continuum of criminal thinking patterns, the drug user is the most extreme.*) Just as he lacked courage in crime, so did he lack courage and tenacity in change. The user lied more and showed greater inertia and less endurance of the requirements of change than did the criminal who was a nonuser. There seemed to be a quicker atrophy of the will to change and, of course, there was the immediate relief of drugs.

Our program requires the same of all criminals — the elimination of thinking errors and their replacement by the new thinking processes of responsibility. These new patterns are implemented with the format described in Volume II. Long efforts to change the drug user have destroyed our illusions about it being easier to change him than it is to change the nonuser. Through persistence and by improving our techniques in working with both users and nonusers, we have succeeded in effecting total basic change in some drug-using criminals, as measured by years of follow-up. Whoever attempts to achieve change in a drug-using criminal will find, as we have, that he faces a herculean task.

CONCLUSION

It is important that, while reading this book, the reader bear in mind the entire context of what we are reporting. That is, we are discussing substance abuse among people who were lawbreakers before drugs were a part of their lives. We are not asserting that every person who uses an illegal drug has a "criminal personality." It is true that in the eyes of the law, use of illicit substances is, by definition, a criminal offense. But, as we have indicated in Volumes I and II, our work is a study of minds, not of laws. We have written an entire volume about the criminal who is also a drug user for two reasons. One is that numerous misconceptions persist as to why these individuals use drugs. Secondly, there is insufficient understanding of the effects of these drugs on the mental processes of criminals. We found that only after we abandoned our own misconceptions and developed a clearer understanding of the drug user's mental processes were we able to be effective in helping him become a responsible human being.

*For a discussion of our concept of the continuum of criminality, see Chapter 4 of Volume I.

Chapter 2

Man and Drugs:
A Perspective on Drug Abuse

The literature review presented in this chapter is designed as a conceptual history that highlights controversies about drug use,* with special emphasis on the relationships between drugs and crime, drugs and sexual behavior, and drugs and psychosis. Rather than attempt to present an exhaustive literature study, we have selected representative studies from a very large literature that contains divergent findings and conclusions.

SINCE PRIMITIVE CIVILIZATION man has sought to alter his state of consciousness and behavior through use of naturally grown or synthetically produced psychoactive substances. Through medical and religious practices, accidentally discovered drugs became useful tools for altering mental and spiritual states, alleviating pain, and treating disease. Widespread nonmedical use of psychoactive drugs (along with social, cultural, and legal sanctions against it) has given rise to the current drug-abuse phenomenon that is a focal point of social concern.

The search for mind-altering substances, whether naturally grown or synthetically created, has led to the use of materials as diverse as lighter fluid and extracts of cactus. Fink et al. (1967, p. 143) pointed out that in almost all known cultures man has used intoxicating and mind-altering substances to seek pleasure or to relieve anxiety. The use of alcohol, the "grandfather" of all psychoactive substances, has been dated from around 6400 B.C. (Quimby 1970). Opium, considered a substance of "joy" by the Sumerians, was used in 4000 B.C. in Mesopotamia. De Ropp (1957) stated that instead of exercising the self-discipline called for by religion and philosophy, contemporary man has sought a "shortcut to happiness," seeking to achieve a desired condition by "a procedure no more laborious than the swallowing of a pill." Poets and writers, early and contemporary, have described drug states and what man has sought through drugs.

---

*Throughout our work with the drug-using criminals, we have used the term *drug user*. Henceforth, we shall speak of *drug user* and drug users, except when representing another author's views. Then we shall adhere to his terminology. In most cases, we are describing illegal drug use.

> Happiness might now be bought for a penny . . . potable ecstasies might
> be corked up in a pint bottle and peace of mind sent down by mail. (De
> Quincey's *Confessions of an English Opium Eater,* 1818, cited by Cohen
> 1968, p. 149)

Elizabeth Barrett Browning, Swinburne, and Poe spoke glowingly of the extract of the Oriental poppy capsule in terms similar to those used by contemporary advocates of LSD (Cohen, 1968).

The list of drugs used for mind-altering properties throughout recorded
history is lengthy. Farnsworth (1972) observed that 174 species or varieties of
plants have been used for their "euphoria-inducing" effects. Some substances
indigenous to specific regions have found markets in other parts of the world.
In the fifteenth and sixteenth centuries, European explorers found a variety
of mind-altering substances. The only region lacking in these drugs until
comparatively recently was the infertile Arctic region, where the white man
introduced the Eskimos to alcohol and then to other drugs (Weil 1972). The
most nearly ubiquitous and most abused substance is alcohol (Glatt 1974,
p. 7). Some substances are still found mainly in their areas of origin, such as
kava, a South Seas shrub of the genus *Piper,* and various mushrooms endemic to particular regions.

> All the vegetable sedatives and narcotics, all the euphorics that grow on
> trees, the hallucinogens that ripen in berries or can be squeezed from
> roots—all without exception, have been known and systematically used
> by human beings from time immemorial. And to these natural modifiers
> of consciousness, modern science has added its quota of synthetics.
> (Huxley 1954, pp. 51–52)

Psychoactive properties of plants were discovered by accident when the extracts from these plants were utilized during religious ceremonies, as man
sought to embrace a transcendent and universal force and to achieve a higher
plane of being. Substances that helped to gratify the desire for transcendence
were imbued with a divine quality. For example, the coca plant (whose leaves
yield cocaine and related alkaloids) was considered by the Peruvian Incas to
be a living representative of one of the gods, and the fields in which it grew
were regarded as holy (Becker 1963). Drugs are still used to achieve or contribute to religious experiences. Cults have formed around hallucinogenic
drugs (Blum et al. 1970).

Some drugs used for religious purposes were eventually recognized as having medicinal properties. Since the Middle Ages, drugs first used for medicinal reasons have been abused as their ability to produce an altered state of
consciousness were discovered. Conversely, some drugs used "recrea-

tionally" by man for centuries were later found to be beneficial medically. The coca plant was used recreationally by South American Indians 315 years before cocaine's medical use as an anesthetic was discovered by Koller in 1884 (Becker 1963, p. 321). Coca leaves were also used by the Indians for their stimulant properties. Recreational use of chloroform, discovered in 1831, was followed by its use as an anesthetic by Simpson in 1847.* LSD has been used in psychotherapy for psychopaths (Pollard et al. 1965), alcoholics (Ludwig et al. 1969; Savage and McCabe 1971, p. 150), autistic children (Domino 1975, p. 7), and cancer patients (Pahnke et al. 1970). Its abuse as a psychedelic substance is well known. Another drug that passed through stages of abuse and legitimate medical use is nitrous oxide, or "laughing gas," discovered by Davy in 1776. In 1799 Davy (see Lynn et al. 1972) proposed the use of nitrous oxide as an anesthetic in surgery. In 1969, it was used to aerate drinks and later to make dairy products effervescent. Lynn et al. (1972) reported that recreational use of nitrous oxide was once again on the rise, and Brecher (1972, p. 314) cited reports of nitrous oxide parties. Conversely, a movement has been in process to legalize marijuana use to relieve pain in cancer patients.

Drugs have been synthesized for medical purposes and later abused.† The literature contains many references to "iatrogenic addiction." This occurs when a physician prescribes a drug such as morphine for legitimate medical purposes, but the patient becomes dependent on it and requires larger and more frequent doses, even when the drug is no longer needed for relief. An example is amphetamine, which was synthesized in 1927 and prescribed to treat obesity, mild depression, epilepsy, parkinsonism, narcolepsy, and hyperkinetic reactions in children. A dependence on this substance may develop as a result of illict use or "iatrogenic addiction." The same is true of barbiturates.

Drugs that are ostensibly more innocuous are also being abused. In a report on Dramamine (dimenhydrinate) abuse, Malcolm and Miller (1972) cited studies indicating that antihistamines were being used as hallucinogens. Jacobs (1974) and Rosenberg (1975) observed that Asthmador (active ingredients, hyoscyamine and scopalamine), a nonprescription medicine for the relief of asthma, was being used as a hallucinogen. It is legal, easy to obtain, and inexpensive. Cough medicines containing codeine have long been abused, especially when preferred drugs were unavailable. Maletzky (1974)

---

*News reports indicated that chloroform began to make a comeback as a recreational drug (*The Washington Star* and *The Washington Daily News* 7/1/73; *Parade* 9/30/73).

†The Drug Enforcement Administration (1976) listed forty-nine different drugs as representative types of "stimulants." It also listed seventy-eight "depressants."

reported addiction to Darvon (*D*-propoxyphene hydrochloride) by people regarded as neither "addiction-prone nor psychiatrically ill." Tennant (1973) found that the nonmedical use of Darvon by American soldiers in West Germany had reached "epidemic proportions."

An increasing array of drugs has become available. Some are new preparations of earlier available substances. For example, opium, which can be eaten, smoked, or drunk in raw form, can be injected or ingested when processed into morphine. If further processed into heroin, it can be snorted or injected. Some drugs have been synthesized in the laboratory and used expressly for their mind-altering properties. LSD is an example of the class of drugs called "psychotomimetic" because of their ability to produce "psychotic-like" phenomena in the user. These hallucinogens, and other products such as glue, gasoline, and lighter fluid, have been used for their mind-altering properites.

Over the years the use of drugs has been subject to social, cultural, and legal sanction. At one time coffee drinking was illegal in Turkey and resulted in severe penalties. Opium smoking among the Chinese and hashish smoking among the people of India have been as socially acceptable as the consumption of alcoholic beverages in the United States (Maurer and Vogel 1967, p. 14). We shall not discuss aspects of cultural relativism in this review chapter but instead shall concentrate on what the individual wants from drugs and on the effects that drugs have on him. We shall present controversies regarding the organic, sociologic, and psychologic effects of drug use and discuss the concept of the "drug-abusing personality" and the relationship between drugs and crime. In the review of factors that contribute to drug use, we shall not dwell at length on those that have been presented in Chapter 2 of Volume I as causal factors in criminality, nor shall we discuss the effects of drugs prescribed appropriately for medical or psychological conditions.

INCIDENCE OF DRUG USE

Scores of studies exist on the incidence of drug use. Most populations sampled have consisted of students and military personnel (e.g., Bramberg and Rodgers 1946; Imperi et al. 1968; Gossett et al. 1971; Buechler 1972; Johnston et al. 1977). A problem with many incidence figures is that they do not differentiate between the person who tries a drug only once and the person who uses drugs more heavily. For example, Pollock (1972), in a questionnaire study, reported that 61.5 percent of a combined questionnaire sample of first- and second-year medical students had had experience with marijuana. However, the term *experience* was applied to "current users, past users, and also those who have only experimented once or twice," whereas the term *inexperience* designated those who had never used marijuana. Similarly, King (1969, 1970a), in his study at Dartmouth, designated as a user any student who had used a drug at least once. In a questionnaire study Seiden (1975) found that 76 percent of public health students had tried marijuana at least once. The drug-use figure dropped to 43 percent when students were asked whether they were using marijuana at the time of the survey. Still, it was unclear what fraction of the 43 percent were regular users, as opposed to sporadic users. The same question arises with respect to a report in *U.S. Medicine* (3/1/75). A poll showed that 18 percent of American adults 18 years of age and older said that they "had tried" marijuana but that only 8 percent were current users. What is a current user? King (1970b) made two important methodologic points about the use of questionnaires: It is often difficult to determine whether the respondent sample is representative of the population being studied (the presence of bias in the group that elects to return a questionnaire must be considered), and there is no check on the validity of self-report responses.

Drug use has sporadically alarmed the nation. In 1891 Lett declared, "The habitual consumption of opium and its products does exist to a very alarming extent in this country." A year later Crothers (1892) stated, "This disease is all about us and may invade our home and firesides any time." Describing the incidence of opiate addiction before the turn of the century, Bowman (1963) observed: "It is probable that the greatest amount of opium per capita was consumed from about 1860 to 1875 and that there was a slow and steady decrease of its use from then on" (p. 145). Bender (1963) pointed out that between 1910 and 1920 the United States experienced a "wave" of adolescent heroin "addiction." Before that, the use had been primarily of morphine.

Drug use is so pervasive that it has come to be regarded by some as the norm — "a very real part of coming of age in Western society" (Millman and Khuri 1973, p. 151). Bartollas and Miller (1978, p 52) noted, "The fact that both boys and girls perceive of the use of marijuana as normal is important in the increased use of drugs." That marijuana abuse has become institutionalized "at all levels of the contemporary youth and adult culture" was affirmed by Hahn (1978, p. 146). He observed that while mainly college students and social protestors used the substance in the 1960s and early 1970s, marijuana smokers "today are doctors, lawyers, investment counselors, and corporation junior executives."

Winick (1965) has said that addiction to narcotics is a problem mainly of adolescents and young adults. According to his "maturing out" hypothesis, most narcotic users stop taking drugs in their mid-thirties. Winick stated that early in life drugs provide the addict with an in-group, a special vocabulary, and a means of absorbing sexual and aggressive impulses. By the mid-thirties, "such needs are less urgent, and the person seems to drift away from drug use" (p. 8). He also said that only 7.26 percent of drug addicts take opiates for fifteen years or more and fail to "mature out." Bailey (1968) took a diametrically opposite view: "A more plausible explanation might be termed the "smartening up" hypothesis which maintains that old addicts do not become cured, they just get smarter" (p. 134). Bailey maintained that older addicts have slowed down and are therefore less visible. Furthermore, with the development of physical problems, they can more easily obtain drugs through physicians.

Almost endlessly, one can cite studies that offer a variety of statistical findings. By and large, statistical studies do not contribute valid and reliable information. A sample is often a respondent subgroup within a student group. There are few validity checks on questionnaire responses. Even if the data are valid, it is often difficult to determine whether the respondents are "experimental" users, who try a drug once or twice out of curiosity, or regular drug users. Rather than cite more of the many studies containing incidence data, we shall review theories that attempt to explain drug use.

THE ORGANIC VIEWPOINT: PHYSICAL DEPENDENCE

Much has been published on iatrogenic, or medically induced, addiction. Some patients become dependent on drugs, mainly opiates, prescribed for treatment by their physicians. A person who takes prescribed amphetamines to lose weight, for example, may begin using them for kicks and become dependent upon them later (Committee on Alcoholism and Addiction of the American Medical Association 1969, p. 111).

According to some, genetic factors play a role in a person's becoming dependent on drugs. There was considerable thinking along this line at the end of the nineteenth century.

> The children of both alcohol and opium inebriates display many forms of brain degeneration. The paranoiacs, criminals, prostitutes, paupers, and the army of defects, all build up a diathesis and favoring soil for the opium craze. Descendants from such parents will always be markedly defective. (Crothers 1892, p. 228)

Sudduth (1896), a physician, believed that some narcotic addicts owed their condition to hereditary factors, but he expressed contempt for this group of people: "They have no desire to reform and their course is continuously, progressively downward. . . . They are wholly given over to evil ways and the sooner they end their days the better for themselves and mankind at large" (p. 797). The genetic point of view was not held exclusively by practitioners of the nineteenth century. Kielholz and Battegay (1963), describing drug addicts in Switzerland, stated that the hereditary background of this group is "considerably more tainted than that of the general population."

Lindesmith (1968) observed that some experts who held a genetic viewpoint do so no longer because of the lack of evidence:

> In the older literature of addiction a significant aspect of the attempt to show that addicts constituted a different breed of human beings from non-addicts included the investigation of their genealogical histories . . . [but] when the necessity of controlled comparisons was recognized and applied, virtually all of the claims which had been made concerning the unusual prevalence of hereditary defects in addicts dissolved. (p. 172)

Weil (1972) has presented a "drive" theory as to why people take drugs:

> The desire to alter consciousness is an innate psychological drive, and we should seek positive ways to fulfill it. It is my belief that a desire to alter consciousness periodically is an innate, normal drive analogous to hunger or to the sexual drive. Drugs are merely one means of satisfying this drive. (p. 19)

Weil stated that very young children have a "need for periods of nonordinary consciousness." They achieve this by measures such as whirling themselves around and hyperventilation. He regarded the use of illegal drugs as "nothing more than a logical continuation of a developmental sequence going back to early childhood" and stated that this drive arises from the "neurological structure of the human brain."

The modern physiologic view is couched mainly in terms of physical dependence. Isbell and White (1953) viewed physical dependence as a function of "an altered physiologic state which requires continued administration of a drug to prevent the appearance of a characteristic illness, termed an 'abstinence syndrome'." De Ropp (1957) stressed that such dependence is "as real and as material as man's physical dependence on food, air, water, or the essential vitamins which his body cannot manufacture for itself. . . . It is a physico-chemical reality" (p. 116). Dole and Nyswander (1967) emphasized that addiction is a metabolic dysfunction and maintained that physical dependence is the major reinforcer of drug use. They pointed out that even long after an addict is detoxified, metabolic and neurophysiologic changes persist; in other words, with respect to "relapse," neurochemical changes outweigh psychological factors. Stimmel and Kreek (1975, p. 96) observed that physical dependence can result in antisocial behavior — the addict resorts to crime to support his "pharmacologic needs."

Many authors have stressed that psychological processes are mediated by physiologic events and that the latter need further study if phenomena such as drug dependence are to be understood. No one has been able to identify precisely the physiologic events that occur in drug dependence. Some authors have described a "cellular model" of addiction:

> These theories begin with the unchallengeable fact — on which all schools of thought are agreed — that the acute withdrawal symptoms suffered after an addict is deprived of his drug are genuinely biochemical in origin. The cause of these immediate withdrawal symptoms is in the structure of the chemical molecule and its effect on cells of the nervous system. Exposed regularly to opiate molecules the human nervous system adjusts to their presence — that is, becomes dependent upon them. If they are withdrawn, the nervous system becomes very seriously disturbed. (Brecher 1972, p. 68)

> Tolerance is now believed to be due to the fact that these substances occupy receptors on certain myelinated neurons and exert a pharmacologic or pathologic effect after occupation. Tolerance may be the result either of maximal saturation of cellular receptors or of increased excitability of the cell body or of both. (Lehmann 1963, p. 173)

Lehmann, referring to laboratory cerebral studies of self-stimulation conducted with animals, stated that it is conceivable that an addicting drug may stimulate the "pleasure or award centers" in the brain. This may induce a self-perpetuating cycle of "compulsive pleasure-seeking behavior," in which the subject continually seeks out the addicting agent. Lehmann pointed out, however, that this is speculative, inasmuch as the presence of such award centers in the human brain has not been demonstrated.

Organic theories have had an impact on the treatment of drug-dependent people, especially where it is believed that narcotic addiction is, in the main, a metabolic deficiency.

THE PSYCHOLOGIC VIEWPOINTS

> What men say they seek with drugs is also what they say they seek without them. (Blum et al. 1970, p. 8)

Many investigators have studied the psychological makeup of those who use drugs. Fenichel (1945, p. 375) and, twenty-five years later, Krystal and Raskin (1970, p. 10) asserted that addiction is not determined by the chemical effect of the drug but, rather, by the "psychological structure" of the human being. Those who address themselves primarily to psychological issues agree that the environment creates pressures. However, their focus, both in investigation and in treatment, is on how the individual responds to those pressures. We shall first present the psychoanalytic position and then discuss two specific aspects common to psychological viewpoints — that the drug user wishes to escape from mental states through drugs and that he seeks new mental states through drugs. We shall also review attempts to conceptualize a personality type of the drug user.

THE PSYCHOANALYTIC VIEWPOINT

According to psychoanalytic theory, the regressive aspects of mental life account in large part for drug dependence.* The drug user has failed to resolve very early conflicts and thus has unconsciously retreated to an earlier developmental level. He tries to resolve these conflicts through drug use. Cameron (1963, p. 678) described the addict's attempting through artificial means (drugs) to "reinstate the all around satisfaction that infants probably experience when they are pacified, well fed and contented." The drug is viewed as giving "physiological support" in the attempt to reestablish the "carefree, passive state of Nirvana, of early infancy, when the child's needs are satisfied at the mother's breast" (Alexander and Shapiro 1952, p. 135). Meerloo (1952, p. 257) referred to the "regressive ecstasy" in which the addict, like an infant, wants to "live in his golden age of omnipotent dependence." Arieti (1967, p. 263) described the addict as "motivated at the level of the pleasure principle" to satisfy intense bodily needs. The narcissism of the oral stage is seen as a central feature of the addict's personality. He always has to be the recipient, never the giver.

> People and objects external to themselves are but sources and providers of supplies which can be "taken in." Their need is to find object-substitutes which produce a status of infantile satiation-fusion. This bliss, though, lasts only a short time and then new supplies have to be ingested. The much desired fulfillment of the ingestions — introjections of the object — repeatedly fails. (Krystal and Raskin 1970, p. 58)

Savitt (1963) pushed the regression to a preoral stage, in that through the act of injection an addict tries to restore the mother-fetus relationship.

The vascular system is the most direct avenue for the incorporation of

---

*We are highlighting specific factors that psychoanalysts have regarded as significant in drug use. This is not intended to be a comprehensive review of the psychoanalytic theory of drug use.

nutritive supplies. In medical and surgical emergencies life-saving measures are often instituted by infusions and transfusions. The addict bypasses the oral route and unwittingly initiates the fetal relationships with the mother by a symbolic representation. It is a restitutive attempt through an archaic introjective mechanism to re-establish the lost object relationship. (p. 54)

Savitt stated that the "elation" of the regressive aspect is overstressed in proportion to sleep, so the "euphoria" is often short-lived. The addict "goes on the nod" as a "surcease from anxiety." Although Menninger (1963) described the regression as a "partial ego failure," Savitt perceived the drug as restoring "the integrity of the ego."* However, the addict's ego has never developed very extensively. Rather, he has a "fixated, archaic, infantile ego" by which he survives from feeding to feeding.

Wieder and Kaplan (1969) have pointed out that different drugs induce different regressive states. The "narcissistic regressive phenomenon of the symbiotic state" is similar to the opiate-induced mental state. LSD states may be compared with "autistic phase" phenomena, and amphetamine states are seen as "reminiscent of the 'practicing period' of the separation-individuation phase."

When an individual finds an agent that chemically facilitates his preexisting preferential mode of conflict solution, it becomes his drug of choice. The drug induces a regressive state, but the drug taker supplies the regressive tendencies. The fixations and regressions that occurred prior to drug-taking and the unconscious wish to regress to a specific developmental level are among the determinants of drug choice. (p. 429)

Oedipal aspects of addiction have also received considerable attention.† The dynamics of the wish for something forbidden, the fear of being found out, and then expiation through punishment are enacted in the adult addict's life.

Anxiety and guilt would follow that mother would find out. To be "found out" by mother means something special to the addict: he has forced mother to make a choice between father and him. This inability to cope with the oedipal situation causes him to be "hooked" (addicted).

*The term *ego* in psychoanalysis refers to the part of the personality that mediates between instinct and reality. It allows a person to achieve gratification of instinctual impulses within socially acceptable bounds.

†The oedipal period (roughly at ages three to five) is charcterized by the child's wanting exclusive possession of the parent of the opposite sex and a fear of retaliation by the parent of the same sex.

The period of "being hooked" is punishment for his unconscious incestuous wishes. Following this, he is ready to "kick the habit" (withdraw from drugs), that is to give up mother and "be clean." (Thorpe 1956, p. 68)

Oedipal dynamics come to the fore in the following analysis of a patient by Wieder and Kaplan (1969):

The psychodynamic meaning of *taking the drug* (marijuana) could now be further understood as representing fulfillment of forbidden, dangerous impulses of the active oedipal constellation, while simultaneously producing a self-inflicted punishment. . . . At different times, the drug symbolically represented phallus, breast, the incorporated object of the powerful mother, or the object over whom he exerted mastery and which on other occasions dominated him. (pp. 408, 411)

Partly responsible for a fixation at the oedipal stage was this drug user's lack of an effective father. Nyswander (1956) pointed out that the addict's self-esteem suffers because of his "inability to identify with the father and feel his own strength in the relationship."

Freud, in an 1897 letter to Fliess (cited by Yorke 1970), emphasized the link between addiction and masturbation. "It has dawned upon me that masturbation is the one major habit, the 'primal addiction' and that it is only as a substitute and replacement for it that the other addictions for alcohol, morphine, tobacco, etc. came into existence" (p. 142). Thus, masturbation was viewed as the "oldest addiction of all" (Yorke). LaTendresse (1968) suggested that an understanding of masturbation can be of considerable assistance in understanding addiction. Rado (1933, p. 11) regarded the "artificial sexual organization" of the addict as being "autoerotic and modeled on infantile masturbation."

Thorpe (1965, p. 68) pointed out that for the addict the erogenous zones appear to be the mouth and skin. Leech (1970, p. 34) held that according to the classical psychoanalytic view "the process of injection replaces intercourse as the focal point of sexual experience."

Because the addict's sexual life is dominated by aspects of the oral stage of psychosexual development, he is seen as having a shaky self-image and a primitive and confused sexual identity, and as trying to resolve basic issues of sexual identity through addiction and the accompanying lifestyle. Thorpe (1956) pointed out that addicts reassure each other of their masculinity by calling one another "man." Maglin (1974) noted that heroin may in fact become a "more or less adequate sex substitute."

A final mechanism put forth is the gratification of sadistic and masochistic striving via drug addiction. Meerloo (1952) described the addict's unconscious drive toward self-destruction:

> On the one hand, ecstasy expands the ego and silences the hostile voice of conscience (the condeming super ego): but it also induces the oceanic sensations of merging with the universe which, in the final analysis, are antithetical to self-preservation. (p. 257)

Rado (1957) maintained that the drug addict's unconscious mind drives him to self-destruction to "placate his conscience." Some writers have observed the gratification of masochistic aspects of the personality in periods of abstinence. Fort (1954) believed that the withdrawal period served for many patients as a "period of suffering which expiates the guilt," thus relieving masochistic desires. In a frequently cited article, Glover (1932, p. 320) pointed out how sadism combines with libidinal factors in addiction. Drugs "cure" through destruction. That is, they destroy the "dangerous psychic state" in which the addict has strong impulses of hate and in which he is making an "identification with objects toward whom he is ambivalent."

DRUGS USED TO DEFEND AGAINST PAINFUL MENTAL STATES

Whatever psychodynamics are cited as present in the etiology of drug addiction, there is a literature that supports the view that addicts are psychologically disturbed individuals. For example, Rounsaville et al. (1982) reported that 86.9 percent of the opiate addicts in their study "met diagnostic criteria for at least one psychiatric disorder other than drug abuse at some time in their lives." Certain authors assert that some people turn to drugs to cope with life stresses. They maintain that in such cases drug use serves an adaptive purpose. Gerard and Kornetsky (1954) observed that addicts use drugs as "a successful and malignant way of coping with difficulties." Glover (1932) stated that drug addiction acts as a "protection against psychotic reactions in states of regression." Krystal and Raskin (1970, p. 12) indicated that drugs may provide "the sole adjustive mechanism to living problems the person has available to himself at the moment." Stanton (1972) said that because of their tranquilizing effects, some illicit drugs may help particular types of people, such as soldiers in combat, function under stress. Khantzian (1974) contended that opiates are used to cope with anxiety, disappointment, frustration, and other painful mental states. He observed that because the addict lacks the familiar neurotic and characterologic defenses, he resorts to "an extraordinary solution through the powerful action of the drug" (p. 162).

Reichard (1947) cited the "degree of discomfort" as an important factor in determining who will use drugs, "discomfort" being synonymous with "dissatisfaction, frustration, unhappiness [and] tension." However, as he pointed out, not everyone experiencing these states turns to drugs. For some, tension acts as a "goad to socially valuable activity"; for others, it is an impetus for "socially unacceptable, even dangerous, behavior." According to Reichard, almost anyone can become addicted if "discomfort becomes intolerable." He stated that although many people have adequate controls and strengths, every personality has its "breaking point" in the face of increasing stress.

According to most authors who address psychological issues, drugs permit a person to "escape" from anxiety or depression. Wikler and Rasor (1953) observed that through drugs neurotics seek relief from anxiety and psychotics try to lift themselves out of depression. Nyswander (1956), commenting on the work of Wikler, pointed out that addicts use drugs to achieve normality because they have difficulty in coping with life stresses. "Such a term as 'feeling normal' commonly used by addicts to describe the effect of drugs, really means to them a gratification of primary needs: hunger and sexual urges and removal of the fear of pain" (p. 68). Levy (1968, p. 55) said that drug use is an attempt to "escape the experience of anxiety through narcotizing it." Brecher (1972, p. 14) underscored the idea that the ex-addict who returns to drugs is not a "pleasure-craving hedonist" but "an anxious, depressed patient who desperately craves a return to a *normal* mood and state of mind."

Most authors believe that the drug user is a depressed person who has strong feelings of inadequacy. Hekimian and Gershon (1968) stated that "the search for euphoria suggests that large numbers of all drug abusers have inherent depressive factors in their personality." A person may use drugs to deny his own inadequacy and feelings of inferiority (Robbins et al. 1969, Looney 1972). Blatt et al. (1984) found that "issues of self-criticism are central in opiate addiction." Another component of the drug user's depression is loneliness due to his "inability to enter prolonged, close or friendly relationships" (Gerard and Kornetsky 1955).

Some writers have particularized drug use as an attempt to deal with the anxiety of growing-up in a disturbed family. A common view is that a disturbed, anxious youngster later acts out his problems and tries to dispel anxiety by drug use. His use of drugs is a statement that he has differentiated his values from those of his parents (Cameron 1969). Lipinski (1972) also maintained that drug use may be an outcome of a conflict over dependence and an attempt to assert one's personal autonomy.

One specific source of anxiety that the drug user tries to overcome is sexuality. There are two opposite viewpoints on this. Nyswander (1956, p. 65) pointed out that some adolescents, frightened by their emerging sexual desires, take narcotics to "diminish sexual activity to the zero point." But it is also said that drugs are used as a sexual disinhibitor (Cohen 1969a) and as a means to attain a "fantastic" type of sexual gratification (Freedman 1967). We shall say more later about the effects of specific drugs on sexuality.

DRUGS USED TO ACHIEVE EXPANDED MENTAL STATES

Many writers emphasize curiosity as the main self-reported motive for a person's first use of drugs. Brotman and Suffet (1970) found that 53 percent of a group of marijuana users said that they first tried the drug out of curiosity. Twenty-six percent of California Institute of Technology marijuana users surveyed gave the same response (Eells 1968). Lipinski (1972) observed that curiosity is aroused by reading about, hearing about, or being present during others' drug experiences. Feldman and Feldman (1972), believing that curiosity is itself a drive, related addiction to the exploratory behavior of the curious person. They observed that, among prison inmates, the addicts were more curious than nonaddicts.

A second explanation is that those trying drugs for the first time are seeking pleasure. Brotman and Suffet (1970) said that 12 percent of their group of marijuana users stated this to be the case. Lipinski (1972) pointed out that pleasure, rather than being an internal motive, is a product of an expectation based on what one hears from others.

Drug users are said to be searching for something that will transport them beyond the mundane aspects of life into something new and exciting. Cohen (1969b, p. 16) stated that many LSD users are simply in search of a "high" and that there is no pretense of a deeper, more significant motivation. Some writers view drug use as part of an experience-for-the-sake-of-experience cult, particularly where a change in awareness of one's state of consciousness is anticipated and valued (Ewing 1972, Weil 1972a). Some drug users seek mental states beyond the normal, a transcendence of the ordinary, a "goal which is just beyond their grasp" (Griffith 1967), "a taste of the infinite" (Baudelaire, cited by De Ropp, 1957, pp. 66, 115).

Most writers describe these mental states as producing "euphoria." Wikler (1952) stated that euphoria can be produced by several different mechanisms. Primary needs may be gratified directly by "opiate-like" drugs. Another mechanism is the release of inhibitions to permit the gratification of "secondary needs," such as narcissism, exhibitionism, sadism, and masochism. Alcohol, barbiturates, cocaine, and amphetamines have this effect. The third mechanism by which euphoria is attained operates when the dosage is high enough to impair the user's sensorium to the extent that he can deny "obvious, realistic sources of anxiety." Ausubel (1958) and Louria (1971) have viewed the seeking of a high as a form of pure hedonism. McMorris (1966) perceived the drug user as seeking a "physical and mental 'thrill' of a quasi-sexual nature." Greaves (1974, p. 271) said that people who become drug dependent do not know how to "provide themselves with usual forms of euphoric experience" and so use drugs as a substitute.

Zimmering et al. (1951, p. 27) observed that adolescent heroin addicts "live a rich fantasy life, the content of which is predominantly grandiose, promising great wealth and power which they administer with benevolent patronage." Robbins et al. (1969) stated that by smoking a few marijuana cigarettes, the "insecure, inadequate person . . . can now perceive himself as an adventurous and daring individual."

It has also been asserted that there is a "kick" or thrill in the mere act of drug use. In Eells's study at the California Institute of Technology (1968), 14.2 percent of undergraduate marijuana users and 16.9 percent of LSD users reported using the drug for "kicks." Redlich and Freedman (1966) mentioned the value placed on the process of procurement: "One psychological factor to be considered is the powerful motive of 'hustling'; many addicts seem to value the search for illicit drugs and even prefer this highly absorbing chase to assured medical sources of supply" (p. 731).

Other effects that drug users are said to seek are heightened sensitivity to music and art (Eddy et al. 1965), greater sociability (Stanton 1972), increased confidence (Knapp 1952), and relaxation (Brotman and Suffet 1970).

For purposes of exposition, we have presented two objectives of using drugs as though they are two discrete entities — that is, either a person seeks to escape a bad situation or he is in pursuit of a "euphoric" experience. In most cases the two objectives are linked. A person seeks an expanded mental state as a means of escaping a painful mental state (Cavan 1962, p. 160; Jersild et al. 1978, p. 455). However, the emphasis in the literature is on what the user seeks to escape rather than on the resultant state of mind that he achieves.

CONCEPTUALIZING A DRUG-USER PERSONALITY

Some writers have presented a distinct profile of a drug-user personality based on their studies of persons already known to be drug users. The features of these people are described variously as neurotic, psychopathic or sociopathic, psychotic, or as a mixture of these.*

Distinctions have been made between the psychopath who uses drugs for thrills and the neurotic. Lehmann (1963) described the neurotic's use of drugs as "a misguided effort to cope with his crippling symptoms." Other writers have pointed out the same phenomenon:

*The Diagnostic and Statistical Manual of the American Psychiatric Association (1981) lists both "drug dependence" and "nondependent abuse of drugs" as separate, descriptive diagnostic categories. But use of illicit drugs is also listed as an aspect of behavior of the person diagnosed as having an "antisocial personality disorder."

The promise of becoming freed of neurotic conflict with its fears, waste of energy, and feelings of futility is most appealing. It seems such an effortless and fulfilling experience. . . . They believe that these drugs are the last resource. (Levy 1968, p. 51)

Fenichel (1945, pp. 375–380) included drug addiction among the "impulse neuroses." He asserted that an "oral dependence on outer supplies" is the central feature of the addict. Users have been described in terms of their prevalent "oral" characteristics, especially passivity (Coodley 1961; Van Kaam 1968; Hendin 1975, p. 171) and dependency (Fiddle 1967, p. 27).

Kaplan and Wogan (1978) cautioned that the "neurosis-linked theories of addiction" are insufficient and dated. "Addiction in Freud's time may well have been a symptom of a neurotic id-disorder while in the contemporary age it may result from rebellion against the superego" (p. 324). These writers go on to point out that because the psychodynamics of addiction vary, "stereotyped thinking about the 'addict personality' is probably counterproductive."

For at least fifty years, psychiatric profiles of drug users have emphasized preponderantly their psychopathic features (Kolb 1925a, 1925b; Gaskill 1945; Pierce 1969; Feldman and Feldman 1972; Cohen and Klein 1972). In 1937 Adams stated: "Ordinarily, then, addiction is a sign of a mental makeup which is not entirely normal. . . . We shall not go wrong, then, in accepting as a fact the existence of this psychopathic basis in a large majority of the victims of drug addiction" (Cited by Lindesmith 1968, p. 159). Later Levy (1968) observed of teenage drug users: "They all manifested the triad observed by Kelman in patients in whom the psychopathic process is operating, namely fragmented relatedness, intense egocentricity, and sick individualism" (p. 52). Isbell (1965) stated that the valuation of addiction and its prevention may depend on advances in knowledge and sociopathy. Isbell commented, "It may be that in the United States addiction is simply another manifestation of delinquent or antisocial behavior."

Chein et al. (1964, pp. 195–196) asserted that drug addiction spans many diagnostic categories. They mentioned four in which drug addiction is likely: overt schizophrenia, incipient or borderline schizophrenia, delinquency-dominated character disorder, and inadequate personality. The term *schizoid* is often encountered in psychiatric literature about drug users (e.g., Ellinwood 1967; Ungerleider et al. 1968). McCaree and Steffenhagen (1969), using the Minnesota Multiphasic Personality Inventory (MMPI) to study personality factors in college drug users, found the "gross multiple user" to be high on the "Sc" (schizophrenia) scale.* This was interpreted not as a sign of overt psychosis but, rather, as evidence of schizoid personality characteris-

---

*Kilpatrick et al. (1974) pointed out that the MMPI has been "the most popular instrument" for assessing personality in heroin addicts, LSD users, and marijuana smokers.

tics such as withdrawal and poor interpersonal relations, aloofness, and an inability to express emotions.

Some in the drug field believe that diagnostic categories of psychopathology are not useful in describing or understanding the drug user. Monroe et al. (1971) stated that addicts civilly committed under the Narcotic Addict Rehabilitation Act "span the entire spectrum of psychiatric disturbances." They stated that the psychopathic labels are not appropriate for the drug-dependent group.

Some writers have described particular characteristics of people who become drug dependent. These features are unrelated to diagnostic categories; rather, they are part of a personality profile of the drug addict. A frequent observation is that the addict is irresponsible. Swatos (1972), reviewing literature of the nineteenth century, noted that "an amazing number of sources take great pains to point out that the addict is by virtue of his drug use an inveterate liar and absolutely untrustworthy." This characteristic is recognized today by nearly all who construct a profile of the drug addict. The immaturity of the addict has also been cited widely (Ausubel 1958, pp. 41–42; Looney 1972; Glatt 1974, p. 22). Mills (1966) cited the addict's pattern of blaming others, and Fiddle (1967) observed that the addict views himself as a victim. Other features are the addict's lack of goals (Van Kaam 1968), his intolerance of frustration (Ausubel 1958, p. 42), and his general insecurity and psychologic inadequacy (De Ropp 1957, p. 157). The addict's sense of inadequacy and inferiority are pointed out by nearly every writer. Gerard and Kornetsky (1954) found that the "prevalent mood" of the adolescent drug addicts whom they studied was "depressive," irrespective of formal psychiatric diagnosis. "Feelings of guilt, inadequacy, unworthiness, pessimism and futility were commonly expressed. Self-esteem was lowered. . . . These were feelings of long duration, preceeding drug addiction" (p. 120).

Some behavioral scientists have oriented their investigations of characteristics toward predicting who will use drugs. Smith (1972) claimed that he had found factors that were 81 percent effective in making this determination: rebelliousness-obedience (measured by self-report and peer rating), academic performance, and cigarette smoking. S. Cohen (1969b, pp. 107–108) stated that many youngsters with a "so-called addictive personality profile" are not and will not become drug dependent. He then described types of people "who may have difficulties with drugs." One type is the "emotionally immature person (who is) passive and dependent in his dealings with others." Another potential drug user mentioned by Cohen is the "impulse-ridden, angry young man who will try anything once and does." Other categories of people susceptible to drugs include individuals "with a borderline personality," "depressed, tormented, and alienated people," and adolescents under "peer-group enticement." "In addition, individuals having quite stable character structures can become heavily involved (in drugs) if their life situation is deplorable — or if they think it is" (p. 109).

CRITICISMS OF PSYCHOLOGICAL EXPLANATIONS

In Chapter 2 of Volume I we described some limitations of psychoanalytic theory as it has been applied to exploring causes of criminality. We specifically criticized the tenuousness of some of the explanatory concepts of the theory. These same criticisms have been expressed regarding the application of psychoanalytic theory to the drug user.

Yorke (1970) pointed out that Anna Freud believed that analysts were puzzled by drug addiction:

> [Anna Freud] felt that analysts were baffled at all times by addictive states and sought to explain them in terms of the prevailing interest of the period — for example, the mother-child relationship was invoked when symbiosis became a leading psychoanalytic preoccupation. (p. 156)

Robbins et al. (1969) stated that the psychoanalytic system cannot account for multiple drug use.

> The system could not account for the concurrent presence of two diseases that were supposedly caused by contradictory sets of dynamics. . . . It is difficult to explain how they can be fixated at one level of development at one time, only to be fixated at another level within a matter of hours. (p. 3)

For example, a person might use alcohol and LSD at different times. According to psychoanalytic theory, he would be fixated both at the "autistic phase" of development (explaining the LSD use) and also at a later stage of psychosexual development (explaining the alcohol use). Bartlett (1975) concluded that psychoanalytic concepts were insufficient and too obscure to explain addiction.

> The familial concepts of superego lacunae, suffusion of id impulses, and oral fixations do not adequately explain either the precocities or deficiencies in these *children, and may obscure the realities of the familial and social contexts of their development.* They suffer all kinds of lacunae. (p. 264)

With respect to the idea that people take drugs to reach mental states that they regard as normal, critics have pointed out that normality is not at all what the drug user seeks. As Brown (1961, p. 55) observed, there would be no value in continuing to use narcotics if all the addict derived was feeling normal. In fact, Brown contended, it is precisely "normalcy" to which the addict objects. Lindesmith (1968) agreed: "If the user only succeeds in feeling normal, one is compelled to wonder why he should go around spending twenty to fifty dollars a day for his non-effect" (p. 44). It has been argued that although the drug user may be considered mentally unstable, most persons who are mentally unstable do not become drug users (Berger and Potterfield 1969). Put another way: "No one knows why one adolescent chooses to try drugs as an answer to his feelings of inadequacy whereas others may become depressed, fail in school work, or take up fast driving (Blaine 1966, p. 73). Brill et al. (1971), in their study of college marijuana users, found no significant differences between users and nonusers in measures of anxiety, depression, and ego strength. Certainly no diagnostic category is especially populated with heavy users of drugs. Nyswander (1974), who regards drug dependence as organically determined, stated that: "The range of personal characteristics in addicts is as varied as in any other group; comparisons of addicts with other population groups have failed to differentiate between [addicts] and others." A few writers object to current psychological formulations because they omit considerations of choice and will. S. Cohen (1964) and others have recognized that will plays a role in drug-induced states. He observed that the "exercise of will" even when one is under the influence of LSD can "prevent the breakdown of ego boundaries."

Confusion occurs when investigators do not differentiate between personalities before and after drug use. As Redlich and Freedman (1966, p. 729) pointed out, the fact that most personality descriptions are based on syndromes encountered after addiction is well established. In 1928, Terry and Pellens commented on this very issue:

> The evidence in support of such [a posteriori] statements . . . has been secured *after* the development of the addiction and was not based on a knowledge of the individual's condition *prior* to his addiction. In other words, the pre-addict has not been studied, and the traits, ethical standards, and intellectual capacities based on *post hoc* findings may or may not have *propter hoc* significance. (p. 514)

Brill and Lieberman (1969, p. 191) cautioned that anyone who thinks that addicts are psychologically disturbed will look for and find the traits that he wants to see.

Many professionals studying drug use and treating drug users believe that current theories do not offer cogent explanations for drug use. With respect to addiction, Wilson (1975) stated: "No generally accepted theory supported by well-established facts exists to explain why only some persons become addicts" (p. 132). Some observers have said that the entire definition of the problem has changed — that there is a new type of drug user. Bean (1974, p. 120) devoted a great deal of attention to this issue. He maintained that there has been a shift in drug users from the "repentant deviants" of the 1930s to the "enemy deviants" of the 1960s. Kaufman (1973) has described the "emergence of several new types of addicts":

> Within the past few years, there has been an emergence of several new types of addicts. The new addict is frequently younger than in previous years. He may come from the armed forces in Viet Nam, our leading preparatory schools and universities, and urban and rural middle class areas across the country. The products of these different backgrounds are very different people with very different ego structures, causes of addiction and needs for treatment. (p. 16)

Babor et al. (1974) are among investigators who have been critical of the methods used for studying the drug user. They said that there has been an "over-dependence" on self-reports and psychologic tests and not enough observational study to assess personality. Milby (1981, p. 31) pointed out that research data may be biased because of a reliance on captive populations of opiate addicts.

There does not appear to be a clear-cut personality profile that differentiates the drug user from the person who does not use drugs. As Glass (1974, p. 21) put it, "There is no such person as 'the' addict. . . . Among drug abusers one finds all kinds of personalities." The addict and the person who does not use drugs manifest many of the same personality patterns (Nyswander 1956, p. 65; Lindesmith 1968, p. 164; Robbins et al., 1969). Millman and Khuri (1973, p. 153) have found "no evidence that [the adolescent addict] was any different from his peers prior to addiction." Accordingly, they do not believe that there is a "preaddictive personality type." Burroughs (in Lindesmith 1968) stated that there is no more a preaddictive personality than there is a "pre-malarial personality." The issues of paramount significance to many are prediction and prevention. Glasscote et al. (1972) said that present knowledge is insufficient for effective prediction:

> Each . . . characteristic is no doubt applicable to some people who abuse drugs. And there may be various other characteristics that apply to some drug users. . . . The problem, in any case, is that *none* of these characteristics . . . predicts for us who will become a drug abuser. . . . Most essentially, there are countless "immature" people who do not resort to illegal drugs. And so on. Among commonly cited causes of drug abuse, *none* predicts the inevitable use of drugs. (p. 22)

THE SOCIOLOGIC VIEWPOINT

Drug use has been viewed as a response by the individual to the conditions of his environment. Sociologists contend that there is a cause-effect relationship, i.e., because of particular circumstances, a person turns to drugs. This position has been summarized by Brecher (1972):

> These views hold in general that society creates addicts and causes ex-addicts to relapse into addiction again. The sense of hopelessness and defeat among dwellers in our city slums, the sense, among young people today, of impotence to effect change, the need of young people to belong to a group and their consequent drift into groups of heroin users — countless sociological factors such as these are cited to explain both addiction and relapse following "cure." An addict relapses, according to some sociological theories, because he returns to the same neighborhood where he became addicted and associates with addicts once more. What these theories have in common is the belief that the secret of addiction lies in the social context. (p. 67)

For decades "contagion" has been regarded as a significant, causative factor. People in the field have viewed drug dependence as comparable to a communicable disease. "The large number of heroin addicts in New York City (over 150,000), and the mode of spread from areas of high drug usage with the addicts serving as carriers to infect susceptibles are typical of an epidemic" (Dole 1973, p. 206). Hekimian and Gersohn (1968) found that "influence by friends and environment" is a "contagious and endemic factor." The "group-social" aspect was seen by Haines and McLaughlin (1952) as causative of the use of both addicting and nonaddicting drugs. The discussion of "contagion" is often couched in terms of norms in the peer subculture. Kandel (1973) pointed out that "peer behavior" is the "crucial determining factor" in adolescent drug use. She observed that both the decision to use drugs and the extent of use is related to what one's friends do. According to her findings, what one's peers do outweighs parental influence. "When faced with conflict, adolescents are much more responsive to peers than to parents. Thus 56 percent of adolescents use marijuana when their best friends use marijuana although their parents have never used any psychoactive drugs" (p. 1069). Meyer (1972, p. 6) suggested that the best social predictor for one's use of any drug is the drug-use history of one's close friends.

Many believe that the peer subculture is responsible for its members' advancing from "lesser drugs," such as marijuana, to heroin (Select Committee on Crime 1970; Subcommittee on Alcoholism and Narcotics 1972, p. 30). A practice of proselytizing among users was noted by Fisher (1968, p. 75), especially by those who use LSD.

It has been maintained that youngsters continue to use drugs to receive the acceptance from their peers that they do not receive elsewhere.

> The neglecting family, the one which gives too little gratification, which seems not to care or be able to care for the addict, exists in (the) middle class population. . . . While the addict may have had the physical needs cared for, emotionally he is starved. His involvement with the drug culture provides him with a family that cares in some way, and a means to be gratified — by taking the drug. (Fram and Hoffman 1973, p. 612)

Scherer et al. (1972) found that those who use hard drugs have a higher need for social approval than do those who use soft drugs or none at all. Zimmering et al. (1951, p. 22) stated that once a person begins to use heroin, he continues because of his "need of social acceptance and status." Anglin et al. (1983) pointed out that drug use may be *necessary* to gain acceptance within a particular group. They go on to note that once the individual gains entry, he is influenced further by the members of that group. Becoming a part of an ingroup reinforces more drug use as well as other types of antisocial behavior.

Poverty has long been considered a cause of drug use; the person who is locked into the hopeless, desperate, frustrating condition of the ghetto is seen as especially susceptible to drugs. Stimmel (1972) noted that most addicts come from low socioeconomic groups. Some observers contend that when inhabitants of the slums discover that the American dream is only a fantasy, they become frustrated and turn to drugs and crime. Drugs offer escape from the oppressive reality of their environment. "What better foundation can be laid for a willingness to experiment with the alchemical stuff that offers the promise of transforming the fantasy, for awhile at least, into an isotope of reality" (Chein et al. 1964, p. 79). Cloward and Ohlin (1960) added another dimension to the idea that disadvantaged groups lack a legitimate opportunity to achieve socially prescribed goals. They identified a "retreatist" subculture in which those who have failed to achieve goals, such as wealth and status, turn to drugs.

Problems in family living are regarded as causal factors in drug use. It has been pointed out that drug use is greater among adolescents from broken homes than among those from stable homes (Haastrup and Thomsen 1972; Rollins and Holden 1972). Chein (1965) studied four groups of eighth-grade boys: delinquent nondrug users, drug users with a prior history of delinquency, drug users with no prior history of delinquency, and boys who were neither delinquent nor drug users. The boys in the last group were reared in more cohesive families. Chein observed that "these boys seemed to be actively resisting the pull of their neighborhood environment" (p. 111). In the discussion of family problems, Haines and McLaughlin (1952) pointed to the lack of acceptable role models for youngsters growing up in disrupted homes. Male addicts are often said to have weak fathers who are either physically or emotionally absent and mothers who are domineering, inconsistent, and seductive (Fort 1954; Redlich and Freedman 1966, p. 730; Seldin 1972). Unstable homes are seen not as a phenomenon of the slums alone but as a problem at all socioeconomic levels.

Attention has turned to assessing etiologic factors in drug use among the more privileged classes of society, who are believed to be suffering a form of deprivation different from that of ghetto residents.

> We may have to take a second look at what we mean by deprivation and consider that many of our young people who "have everything" may indeed be missing much of what is necessary to healthy growth and development. . . . When drugs are needed to feel "high," it suggests that there are too few opportunities to feel exhilaration by life without drugs. (Child Study Association of America Wel-Met 1971, p. 26)

Drug use has been viewed as a consequence of alienation and boredom among the affluent.* Glasscote et al. (1972, p. 21) commented on the irony of a situation in which more people are bored "at a time when the variety of sensory stimuli is the greatest ever known, and when more people than ever before have the money to gain access to them." The push for achievement and status is meaningless to some people. This may be because "unrealistic and excessive aspirations are likely to be a heavy burden for even the most intact ego" (Gerard and Kornetsky 1955). Others, although they may have the emotional and intellectual resources to compete and succeed, eschew what they perceive as a "closed room" with a rat race going on in the middle (Goodman 1960, p. 159). The 1973 National Commission on Marihuana and Drug Abuse pointed out that more than any other factor a "sense of purposelessness and meaninglessness in living" contributes to taking drugs (p. 104). This lack of purpose has been attributed to an ideologic void that the upcoming generation regards as characterizing its predecessors.

> Forced to confront a meaningless (or finished) contest, they may decide to invent a new game rather than join the old as opponents to a team that has lost its spirit. Even to picket the old game for having unfair rules is still political action, because one must go to the old stadium. . . . These people are busy inventing a new myth, that is, a new reality. (Messer 1970, pp. 163, 167)

---

*Alienation is actually a psychologic state. Sociologists emphasize aspects of the environment that they regard as producing a mental state of alienation.

Messer has said that youngsters who come from homes where "the dream of success has become a reality" turn around and say, "O.K., I've had enough; what else can you show me?" They find that they have to create a "new reality." Drugs appear to offer a path to meaning (Horman 1973) or an antidote to a sense of powerlessness (Rollins and Holden 1972).

> The origins of drugs in the young cannot be stated in terms of simple causality. Among the most important of the many variables are an often unrecognized sense of injustice concerning nonperson status and the lack of importance, dignity and personal worth. (Freedman 1972, p. 419)

Drug use is regarded as a form of rebellion against the established order. This has been said to be as true of affluent youngsters who decide to experiment (Blaine 1966, p. 68) as of drug-using soldiers in the army (Stanton 1972). Finding that drug use frustrates and alarms those in authority, they engage in it as a means of expressing hostility toward the establishment (Ausubel 1958; Berger and Potterfield 1969; Group for the Advancement of Psychiatry, 1971; Glatt 1974, p. 34). McGlothlin (1975, p. 46) stated that "normal curiosity and rebelliousness" are more often factors in beginning drug use than are adverse family situations or personality defects. Although the marijuana user, for example, may be said to be rebelling against an order, he is also perceived as moving toward establishment of an order of his own. Goodman (1960, p. 156) described how the Beat Generation of the fifties resigned from society to "form peaceful brotherhoods of pure experience." Schofield (1971, p. 183) has emphasized that a thoughtful search for new values and standards accompanies the rebellion. Many others have commented on this aspect of drug use.

Bartlett (1975, p. 281) observed that drug addiction is a partial expression of a social era of anxiety and cynicism. Freedman (1972) stated that problems resulting from the technologic revolution and urbanization have contributed to widespread drug use. Indeed, modern technology itself has produced a plethora of drugs from which to select an agent to allay anxiety.

> This proliferating technology produces an ever-widening range of options for those who are otherwise predisposed to use drugs. In the field of addiction and drug use, supply tends to create a demand as well as vice versa so that in a special way secularization increases the momentum of drug use. (Fiddle 1967, p. 328)

Peele (1975, p. 43) has stated that opiates appeal to Americans who believe that they cannot control their destinies. Yet the effect of opiate use makes this sense of helplessness even greater because the user is less able to cope effectively.

The belief that drug use is in great part a response to the pressures of modern life was expressed in 1926 by Cantala, who indicated that at that time the pressures of "modern civilization" were contributing to drug dependence.

Social institutions come under indictment for fostering conditions that contribute to drug use. Schools especially are criticized when any social problem arises. The factors in the school's contribution are seen as being the same for crime and drug use.* For example, it is alleged that the pressures are too great and that what is taught has little relevance to many students. In an article on boys who are glue sniffers, Rubin and Babbs (1970) stated that the "educational process itself often fails to relate realistically to the circumstances of the boys' immediate environment." In a world of middle-class teachers and middle-class expectations, "disadvantaged" youngsters are seen as failing, developing a poor self-concept and then compensating in some way through drug use. At the graduate level, the medical student who is said to experience a lack of challenge turns to drugs.

> Through the usage of marijuana the medical student is possibly afforded an opportunity to escape from the world of objectivity that surrounds and conceivably haunts him. It enables him to perceive new sensations that are lacking in his daily routine. . . . The problem is not that a great percentage of our nation's medical students occasionally use marijuana but of a lack of challenging and stimulating experiences within the medical school that disposes some students to seek this in marijuana and other drugs. (Polakoff and Lowinger 1972, pp. 187–188)

The mass media come in for their share of the blame for contributing to drug use. Schroeder (1980, p. 63) asserted, "The entertainment and news media have helped focus youthful attention on drug-taking." Hanneman (1973) found that college students became initially aware of drugs other than marijuana and amphetamines more through "media content and drug abuse ads" than through other sources. Fort (1973) has pointed out that drug use is portrayed as an acceptable part of life. Taqi (1973, pp. 27–28), writing about the popularity of films with drug themes in the late 1960s and early 1970s, said that "young people follow the fashions of their times, and one of today's fashions seems to be drug-taking. Drug films . . . reflect that fashion and to some extent keep it alive and in the public eye." Nail and Gunderson (1972) have scored the media for "glorifying drug-oriented life styles." Millman and

*See Volume I, Chapter 2.

Khuri (1973, p. 157) pointed out that "until recently the mystique and romance of the dealer and user of drugs were very pervasive indeed." They stated that it is now "less fashionable" to be a drug user, partly because of the current "media onslaught." A far-reaching criticism of the media was made by Starratt (1971), who maintained that America's youngsters are particularly vulnerable to the appeal of drugs because they have only a "*symbolic* contact with reality until their early twenties."

> They see pictures on a TV set, they read books, they hear lectures, they look at photographs in magazines. But they find it impossible to get beyond these symbols to honest-to-God contact with reality. They have knowledge *about* life, but they lack first-hand acquaintance *with* life. So they get tired of the vicarious thrill of watching television. They want some first-hand experience. And the thrill of forbidden fruit as a first-hand experience is available on the drug scene. (p. 83)

It has been contended that so much publicity has been given to drugs, particularly the psychedelics, that instead of deterring their use, it has encouraged it.

> Most authorities agree that the tremendous and almost unprecedented early publicity given to the sensory-enhancing and psychic effects of LSD and its evangelical prophets added to the "contagious" nature of drug taking. (Group for the Advancement of Psychiatry 1971, p. 271)

During the late 1960s and early 1970s, radio stations were under pressure to stop playing popular music that might be interpreted as glorifying the drug experience.

Also severely criticized has been advertising that promotes such ideas as "relief is only a swallow away" (Group for the Advancement of Psychiatry 1971; Ewing 1972; Nail and Gunderson 1972; Goldberg and Meyers 1980). Frank, a physician quoted in *U.S. Medicine* (1/1/74), stated that addicts try to solve problems the way television advertisements tell them to — with drugs. Sebald (1972) has said that he views the "basic Western idea of instantaneous results" as having miscarried. He pointed to a long list of "instant" features of American life, from the "instant energy" of a breakfast cereal to the "instant prayer" of "Dial-a-Prayer." Included in this presentation was a comment that "drug dependence for instantaneous results" had become an "entirely acceptable, if not hallowed, style of life." Sebald viewed youth's psychedelic-drug use as being in line with this aspect of American life and stated that "youth simply is not used to expenditure of effort and delay" (p. 346). Although he did not claim the instancy feature as a total explanation, Sebald viewed it as "an important ingredient and a surprisingly neglected one" in explaining contemporary drug use.

Society has been blamed in other ways for creating a climate of drug use. Nail and Gunderson (1972) pointed to various social, economic, and national problems, including racial strife, poverty, and the Vietnam war. A symposium sponsored by the Washington, D.C. chapters of the Association of Black Psychologists and the Association of Black Social Workers blamed white supremacy for drug addiction in blacks (*Washington Post* 11/9/73). Maglin (1974) maintained that the "sexist bias of society" puts female addicts in an even worse position than male addicts. Goodman (1960, p. 187) observed that the older generation is blamed for providing a poor example and creating or worsening unfavorable living conditions: "You squares dropped the atom bomb, don't you dare criticize my smoking marijuana."

Brecher (1972) pointed out that much information passed on to guide and inform young people is not factual. Thus, he maintained, young people "were left to flounder without guidance they could trust" (p. 498). Kaufman et al. (1969) stated that, worse yet, some of the warnings served as lures, and a great deal of the material was simply not believable because it did not correspond to the real-life experience of the drug user. This reduced the credibility of the establishment even more.

> The horrible reactions to marijuana predicted by various authorities were virtually never seen. The runaways generally took this to mean that all the widely advertised dangers of drugs were establishment lies. This further alienated them from the social structure and made them more willing to experiment with all sorts of chemicals. (p. 719)

In attempting to look at values of society in historical perspective, writers have pointed to the present era as a permissive one. However, such an observation also was made in 1926 when Wallis blamed the widespread use of drugs on the "I'll try anything once attitude of today's youth" (p. 22). If it is not permissiveness, then it is the lack of it that is observed as complicating the drug problem. In 1939, Barnes stated that many authorities believed that "more drug addiction is caused by the laws which have been passed to repress it than by any other single factor" (p. 807). In 1968, Lindesmith commented on the role that the addict is "forced"into partly because of the legal climate.

> The social behavior of the addict everywhere depends on the legal and social context in which it occurs, not on the biochemistry of the drug. . . . The personal and social characteristics of the American addict are not directly determined by the pharmacological effect of the drug, but are consequences of the role which he is forced to adopt in our society, that is of his social, economic, and legal situation. (pp. 44–45)

A report of the New York Academy of Medicine, cited by DeRopp (1957), took the position that "laws now in force more or less compel the addict to take to crime because they regard him as a criminal" (p. 158). This is still widely held. Cohn (1984) stated:

> That we have criminalized the use and abuse of illicit substances suggests that much of the crime problem is a product of our own misguided public policy. . . . The criminalization of deviance may even help to push the deviant into a criminal career. (p. 17)

The law is seen as making the addict a criminal, not only in his use of illegal drugs per se but also in the type of life that he has to lead to acquire the drugs that are so hard to obtain.

The idea that the addict is forced into crime to support his habit has had wide circulation and acceptance. In 1957, Chein and Rosenfeld stated, "The high cost of heroin . . . forces specific delinquency against property for cash returns" (p. 54). A quarter of a century later, Weissman (1982, p. 72) made the same observation: "Under our prevailing criminalization of drug-use system, society forces addicts to practice income-generating criminal behaviors."

England has confronted this aspect of the drug-use problem through an alteration of laws to allow addicts to procure drugs legally under medical supervision. The British system will be reviewed in Chapter 7.

A comprehensive treatment (from a sociologic perspective) of the effect of drug laws is Johnson's *Marihuana Users and Drug Subcultures* (1973). Johnson did not write the book as a treatise on drug laws but, rather, as a sociologic study of drug subcultures. He emphasized the primacy of the subculture in marijuana use and contended that drug laws seemed to encourage interlocking subcultures of sellers and buyers who otherwise might not have contact. The author argued that if cannabis were legally available, the illicit drug market would be undermined.

> In short, the findings suggest that legal cannabis might be an important ingredient in dissolving the glue that holds drug subcultures together. Legal cannabis would undermine the illicit drug market and, at the same time, undercut the social processes by which students are recruited into, and maintained in, each subculture. (pp. 204–205)

Availability, an obvious determinant of drug use, is seen as varying with the economic and social character of the environment. The ghetto inhabitant of the inner city is described as having access because of the ubiquitous presence of a "pusher." Sharoff (1968) observed that the incidence of addiction is high among doctors, nurses, and dentists — in fact, ten times that in the general community, not because medical people are more susceptible but because they have greater access. Suburbanites are seen as having access to drugs because they have money to buy them. Some authors (e.g., Berger and Potterfield 1969) describe addiction in the suburbs as "hidden," because the user can afford to buy what he wants without resorting to criminal means; he does not run afoul of the law.

One observer (Schofield, 1971, p. 108) ventured the opinion that no matter how disturbed a person is, if he was born in a remote village and remained there all his life, he would be unlikely to use a multiplicity of drugs simply because they would not be in his environment. Drugs drift in and out of vogue mainly on the basis of availability. During the late 1960s and early 1970s marijuana use became widespread. In the late 1970s reports began to appear that cited the resurgence of alcohol consumption because it is legal, less expensive, and generally more available than other drugs. Then, in the 1980s, there was a surge in cocaine use as both the street reputation and availability of the drug increased.

All these factors have been regarded, at one time or another, as contributing to drug use, either singly or in combination. The causal links have ranged from the very specific, such as "contagion," to the less precisely defined "deep-seated pathology" in society. In the 1970s and 1980s, the "something's rotten in America" view has attracted more subscribers than perhaps any other view.

> Many, many older Americans are asking, "Why are young people so interested in drugs?" The first level answer is that we live in a drug-ridden, drug-saturated, drug-obsessed society, where from infancy onward we are taught to accept and live the industrial slogan of *better living through chemistry*. The use or abuse of marijuana or any other drug should be seen as a barometer of society, often reflecting deep-seated pathology and alienation. (J. Fort 1973, p. 339)

As we have indicated, most writers do not emphasize a single sociologic cause but, rather, explain drug use in terms of a combination of factors. Chein et al. (1964, p. 71) noted that social causation is complex, and that it is not feasible to identify one or two clear-cut factors, such as poverty and disrupted family life. Instead, they maintained that it is the "entire complex of unwholesome factors" that contributes to drug use.

CRITICISMS OF THE SOCIOLOGIC POSITION

Critics of the sociologic position assert that one's environment is far less significant than one's response to that environment. They point to the many broken homes in which there is no drug use or to the intact, psychologically secure family in which there is drug use. The second criticism is that some of the correlations are not valid when subjected to careful scrutiny. For example, drug use in the military services has been regarded as a direct result of various pressures, including that of boredom while one is stationed at a base and not in combat. Yet closer investigations have revealed that many soldiers used drugs before they entered the armed forces.

Some writers have rejected the "contagion" theory on the grounds that the individual selects the company he keeps and has a choice as to which pressures he will submit to. Chein et al. (1964) observed that a youngster may attach himself to a variety of peer groups. "In attaching himself to one [peer group] rather than to another, he selects the environment that will influence him. That is, in the very process of choice he reveals the influences to which he is more-or-less open" (p. 138). Chein et al. pointed out that some youths actively seek drugs for the first time on their own initiative — they go to drugs; drugs do not come to them. As Sharoff (1968) put it, "Not all susceptible individuals succumb, whether it be to malaria, tuberculosis or drugs." Wilson (1983, p. 202) emphasized the role of choice: "We do not choose to contract smallpox from a friend, but we do choose to use heroin offered by a friend." Ploscowe (1961, p 51) observed that "through an effort of will, strength of character or force of personality" many people who are exposed to drugs reject having anything to do with them. King (1970), writing about student drug use, said that neither knowing someone who has used marijuana nor having the opportunity to try the drug "automatically seduces all students into using the drug." Glass (1974, p. 28) observed that the drug user "voluntarily and willingly joins certain cultures which seem meaningful to him."

During the 1960s and early 1970s, there was much discussion of an "epidemic" of drug use among American military personnel, especially in Vietnam and Germany. This was also true of armed forces personnel stationed at home. The "contagion" and environmental-influence arguments were the most frequent explanations. Tennant et al. (1972) obtained 3,553 questionnaires completed by Army personnel and conducted more than 400 personal interviews with drug users. Their findings did not support environmental-influence explanations.

> Of the military drug users, 78 percent had first used drugs before coming to West Germany and 65 percent had first used drugs before starting military service. This leaves approximately 22 percent of drug users who presumably used drugs for the first time in West Germany. There is, of course, no way to know whether these individuals represent a group who would not have otherwise used drugs. (p. 382)

The family has been cited as having a decisive influence on whether one uses drugs. Friedman et al. (1980) said that the widely held view that family problems propel the adolescent into drug use may be in error. They noted that perhaps it is the drug use of the adolescent that creates the family problems. In a study of drug users admitted to a psychiatric hospital, Hekimian and Gershon (1968) concluded that there was no familial basis for narcotic addiction. Glaser et al. (1971) reported a study in which they examined the differences between addicted and nonaddicted members of the same families. These investigators noted that differences emerged very early in life. The addicts-to-be were involved in "the illegitimate opportunity structure of the streets at an early age," whereas their responsible siblings "early eschewed the illegitimate world and sought conventional employment." Studies of child-rearing practices have yielded no consistent pattern with respect to explaining addiction. Gerard and Kornetsky (1954) studied thirty-two male adolescent narcotic addicts at Lexington. They found that 40 percent had mothers who could be described as "excessively controlling and strict," and 48 percent had mothers who were "excessively indulgent." The authors did point out that the fathers of 60 percent of the addicts had played a minimal role in their sons' lives. However, the authors did not state whether this was attributable to the fathers' irresponsibility or to the addicts' rejection of their fathers. Another observation made of these youthful addicts was that "manifest instability of the home did not commonly occur."

Many writers have observed that drug use cannot be explained by poverty. Gossett et al. (1971) found that drug use of most types was more frequent in middle- and upper-middle-income groups than in lower socioeconomic groups. The observation that substantial drug use occurs in areas of relative affluence has appeared so often (e.g., Gerard and Kornetsky 1954, 1955; Berger and Potterfield 1969) that today one rarely finds an unequivocal statement that poverty is a primary causal factor.

> The young heroin user from the suburbs did not take up his habit because rats ran across his bedroom floor. Within the slums, where rats are plentiful, there are many more people who do *not* take up drugs than who do. (Glasscote et al. 1972, p. 22)

> On the contrary, those noticed in the 1960s were often construed as "middle-class dropouts" whose addiction, far from being explicable in terms of some material disadvantage, appears to have been motivated by the deliberate rejection of middle-class norms and opportunities. (Dr. David V. Hawks, cited by May 1972, p. 349)

Similar observations were made in a Japanese study (Hemmi 1965), in which 70 percent of addicted prisoners came from middle-class homes.

In accounting for drug use by the economically and culturally better-off, some writers have described boredom, alienation, and rebellion against the established order. Yet Glasscote et al. (1972, p. 22) pointed out that many people who are bored and rebellious do not use drugs. Ewing (1972) suggested that those who use marijuana do so less as a mode of rebellion than as part of a search for new experiences and meaning.

Opinions about the importance of availability of drugs have been countered by the contention that a person's attitudinal predisposition is of overriding importance (Ausubel 1958, p. 34). As Robbins et al. (1969) pointed out, a decision has to be made initially to try drugs. Availability determines only which substance is to be used. J. P. Fort (1954) asserted that the drug user is not a victim of the drug peddler. "Although the young addict is often described as the victim of unscrupulous drug peddlers who have urged or tricked him into taking drugs, I have almost never seen such a case" (p. 252).

A major problem with sociologic theories of causation is that they do not enable one to predict who will become a drug user. Berger and Potterfield (1969, p. 40) reported that "racial origin, sex, age, educational background, economic status, or social position are not factors of primary importance in determining whether or not an individual will become a drug abuser."

Those who reject sociologic explanations of drug use do so primarily because they believe that psychologic factors play a more important role. Mahon's (1974) survey of explanations of drug use resulted in this "Eschewment of Theory Theory."

> It appears that as far as drug dependence theories are concerned, you pay your money and you take your choice. . . . There is no single theory that can adequately unravel the puzzle and establish the true cause. If this is the case, then such a scientific chase for the theoretical Holy Grail is doomed to failure, and The Eschewment of Theory Theory is the best of a bad bunch. (pp. 318–319)

From our findings in the following chapters we shall explain why we too have ceased searching for causes.*

DRUG EFFECTS

Some investigators claim that drug effects are attributable primarily to the pharmacologic properties of a drug. Others assert that the personality of the user is the critical factor. Most conclude that both are important in

---

*In Chapter 1 of Volume I, we discussed how our search for a cause of criminality not only ended in futility but was counterproductive to effective change in the criminal.

producing a drug's effects.* Proponents of the importance of pharmacologic factors emphasize the "reinforcing effects" of the physiologic changes. For example, Crowley (1972) cited the "intense physical pleasure" and the "rush" that occur with the injection of methamphetamine.

The controversy centers around whether pharmacologic substances produce psychic effects. Can a drug, by inducing a physiologic change, bring out something in a person that is alien to his nature? McCarthy (1971) reported that after taking psilocybin, a "respectable family man" ran naked through the hospital, molesting the nursing staff. The clear implication was that the drug did something to the man to bring out behavior that had been foreign to his previous conduct. The issue is raised in an editorial of *The British Journal of Criminology* (1967): "The problem is clearly two-sided; whether on the one hand the use of drugs loosens the passions of brute man or whether only demented addicts commit crimes in order to maintain their life-line to drug intoxication. Needless to say the evidence is equally equivocal" (p. 367).

Arguing the importance of the psychologic determinants of drug effects, some writers point out that a particular drug itself is not responsible for the personality alteration. That is, drug users will switch from a preferred drug to another if the former is not available. Glatt (1974, p. 312) stated that "today's drug abuser . . . is a polydrug abuser for whom 'everything goes.' "

It has been pointed out that the ritual of drug administration is often as psychologically important as the drug itself. "[Heroin addicts] repeatedly claim that the ritual of fixing (i.e., preparation of the injection) and the 'needle' (i.e., the actual injecting) are as important as the drug itself, and some asked for intravenous injection of anything, even water" (Thomson and Rathod 1968, p. 297). Levine (1974) described people who are "addicted" to the use of hypodermic needles. Glatt (1974, p. 20) also observed "dependence" on the needle. Speaking of the conditioning aspect (rather than the pharmacology), Levine pointed out that for the "needle freaks" the attraction of the ritual itself is strong enough to produce the drug effect. He viewed injection by such people as a "medium for the expression of and a defense against an unconscious sexual identity conflict."

Many experts regard the mental predisposition of the user as the critical determinant of the effects experienced when drugs are used. Walters et al. (1972) contended that a person is as he is "before he even inhaled his first puff or swallowed his first tablet. . . . It is not the drug which determines the use, but the *personality* of the user that determines the drug, and the use to which

---

*Our survey is of the professional literature. Ashley (1975) has claimed that in the literature proper accord is not given to the accounts of drug users. He said that the scientific model "views subjective experience with great suspicion" (p. 167). Ashley believes that to be accurate in studying drug effects, one needs to have firsthand knowledge, i.e., personal experience.

he puts it" (p. 96). De Ropp (1957, p. 133) pointed out that the effect of alcohol depends on the person, not on the alcohol; it's "not in the whiskey bottle, but in the psyche." To paraphrase a homily of St. John Chrysostom (cited in De Ropp 1957, p. 133), blaming drugs for the abuse problem is like blaming the night for thievery. Blum et al. (1970, p.289) and Bloomquist (1971, p. 202) stated that it is unlikely that a well-adjusted person would suddenly become violent under the influence of a drug. They believe that drugs bring out only the personality features already present.

> This is the remarkable thing about Cannabis. Whatever you were before you took the drug, whatever you had in mind as the goal to reach while on it, is increased and enhanced by the use of the drug. If one wishes to pray, one may think he is in intimate contact with the Eternal; if one wishes to copulate, he can pretend he is a satyr or she a nymph. (Bloomquist 1971, p. 367)

Most writers assert that prior knowledge, expectations, and current desires all interact to create the specific effect of a drug. Freedman (1967) observed that subjects given barbiturates but told that they are stimulants respond with activity, as though they had received "pep pills." Conversely, an active subject will drop off to sleep if given a stimulant that he is told is a sedative. Smith (1964) observed that given suitable mental set and social setting, drugs can induce religious experiences. "Among subjects who have strong religious inclinations to begin with, the proportion of those having religious experience jumps to three-fourths. If they take (drugs) in settings which are religious too, the ratio soars to nine out of ten" (p. 156). Ungerleider et al. (1968) reported that people now have "psychedelic experiences" in groups in the "proper setting," where they even hallucinate without using drugs at all. Finally, Weil (1972) has stated that the most important fact to emerge from drug research in this century is that "individual responses result from set and setting as much as from the drug itself. (It is) impossible to talk meaningfully about the effects of psychoactive drugs except by reference to their effects on specific individuals on specific occasions" (p. 330).

THE NATURE OF ADDICTION

Addiction applies to both physical and psychologic changes. The World Health Organization (Expert Committee, 1950) defined addiction as

> a state of periodic and chronic intoxication detrimental to the individual and to society, produced by the repeated consumption of a drug (natural or synthetic). Its characteristics include:
> (1) An overpowering desire or need (compulsion) to continue taking the drug and to obtain it by any means;

(2) A tendency to increase the dose;

(3) A psychic (psychological) and sometimes a physical dependence on the effects of the drug.

In 1965 the World Health Organization substituted the term *dependence* for *addiction* (Eddy et al. 1965). The problem was that the term *addiction* was being loosely applied to the misuse of almost any drug outside legitimate medical practice. The National Commission on Marihuana and Drug Abuse (1973) also elected to speak of a broad concept of drug *dependence* rather than use the term *addiction.* The Commission pointed out that "most people who use psychoactive drugs do not succumb entirely to the pharmacologic properties of drugs" (p. 139) but use them for psychologic reasons. Irwin's (1970, p. 1) definitions of "physical dependence" and "psychologic dependence" are representative of how these concepts are defined in the literature:

Physical dependence: Dependence of the body tissues on the continued presence of a drug (even in the absence of psychologic dependence), revealed by disturbing or life-threatening withdrawal systems that develop when the drug is discontinued.

Psychologic dependence: A tendency or craving for the repeated or compulsive use (not necessarily abuse) of an agent because its effects are deemed pleasureable or satisfying.

Irwin pointed out that one could become dependent on activities other than drug use, such as eating or television watching.*

Van Kaam (1968) observed that the phenonenom of addiction "seems to be related more to the passive rather than the active dimension of man's life." However, some authors (Brown 1961; Chein et al. 1964; Scher 1966) have contended that the active search for euphoria is a major characteristic of addiction. Others have identified as hallmarks of addiction such factors as the presence of withdrawal symptoms (Ausubel 1958; Farber 1968; Lindesmith 1968), the tendency to relapse after a period of abstinence (Nyswander 1956; Kolb, 1962), and tolerance (Expert Committee 1950). The last of these, *tolerance,* is an especially important feature. This term refers to the need for increasingly large and more frequent doses of a drug to obtain the desired effect. It is explained largely as a physiologic phenomenon, although the specific mechanisms by which tolerance occurs are largely unidentified.

---

*Peele (1975, p. 43) argued that in the United States addiction is a way of life, whether it is to pets, television, food, or doctors. Some addictions are necessary, such as food and love; others are not, such as heroin and nicotine.

(Tolerance) may be due to an increased rate of biotransformation of drug to less active and more readily excretable substances ("biochemical tolerance"), to adaptive changes in cells of the central nervous system ("tissue tolerance"), or to both. (Isbell 1972, p. 38)

In some cases there appears to be an increase in the activity of the enzyme system that deactivates the drug. Another possibility is that tolerance occurs because of an exhaustion of stores of the endogenous agent causing the effect. For most drugs, there is little knowledge of the underlying process. (Ray 1972, p. 64)

It has been contended that craving is a definitive feature of addiction. A craving for drugs evolves into a conditioned response that "becomes independent of the physiological conditions of tolerance and physical dependence, and predisposes the individual to return to the drug even after a lapse of years" (Lindesmith 1968, p. 55). *Craving* is a term that appears often in the literature but is not precisely defined. That the phenomenon is important is attested to by the fact that for more than twenty years it has been regarded as the feature of drug use that enables one to make a distinction between addiction and habituation.

Milby (1981) reviewed explanations of physiologic processes by which drug addiction may occur. These include theories of receptor-site action, altered metabolic disposition, and cellular adaptation. He stated that no theory so far is capable of explaining "the full range of phenomena" that occur in addiction. His conclusion is, "The conditioning theories hold sway not so much because of their scientific superiority as by default in comparison to the alternatives."

Finally, addiction has been viewed as being dependent upon the expectations of the individual:

Both the advance knowledge of the properties of drugs and social interpretation of his reactions to them influence the subsequent course of the individual's addiction. Thus, although he may actually be physically dependent on opiates, he may not regard himself as an addict ("hooked") if he does not know about dependence and withdrawal symptoms, and if no one points these out to him as evidence of addiction. (Ausubel 1958, pp. 66–67)

Lindesmith (1968), arguing against the contention that addiction is derived solely from the effects of an opiate on the body, stated:

Addiction occurs only when opiates are used to relieve withdrawal distress, after this distress has been properly understood or interpreted, that is to say, after it had been represented to the individual in terms of the linguistic symbols and cultural patterns which have grown up around the opiate habit. (p. 191)

In this and in succeeding chapters we do not use the term *addiction* except when referring to another author's work. The term has become so ambiguous as to have as many meanings as there are authorities using it. In Chapter 4 we shall discuss the concept of drug dependence from the perspective of our findings.

Each of the following subsections reviews briefly the most commonly cited effects of a *class* of drugs, rather than focusing on differences among individual drugs within a class We shall cite controversies surrounding these effects, which include physical changes, perceptual alterations, mood changes, and effects on cognitive functioning and interpersonal transactions. The relationship of drugs to crime, sexuality, and psychosis will be treated at greater length.

OPIATES

Opium is a natural substance that is processed to produce morphine, heroin, codeine, and other derivatives. There are at least seventy-two opiates; they range from crude to totally synthetic preparations (Kramer 1969). Some synthetic opiates that are closely related to morphine and heroin in their effects are meperidine (e.g., Demerol), hydromorphone (e.g., Dilaudid), oxycodone (e.g., Percodan), and methadone (e.g., Dolophine). The opiates are considered highly addicting, with physical dependence developing within a week (Redlich and Freedman 1966, p. 737). Scher (1966, p. 542) observed that the opiate addict is always struggling with the "three-pronged issue of maintaining euphoria, limiting tolerance, and avoiding withdrawal."

We have chosen to discuss mainly heroin as representative of the class of opiates. Its effects are similar to those of other opiates, and heroin is the substance that most dominates the illegal market for opiates in the United States.

According to Louria (1967), when the addict buys heroin on the street, he is getting only 1 to 2 percent heroin; the rest consists of adulterants, such as quinine, baking soda, milk sugar, cornstarch, or almost any other white, pow-

---

*While the term *opiate* refers to substances that are derived from the naturally growing opium poppy, it is often used interchangeably with the term *narcotic,* which may be applied to any drug that alleviates pain, induces drowsiness (or coma in large doses), and numbs the senses (Lingeman 1974).

dery substance. The purity range is anywhere from 1 to 30 percent, according to the Task Force on Narcotics and Drug Abuse (1967). Because of the variability in heroin purity, the addict does not know what he is getting and risks overdosing himself.

Heroin is bought ready for use. Other opiates sometimes have to be processed by boiling and straining. Lerner and Oerther (1967) reported that addicts do this with paregoric to remove the camphor. Williams (1974) stated that cough syrups are also boiled to provide a more concentrated supply of codeine. Addicts have used both paregoric and codeine to maintain themselves until they could obtain heroin.

Weppner (1971) reported that after heroin, codeine is the most abused narcotic. It is relatively inexpensive and provides a reliable "high," compared with the fluctuating quality of street heroin.

Heroin is injected intravenously ("mainline"), injected subcutaneously ("skin-popped"), or inhaled ("snorted").* Irwin (1970) stated that the opiates act primarily on the central and parasympathetic nervous system. Eidelberg (1975) presented a comprehensive review of studies that report the acute effects of opiates on the cerebral cortex, limbic structures, basal ganglia and thalamus, hypothalamus, brain stem, spinal cord, and the nerve, muscle and peripheral autonomic system.

When an opiate is injected intravenously, the user experiences what has been variously termed a *thrill,* a *flash,* and a *rush.†* The sensation is intensely pleasurable, the effect being a feeling of warmth and fullness in the stomach, skin, or genitals (Chessick 1960; Wikler 1967; Long and Pena 1968; Williams 1974). Kaplan (1983) noted that the rush is described as "a violent, orgasmic experience." Feldman (1970) has called the "flash" a "combination of cocoon-comfort and an inexplicable physical ascendency to a 'high.' " He asserted that this phenomenon is the "incentive" for the neophyte addict to "move on to the next phase of his career."‡ The pursuit of this high then becomes all-important. "The (addict) seeks and obtains an unnatural euphoria every time he injects the narcotic and this elation is the principal cause of drug enslavement" (Brown 1961, p. 55).

Lindesmith (1968, pp. 23–45) stated that other than the pleasurable sensations occurring within five or ten minutes after the injection, the opiates do not produce an unusual state of mind. In fact, during the four hours (typically) between injections, addicts claim to "feel normal." The euphoric state

---

*Other ways of using opiates include smoking, eating, use of suppositories, rubbing on the gums, and rubbing in the eye sockets.

†Rado (1933) referred to the effect as "pharmacogenic elation."

‡Zimmering et al. (1951) observed that the first time a person uses heroin, he is likely to experience nausea, vomiting, and anxiety.

or "high" has been described as one in which a person has no worries (Chessick 1960), has bodily comfort, and has a sense of well-being (Alcohol, Drug Abuse, and Mental Health Administration 1975). Chein et al. (1964, p. 232) described the euphoria as an "enjoyment of negatives." That is, the addict is in less distress than he was earlier. He feels "out of this world," as though all his needs are taken care of. The Alcohol, Drug Abuse, and Mental Health Administration also characterized the euphoric state as being an absence of pain or distress. The tranquility and somnolence of the high have also been described. Kaplan (1983, p. 23) reported the high to be "a warm, drowsy, extremely pleasant state" that can last as long as five hours. The period of drowsiness or "nod" is usually referred to as distinct from the high. Long and Penna (1968) have called the nod a "dreamy state of imperturbability." Nyswander (1956), Wikler (1967), and Long and Penna (1968) noted that sleep comes without difficulty, although the addict can be awakened easily. Fiddle (1967, p. 35) and Sutter (1969, p. 824) have noted that the nod is not really a state of euphoria but one of "nothingness." Others have said that far from being a state of nothingness, the nod is a state that facilitates fantasy.

Many psychologic effects of heroin have been documented. According to the Task Force on Narcotics and Drug Abuse (1967), heroin is primarily a depressant. It alleviates anxiety and tension, diminishes primary drives (such as hunger and sex), and may produce drowsiness and apathy, impair concentration, and reduce physical activity. Ausubel (1958, p. 44) found that addicts experience "increased self-confidence and feelings of self-esteem, decreased anxiety, and grandiose fantasies of wealth, power, and omnipotence." Zimmering et al. (1951) observed that addicts experience a sense of being at ease with the world and have an "excessive fantasy life." Chessick (1960) stated that addicts often believe that under the influence of opiates they are more creative, especially in artistic endeavors.

Maurer and Vogel (1967, p. 82) stated that the pleasure opiates offer gives way to a "driving necessity" to obtain more drugs to avoid the distress of withdrawal. The addict is said to be "lethargic and indifferent to his environment" only until the need for the drug is pressing; then his activities revolve around drug acquisition (Smith, Kline & French Laboratories 1967). Cohen (1969) said that many "established addicts" are concerned more with avoiding withdrawal symptoms than with attaining a "positive elevation of mood."

The literature contains marked differences in emphasis and sometimes in basic conceptualization as to whether the addict uses heroin to escape from distress or to achieve a different plane of existence. Some reports state that he seeks to escape adversity so as to be at ease in the world, while others indicate that he seeks an extremely exciting and elated state. In either case, most studies rely on subjective evaluations or self-reports of mood or on overt expressions of attitude in behavior, not on a study of cognition.

CRIME

Discussion of the relationship between crime and drugs has centered mostly upon a linkage between addiction to opiates and antisocial behavior. The prevailing view is that most crimes committed by addicts are for the purpose of supporting drug habits.

> Some responsible authorities state the physical and psychological dependence of addicts on narcotic drugs, the compulsion to obtain them, and the high price of the drugs on the illicit market are predominantly responsible for the crimes committed by addicts. Others claim that the drug itself is responsible for criminal behavior. The weight of evidence is so heavily in favor of the former point of view that the question can hardly be called a controversial one. (ABA-AMA 1961, p. 1965)

> The nondrug offenses in which the heroin addict typically becomes involved are of the fund-raising variety. Assaultive or violent acts, contrary to popular belief, are the exception rather than the rule for the heroin addict, whose drug has a calming and depressant effect. (Task Force on Narcotics and Drug Abuse 1967, p. 10)

> Most male addicts steal to maintain themselves and their habit, while female addicts resort to either prostitution or shoplifting. (Ray 1972, p. 195)

> The poorer addict is too readily forced into a life of crime to meet his increasing needs for narcotics. (Nyswander 1974, p. 395)

Many authorities acknowledge that crime may have preceded drug addiction but claim nevertheless that the amount of crime has spiraled because of the demands of the drug habit.

> If we assume that a heroin-dependent person has a daily habit of $20 (the lowest daily estimate found but one amounting to $7,300 per year), we can also assume that it would be relatively impossible for him to support his habit without supplementing his income through illegal means. (National Commission on Marihuana and Drug Abuse 1973, p. 175)

Kolb (1925) was one of the earliest authorities to point out that an addict was a criminal before he became addicted. He stated that "no opiate ever directly influenced addicts to commit violent crimes." Pierce (1969) found that 75 percent of the incarcerated British male adult heroin addicts whom he studied had court convictions that predated their addiction to narcotics.

James and D'Orban (1970) stated that many researchers in Great Britain had concluded that thievery precedes addiction. Wilson (1983, p. 204) stated that studies of "known addicts" indicate that between 50 and 75 percent were delinquent before they began using drugs. Taylor and Albright (1981) specified that among 1,328 heroin users "nondrug criminality predates heroin use by about five years." Statistics compiled from official records do not reveal the extent of crime before or during drug use.

Much has been written on the association between opiate use and violence. The most frequently articulated view is that addicts are unlikely to be violent. Kolb (1925) declared: "The heroin hero is a myth. Both heroin and morphine in large doses change drunken, fighting psychopaths into sober, cowardly, nonaggressive idlers" (p. 88). In 1940, Lindesmith said that the public stands "in virtually no danger of violence at the hands of drug users" (referring to heroin addicts). Hesse (1964, p. 57) said that heroin produces cowardice. Halleck (1967, p. 155) claimed that heroin is "an almost perfect tranquilizer." The ABA-AMA (1961, p. 165) stated that crimes of violence are rarely committed by addicts. Hoffman (1975, p. 75) observed that heroin-produced euphoria has been characterized as "a feeling of sublime contentment." Reed (1980) noted that addicts are more likely to commit crimes against property than against the person. He maintained, "Assaultive crime is not especially addiction-related."

However, there are some data that directly contradict the position that opiate use is not conducive to violence. Fry (1985) found that among a Swedish birth cohort studied for criminal involvement, "intravenous male drug users" accounted for nearly one-third of the violent crimes, and female intravenous users accounted for 45 percent of the violent crimes. Observing patients on experimental research wards for sixty days, Babor et al. (1974) found that

> the findings do not support the hypothesis that chronic heroin use functions to suppress interpersonal hostility. On the contrary, patients showed a tendency to express more hostility after higher doses of heroin. . . . While it is possible that heroin may suppress hostility temporarily after an acute dose, it appears that the cumulative effect of addiction is to increase the frequency of hostile verbal behavior. This is undoubtedly related to increases in physical discomfort experienced during this time. (p. 10)

The period of withdrawal is observed to be the time at which the addict is said to pose the greatest danger (Wallis 1926). Tinklenberg and Stillman (1970, p. 353) contended that although opiate use is "not associated with a generalized increase in violence," users may become more violent during withdrawal and "are likely to be drawn into the criminal world where violence is inherent."

SEXUAL BEHAVIOR

Most published reports indicate that sexual desire (heterosexuality, homosexuality, and autoeroticism) is reduced or eliminated by opiate use (Wikler and Rasor 1953; Savitt 1963, p. 52; Milby 1981, p. 41). Zimmering et al. (1951) said that adolescent heroin addicts, in referring to this phenomenon, said, "We lose our nature." Some writers have asserted that the inhibition of sexual desire in the opiate addict tends to remove him from the category of psychopathic sex offenders (Maurer and Vogel 1967, p. 247). Gebhard (1972) said that the use of morphine and heroin is extremely rare among sex offenders. Hoffman (1975, p. 77) stated, "The central nervous system effects of heroin are such that sexual desire is minimal or absent."

It has been observed that although the sex drive is reduced almost to the point of total elimination, a secondary effect on sex is the prolongation of erection and the delay of orgasm (Fiddle 1967, p. 33).

> In both males and females, opiates have a general tendency to reduce or obliterate sexual desire. . . . The use of opium, especially by smoking, appears to enable some men to maintain erections for several hours, and although sexual relations may take place after smoking, orgasm is usually absent. Similar effects are reported from heroin, and cases are known where women encourage their men to use heroin for this reason. At the same time, most male addicts do not feel the active desire for intercourse, although they may indulge in it to please their companions. (Maurer and Vogel 1967, p. 86)

Fiddle (1967) has observed that an addict who thinks that he is sexually incompetent can use heroin and then delay orgasm long enough to satisfy more than one woman. Nyswander (1956, p. 46) stated that morphine enables some people to achieve sexual satisfaction without their usual accompanying anxiety about performance. Lindesmith (1965) mentioned that in some cultures opium has been used "to prolong sexual pleasure by delaying the orgasm, to restore fertility or cure impotence." Hendin (1975) said of three student users: "Heroin serves to relieve sexual anxiety and make orgasm irrelevant, permitting them to take pride merely in sustaining an erection" (p. 197).

PSYCHOSIS

We have found nothing in the literature reporting psychosis as a consequence of opiate use. Nor is there any indication that physically dependent users have a personality that is predisposed to psychosis. Ling et al. (1973) found a "lack of major psychoses" among sixty subjects who had been physically dependent on heroin for an average of 13.6 years. Furthermore, the investigators regarded psychosis as a condition that would interfere with the addict's lifestyle.

> Major psychoses appeared to be unusual among the chronic addicts. Beyond the factor of simple bias one is tempted to speculate that the disabling nature of a serious psychiatric illness makes it difficult for the sufferer to keep up with the demands of a chronic addictive state. (p. 432)

COCAINE

Cocaine, derived from the coca plant, has been called "the strongest stimulant known to man" (Ferguson 1975, p. 155).* Cocaine is administered orally, intravenously, and by snorting. Some authorities contend that the drug is not physically addicting, and it does not produce tolerance (Ewing 1967; Altshuler and Burch 1976; Carr and Meyers 1980, p. 185). With regard to addiction, Brecher (1972, p. 276) has said that cocaine resembles tobacco more than it resembles opiates or alcohol. Ashley (1975) asserted that the heavy physical dependence on the drug cited by almost all current authorities is not experienced by most cocaine users.† Yet there are others who contend that cocaine can produce tolerance, psychologic dependence, and physiologic dependence (Eddy et al. 1971; Julien 1978, p. 87).

In 1885 Freud described the stimulant properties of cocaine and how it caused the disappearance of fatigue and hunger. He advocated use of the drug to alleviate symptoms of morphine withdrawal. Redlich and Freedman (1966) and others have commented on the physical indefatigability of the cocaine user.

According to Ashley (1975), three distinct components comprise a cocaine "high": increased energy, clarity of mind, and euphoria. The National Clearinghouse for Drug Abuse Information (1972) stated that cocaine produces feelings of euphoria that are stronger than those of most other psychoactive agents, including heroin. Ferguson (1975) reported that the drug produces "feelings of intense psychic energy and self-confidence." The user "ascends to extreme heights of mood elevation, elation, and grandiosity." Eddy et al. (1971) and Williams (1974, p. 281) stated that the drug induces a feeling of tremendous muscular and mental power — so much so that the user overestimates his capabilities. Grinspoon and Bakalar (1976, p. 226) graphically con-

---

*Although cocaine is classified legally as a narcotic, its effects more closely resemble those of the central nervous system stimulants (Brecher 1972, p. 271).

†Ashley (1975) has presented a detailed history of the drug's use and an account of the drug's effects.

trasted the quality of experience of users on opiates versus those on cocaine: "If the opiate addict thinks of himself as a kind of Buddhist attaining Nirvana, the cocaine abuser is more likely to see himself as a Nietzschean superman realizing his will to power."

The effect of the "high" does not last long. The user experiences "a violent rush of excitation" and then "tremendous depression" (National Clearinghouse 1972). The depression can follow exhilaration within thirty minutes, so the user resorts to more cocaine. Thus a cycle is established in which cocaine is used repeatedly and in ever increasing amounts (Ferguson 1975). But during the early 1980s cocaine, which had been known as the "drug of celebrities," became much more widely available in the streets.*

Because its effects are so brief, cocaine is often used in combination with heroin, a longer-lasting euphoriant. The combination is called a "speedball" (Bewley 1965; National Institute of Mental Health 1971). According to Brecher (1972, p. 276), the mixture not only relieves the "excess agitation and tension" produced by cocaine alone, but enhances the "rush."

CRIME

Cocaine is an energizer, and as an energizer it is said to have the same effect as amphetamines on criminality. Kolb (1925) observed:

> A criminal who takes cocaine is for the time being more efficient as a criminal unless he takes too much. The drug does not arouse criminal impulses in anyone, but it enhances the criminal's mental and physical energy so that he is more likely to convert his abnormal impulse into action. (p. 76)

Ewing (1967, p. 1009) has said that violence is a frequent outcome of the use of large doses of the drug. The National Clearinghouse (1972) stated that in a "hyperexcited, toxic" cocaine state, the user may become irrational and violent. Williams (1974, p. 281) has said that cocaine is used by criminals to "bolster their courage before they commit major crime." It is a "means of achieving the proper mental state, of degree of nerve, prior to the commission of the crime" (p. 82). Grinspoon and Bakalar (1976, p. 226) made the point that cocaine as a central nervous stimulant may facilitate any action that is being contemplated, "whether it be a public speech, a stage show, or a robbery." The predispostion of the user is critical. "The drug can obviously exacerbate tendencies toward paranoia and violence that are already present

---

*A colorful narrative of the role of cocaine in the life of the street user has been written by Olden (1973).

in its users or encouraged by a criminal milieu" (p. 227). On the other hand, Weil (1975) said, "I have never seen cocaine produce real aggression, violence, or psychosis." And Carr and Meyers (1980, p. 186) asserted: "The relationship of cocaine to violence derives more from fears and the long-standing bias against the drug than from any empirical data."

SEXUAL BEHAVIOR

There is little in the current literature about the effects of cocaine on sexuality. Eiswirth et al. (1972) stated that cocaine is believed by many to act as an aphrodisiac. Gay et al. (1973, p. 1037) have said: "The chronic cocaine user comes much closer to fitting the picture of a 'sex-crazed, depraved dope fiend' than do the narcotic addicts to whom the description is classically applied." Ferguson (1975, p. 155) indicated that as the drug intensifies emotional states of various kinds, it produces in the user "feelings of intense sexuality." Resnick and Schuyten-Resnick (1976, p. 221) cited both an increased intensity of sexual feelings and a heightened ability to fantasize. Grinspoon and Bakalar (1975, p. 105) commented, "Cocaine, like other stimulants, often heightens sexual interest and sexual powers in the short run." Phillips and Wynne (1976) stated that the user who expects cocaine to be an aphrodisiac is likely to discover that he can prolong intercourse with a delayed orgasm and then experience an increased intensity of orgasm.

PSYCHOSIS

There are numerous references to psychotic reactions resulting from cocaine use, especially to the paranoid ideation experienced by those who use the drug in high doses over a prolonged period (Kiev 1975; Millman 1982; Holbrook 1983, p. 63). Both Ewing and Williams (1974) mentioned tactile hallucinations, a common one being foreign bodies under the skin. The most frequently observed phenomenon has been psychotic reaction with paranoid and megalomaniac delusions – a condition similar to the amphetamine psychosis (Redlich and Freedman 1966, p. 739; Maurer and Vogel 1967, p. 132). Post (1975) has observed an orderly progression of clinical syndromes associated with cocaine psychosis (euphoria, dysphoria, and schizophreniform psychosis) related to dosage, chronicity, and genetic and experiential predispositions. Symptoms in his continuum model include hyperactivity, insomnia, apathy, hallucinations, paranoid delusion, and proneness to violence.

However, Ashley (1975) averred that reports of such adverse reactions are either dated or in error. He contended that current users almost never report hallucinations or paranoid reactions. The cocaine user who takes large doses of the drug over an extended period may experience visual, auditory, or tactile sensations. But these are not hallucinations, inasmuch as the user does not believe that what he experiences is real.

AMPHETAMINES AND AMPHETAMINE-LIKE COMPOUNDS

The most widely abused amphetamine stimulants* are:

amphetamine (Benzedrine)
methamphetamine (Methedrine and Desoxyn)
dextroamphetamine (Dexedrine)
phenmetrazine (Preludin)
mephentermine (Wyamine)

The literature refers mostly to amphetamines as a class and does not discuss each member individually. Amphetamines can be injected, ingested, or snorted. An enormous tolerance is built up in a short time (Shick et al. 1973, Yatsu et al. 1975). Grinspoon and Hedblom (1975, p. 198) stated, "Contrary to much medical and popular opinion, the amphetamines are probably as addicting as heroin.† These writers affirmed that amphetamines cause physical dependence and that the user experiences gradual development of withdrawal symptoms.

> We believe amphetamines do cause physical dependence, unless "physical dependence" is regarded as synonymous with "dependence produced by opiates." It is true that the amphetamine abstinence syndrome is not always so obviously painful or apparently life-threatening as the opiate or barbiturate abstinence syndrome. The difference appears to be related to the rate at which different drugs are eliminated from the body. (p. 159)

The user experiences increased sweating, quicker breathing, and raised blood pressure as the central nervous system is stimulated (Irwin 1970). Appetite for food is suppressed (Ferguson 1975). The most important physical effect is the rush (also called the "flash" or "splash"). Ray (1972, p. 171) pointed out that the amphetamine rush is different from the "drowsy, drifting effect" of the heroin rush. As the drug is injected directly into the bloodstream, there is a feeling of exhilaration and of the blood pounding

---

*Wiley (1971) reported also heavy use of methylphenidate (Ritalin), called by users "West Coast."

†Grinspoon and Hedblom (1975) in a 300-page book, have covered many aspects of amphetamine usage, including pharmacogenic properties; the effect of amphetamines on mood, performance, and other aspects of personality, habituation, dependence, addiction, and treatment of hyperkinetic children.

through the body. The rush has been compared to an orgasm all over the body (Clement et al. 1970, Ferguson 1975).

There is an increase in alertness, arousal, and physical activity, and the user becomes talkative and restless (Irwin 1970). He is oversensitive to stimuli and is jumpy and anxious. "The body is in a general state of stress as if it were extremely threatened or expecting a violent fight" (National Institute of Mental Health 1971). The user experiences a feeling of elation and is overconfident (Long and Penna 1968; Kiev 1975; Pittel and Hafer 1973). When the user comes down from this state of exhilaration, there is an intense depression, or "crash," which for many is relieved only by reinjection of the drug (National Clearinghouse 1970). Consequently, the user starts another "speed binge" or "amphetamine run," and the high–depression cycle starts again (Clement et al. 1970). It has been reported (Vista Hill Psychiatric Foundation 1972) that some amphetamine users inject heroine with methamphetamine to help them "come down" more gradually. This combination of drugs is called the "poor man's speedball." Ferguson (1975) mentioned five types of psychologic consequences that may follow amphetamine use: anxiety reaction, amphetamine psychosis, exhaustion syndrome, prolonged depression, and prolonged hallucinosis.

CRIME

Amphetamine use is viewed as having a direct causal relationship to crimes of violence. Seevers (1969) stated that antisocial behavior occurs as "a manifestation of the direct action of the drug." Grinspoon and Hedblom (1975, p. 202) observed that the pharmacologic properties of amphetamines "appear to make (them) uniquely criminogenic. . . . Since the amphetamines have psychopharmacological properties which potentiate or disinhibit aggressive impulses and promote paranoid thinking and even delusions, they have much greater potential for producing violence than opiates or marihuana" (p. 189). These authors also observed that in 1968 after the Haight-Ashbury district of San Francisco became the "speed capital of the world," crime and violence increased dramatically.

It is the energizing property of amphetamines that is regarded by some as enhancing the "tendency to take physical action quickly" (Tinklenberg and Stillman 1970, p. 338). Milkman and Frosch (1977, p. 22) observed: The energizing effects of amphetamine serve the user's needs to feel active and potent in the face of an environment perceived as hostile and threatening." Crime, then is a natural outlet for drug-induced overactivity: "On a typical run (prolonged heavy use) of speed, there develops severe paranoia . . . . a marked tendency to violence sometimes tragically leading to murder, and serious physical deterioration" (Fort 1971, p. 14). Girdano and Girdano (1976,

p. 122) asserted that "extreme hyperactivity, fatigue, paranoia, and the social condition" all contribute to violent behavior when a person uses high doses of amphetamines. Comparing amphetamines with marijuana, Schofield (1971) said: "Amphetamines increase courage and energy, but a man under the influence of cannabis prefers to sit still and enjoy himself passively" (p. 69). Seevers (1969) also observed that amphetamines increase courage, referring to the building of "false bravery" through amphetamine use.

Greene et al. (1973) studied 320 men who had been arrested for a variety of crimes; all had used amphetamines. They found that 300, or 93.7 percent, of this group had also used opiates. Opiate use came first and was supplemented by amphetamines as addicts attempted to improve the "high" obtained from poor-quality heroin. What they sought was an enhanced opiate effect, not an amphetamine effect. Greene et al., considering the arrest reports of their subjects, noted that these amphetamine users appeared to be no more likely to commit violent crimes than nonamphetamine users. They speculated that the opiates counteracted the excitatory effects of amphetamines. Another possibility suggested was that violent crimes were in fact committed, but the amphetamine users had not been apprehended.

SEXUAL BEHAVIOR

Most writings that we surveyed emphasize that the variety of effects on sexual behavior attributable to amphetamines is related to personality factors, setting, and dosage. In a study of "amphetamine addiction and disturbed sexuality," Bell and Trethowan (1961) found that five of thirteen subjects experienced an increase in sex drive, three a decrease, and five no change. They concluded that the drug effect was related to "the preexisting sexual adjustment of the individual concerned." These investigators and Ellinwood (1967) found that the relationship between amphetamine use and sexual behavior was also based on dosage and setting. Cohen (1969, p. 94) reported that "sexual interest may be enhanced or diminished." Angrist and Gershon (1969) stated that "increased promiscuity, compulsive masturbation, prostitution and intensification of sado-masochistic fantasies were all reported as consistent sequelae" of amphetamine use. The Vista Hill Psychiatric Foundation (February 1972) reported "marathon sexual activity" by some users of amphetamines: "Orgasm and ejaculation are delayed or impossible to achieve. As a result, marathon sexual activity is described by some 'speed freaks.' Others report a complete absence of sexual interest." Ferguson (1975, p. 127) stated that the sexual interest of amphetamine users is increased, but ejaculation and orgasm are delayed. Grinspoon and Hedblom (1975, p. 96) concluded: "Amphetamines' sexual effects seem as varied as those of alcohol, and depend as much on dosage, personality, and setting."

PSYCHOSIS

The National Clearinghouse (1970) stated that a paranoid psychotic state from amphetamine abuse can last long beyond the period of actual drug use. Redlich and Freedman (1966) and Connell (1966) observed that chronic high doses of amphetamines produce an acute psychosis with "lively visual or auditory hallucinations and paranoid delusions." Such a psychosis is hard to distinguish from schizophrenic psychoses. The paranoid feature of the amphetamine psychosis has been described by many (Cohen 1969, p. 92; Kalant 1973; Kiev 1975, p. 59).* "The characteristic clinical picture of amphetamine psychosis emerging from the study of world literature is one of paranoid delusions as the most common feature with hallucinations of various kinds" (Glass 1974, p. 126). Some people believe that paranoid reactions make the amphetamine user more likely to become indiscriminately violent. Ellinwood (1968) observed a striking similarity between the symptoms of amphetamine psychosis and those of the psychosis associated with temporal lobe epilepsy.

DEPRESSANTS

This class of drugs includes the barbiturates and other drugs that are not barbiturates but have almost identical clinical effects. These drugs (ingested or injected) produce physiologic and psychologic dependence. Some professionals believe that barbiturate dependence is more difficult to cure than narcotic dependence (National Institute of Mental Health 1969). Woolf (1983, p. 42) noted that chronic barbiturate abusers can die during untreated barbiturate withdrawal.† The most commonly abused sedative-hypnotics are:

pentobarbital (Nembutal) — "yellow jackets"
secobarbital (Seconal) — "red devils"
amobarbital (Amytal) — "blue devils"
combination of secobarbital and amobarbital (Tuinal) — "rainbows"
glutethimide (Doriden)
chloral hydrate (Noctec) — "Mickey Finn"
methaqualone (Quaalude, Sopor)

---

*Angrist et al. (1970) described three cases of psychosis caused by the abuse of the Wyamine (mephentermine) inhalant. The condition was similar to other amphetamine psychosis and to paranoid schizophrenia.

†Tragic effects of sedative-hypnotic addiction are cited in the literature. Suicides have been reported (AMA-CAA 1965, *U.S. Medicine* 5/15/72), and Ray (1972, p. 176) stated that barbiturates are the "most frequently used class of drugs for suicides."

All these drugs are referred to as "downers" because they have a depressant effect on the central nervous system, producing in some users drowsiness and sleep (Ewing 1967). Carrol (1974) stated that such depressants are not used to seek out novel forms of experience but, rather, to reduce unwanted, excessive environmental stimulation. However, another set of effects has been cited. Wesson and Smith (1977, p. 67) reported that some people use barbiturates chiefly to become less inhibited. Long and Penna (1968) stated that sedative-hypnotics produce a type of euphoria — a "feeling of elation, tranquility and well-being." Irwin (1970) said that the state was similar to that produced by alcohol, the effects being talkativeness, loss of inhibitions, faulty judgment, and changeability in emotional state. Ewing (1967), Irwin (1970), and Kiev (1975) also observed that some users become quarrelsome and belligerent.

Pascarelli (1973) said that the use of methaqualone (Quaalude or Sopor) had reached "the proportions of a countrywide epidemic." This drug was synthesized in India in 1955 and introduced into American pharmaceutical use in 1965. Quaalude was alleged to be nonaddicting. Kempton and Kempton (1973) stated that methaqualone is preferred by users to barbiturates because its euphoric effects are alleged to be psychedelic, a quality not attributed to the latter. Hendin (1975, p. 195) quoted a user in his study as saying about methaqualone: "You learn to resist the initial sedative effect and then the drug comes to be like a stimulant."

Chambers (1969) stated that one of every three narcotic-abusing patients was also addicted to sedative-hypnotics. Doriden, a nonbarbiturate sedative, was the most common. Raynes (1973) reported that 223 of 400 patients (55 percent) admitted to Boston City Hospital's Drug Detoxification Unit had abused barbiturates. This facility had been treating primarily drug users physically dependent on heroin. Raynes observed that the frequent use of barbiturates by heroin addicts "may well represent a shift from impure and less available heroin" (p. 997). Mitcheson (1970) described the extensive use of barbiturates by heroin addicts in Great Britain. They used barbiturates to sleep better, to avoid symptoms of heroin withdrawal, or for "kicks." These addicts claimed to be using sedatives because of reduced availability of amphetamines, heroin, and cocaine.

Many users of amphetamines also used barbiturates. Ray (1972, p. 170) pointed out that barbiturates are used to combat the nervousness produced by amphetamines. Brecher (1972, p. 279) observed that barbiturates are used to alleviate the depression of "coming down" from amphetamines.

CRIME

The literature on depressants and crime is sparse. Hendin (1975, p. 195) noted that youthful sedative abusers were prone to "express hostility without remorse or inhibition." Tinklenberg and Stillman (1970, p. 343) and the National Commission on Marihuana and Drug Abuse (1973, p. 160) have noted a link between high dosages of barbiturates and violent crime, although as the Commission pointed out, it was observed in people "who are prone toward violence in a non-drugged state." In a 1974 study Tinklenberg et al. found that, other than alcohol, secobarbital was "the specific drug most likely to enhance assaultive tendencies," despite the fact that it was used less frequently than most other drugs. Spotts and Shonty (1982) noted that abusers of depressants describe "an alarming incidence of fights, barroom brawls, accidents, and car wrecks." Gerald and Schwirian (1973) presented a different finding: "We find little evidence to suggest that our respondents exhibit an aggressive antisocial behavioral tendency" (p. 630).

SEXUAL BEHAVIOR

Current literature contains little about depressants and sexual behavior. When methaqualone became popular in the early 1970s, one of its touted effects was that it was the "love drug," allegedly possessing aphrodisiac qualities (Zwerdling 1972; Kempton and Kempton 1973; Pascarelli 1973; Swartzburg et al. 1973). According to street mythology, the difference between Sopors and other downers is that Sopors are a sex drug. Unlike most barbiturates, the myth has it, "Sopors don't impair sexual performance—if you can stay awake, that is" (Cameron 1973, p. 24). Most experts believe that the "love drug" statements constitute a myth. Inaba et al. (1973) quoted one patient as saying what was true for many others: "I never get off and it's also hard to get it up" (a reference to ejaculation and erection). However, Wesson and Smith (1977, p. 72) reported that men "self-medicated" themselves for premature ejaculation and women did the same "to reduce their sexual inhibitions so they could experience orgasm."

PSYCHOSIS

The only reference we found to a psychotic reaction to barbiturates was Ray's observation (1972, p. 175) that psychosis may occur as part of a withdrawal reaction.

VOLATILE SUBSTANCES

The National Institute of Mental Health (1971) divided volatile substances that are often abused by inhalation of fumes into three groups: commercial solvents, aerosols, and anesthetics. Rubin and Babbs (1970) listed as the most commonly abused substances gasoline, paint thinner, paint, lacquer thinner, cigarette-lighter fluid, marking pencils, and model-airplane glue. Wilde

(1975) reported that aerosol spray paints with metallic particles were being inhaled for purposes of intoxication. Preble and Laury (1967) said that plastic cements used in assembling models were the most popular substances for abuse. Unlike many drugs, these substances are inexpensive and legal (Alex 1968).*

Researchers give the same reasons for use of these substances as they do for use of other drugs. From a sociologic standpoint, Rubin and Babbs (1970) pointed out that the boys whom they studied could gain acceptance from their peers for glue sniffing and receive the "positive attention that had been witheld by . . . family and school." Wilson (1968) stated that glue sniffing is a socioeconomic phenomenon by which the "have-nots" of society escape the awareness of all they are lacking.

Commenting on the psychology of the glue sniffer, Gioscia (1968) emphasized its regressive aspect. He referred to a "primitive respiratory incorporation" in which there is an unconscious effort to "breathe in, more rapidly, some childish image of a happy life." Gioscia observed that the inhaler may ultimately reach an "extremely infantile psychotomimetic state."

The user seeks exhilaration or euphoria, "a pleasurable oblivion from reality" (Ackerly and Gibson 1964). Irwin (1970) said that the user experiences floating sensations, reckless abandon, a breakdown of inhibitions, and intense feelings of well-being. Inhalation of volatile substances also provides the user with a tremendous sense of power (Irwin 1970; Ferguson 1975). Clinger and Johnson (1951) reported that a thirteen-year-old inhaler of gasoline vapors had the fantasy that he could move massive machinery up a mountain and that he could see for extraordinary distances. Sokol (cited by Williams 1967, p. 156) quoted a thirteen-year-old glue sniffer: "When I sniff the stuff, I'm second to God. I'm in a different world. All of my problems are forgotten."

The euphoria induced by volatile substances increases until the sniffer has become "drunk" (Allen 1966). Then he experiences much the same effects as those that are evident in acute alcoholism — slurred speech, confusion, and depression (Ferguson 1975). Allen (1966) described the user's experiencing double vision and a lack of coordination. According to some sources, the user of volatile substances does not recall what happened during his "intoxication" (National Institute of Mental Health 1971). He may go into a complete stupor (Preble and Laury 1967). Lewis et al. (1978) reported a case of ir-

---

*An international conference in 1976 was told that in the United States inhalation of volatile substances is the "fastest growing and most widespread problem of substance abuse" (*Washington Post* 7/26/76). The *Post,* editorializing on this report, pointed out: "The cans of hairspray and metallic paints are themselves cheap by the standard of the hallucinogenic marketplace. Furthermore, they are readily and widely available. Any youngster with a weakness for such abuse can easily find the substance of his or her choice."

reversible brain damage as a result of prolonged sniffing of the solvent toluene. Bass (1970) reported an "epidemic" of 110 deaths of youths who sniffed solvents.

CRIME

While there is a general lack of information about the relationship between use of volatile substances and the commission of crime (National Commission of Marihuana and Drug Abuse 1973, p. 164), some investigators believe that there is a causal link between inhalation of these substances and acts of violence (Tolan and Lingl 1964; Cohen 1969, p. 102). Friedman and Friedman (1973) reported on cases of assaultive behavior and violence among glue sniffers whom they studied. Hoffman (1975, p. 135) stated that accompanying volatile-substance-usage effects (such as ataxia, giddiness, and euphoria) is "a sense of reckless abandon and omnipotence, often leading to impulsive and destructive behavior."

Krug et al. (1965, p. 44) included in their typology of glue sniffers "the child who becomes 'addicted' to the glue vapor and will steal, lie, etc., to obtain a supply of glue or other solvent." Hahn (1978) reported:

> Behavior is altered emphatically as glue sniffers tend to deteriorate in their ability to effectively control their impulses. When under the influence of these toxic vapors, the youthful inhalers become extremely aggressive, easily sexually aroused, and have little respect for authority or the personal and property rights of others. (p. 158)

SEXUAL BEHAVIOR

A sexual aspect of the "excitation" experienced by users of volatile substances has been cited. Clinger and Johnson (1951) reported that for a 16-year-old who inhaled gasoline vapors, sexual fantasy was a "specific objective of inhalation." Massengale et al. (1963) said that glue sniffing reduces anxieties and lessens inhibitions that normally accompany sexual impulses. Ackerly and Gibson (1964) stated that "usually either a suggestion or evidence of sexual activities" is associated with the sniffing of lighter fluid. Schroeder (1980, p. 117) noted that inhalation of nitrates (used to dilate blood vessels) is reputed to enhance sexual performance.

PSYCHOSIS

The vivid hallucinations in color experienced by inhalers of volatile substances (e.g., Long and Penna 1968, Irwin 1970, National Institute of Mental Health 1971) have not been regarded as manifestations of psychosis. Tolan and Lingl (1964) reported toxic psychosis associated with gasoline inhalation by two teenagers. The investigators stated that this was comparable with the "model psychoses" evoked by LSD-25 and psilocybin. The youngsters in the study experienced spatial distortions, hyperacusis, light-headedness, grandiosity, a dreamlike state, and hallucinations that were visual, auditory, and tactile.

MARIJUANA

In the 1930s marijuana use was of national concern. According to some (e.g., Gomila and Lambou 1938, p. 27), it was the "greatest problem facing narcotics authorities." It was observed in 1971 that "smoking marijuana has become a major national pastime" (Snyder, p. 72). Statistics during the mid-1970s (National Institute on Drug Abuse 1976, p. 2) indicated that for the first time a majority of a particular age group had tried marijuana: 53 percent of young adults eighteen to twenty-five years old had used it at least once.* Hahn (1978, p. 150) noted that between 25 and 30 million Americans had "experimented" with the drug. Summing up the increasing prevalence of marijuana use, Ray (1978, p. 417) asserted, "Has the world gone to pot? It sure has." Perhaps because of its widespread availability, the pendulum has swung from regarding marijuana as a menace to what the editor of a pediatric journal called a "current all too prevalent laissez-faire attitude about this problem" (see editor's note in Schwartz, 1984).

Although addiction to the drug was considered rare, it was believed to occur when the drug was used over an extended period. Today marijuana is considered nonaddicting. But there is disagreement as to whether there is a tolerance effect or physical dependence and, if so, to what extent. The Institute of Medicine (1982, p. 26) stated, "Tolerance can develop rapidly after only a few small doses." Apster (1978) stated flatly that marijuana does not produce physical dependence. However, the National Institute on Drug Abuse (1976, p. 6) stated that physical dependence can occur, but only when unusually high doses of tetrahydrocannabinol (THC, the principal psychoactive component of marijuana) are administered under research conditions.

The marijuana "high" has been characterized in many ways. Winick (1971) observed that what the user gets out of it may be implied in the colloquial names for the drug — "joy stick" and "locoweed." Effects vary according to the personality of the user, the dosage, and the span of time. Some subjective aspects of the reported euphoria are the sensation of floating in air (Allentuck and Bowman 1942) and falling on waves (Winick 1971), a feeling of warmth and joy (Ferguson 1975), and an increased sense of well-being (National Commission on Marihuana and Drug Abuse 1972).

---

*However, only 25 percent had tried the drug during the last month of the survey. Thus this is not a statement on the chronicity of usage.

There is frequent mention of the hallucinogenic effects of the drug, especially at high doses (e.g., Chopra 1969). De Ropp (1968) described the positive effects of hashish.*

> The spirit of hashish on one's good days . . . is playful as a kitten, puckish, jocular, a conjurer performing quaint tricks that one never would have thought possible. The tricks are associated with the self-sense, that mixed bag of awareness, of muscle tone, vision, hearing, touch, taste, smell that gives us the overall sensation of "I am." (p. 37)

Sensations seem "newer, sharper, and more intense" (Kaplan 1970). This applies to colors and the enjoyment of music. The appetite is increased, there is a craving for sweets, and food tastes better (Allentuck and Bowman 1942; Snyder 1971; Kiev 1975). The user's perception of time and space changes. Time intervals are estimated by the user to be far greater than they actually are (National Institute of Mental Health 1971; Snyder 1972; Balis 1974). "Along with the euphoria, this slowing of subjective time is probably the most dramatic effect of ordinary marijuana use" (Kaplan 1970, p. 67).

Users claim that marijuana helps them to relax (National Commission on Marihuana and Drug Abuse 1972; Kiev 1975). Another positive effect cited is increased sociability (Eddy et al. 1971; Kiev 1975). This has been called a "loss of inhibitions" (Winick 1971; Ferguson 1975).

Other benefits claimed by marijuana users are enhancement of aesthetic appreciation (Kaplan 1970; Eddy et al. 1971; Balis 1974), originality and creativity (Balis 1974), and insight. "The merciless spirit of hashish strips from all art forms the overlay of egotism, illuminating with a pitiless radiance the underlying reality. For genuine artistic creation its praise is unqualified" (De Ropp 1968, p. 39). Baudelaire (Solomon 1966) spoke of pantheistic visions from hashish. However, Kiev (1975) said that insights from marijuana "contribute little to personality maturation or responsible behavior." Snyder (1971) pointed out that although the marijuana user believes that he has greater understanding of others when he uses the drug, studies have demonstrated that he is more perceptive when sober.

A negative effect from the standpoint of society is what has been termed the "amotivational syndrome." Bejerot (1972) observed that the heavy hashish smoker loses interest in school or work: "He becomes passive and is very inclined to glide into a life of daydreams" (p. 23). The American Academy of Pediatrics Committee on Drugs (1975) observed that long-term regular users of marijuana are "motivated" to obtain the drug, but to do little else; they drop out and become apathetic. Kiev (1975, pp. 51–52) has said that even if

---

*Marijuana is derived from the flowering tops, stems, and leaves of the female hemp plant. Hashish is the plant's pure resinous exudate.

marijuana smoking does not cause withdrawal from society, its effects may result in the user's deemphasizing achievement and mastery of reality. The National Institute on Drug Abuse (1976) stated that it is questionable whether marijuana causes a change in values; it may well be that the change comes first and that marijuana use is a consequence.

Halikas (1974) noted that the most commonly cited adverse reaction to marijuana use is the "panic anxiety reaction." The clinical picture is one of "prominent anxiety and panic features, physiological concomitants of anxiety, psychological and physiological symptoms of intoxication, and a relatively clear sensorium."

> This reaction is self-limited, lasting from several minutes to several hours. It is said to occur most frequently in novice users, highly suggestible users, users in a strange or threatening situation (such as a clinical laboratory), and in regular users receiving an unexpectedly large dose. (p. 280)

Nahas (1973) has warned that the dangers of marijuana use include psychologic dependence, possible precipitation of psychosis, and a decrease in productivity, efficiency, and dependability. A more ominous prospect that only later studies can refute or confirm is brain damage. "One cannot exclude the possibility that the repetitive impairment of [brain biochemistry] by frequent *Cannabis* intoxication during adolescence might after a few years induce permanent changes in patterns of thinking or of behavior" (p. 110).

Some studies report that the user's memory and attention are impaired.* Kaplan (1970) said that marijuana use adversely affects immediate memory and decreases ability to perform complex tasks that require sustained concentration. The National Commission on Marihuana and Drug Abuse (1972) pointed out that impairment of cognitive and psychomotor performance is dose-related. Long and Penna (1968) stated that memory deteriorates and attention is interfered with by confusion resulting from the use of marijuana. On the other hand, Rubin and Comitas (1976, pp. 119, 123) found no difference between cannabis smokers and nonsmokers on tests of attention and memory.

The "stepping-stone" or "escalation" theory (that there is a direct causal relationship between early marijuana use and later use of opiates) has generated much controversy. Jones (1971, p. 18) stated: "The statistical case for a progression from marijuana to more powerful drugs is so strong that cause

---

*For a review of marijuana's physiologic effects, neurologic effects, and effects on mental and motor performance and driving, see the publication of the National Institute on Drug Abuse (1976).

and effect relationships are a mandatory tentative conclusion." Kandel (1984) published follow-up findings from surveying a cohort representative of tenth- and eleventh-grade public school teenagers in New York State. She found, "The more intense the current involvement in marijuana, the greater the number of different illicit drugs that had been used." This supported what she termed "one of the best-established findings in drug research — i.e., "the strong association between the use of marijuana and other illicit drugs."

Generally, a cause-effect relationship of this nature receives little support in the literature. Although some investigators (e.g., Chappel 1966; Ball et al. 1968; Pillard 1970) have noted a statistical relationship between early marijuana use and later use of heroin, the prevailing view is that such a correlation does not demonstrate a causal relationship. Goode (1974), in a lengthy article on the stepping-stone theory, asserted: "The greater tendency of marijuana users, and especially regular and heavy users, to also use dangerous drugs may be taken as an established fact" (p. 316). However, Goode warned: "A correlation, even a strong and unambiguous one, is not a demonstration of causality; it is a fallacy to automatically equate correlation with cause" (p. 320). Weil (1972, p. 61) pointed out that while many addicts used marijuana before trying heroin, they also tended to use tobacco and alcohol before trying marijuana. By implication one might conclude that cigarette smoking, as much as marijuana use, leads to heroin addiction.

There are those who regard marijuana as safe relative to other drugs. Grinspoon (1977) affirmed that the substance "is not addicting, is not criminogenic, and does not lead to sexual excess" (p. 323). He urged that the social use of marijuana be legalized and predicted that this would happen by the end of the 1980s. But there are others who continue to have a less sanguine view of marijuana use. Schwartz (1984) called marijuana an "underestimated, deceptive, potent crude drug." He warned, "Acute or chronic marijuana use may impede cognitive and emotional maturation of the adolescent user." A body of findings is emerging that documents marijuana's adverse impact on health. Of concern is the effect of marijuana on intellectual performance, the cardiovascular system, the immune system, the functioning of the lungs, chromosomes, testosterone levels in males, and the drug's cancer-causing potential.* We shall limit our survey to the controversy over the alleged link between marijuana and crime, sex, and psychosis.

CRIME

The effect of marijuana use on criminality is surrounded by controversy. Some authors assert that no direct relationship exists between the two

---

*The Addiction Research Foundation (1983) has published an annotated bibliography of 1,719 papers on the health risks of marijuana.

(Ausubel 1958, pp. 68, 103; Maurer and Vogel 1967, p. 282; Simmons 1967). Others assert that marijuana inhibits and deters violence. Kaplan (1970) stated that if long-term use of marijuana has any effect on aggressiveness, it is to reduce it and render the user more passive. Schofield (1971) has observed that cannabis produces "lethargy and passive behavior." Hendin (1975, p. 170) referred to the function of marijuana as a subduer of rage and fear.

To the argument sometimes advanced that cannabis is used to fortify the criminal's courage, Schofield stated that "pot is taken so as to have a calming effect" and that its ultimate effect would be to make a criminal less efficient. He concluded by stating: "At any event cannabis does not have some mysterious power which forces people to perpetrate crimes which they would not otherwise commit" (p. 118). The National Commission on Marihuana and Drug Abuse (1972) reported the following: "Some users commit crimes more frequently than nonusers not because they use marihuana, but because they happen to be the kinds of people who would be expected to have a higher crime rate, wholly apart from the use of marihuana" (p. 77). Finally, the National Institute on Drug Abuse (1976, p. 90) stated that there is virtually no evidence that marijuana causes crime. In fact, research findings indicate that subjects acutely or chronically intoxicated with the drug show a decrease in "expressed and experienced hostility."

Tinklenberg (1974, p. 348) examining case reports, observed that the sedative effects of marijuana are most prominently cited. At the conclusion of his own review of literature on marijuana and aggression, this investigator asserted:

> Contrary to many central nervous system depressants, marijuana may exert influences that tend to inhibit brain mechanisms subserving assaultiveness. There is suggestive evidence, at any rate, that the use of marijuana facilitates acquiescence in some individuals and hence reduces the possibilities for human aggression. (p. 354)

There are those who believe that there is a direct causal relationship between marijuana use and crime. Gomila and Lambou (1938, p. 31) described the occurrence in New Orleans of a "crime wave which unquestionably was aggravated by the influence of this drug habit." In 1939 Barnes warned of the dangers of "locoweed":

> The effects of marijuana are far more direct and dangerous than those of any type of narcotic drug. It destroys all sense of restraint and self-control and incites its users to crimes of violence and sex degeneracy. It heads innocent girls to prostitution and boys toward gangs and rackets. A large number of recent and loathsome and degenerate crimes of vio-

lence have been proved to be directly attributable to marijuana. Here is a real menace to the safety of the nation. . . . Here is a field to which alarmists and fanatics in the matter of drug addiction may legitimately turn their attention. (p. 816)

Gaskill (1945) spoke of the "tendency of the drug to result in criminal activities." He cited the fact that in India the chief users of marijuana are the "coolies," who "often become violent and aggressive under its influence." Williams (1967, p. 141) maintained that marijuana "destroys the brain and distorts the mind . . . and is the immediate and direct cause of the crime committed." Others who related marijuana and crime causally include Wolff (1949) and McMorris (1966). Robins et al. (1970, p. 169) stated that twice as many adolescent marijuana users as nonusers showed three or more indices of violence.*

Some reports emphasize the danger of marijuana as a disinhibitor rather than declaring that it is directly reponsible for crime (Brown 1961, p. 60; Winick 1971, p. 233). MacDonald (1976) said that if antisocial tendencies are present in a person, marijuana use will bring them to the fore:

The smoking of marijuana and crimes against the person may have a common background in personality disorder and a subculture of violence. Marijuana may give rise to feelings of self-confidence and bravado which might well encourage someone who is already so inclined to use a gun to supplement his income. (p. 250)

Charen and Perelman (1946) said the following about sixty marijuana addicts: "These men had traits of character which lead to conflict with the law. Basically the urge for criminal activity must be present. Use of marijuana lessens or eliminates anxieties which interfere with the urge for lawlessness" (p. 677). Cohen (1964, p. 15) observed that marginally adjusted people use the drug either "for 'kicks' or to work up enough courage to commit a felony." Maurer and Vogel (1967, p. 282) asserted that: "whatever you are before you smoke marijuana, the drug will only make you more so." McGlothlin and West (1968) stated that there appears to be "some validity" to the assertion that "professional criminals use marijuana as a means of fortifying themselves in their criminal operations."

The predominant view today is that the personality of the user is the crucial variable in the relationship between marijuana use and antisocial behavior.

---

*Robins et al. were referring to their nine measures of violent behavior and fantasy: e.g., have you ever been hurt in a fight, have you ever felt like killing someone, do you throw or break things when angry?

"If the user is not prone to violence or crime and if he does not develop a drug-induced psychosis, he will not, except for the infraction of narcotics laws, normally resort to violent or criminal behavior" (Bloomquist 1971, p. 202).

SEXUAL BEHAVIOR

Opler (1972) viewed the relationship between marijuana use and sexual behavior in terms of cultural mores and conceptions of social deviance. In his opinion social and behavioral conditioning is more significant than psychologic predisposition, and both marijuana use and sexual experimentation are parts of the youth subculture rather than causes of each other.

There has been considerable mention of the aphrodisiac qualities of marijuana. Lewin (1964, p. 117) said that it is smoked "to increase the sexual functions or to experience voluptuous sensations in the trance state." The National Commission on Marihuana and Drug Abuse (1972) stated that it appears to intensify the sex experience, although its effects may be largely psychologic. Zinberg (1984, p. 88) stated that, in interviews, marijuana users said that sexual activity was more enjoyable when they were "stoned." Berke and Hernton (1974), after providing an account of marijuana's enhancement of sexual experience, asserted: "We must conclude that cannabis has a direct physical effect which increases sexual staying power to such a point that the pleasure of the sexual climax may be felt to be almost unbearable" (p. 145). Winick (1971) stated that a sexual experience may seem more intense because of the marijuana user's distorted sense of time. The slowing of time seems to prolong the period of contact.

Of course, it is possible that a high degree of sexual activity preceded drug use. In a study of drug users on a college campus, Goode (1972) found that they were likely to have had sexual intercourse earlier in life than nonusers, to have it more frequently, and to have it with a greater number of partners.

The National Commission on Marihuana and Drug Abuse (1973, p. 159) found that "marihuana is not an aphrodisiac and does not chemically induce sexual arousal." Finally, the National Institute on Drug Abuse (1976, p. 82) reported that large doses or long-term use of the drug may diminish sexual interest and potency in males.

Some authorities affirm that the effect depends on the user: "Marijuana does not create anew; it only activates what is latent" (Goode 1969). Alexander Trocchi, a novelist quoted by Schofield (1971), said:

> If one is sexually bent, if it occurs to one that it would be pleasant to make love, the judicious use of the drug will stimulate the desire and heighten the pleasure immeasurably, for it is perhaps the principal effect of

marijuana to take one more intensely into whatever the experience. (pp. 124-125)

Ferguson (1975) affirmed this in his statement that marijuana influences sexual responsiveness by releasing the user's inhibitions.

PSYCHOSIS

The literature reveals a controversy as to whether marijuana can precipitate a psychosis in a person with no known tendency to psychosis or whether it does so only in individuals with a psychotic predisposition.

Talbott and Teague (1969) observed twelve cases of acute toxic psychosis produced on first exposure to marijuana. This occurred in American soldiers in Vietnam who inhaled smoke from cigarettes containing cannabis derivatives. The recovery from the psychosis was complete, and the symptoms did not recur. The investigators raised the question of whether it might have been the conditions in Vietnam that were predisposing. A study that received considerable publicity and created controversy was that of Kilansky and Moore (1971). These physicians studied thirty-eight patients who each smoked two or more marijuana cigarettes a week. Before using the drug, the patients had no predisposition to mental illness. The investigators concluded: "It is our impression that our study demonstrates the possibility that moderate-to-heavy use of marijuana in adolescents and young people without predisposition to psychotic illness may lead to ego decompensation ranging from mild ego disturbance to psychosis" (p. 492). Bejerot (1972) observed an increase in the number of hashish psychoses in Sweden. He asserted that these were more serious than amphetamine psychoses in that psychotic conditions from hashish sometimes became chronic. And Ferguson (1975, p. 95) stated that large enough doses of marijuana cause psychotic reactions in almost any person. Weil (1973) affirmed that in people with no history of mental disorder or drug experimentation, toxic psychosis occurs only if marijuana is ingested rather than smoked. In people with a history of psychosis, however, he said that marijuana may precipitate a psychotic break (although he never saw such a case). Finally, he reported, people who have a history of drug experimentation but no mental disorder may experience "flashbacks" or delayed psychotic reactions.

Halikas (1974, pp. 281-285) asserted that a "marijuana psychosis" (also called "toxic psychosis," "hemp psychosis," "acute psychotic reactions," or "acute schizophrenic decompensation") is actually a "classic acute brain reaction to an exogenous toxin." This marijuana brain syndrome is characterized by clinical features similar to those of other acute toxic brain syndromes. Of course, unique features in the syndrome appear as a consequence of individual differences in intelligence, personality, and life problems.

In reviewing the literature on marijuana-induced psychosis, Grinspoon (1977, p. 265) stated that what is often glossed over is that "the affected individuals have had preexisting psychiatric disturbances and have also taken other drugs." Thus the alleged cause-affect connection between marijuana and psychosis is thrown into question. Szymanski (1981) cited four cases that he regarded as documenting that "depersonalization can be a prolonged, severe, and continuous sequel of marijuana use." He added that this is true "especially when use occurs at the time of exposure to psychosocial stresses or significant life events." Others had concurred that, in a stable person, the drug does not produce adverse psychological reactions including psychosis *de novo* (e.g., Bloomquist 1971; Winick 1971; Nahas 1973, pp. 240–241; Institute of Medicine, 1982).

HALLUCINOGENS, OR PSYCHOTOMIMETIC DRUGS

The literature on hallucinogenic drugs ranges from extensive coverage of the well-known and widely used to mere mention of some that are obscure. The substances most often discussed are lysergic acid diethylamide (LSD, a synthetic substance), psilocybin (usually produced synthetically, although obtainable from a mushroom), and mescaline (from the tubercles of the mescal or peyote cactus). Phencyclidine (PCP, an animal tranquilizer) began to draw a great deal of attention as its use sharply increased in the mid-1970s.* Less attention is devoted to dimethyltryptamine (DMT), dipropyltryptamine (DPT), dimethoxyphenylisopropylamine (DOM or STP), diethyltryptamine (DET), morning glory seeds, and the household spices, nutmeg and mace.

Until relatively recently, the most extensive literature was on LSD because, as Wells (1974) pointed out, it was the most easily available of the major hallucinogens and "the principal material of the psychedelic cult." Williams (1974) has said that LSD seems to affect the concentrations of some chemicals in the brain and produces changes in the brain's electric activity. The nature of the effects is roughly correlated with the dosage; tolerance develops rapidly, and repeated daily doses become totally ineffective within three to four days (Ray 1978, p. 356). McGlothlin (1973, p. 84) stated that LSD cannot be used more than twice a week without losing much of its impact. Scher (1966) said that most users discontinue using the drug because of its progressively reduced effectiveness. Julien (1978, p. 159) noted that even when the drug is used heavily over a prolonged period, physical dependence does not develop.

McGlothlin and Arnold (1971) described in general terms the acute effect of hallucinogens. Although they were discussing LSD, this statement applies

*The Drug Enforcement Administration (1977) reported that its sources showed that during the last three months of 1976, 43 percent of all hallucinogens used were PCP.

as well to other drugs of the same class. "The primary impact is a temporary suspension of mechanisms which provide structure and stability to man's perception of self-image, environment, beliefs, and values in the normal state of consciousness" (p. 40). All writers describe the perceptual changes in their accounts of hallucinogenic drug effects. Perhaps the best-known firsthand description is that of Huxley (1954) in *The Doors of Perception.* An effect widely experienced is synesthesia, in which one "hears" colors, "sees" sounds, and perceives in other combinations of senses (Irwin 1970; Balis 1974; Wells 1974). Ludwig and Levine (1966) observed that perception and mood are interwoven in a synesthetic experience, so that a change in one causes a change in the other. The user of hallucinogens experiences a heightened sensory acuity — colors are more intense, smells are stronger, and the senses of touch, taste, and hearing are enhanced. Visual space may appear to become alternately larger and smaller, and sounds may be hard to localize and understand (Siegel 1973). Balis (1974) stated that there is a splitting of the self into an "observing monitor" and "an experiencing self." In the course of the hallucinogenic experience, there may be a loss of body boundaries as the user thinks that he is merging with his environment. Consequently, a change in body image may occur (Wells 1974). Another perceptual alteration is the change in estimation of time. Siegel (1973) reported that time may slow up, stop entirely, accelerate, or go backward (see also Ludwig and Levine 1966, Wells 1974). Siegel (1973) and Balis (1974) also reported spatial distortions. It is noted by some (National Institute of Mental Health 1971) that perceptual changes may appear long after the drug has worn off. "Flashbacks" may occur days, weeks, or even months after the drug experience.

Another category of hallucinogenic drug effects is the impairment of cognitive functioning. Balis (1974) reported decrements in memory, attention, recognition, recall, problem solving, and comprehension. In great part, this is attributable to the user's preoccupation with subjective experience (Ludwig and Levine 1966). In fact, Wells (1974) has said that the user of hallucinogens is thinking in "alogical" or "prelogical" modes.

Marked changes transpire in the emotional state of the hallucinogen user. Strong emotions ranging from bliss to horror may be experienced within a single hallucinogenic session (National Clearinghouse For Drug Abuse Information 1970; Pollard et al. 1965). Emotional reactions are intensified, and mood swings may be very rapid (Terrill 1964, Irwin 1970). Kiev (1975) stated that hallucinogens may intensify existing neuroses, such as depression. Domino (1975, p. 7) listed depersonalization and acute panic reactions as among the side effects of LSD.

Some writers point to the suggestibility of people under the influence of hallucinogens (National Clearinghouse 1970; Long and Penna 1968). McGlothlin (1973, p. 96) had said that LSD is an "effective agent for facilitating the rapid assimilation of a new set of beliefs and values by large numbers of young persons." Users of hallucinogens report discovering extraordinary meanings and deep insights. The most ordinary objects are endowed with profound significance (De Ropp 1957, p. 53). Girdano and Girdano (1976, p. 90) stated that LSD users perceive an increase in their creativity while on the drug but that in reality products of their creative efforts prove to be inferior in quality to those originated and carried out when they were not on drugs. Berger and Potterfield (1969) and the National Institute of Mental Health (1971) also noted an impairment in creativity among users of hallucinogens. Williams (1974, p. 359) stated that some users report a sense of rebirth or new insights but later are unable to explain the experience to others. Reports of religious experiences are mainly transcendental rather than theistic in content (Gioscia 1969).*

According to the National Clearinghouse (1973, 1975), between 1967 and 1970 use of mescaline and psilocybin increased following publicity about possible chromosome damage caused by LSD. The literature on mescaline, the primary active ingredient of the peyote cactus, is not as voluminous as the literature on LSD, but it is older (mescaline being a natural substance and LSD a comparatively recent synthetic). In 1926 Kluver recorded in detail visual aspects of his mescaline experiences. Marshall and Wells (1937) described a "riot of colour," geometric forms, and prolonged after-images. Thale et al. (1950) made other observations on the visual experience, relating color vividness and degree of distortion of perception to size of dose. Other observations on behavior under mescaline do not differ from those made on behavior under LSD. Smith (1959), describing his use of LSD, reported lassitude, "nondecision," an altered time sequence, and a sense of the unreliability of his usual thought patterns. Guarner (1966) stated that the mescaline user experiences a disintegration of the ego — depersonalization and a fusion of self with object.

Similar observations have been made of the effects of psilocybin, a substance found in several species of mushrooms. Leary et al. (1963) asserted that reactions to psilocybin are milder and briefer than those to LSD or mescaline. Rinkel et al. (1960) described alterations in visual and time perception and depersonalization. Rynearson et al. (1968) mentioned distortions in vision, hearing, and touch; sensations of numbness, lightness, and heaviness; and uncontrolled laughter. As is the case with mescaline, no major differences were observed between psilocybin and LSD.

In the literature occasional reports appear about common household substances that are hallucinogenic when ingested. Hafen (1973) cited nutmeg's

---

*Wells (1974, pp. 189-212) has written on psychedelic drug use and religious experience. He provided both an historical perspective and a review of some recent studies.

serving as a substitute for drugs that are illegal and expensive. Reactions to nutmeg were reported to vary from no mental changes to "full-blown hallucinogenic experiences." Wells (1974, p. 34) said that the abuser of nutmeg is nauseated "until the sense of well-being and euphoria supervenes." The user may have exotic visions and beautiful experiences or "disturbing and frightening perceptual effects" and "an engulfing feeling of being unwell."

In the 1980's, phencyclidine, known as PCP, killer weed (KW), or angel dust became readily available and was widely regarded as the most dangerous drug being abused on the streets. The drug was synthesized in 1957. By the mid-1960s, veterinary use of the substance as an analgesic-anesthetic for animals was still permitted by law, but the substance was outlawed for human use. In 1978, the manufacturer ceased production. But by then PCP was being produced illicitly and inexpensively in laboratories throughout the country. The effects of using this drug are varied and often unpredictable. Associated with PCP use are disorientation, bizarre behavior, and often violent destructiveness toward others or towards the self. Schroeder (1980, p. 117) noted, "The unpredictability of the drug may be part of its attraction for young drug experimenters."

CRIME

Until phencyclidine (PCP) abuse became widespread, literature was sparse on the relationship between the use of hallucinogens and the commission of crimes. Some sources refer to suicide and homicide being outcomes of hallucinogen use (Committee on Alcoholism and Drug Dependence of the AMA 1969; Barter and Reite 1969). Reich and Hepps (1972) reported a homicide by a twenty-two-year-old student who became psychotic on LSD. They said that it was not clear why this occurred; he had had two "bad trips," but twenty benign ones. The investigators suggested that his character structure may have made him "susceptible to the adverse effects of LSD." Klepfisz and Racy (1973) reported another instance of homicide by a twenty-two-year-old. They also were unclear if the drug "exacerbated an underlying psychosis or bore a more direct causal relation to the homicide."

As LSD became increasingly available and more widely used, reports appeared in the press of homicide by people who were said to have been under the influence of the drug (e.g., *National Observer* 11/20/71). Most notorious were the reports of the violence perpetrated by devotees of an LSD cult on the West Coast in the 1960s.

Similarly, an association between PCP use and violent behavior became well documented as health service providers acquired experience with users of that drug. Violence is directed both toward others and the self (Burns and

Lerner 1978; Fauman and Fauman 1979; Wright 1980; Helig et al. 1982). Numerous PCP-related deaths are a result of homicide or suicide that have occurred while the person was on the drug. But Davis (1982) stated that the media have greatly exaggerated the association between PCP and violence. She pointed out that many users of the drug who suffer no adverse PCP reactions do not come to the attention of the authorities or the media.

SEXUAL BEHAVIOR

There is little discussion in the literature of specific effects of hallucinogens on sexual behavior. Writing on the subject centers around a controversy as to whether these drugs inhibit or facilitate sexual activity.

Fisher (1968, p. 75) stated that LSD inhibits sex. He contended that while on LSD most users are "quite passive, suggestible, and rarely concerned about sex." Hoffman (1975, p. 11) said that although erotic thoughts may emerge while the user is on a hallucinogen, he is so preoccupied with his own introspection and fantasy that he is unlikely "to bother with others." However, others have commented on LSD's enhancing the sexual activity of the user. According to Freedman (1967), Leary called LSD "the most powerful aphrodisiac ever discovered by man" and believed that LSD not only increases and intensifies sexual response in a person without major sexual problems but also is of great value for people suffering from sexual inhibitions. Wells (1974) raised the question of whether it is the drug that produces erotic desires in the young or whether the young people who use it are at a stage in life in which the sex drive is already at a maximum. Cohen (1969, p. 22) denied that LSD is an aphrodisiac, but simply called it a "disinhibitor," in that it "permits loosening of superego controls" so that sexual activity may be indulged in more readily. Cattell (1954) observed that in several instances psychiatric patients who used mescaline showed less inhibited sexual behavior.

PSYCHOSIS

The hallucinogens are termed "psychotomimetic" drugs because their effects mimic psychosis. Ray (1972, p. 224) stated that LSD may mimic the biochemical process of schizophrenia. Kiev (1975, p. 70) asserted that any of the hallucinogens can trigger psychotic episodes that may recur months later. Cases of extended psychoses began to be reported in the mid-1960s as use of hallucinogens increased (*Psychiatric Progress* 1969). Glass and Bowers (1970) reported four cases of chronic psychosis in young men who had taken large quantities of hallucinogens over a long period; they reported that the men suffered from "a chronic, ego-syntonic psychotic syndrome" that resisted inpatient treatment. Fink et al. (1967) cited three cases in which psychosis induced by morning glory seeds resembled schizophrenia and various toxic psychoses. There is a considerable literature on acute psychotic states produced by phencyclidine. Holbrook (1983, p. 95) reported that in a PCP-induced psychosis the user may experience hallucinations, delusions of grandiosity or persecution, and may be highly unpredictable in his behavior. The psychotic episode may last one month or longer.

Hekimian and Gershon (1968) stated that drug users who already have an underlying psychotic process appear to prefer hallucinogens to other drugs. The National Institute of Mental Health (1971) stated that the people who seek "instant insight" to solve their problems are often attracted to LSD and are people "most susceptible to an LSD-precipitated breakdown." Leech (1970, p. 53) noted that psychosis may appear when "the unprepared person is faced with the terrors of ego-loss combined with an inability to return to ordinary consciousness." Blaine (1966) noted the lack of predictability with respect to the individual's response: "At present there is no known method of predicting for whom such an experience will consist of one short episode, and for whom it may mark the beginning of a life-time struggle against a crippling and terrifying emotional illness" (p. 77).

POLYDRUG USE

We have presented each class of drugs as a distinct entity. That is, we have discussed the opiate "addict," cocaine user, amphetamine user, depressant user, volatile substance user, marijuana user, and hallucinogen user. An accurate picture of the "drug scene" shows that people who use drugs illegitimately often use more than one. They may use several different drugs separately over time or several drugs at once. The choice of drugs is dictated by availability, fads, and most important, the specific effects desired.

Johnston (1973), reporting the results of a large-scale study of high school males who used drugs, found that "knowing that a young man is more than an experimental user of one of those drugs makes it quite likely that he also is a user of each of the others" (p. 56). Johnston discovered that all youths who had had more than "experimental contact" with heroin had also used marijuana, hallucinogens, amphetamines, and barbiturates. He also reported:

(1) Of those who used hallucinogens more than once or twice during the year, most (84%) also used amphetamines and the majority (60%) also used barbiturates.
(2) Of those who had used amphetamines more than once or twice, 69% also used hallucinogens and 18% used barbiturates.
(3) Of those using barbiturates more than experimentally, most (74%) used hallucinogens and nearly all (90%) used amphetamines.

Gould et al. (1977), surveying 1,094 high school students, found that the use of each of nine drugs was highly associated with the use of all the others, and that the pattern of use formed the following progression: alcohol, marijuana, hashish, barbiturates, amphetamines, LSD, mescaline, cocaine, and heroin. Frosch (1968), studying patients hospitalized at Bellevue as a result of LSD use, found that 90 percent had experimented with stimulants, two-thirds had taken depressants, and nearly half had experimented with opiates. The New York State Office of Drug Abuse Services (1975) reported that among junior and senior high school students the use of multiple substances is not predominant among marijuana users. However, it is a major pattern among users of other drugs. Four of every five students who admitted using narcotics or hallucinogens had used at least two other drugs.

Different drugs may be combined for 'novel experiences" (Hoffman 1975, p. 81), with users randomly and indiscriminately trying anything. However, most combine drugs for specific effects. Users of opiates combine cocaine with heroin in a "speedball" (Ewing 1967; Williams 1974); cocaine's effects are so brief that the user takes heroin with it to prolong the euphoria (National Clearinghouse 1972). Heroin is also taken with other opiates, such as codeine (Chessick 1960; Scher 1966).

McGlothlin (1975, p. 51) has stated that there was a "lower addiction potential" among users of heroin when they were using other drugs simultaneously.

> In order to attempt to prevent the development of tolerance, some addicts will use the narcotic in conjunction with or alternation with agents such as amphetamines. Such combinations will tend to "normalize" the addict so that he can function in a job. (Scher 1966, p. 542)

A dual addiction to opiates and barbiturates is common (Milby 1981, p. 48). Hamburger (1964) noted that 22.8 percent of narcotic addicts admitted to the federal facility at Lexington, Kentucky, said that they were dependent on barbiturates; another 9.6 percent had been dependent on them in the past. Mitcheson et al. (1970) found that 80 percent of the heroin addicts they studied had also used barbiturates. Forrest and Tarala (1973) stated that among 252 drug users admitted to a hospital in Edinburgh, barbiturates were the drugs of choice. In that city opiates had been difficult to obtain. Barbiturates may provide a temporary substitute for heroin. When the latter becomes available, the addict will return to using it. As the quantity and purity of heroin decreases, barbiturates or amphetamines are used to heighten the effect of the less potent heroin and to ease withdrawal (Ferguson 1975, p. 114; Hoffman 1975, p. 81). Scher (1966) reported that some addicts inject the "bombita," a mixture of heroin, amphetamine sulfate, and secobarbital sodium.

The literature contains reports of use of almost every imaginable combination of drugs. From time to time, most drug users accompany their drug of preference with alcohol (e.g., heroin and alcohol, Chessick 1960). Merry (1967) documented a case of a heroin addict who sniffed glue. Chambers et al. reported that Darvon (D-propoxyphene hydrochloride) prolongs or intensifies the effects of the primary drug. Amphetamine users often take it to mitigate the severe depression that accompanies coming down from an amphetamine high. Woody et al. (1975) stated that diazepam (Valium) has been abused alone or in conjunction with methadone and other narcotics. As we shall point out in discussing the treatment of drug users (Chapter 7), methadone has been used illegitimately in combination with many other substances.

ALCOHOL

There is a vast literature on alcohol abuse. As Ferguson (1975, p. 26) observed, psychic dependence on alcohol occurs in various degrees and is a consequence both of pharmacologic effects and of the personality of the user. Brecher (1972, p. 245) stated that "alcohol is very similar in effect to short-acting barbiturates." Alcohol and barbiturates are "two ways of getting drunk." We are concerned here mainly with the effects of alcohol on crime and sexual behavior. The reader interested in alcohol and psychosis can obtain such information by consulting psychiatric references.

CRIME

Reports are numerous of heavy alcohol use among criminals. McPeek (1944) stated that alcohol use and abuse constitute "accepted incidents in the daily and weekly routine" of antisocial people. Blacker et al. (1965) noted that most of 500 delinquent youths who were referred to a Massachusetts reception center had had "considerable exposure to alcohol"—more so, in fact, than other high school boys: 47 percent were moderate or heavy social drinkers, and 7 percent were designated as "pathological drinkers."

Three different views on the relationship between alcohol and crime were summarized by Haughey and Neilberg (1962): Alcohol is regarded as a primary cause of criminal activity, a secondary cause, or no cause at all. In the first case, alcohol is regarded as a "trigger mechanism," in that it releases hostility leading to crime. This view asserts that the crime would not have been committed if its perpetrator had remained sober. Alcohol is considered a secondary cause in that the criminal behavior stems from long-term addiction to alcohol. The alcohol abuser indulges in petty larceny and forgery to support his "habit." In the third case (the most commonly cited), although a crime may have been committed by a person who was drinking, no causal link is established.

Guze et al. (1968) stated that alcoholism is the "most important psychiatric problem associated with criminal behavior aside from the fundamental issue of sociopathy." They said that sociopathic patterns are "frequently complicated by alcoholism" and concluded that the alcoholism is "associated with extensive and serious criminal behavior." Fort (1968, p. 8) noted that "half of the people in prisons committed their crimes in association with excessive alcohol consumption." Goodwin et al. (1971), in an eight-year follow-up study of convicted male felons, found that if sociopathy was present in boyhood or adolescence, fighting and rage reactions were far more prevalent in alcoholics than in nonalcoholics. And the National Commission on Marihuana and Drug Abuse (1973) reported alcohol and crime in strong association with each other.

There is general agreement that alcohol is a disinhibitor. That is, it "acts to release impulses and lower inhibitions" (J. Kaplan 1984, p. 78). Bacon (1962) pointed out that alcohol can increase the potential for "deviation" in adolescents. Hoffman (1975, p. 101) observed, "Ordinary restraints on speech and behavior are weakened." Taylor and Gammon (1976) reported that in a laboratory setting intoxicated subjects showed a higher level of aggression than did nonintoxicated subjects. Plaut (1962) stated that a criminal act occurs "when the alcohol removes sufficient inhibitions so that the person does things he normally would not do." MacKay (1962) referred to a "loss of impulse control" after drinking that leads to "delinquent acts and aggressive outbursts." Blane (1968, p. 38) pointed out that under the influence of alcohol, the abuser is affected so that "submerged rage may come to the surface." The National Commission on Marihuana and Drug Abuse (1973) reported that some researchers have found that the use of alcohol increases courage in preparation for a crime. Bacon (1962) maintained that alcohol reduces efficiency in a crime. He stated that the number of people who use alcohol excessively may be fairly large "among the failures and 3rd raters of the professional criminal category." However, he observed that in less professional crime the "uninhibiting action" of alcohol, although it does not explain a theft, might have allowed the theft to occur.

Of longstanding concern is the outbreak of violence when alcohol is used to excess. Berry and Boland (1977, p. 147) stated that an extensive review of research findings has revealed a significant relationship of alcohol use to "criminal homicide, assault, forcible rape, and other sex offenses." In a study of 200 criminals at Sing Sing, Banay (1942) found a higher incidence of assaults by alcoholic criminals than by those in the general-offender group. The Denver High Impact Anticrime Program (1972, pp. 60–61) reported that among adults charged with crime, heavy users of alcohol were more likely to be charged with violent crimes than were light users or nonusers. A number of studies have revealed that alcohol was used immediately before commission of the act by at least half the offenders involved in crimes of assault (Wolfgang 1958; MacDonald 1961; Voss and Hepburn 1968; Tinklenberg 1973). Tinklenberg and Stillman (1970, p. 348) reported that violence was associated with alcohol less frequently than with methamphetamine but more frequently than with marijuana. Greene (1981) presented data indicating that alcoholics "are more violent than other drug users."

It is widely recognized that antisocial behavior precedes drinking (e.g., McPeek 1944; Guze et al. 1968), but drinking makes a bad situation worse. "While most of the men gave a history of antisocial behavior preceding the onset of a drinking problem, excessive drinking nevertheless appeared to intensify or prolong criminal behavior" (Goodwin et al. 1971, p. 144). Guze and Cantwell (1965) also observed the prolongation of criminal behavior in drinkers. Recidivism rates were higher for alcoholic than nonalcoholic criminals. Although it appears that certain crimes would not have been committed if their perpetrators had not been drinking, several writers warn against simple cause-effect explanations. Wolfgang and Strohm (1956) cautioned that

> the associations with the presence of alcohol shown herein should not be construed as causal connections. . . . Although many serious crimes may be committed by men who are drunk, more often drunkenness is rather a complicating factor, and most men who drink or who are drunk do not commit serious crimes, and especially not homicide. (p. 423)

Blacker et al. (1965) stated that "it is not known whether or not the drinking stimulates misbehavior or serves as a functional equivalent to other deviant modes of conduct."

SEXUAL BEHAVIOR

Predominantly, alcohol is seen as releasing sexual inhibitions (Plaut 1962, Quimby 1970). Rada (1975) cited two theories as to how the process of disinhibition occurs. The "disinhibition" theory states that alcohol "decreases ego control, numbs judgment, and releases normally present moral inhibition." The other theory "posits a direct effect of the alcohol on the brain center responsible for sexual and/or aggressive behavior."

An old observation is that alcohol increases sexual desire but detracts from performance.* Shakespeare wrote in Macbeth:

> [Drink] provokes and unprovokes; it provokes the desire, but it takes away from performance. (Act 2, Scene 3)

---

*Lemere, quoted in a *Washington Post* (2/25/73) article on alcoholism, stated that nearly all his alcohol-abusing patients who "complained of impotence still had a strong desire for sex but, much to their chagrin, were unable to perform."

Hoffman (1975, p. 101) observed that with alcohol, "Sexuality, as manifested in speech and purposive behavior, may become overt."

McClelland (1971) reported that drinking among college students "is associated with sexual conquests and high-powered motorcycles or cars." He stated that one who drinks and is "intensely concerned with personal power" finds his sense of power accentuated and that this results in, among other things, "sexual exploits." In addition, there may be fights, accidents, and marital discord, followed by more drinking.

Gebhard et al. (1967) reported that alcohol was a factor in 67 percent of sexual crimes against children and 39 percent of sex offenses against women. Ferracuti (1972) stated that excessive use of alcohol played a role in cases of parent–child incest.

In summary, investigators representing a variety of scientific disciplines have attempted to answer questions about the causes and incidence of drug use and about the effects of drugs on human behavior. Had a comprehensive, *conceptual* history of the many aspects of drug use been available, this historical review would not have been necessary. Because the drug literature is so extensive, we have selected from it themes most relevant to our work. In doing so, we have included representative studies that present opposing sides of controversies.

Every arena of inquiry into human behavior has its vigorous theoretical proponents and critics. The causation of drug use is no exception. Accordingly, one finds organic, psychologic, and sociologic explanations (as well as multifactor theories). Some of these complement one another; others are mutually exclusive.

Divergent viewpoints and contradictory research findings demonstrate that definitive knowledge about drug use is lacking. Nowhere is this more apparent than in the literature on the effects of drugs, specifically on crime, sexual behavior, and psychosis. Like research on causes and incidence of drug use, studies on drug effects raise more questions than they answer. Are opiates depressants or energizers? Is the "rush" mainly a physical or psychologic effect? What is meant by "euphoria"? Are the "nod" and the "high" experiences of lethargy or excitement? Who is likely to experience a "bad trip"? Is the "amotivational syndrome" present before drug use, or is it a consequence of drug use? How does the drug user choose his drug? Are the various drugs really very different in the behavior they facilitate or inhibit? Do drugs facilitate or inhibit sexual activity? Can a drug produce a psychosis *de novo* in a user? Does the addict commit crimes to support his habit, or was the addict first a criminal and only later a drug user? To what extent are the effects of a drug the result of set and setting rather than a consequence of the pharmacologic properties of the drug itself?

Many other questions will undoubtedly have occurred to the reader. In the succeeding chapters we shall provide data that clarify some of the findings and conclusions presented in this survey. Our methods differ from epidemiologic research in that we have worked intensively with a relatively small sample (121) of drug-using criminals and have done so over fifteen years. We believe that our observations will shed more light on the many dark areas of the drug field and that they will provide some fresh insights into the thinking and behavior of the drug user.

BIBLIOGRAPHY

MAN AND DRUGS: A PERSPECTIVE ON DRUG ABUSE

Becker, H. K. (1963). Carl Koller and cocaine. *Psychoanalytic Quarterly* 32:309-373.

Blum, R., and Associates. (1970). *Drugs I: Society and Drugs*. San Francisco: Jossey-Bass.

Brecher, E. M., and the editors of *Consumer Reports*. (1972). *Licit and Illicit Drugs*. Boston: Little, Brown.

Cohen, S. (1968). The cyclic psychedelics. *American Journal of Psychiatry* 125:393-394.

De Ropp, R. S. (1957). *Drugs and the Mind*. New York: St. Martin's Press.

Domino, E. F. (1975). The hallucinogens. In *Medical Aspects of Drug Abuse*, ed. R. W. Richter, pp. 3-15. Hagerstown, MD: Harper and Row.

Drug Enforcement Administration. *Drugs of Abuse*. Washington, D.C.: Drug Enforcement Administration.

Farnsworth, N. R. (1972). Psychotomimetic and related higher plants. *Journal of Psychedelic Drugs* 5:67-74.

Fink, P. J., Goldman, M., and Lyons, I. (1967). Recent trends in substance abuse. *International Journal of the Addictions* 2:143-151 (Reprinted by courtesy of Marcel Dekker, Inc.).

Glatt, M. M. (1974). *A Guide to Addiction and Its Treatment*. New York: Halsted Press.

Huxley, A. (1954). *The Doors of Perception*. New York: Harper.

Jacobs, K. W. (1974). Asthmador: a legal hallucinogen. *International Journal of the Addictions* 9:503-512 (Reprinted by courtesy of Marcel Dekker, Inc.).

Ludwig, A., Levine, J., Stark, L., and Lazar R. (1969). A clinical study of LSD treatment in alcoholism. *American Journal of Psychiatry* 126:59-69.

Lynn, E. J., Walter, R. G., Harris, L. A., and James, M. (1972). Nitrous oxide: it's a gas. *Journal of Psychedelic Drugs* 5:1-7.

Malcolm, R., and Miller, W. C. (1972). Dimenhydrinate (Dramamine) abuse: hallucinogenic experiences with a proprietary antihistamine. *American Journal of Psychiatry* 128:1012-1013.

Maletzky, B. M. (1974). Addiction to propoxyphene (Darvon): a second look. *International Journal of the Addictions* 9:775–784 (Reprinted by courtesy of Marcel Dekker, Inc.).

Maurer, D. W., and Vogel, V. H. (1967). *Narcotics and Narcotic Addiction,* 3rd ed. Springfield, IL: Charles C. Thomas.

Pahnke, W. N., Kurland, A. A., Unger, S., Savage, C., Wolf, S., and Goodman, L. E. (1970). Psychedelic therapy (utilizing LSD) with cancer patients. *Journal of Psychedelic Drugs* 3:63–75.

Parade. (1973). Chloroform parties. September 30.

Pollard, J. C., Uhr, L., and Stern, E. (1965). *Drugs and Phantasy.* Boston: Little, Brown.

Quimby, F. H. (1970). Little known facts about the psychoactive drugs (Part I: alcohol). Multilith from Science Policy Research Division, Congressional Reference Service, Library of Congress, Washington, D.C. (July 22).

Rosenberg, P. (1975). The effects of mood altering drugs: pleasures and pitfalls. In *Fundamentals of Juvenile Criminal Behavior and Drug Abuser,* eds. R. E. Hardy and J. G. Cull, pp. 139–168. Springfield, IL: Charles C. Thomas.

Savage, C., and McCabe, O. L. (1971). Psychedelic (LSD) therapy of drug addiction. In *The Drug Abuse Controversy,* eds. C. C. Brown and C. Savage, pp. 145–166. Baltimore: National Educational Consultants.

Tennant, F. S., Jr. (1973). Complications of propoxyphene abuse. *Archives of Internal Medicine* 132:191–194.

Washington Post (7/9/73). Chloroform: new high.

Washington Post (11/5/76). Entrepreneurs of "organic highs".

Weil, A. T. (1972). *The Natural Mind: A New Way of Looking at Drugs and the Higher Consciousness.* Boston: Houghton Mifflin.

INCIDENCE OF DRUG USE

Bailey, W.C. (1968). Nalline control of addict-probationers. *International Journal of the Addictions* 3:131–137 (Reprinted by courtesy of Marcel Dekker, Inc.).

Bartollas, C., and Miller, S. J. (1978). *The Juvenile Offender: Control, Correction and Treatment.* Boston: Holbrook Press.

Bender, L. (1963). Drug addiction in adolescence. *Comprehensive Psychiatry* 4:181–194.

Black, S., Owens, K, and Wolff, R. (1970). Patterns of drug use: a study of 5,482 subjects. *American Journal of Psychiatry* 127:62–65.

Bowman, K. M. (1963). Past, present and future in the treatment of drug addiction. *Comprehensive Psychiatry* 4:145–149.

Bromberg, W., and Rodgers, T. (1946). Marijuana and aggressive crime. *American Journal of Psychiatry* 102:825–827.

Buechler, K. P. (1972). Drug usage at the secondary and primary school levels. *Journal of Drug Education* 2:179–190.

Crothers, T. D. (1892). Some new studies of the opium disease. *Journal of the American Medical Association* 18:227–230.

Gossett, J. T., Lewis, J., and Phillips, V. (1971). Extent and prevalence of illicit drug use as reported by 56,745 students. *Journal of the American Medical Association* 216:1464–1470.

Hollander, M. (1973). Programs for drug abuse prevention and treatment in a suburban community. In *Drug Abuse and Drug Addiction,* ed. M. Rosenbaum, pp. 47–61. New York: Gordon and Breach Science Publishers.

Johnston, L. D., Bachman, J. G., and O'Malley, P. M. (1977). *Drug Use Among American High School Students 1975–1977.* Rockville, MD: National Institute on Drug Abuse.

King, F. W. (1969). Marijuana and LSD usage among male college students: prevalence rate, frequency, and self-estimates of future use. *Psychiatry* 32:265–267.

———— (1970a). Users and nonusers of marijuana: some attitudinal and behavioral correlates. *Journal of the American College Health Association* 18:213–217.

———— (1970b). Anonymous versus identifiable questionnaires in drug usage surveys. *American Psychologist* 25:982–985.

Lett, S. (1891). Treatment of the opium neurosis. *Journal of the American Medical Association* 17:828–833.

Millman, R. B., and Khuri, E. T. (1973). Drug abuse and the need for alternatives. In *Current Issues in Adolescent Psychiatry,* ed. J.C. Schoolar, pp. 148–167. New York: Brunner/Mazel.

Pollock, S. H. (1972). Attitudes of medical students toward marijuana. *Journal of Psychedelic Drugs* 5:56–61.

Seiden, R. H., Tomlinson, K. R., and O'Carroll, M. (1975). Patterns of marijuana use among public health students. *American Journal of Public Health* 65:613–622.

U.S. Medicine (3/1/75). Adults found "divided" on marijuana.

Winick, C. (1965). Epidemiology of narcotics use. In *Narcotics,* eds. D. M. Wilner and G. G. Kassebaum, pp. 3–18. New York: McGraw-Hill.

THE ORGANIC VIEWPOINT: PHYSICAL DEPENDENCE

Brecher, E. M., and the editors of *Consumer Reports.* (1972). *Licit and Illicit Drugs.* Boston: Little, Brown.

Committee on Alcoholism and Addiction. American Medical Association (1969). Dependence on amphetamines and other stimulant drugs. In *Drug Dependence: A Guide for Physicians.* Chicago: American Medical Association, pp. 111–123.

Crothers, T. D. (1892). Some new studies of the opium disease. *Journal of the American Medical Association* 18:227–230.

De Ropp, R. S. (1957). *Drugs and the Mind.* New York: St. Martin's Press.

Dole, V. P., and Nyswander, M. (1967). Heroin addiction – a metabolic disease. *Archives of Internal Medicine* 120:19–24.

Isbell, H., and White, W. (1953). Clinical characteristics of addictions. *American Journal of Medicine* 14:558–565.

Kielholz, P., and Battegay, R. (1963). The treatment of drug addicts in Switzerland. *Comprehensive Psychiatry* 4:225–235.

Lehmann, H. E. (1963). Phenomenology and pathology of addiction. *Comprehensive Psychiatry* 4:168–180.

Lindesmith, A. R. (1968). *Addiction and Opiates.* Chicago: Aldine.

Stimmel, B., and Kreek, M. J. (1975). Dependence, tolerance and withdrawal. In *Heroin Dependency,* ed. B. Stimmel, pp. 88–97. New York: Stratton Intercontinental Medical Book Corporation.

Sudduth, W. (1896). The psychology of narcotism. *Journal of the American Medical Association* 27:796–798.

Weil, A. T. (1972). *The Natural Mind: A New Way of Looking at Drugs and the Higher Consciousness.* Boston: Houghton Mifflin.

THE PSYCHOLOGIC VIEWPOINTS

Alexander, F., and Shapiro, L. B. (1952). Neuroses, behavior disorders, and perversions. In *Dynamic Psychiatry,* eds. F. Alexander and H. Ross, pp. 117–159. Chicago: University of Chicago Press.

American Psychiatric Association. (1981). Diagnostic and Statistical Manual of Mental Disorders, 3rd ed., Washington, D.C.: American Psychiatric Association.

Arieti, S. (1967). *The Intrapsychic Self.* New York: Basic Books.

Ausubel, D. P. (1958). *Drug Addiction.* New York: Random House.

Babor, T., Meyer, R. E., Mirin, S. M., Davies, M., Valentine, N., and Rawlins, M. (1974). Interpersonal behavior in a small group setting during the heroin addiction cycle. Paper presented at the 127th Annual Meeting of the American Psychiatric Association, Detroit.

Bartlett, D. (1975). The use of multiple family therapy groups with adolescent drug addicts. In *The Adolescent in Group and Family Therapy,* ed. M. Sugar, pp. 262–282. New York: Brunner/Mazel.

Bean, P. (1974). *The Social Control of Drugs.* New York: Halsted Press.

Berger, F. M., and Potterfield, J. (1969). Drug abuse and society. In *Drugs and Youth: Proceedings of the Rutgers Symposium on Drug Abuse,* eds. J. R. Wittenboln et al., pp. 37–43. Springfield, IL: Charles C. Thomas.

Blaine, B. (1966). *Youth and the Hazards of Affluence.* New York: Harper and Row.

Blatt, S. J., Roursaville, B., Eyre, S. L., and Wilber, C. (1984). "The psychodynamics of opiate addiction. *Journal of Nervous and Mental Diseases* 172: 342–352.

Brill, L., and Lieberman, L. (1969). *Authority and Addiction.* Boston: Little, Brown.

Brill, N. Q., Crumpton, E., and Grayson, H. M. (1971). Personality factors in marijuana use. *Archives of General Psychiatry* 24:163–165.

Brotman, R., and Suffet, F. (1970). Marijuana users' views of marijuana use. In *The Psychopathology of Adolescence,* eds. J. Zubin and A. Freedman, pp. 258–272. New York: Grune and Stratton.

Brown, T. T. (1961). *The Enigma of Drug Addiction.* Springfield, IL: Charles C. Thomas.

Cameron, D. C. (1969). Youth and drugs: a world view. In *Drug Dependence: A Guide for Physicians,* American Medical Association. Council on Mental Health, pp. 15–29. Chicago: American Medical Association.

Cameron, N. (1963). *Personality Development and Psychopathology.* Boston: Houghton Mifflin.

Cavan, R. (1962). *Juvenile Delinquency.* Philadelphia: J. B. Lippincott.

Chein, I., Gerard, D. L., Lee, R. S., and Rosenfeld, E. (1964). *The Road to H: Narcotics, Delinquency and Social Policy.* New York: Basic Books.

Cohen, A. Y. (1969). Inside what's happening: sociological, psychological, and spiritual perceptions on the contemporary drug scene. *American Journal of Public Health* 59:2029–2095.

Cohen, M., and Klein, D. F. (1972). Age of onset of drug abuse in psychiatric inpatients. *Archives of General Psychiatry* 26:266–269.

Cohen, S. (1964). *The Beyond Within: The LSD Story.* New York: Atheneum.

———— (1969). *The Drug Dilemma.* New York: McGraw-Hill.

Coodley, A. E. (1961). Current aspects of delinquency and addiction. *Archives of General Psychiatry* 4:632–640.

De Ropp, R. S. (1957). *Drugs and the Mind.* New York: St. Martin's Press.

Eddy, N. B., Halbach, H., Isbell, H., and Seevers, M. H. (1965). Drug dependence: its significance and characteristics. *Bulletin of the World Health Organization* 32:721–733.

Eells, K. (1968). Marijuana and LSD: a survey of one college campus. *Journal of Counseling Psychology* 15:459–467.

Ellinwood, E. H. (1967). Amphetamine psychosis: I. description of the individuals and process. *Journal of Nervous and Mental Disease* 144:273–283.

Ewing, J. A. (1972). Students, sex, and marijuana. *Medical Aspects of Human Sexuality* 4:100–117.

Feldman, D. J., and Feldman, H. S. (1972). On the etiology of narcotic addiction and its relation to curiosity. *Psychosomatics* 13:304–307.

Fenichel, O. (1945). *The Psychoanalytic Theory of Neurosis.* New York: Norton.

Fiddle, S. (1967). *Portraits from a Shooting Gallery.* New York: Harper and Row.

Fort, J. P. (1954). Heroin addiction among young men. *Psychiatry* 17: 251–259.

Freedman, A. M. (1967). Drugs and sexual behavior. *Medical Aspects of Human Sexuality,* November:25–31.

Gaskill, H. S. (1945). Marijuana, an intoxicant. *American Journal of Psychiatry* 102:202–204.

Gerard, D. L., and Kornetsky, C. (1954). A social and psychiatric study of adolescent opiate addicts. *Psychiatric Quarterly* 28:113–125.

———— (1955). Adolescent opiate addiction: a study of control and addict subjects. *Psychiatric Quarterly* 29:457–486.

Glasscote, R. M., Sussex, J. N., Jaffee, J.H ., Ball, J., and Brill, L. (1972). *The Treatment of Drug Abuse.* Washington, D.C.: American Psychiatric Association.

Glatt, M. M. (1974). *A Guide to Addiction and Its Treatment.* New York: Halsted Press.

Glover, E. (1932). On the aetiology of drug-addiction. *International Journal of Psycho-Analysis* 13:298–328.

Greaves, G. (1974). Toward an existential theory of drug abuse. *Journal of Nervous and Mental Disease* 159:263–274.

Griffith, J. (1967). Psychiatric implication of amphetamine drug use. Paper presented at the Nonnarcotic Drug Institute, Southern Illinois University, Edwardsville, IL.

Hekimian, L. J., and Gershon, S. (1968). Characteristics of drug abusers admitted to a psychiatric hospital. *Journal of the American Medical Association* 205:75–80.

Hendin, H. (1975). *The Age of Sensation.* New York: Norton.

Isbell, H. (1965). Perspectives in research in opiate addiction. In *Narcotics,* eds. D. M. Wilner and G. G. Kassebaum, pp. 36–52. New York: McGraw-Hill.

Jersild, A. T., Brook, J. S., and Brook, D. W. (1978). *The Psychology of Adolescence.* New York: Macmillan.

Kaplan, C. D., and Wogan, M. (1978). The psychoanalytic theory of addiction. *The American Journal of Psychoanalysis* 38:317–326.

Kaufman, E. (1973). Group therapy techniques used by the ex-addict therapist. In *Drug Abuse and Drug Addiction,* ed. M. Rosenbaum, pp. 3-19. New York: Gordon and Breach Science Publishers.

Khantzian, E. J., Mack, J. E., and Schatzberg, A. F. (1974). Heroin use as an attempt to cope: clinical observations. *American Journal of Psychiatry* 131:160-164.

Kilpatrick, D. G. et al. (1974). Personality correlates of polydrug abuse. Paper presented at the 82nd Annual Convention of the American Psychological Association, New Orleans.

Knapp, P. H. (1952). Amphetamine and addiction. *Journal of Nervous and Mental Disease* 115:406-432.

Kolb, L. (1925a). Drug addiction in its relation to crime. *Mental Hygiene* 9:74-89.

——— (1925b). Types and characteristics of drug addicts. *Mental Hygiene* 9:300-313.

Krystal, H., and Raskin, H. (1970). *Drug Dependence.* Detroit: Wayne State University Press.

La Tendresse, J. D. (1968) Masturbation and its relation to addiction. *Review of Existential Psychology and Psychiatry* 8:16-27.

Leech, K. (1970). *Pastoral Care and the Drug Scene.* London: S.P.C.K.

Lehmann, H. E. (1963). Phenomenology and pathology of addiction. *Comprehensive Psychiatry* 4:168-180.

Levy, N. (1968). The use of drugs by teenagers for sanctuary and illusion. *American Journal of Psychoanalysis* 28:48-59.

Lindesmith, A. R. (1968). *Addiction and Opiates.* Chicago: Aldine.

Lipinski, E. (1972). Motivation in drug misuse. *Journal of the American Medical Association* 219:171-175.

Looney, M. (1972). The dreams of heroin addicts. *Social Work* 17:23-28.

Louria, D. B. (1971). *Overcoming Drugs.* New York: McGraw-Hill.

McCaree, C. P., and Steffenhagen, R. A. (1969). Personality factors in college drug users. *International Journal of Social Psychiatry* 15:102-106.

McMorris, S. C. (1966). What price euphoria: the case against marijuana. *Medico-Legal Journal* 34:74-79.

Maglin, A. (1974). Sex role differences in heroin addiction. *Social Casework* 160-167.

Maurer, D. W., and Vogel, V. H. (1967). *Narcotics and Narcotic Addiction,* 3rd ed. Springfield, IL: Charles C. Thomas.

Meerloo, J. A. M. (1952). Artificial ecstasy. *Journal of Nervous and Mental Disease* 115:246-266.

Menninger, K. A. (1963). *The Vital Balance.* New York: Viking Press.

Milby, J. B. (1981). *Addictive Behavior and Its Treatment.* New York: Springer Publishing Co.

Millman, R. B., and Khuri, E. T. (1973). Drug abuse and the need for alternatives. In *Current Issues in Adolescent Psychiatry,* ed. V. C. Schoolar, pp. 148-157. New York: Brunner/Mazel.

Mills, J. (1966). The world of needle park. In *Narcotic Addiction,* eds. J. A. O'Donnell and J. C. Ball, pp. 17-23. New York: Harper and Row.

Monroe, J. J., Ross, W. F., and Berzins, J. I. (1971). The decline of the addict as "psychopath": implications for community care. *International Journal of the Addictions* 6:601-608 (Reprinted by courtesy of Marcel Dekker, Inc.).

Nyswander, M. (1956). *The Drug Addict as a Patient.* New York: Grune and Stratton.

—— (1974). Drug addiction. In *American Handbook of Psychiatry,* Vol. 3, eds. S. Arieti and E. B. Brody, pp. 393-403. New York: Basic Books.

Peele, S. (1975). *Love and Addiction.* New York: Taplinger.

Pierce, J. I. (1969). Delinquency and heroin addiction in Britain. *British Journal of Criminology* 9:108-124.

Rado, S. (1933). The psychoanalysis of pharmacothymia (drug addiction). *Psychoanalytic Quarterly* 2:1-23.

—— (1957). Narcotic bondage. *American Journal of Psychiatry* 114:165-170.

Redlich, F. C., and Freedman, D. X. (1966). *The Theory and Practice of Psychiatry.* New York: Basic Books.

Reichard, J. D. (1947). Addiction: some theoretical considerations as to its nature, cause, prevention and treatment. *American Journal of Psychiatry* 103:721-730.

Robbins, L., Robbins, E. S., and Stern, M. (1969). Psychological and environmental factors associated with drug abuse. Paper presented at the Community Conference: *Drug Abuse and Youth.* Beth Israel Medical Center, New York, June.

Rounsaville, B. J., Weissman, M. M., Kleber, H., and Wilber, C. (1982). Heterogeneity of psychiatric diagnosis in treated opiate addicts. *Archives of General Psychiatry* 39:161-166.

Savitt, R. A. (1963). Psychoanalytic studies on addiction: ego structure in narcotic addiction. *Psychoanalytic Quarterly* 32:43-57.

Smith, G. M. (1972). Antecedents of teenage drug use. Department of Psychiatry, Massachusetts General Hospital, Boston (unpublished).

Stanton, M. D. (1972). Drug use in Vietnam. *Archives of General Psychiatry* 26:279-286.

Swatos, W. H. (1972). Opiate addiction in the late nineteenth century: a study of the social problem, using medical journals of the periods. *International Journal of the Addictions* 7:739-753 (Reprinted by courtesy of Marcel Dekker, Inc.).

Terry, C. E., and Pellens, M. (1928). *The Opium Problem.* New York: Bureau of Social Hygiene.

Thorpe, J. J. (1956). Addicts. In *The Fields of Group Psychotherapy*, ed. B. R. Slavson, pp. 59-75. New York: International Universities Press.

Ungerleider, J., Fisher, D. D., Fuller, M., and Caldwell, A. (1968). The "bad trip"—the etiology of adverse LSD reaction. *American Journal of Psychiatry* 124:1483-1490.

Van Kaam, A. (1968). Addiction and existence. *Review of Existential Psychology and Psychiatry* 8:54-64.

Weil, A. T. (1972a). *The Natural Mind: A New Way of Looking at Drugs and the Higher Consciousness.* Boston: Houghton Mifflin.

—— (1972b). Altered states of consciousness. In Drug Abuse Survey Project. *Dealing with Drug Abuse*, pp. 345-394. New York: Praeger.

Wieder, H., and Kaplan, E. H. (1969). Drug use in adolescents. *Psychoanalytic Study of the Child* 24:399-431.

Wikler, A. (1952). Mechanisms of action drugs that modify personality function. *American Journal of Psychiatry* 108:590-599.

Wikler, A. and Rasor, R. (1953). Psychiatric aspects of drug addiction. *American Journal of Medicine* 14:566-570.

Wilson, J. Q. (1975). *Thinking About Crime.* New York: Basic Books.

Yorke, C. (1970). A critical review of some psychoanalytic literature on drug addiction. *British Journal of Medical Psychology* 43:141-159.

Zimmering, P., Toolan, J., Renate, S., and Wortis, S. B. (1951). Heroin addiction in adolescent boys. *Journal of Nervous and Mental Disease* 114:19-34.

THE SOCIOLOGIC VIEWPOINT

Anglin et al. (1983). Drugs and crime. In *Encyclopedia of Crime and Justice*, ed. S. Kadish, pp. 636-663. NY: Free Press.

Ausubel, D. P. (1958). *Drug Addiction.* New York: Random House.

Barnes, H. E. (1939). *Society in Transition.* New York: Prentice-Hall.

Bartlett, D. (1975). The use of multiple family therapy groups with adolescent drug addicts. In *The Adolescent in Group and Family Therapy*, ed. M. Sugar, pp. 267-282. New York: Brunner/Mazel.

Bejerot, N. (1972). *Addiction: An Artificially Induced Drive.* Springfield, IL: Charles C. Thomas.

Berger, F. M., and Potterfield, D. J. (1969). Drug abuse and society. In *Proceedings of the Rutgers Symposium on Drug Abuse*, eds. J.R. Wittenborn et al., pp. 37-43. Springfield, IL: Charles C. Thomas.

Blaine, G. B. (1966). *Youth and the Hazards of Affluence.* New York: Harper and Row.

Brecher, E. M., and the editors of *Consumer Reports.* (1972). *Licit and Illicit Drugs.* Boston: Little, Brown.

Cantala, J. (1926). Opium, heroin, morphine: their kingdoms. In *Narcotic*

Education, ed. H.S. Middlemiss, pp. 232–268. Washington, D.C.: H. S. Middlemiss.

Chein, I. (1965). The use of narcotics as a personal and social problem. In *Narcotics,* eds. D. M. Wilner and G. G. Kassebaum, pp. 103–117. New York: McGraw-Hill.

Chein, I., Gerard, D. L., Lee, R. S., and Rosenfeld, E. (1964). *The Road to H: Narcotics, Delinquency and Social Policy.* New York: Basic Books.

Chein, I., and Rosenfeld, E. (1957). Juvenile narcotics use. *Law and Contemporary Problems* 22:53–54.

Child Study Association of America Wel-Met, Inc. (1971). *You, Your Child and Drugs.* New York: Child Study Press.

Cloward, R. A., and Ohlin, L. E. (1960). *Delinquency and Opportunity: A Theory of Delinquent Gangs.* Glencoe, IL: The Free Press.

Cohn, Alvin D. (1984). Drugs, crime, and criminal justice: state-of-the-art and future directions. *Federal Probation.* XLVIII:13–24.

De Ropp, R. S. (1957). *Drugs and the Mind.* New York: St. Martin's Press.

Dole, V. P. (1973). Heroin addiction—an epidemic disease. Reprinted from *The Harvey Lectures,* Series 67. New York: Academic Press.

Ewing, J. A. (1972). Students, sex, and marijuana. *Medical Aspects of Human Sexuality* 4:100–117.

Fiddle, S. (1967). *Portraits from a Shooting Gallery.* New York: Harper and Row.

Fisher, D. D. (1968). The chronic side effects from LSD. In *The Problems and Prospects of LSD,* ed. J.T. Ungerleider, pp. 69–79. Springfield, IL: Charles C. Thomas.

Fort, J. (1973). Perspective on marijuana. In *Yearbook of Drug Abuse,* eds. L. Brill and E. Harms, pp. 333–366. New York: Behavioral Publications.

Fort, J. P. (1954). Heroin addiction among young men. *Psychiatry* 17: 251–259.

Fram, D. H., and Hoffman, H. A. (1973). Family therapy in the treatment of heroin addiction. In *Proceedings of the 5th National Conference on Methadone Treatment,* Vol. 1, pp. 610–615. New York: National Association for the Prevention of Addiction to Narcotics.

Freedman, A. M. (1972). Drugs and society: an ecological approach. *Comprehensive Psychiatry* 13:411–420.

Friedman, A. S., Pomerance, E., Sanders, R., Santo, Y. and Utada, A. (1980). The structure and problems of the families of adolescent drug abusers. *Contemporary Drug Problems* 9:327–356.

Gerard, D. L., and Kornetsky, C. (1954). A social and psychiatric study of adolescent opiate addicts. *Psychiatric Quarterly* 28:113–125.

——— (1955). Adolescent opiate addiction: a study of control and addict subjects. *Psychiatric Quarterly* 29:457–486.

Glaser, D., Lander, B., and Abbott, W. (1971). Opiate addicted and non-addicted siblings in a slum area. *Social Problems* 18:510-521.

Glasscote, R. M., Sussex, J. N., Jaffee, J. H., Ball, J., and Brill, L. (1972). *The Treatment of Drug Abuse.* Washington, D.C.: American Psychiatric Association.

Glatt, M. M. (1972). The treatment of the withdrawal stage in narcotic addicts by diphenoxylate and chlormethiazole. *International Journal of the Addictions* 7:593-596 (Reprinted by courtesy of Marcel Dekker, Inc.).

———— (1974). *A Guide to Addiction and Its Treatment.* New York: Halsted Press.

Goldberg, P., and Meyers, E. J. (1980). The influence of public understanding and attitudes on drug education and prevention. In The Drug Abuse Council. *The Facts about "Drug Abuse"* New York: Free Press.

Goodman, P. (1960). *Growing Up Absurd.* New York: Vintage.

Gossett, J. T., Lewis, J., and Phillips, V. (1971). Extent and prevalence of illicit drug use as reported by 56,745 students. *Journal of the American Medical Association* 216:1464-1470.

Group for the Advancement of Psychiatry. (1971). *Drug Misuse: A Psychiatric View of a Modern Dilemma,* Vol. 7, No. 80. New York: Group for the Advancement of Psychiatry.

Haastrup, S., and Thomsen, K. (1972). The social backgrounds of young addicts as elicited in interviews with their parents. *Acta Psychiatrica Scandinavica* 48:146-172.

Hanneman, G. J. (1973). Communicating drug-abuse information among college students. *Mental Health Digest* 5:47-51.

Hekimian, L. J., and Gershon, S. (1968). Characteristics of drug abusers admitted to a psychiatric hospital. *Journal of the American Medical Association* 205:75-80.

Hemmi, T. (1965). Narcotic-addict prisoners in Japan. *Corrective Psychiatry and Journal of Social Therapy* 11:87-89.

Horman, R. E. (1973). Alienation and student drug use. *International Journal of the Addictions* 8:325-333 (Reprinted by courtesy of Marcel Dekker, Inc.).

Johnson, B. D. (1973). *Marihuana Users and Drug Subcultures.* New York: Wiley.

Kandel, D. (1973). Adolescent marijuana use: Role of parents and peers. *Science* 181:1067-1070.

Kaufman, J., Allen, J., and Jolyon, L. (1969). Runaways, hippies, and marijuana. *American Journal of Psychiatry* 126:717-720.

King, F. W. (1970). Users and nonusers of marijuana: Some attitudinal and behavioral correlates. *Journal of the American College Health Association* 19:213-217.

Lindesmith, A. R. (1968). *Addiction and Opiates.* Chicago: Aldine.

Maglin, A. (1974). Sex role differences in heroin addiction. *Social Casework* 55: 160–167.

Mahon, T. A. (1974). The "eschewment of theory" theory in drug dependence. *Drug Forum* 3:311–319.

May, E. (1972). Narcotics addiction and control in Great Britain. In *Dealing with Drug Abuse,* Drug Abuse Survey Project, pp. 345–394. New York: Praeger.

McGlothlin, W. H. (1975). Drug use and abuse. In *Annual Review of Psychology,* Vol. 26, eds. M. R. Rosenzweig and L. W. Porter, pp. 45–64. Palo Alto, CA: Annual Reviews.

Messer, M. (1970). Running out of era: some non-pharmacological notes on the psychedelic revolution. In *The New Social Drug: Cultural, Medical, and Legal Perspectives on Marijuana,* ed. D. E. Smith, pp. 157–167. Englewood Cliffs, NJ: Prentice-Hall.

Meyer, R. E. (1972). *Guide to Drug Rehabilitation.* Boston: Beacon Press.

Millman, R. B., and Khuri, E. T. (1973). Drug abuse and the need for alternatives. In *Current Issues in Adolescent Psychiatry,* ed. J. C. Schoollar, pp. 148–157. New York: Brunner/Mazel.

Nail, R. L., and Gunderson, E. K. (1972). Characteristics of hospitalized drug abuse cases in the Naval service. *Journal of Nervous and Mental Disease* 155:91–98.

National Commission on Marihuana and Drug Abuse (1973). *Drug Use in America: Problem in Perspective.* Second Report of the National Commission on Marihuana and Drug Abuse. Washington, D.C.: Government Printing Office.

Peele, S. (1975). *Love and Addiction.* New York: Taplinger.

Ploscowe, M. (1961). Some basic problems in drug addiction and suggestions for research. In *Drug Addiction: Crime or Disease?,* American Bar Association and American Medical Association. Joint Committee on Narcotic Drugs, pp. 15–120. Bloomington, IN: Indiana University Press.

Polakoff, P. L., and Lowinger, P. (1972). Do medical students turn on? *Comprehensive Psychiatry* 13:185–188.

Redlich, F. C., and Freedman, D. X. (1966). *The Theory and Practice of Psychiatry.* New York: Basic Books.

Robbins, L., Robbins, E. S., and Stern, M. (1969). Psychological and environmental factors associated with drug abuse. Paper presented at the Community Conference: *Drug Abuse and Youth,* Beth Israel Medical Center, New York, June.

Rollins, J. H., and Holden, R. H. (1972). Adolescent drug use and the alienation syndrome. Paper presented at the 80th Annual Convention of the American Psychological Association, Honolulu.

Rubin, T., and Babbs, J. (1970). The glue sniffer. *Federal Probation* 34 (September):23-28.

Scherer, S. E., Ettinger, R., and Mudrick, N. (1972). Need for social approval and drug use. *Journal of Consulting and Clinical Psychology* 38:118-121.

Schofield, M. (1971). *The Strange Case of Pot.* Middlesex, England: Penguin Books.

Schroeder, Richard C. (1980). *The Politics of Drugs.* Washington, D.C.: Congressional Quarterly Press.

Sebald, H. (1972). The pursuit of "instantness" in technocratic society and youth's psychedelic drug use. *Adolescence* 7:343-350.

Seldin, N. E. (1972). The family of the addict: a review of the literature. *International Journal of the Addictions* 7:97-107 (Reprinted by courtesy of Marcel Dekker, Inc.).

Select Committee on Crime (1970). *Marijuana: First Report of the Select Committee on Crime.* U.S. Congress. House of Representatives. Washington, D.C.: Government Printing Office.

Sharoff, R. L. (1968). Discussion of Levy, N.J., The use of drugs by teenagers for sanctuary and illusion. *American Journal of Psychoanalysis* 28:48-59.

Stanton, M. D. (1972). Drug use in Vietnam. *Archives of General Psychiatry* 26:279-286.

Starratt, A. B. (1971). Drugs and the new morality. In *The Drug Abuse Controversy,* eds. C. C. Brown and C. Savage, pp. 77-86. Baltimore: National Educational Consultants.

Stimmel, B. (1972). The socioeconomics of heroin dependency. *New England Journal of Medicine* 287:1275-1280.

Subcommittee on Alcoholism and Narcotics. (1972). *Marijuana and Health: Second Annual Report to Congress from the Secretary of Health, Education, and Welfare.* Senate Committee on Labor and Public Welfare. U.S. Congress. Senate. Washington, D.C.: Government Printing Office.

Taqi, S. (1973). The drug cinema. *Addictions* 20:2-29.

Tennant, F. S., Preble, M. R., Groesbeck, C. J., and Banks, N. I. (1972). West Germany. *Military Medicine* 137:381-383.

U.S. Medicine (1/1/74). TV ads bad influence.

Wallis, F. A. (1926). The criminology of drug addiction. In *Narcotic Education,* ed. H. S. Middlemiss, pp. 21-28. Washington, D.C., H. S. Middlemiss.

Washington Post (11/9/73). Symposium blames white supremacy for black addicts.

Washington Post (2/3/74). Alcohol abuse.

Weissman, James C. (1982). Understanding the drugs and crime connection.

In *Criminal Justice and Drugs,* eds. J. C. Weissman and R. L. Du Pont, Port Washington, NY: Kennikat Press.

Wilson, J.Q. (1983). *Thinking About Crime.* New York: Basic Books.

Zimmering, P., Toolan, J., Renate, S., and Wortis, S. B. (1951). Heroin addiction in adolescent boys. *Journal of Nervous and Mental Disease* 114:19-34.

ADDICTION

Ausubel, D. P. (1958). *Drug Addiction.* New York: Random House.

Brown, T. T. (1961). *The Enigma of Drug Addiction.* Springfield, IL: Charles C. Thomas.

Chein, I., Gerard, D. L., Lee, R. S., and Rosenfeld, E. (1964). *The Road to H: Narcotics, Delinquency and Social Policy.* New York: Basic Books.

Eddy, N. B., Halbach, H., Isbell, H., and Seevers, M. H. (1965). Drug dependence: its significance and characteristics. *Bulletin of the World Health Organization* 32:721-733.

Expert Committee on Drugs Liable to Produce Addiction. (1950) *Second Report.* World Health Organization Technical Report Series No. 21. Geneva, Switzerland: World Health Organization.

Farber, L. H. (1968). Ours is the addicted society. *Review of Existential Psychology and Psychiatry* 8:5-16.

Irwin, S. (1970). *Drugs of Abuse: An Introduction to Their Actions and Potential Hazards.* Beloit, WI: Student Association for the Study of Hallucinogens.

Isbell, H. (1972). Pharmacological factors in drug dependence. In *Drug Abuse: Non-medical Use of Dependence-Producing Drugs,* ed. S. Btesh, pp. 35-42. New York: Plenum.

Kolb, L. (1962). *Drug Addiction.* Springfield, IL: Charles C. Thomas.

Lindesmith, A. R. (1968). *Addiction and Opiates.* Chicago: Aldine.

Milby, Jesse B. (1981). *Addictive Behavior and Its Treatment.* NY: Springer Publishing Co.

National Commission on Marihuana and Drug Abuse (1973). *Drug Use in America: The Problem in Perspective.* Washington, D.C.: Government Printing Office.

Nyswander, M. (1956). *The Drug Addict as a Patient.* NY: Grune and Stratton.

Peele, S. (1975). *Love and Addiction.* NY: Taplinger.

Ray, O. S. (1972). *Drugs, Society, and Human Behavior.* Saint Louis: C. V. Mosby.

Scher, J. (1966). Patterns and predictions of addiction and drug abuse. *Archives of General Psychiatry* 15:539-551.

Van Kaam, A. (1968). Addiction and existence. *Review of Existential Psychology and Psychiatry* 8:54-65.

DRUG EFFECTS

Ashley, R. (1975). *Cocaine. Its History, Uses and Effects.* New York: St. Martin's Press.

Bloomquist, E. R. (1971). *Marijuana: The Second Trip.* Beverly Hills, CA: Glencoe Press.

Blum, R., and Associates (1970). *Drugs I: Society and Drugs.* San Francisco: Jossey-Bass.

British Journal of Criminology (1967). Editorial Vol. 7.

Crowley, T. J. (1972). The reinforcers for drug abuse: why people take drugs. *Comprehensive Psychiatry* 13:51–62.

De Ropp, R. S. (1957). *Drugs and the Mind.* New York: St. Martin's Press.

Freedman, A. M. (1967). Drugs and sexual behavior. *Medical Aspects of Human Sexuality* November: 25–31.

Glatt, M. M. (1974). *A Guide to Addiction and Its Treatment.* New York: Halsted Press.

Levine, D. (1974). "Needle freaks": compulsive self-injection by drug users. *American Journal of Psychiatry* 131:297–300.

McCarthy, J. P. (1971). Some less familiar drugs of abuse. *Medical Journal of Australia* 2:1078–1081.

Smith, H. (1964). Do drugs have religious impact? In *LSD: The Consciousness-Expanding Experience,* ed. D. Solomon, pp. 152–1676. New York: Putman.

Thomson, I. G., and Rathod, N. H. (1968). Aversion therapy for heroin dependence. *Lancet* August 17: 382–384.

Ungerleider, J., Fisher, D. D., Fuller, M., and Caldwell, A. (1968). The 'bad trip'—the etiology of adverse LSD reaction. *American Journal of Psychiatry* 124:1483–1490.

Walters, P., Goethals, G., and Pope, H. (1972). Drug use and life-style among 500 college undergraduates. *Archives of General Psychiatry* 26:92–96.

Weil, A. T. (1972). *The Natural Mind: A New Way of Looking at Drugs and the Higher Consciousness.* Boston: Houghton Mifflin.

OPIATES

Ausubel, D. P. (1958). *Drug Addiction.* New York: Random House.

Babor, T., Meyer, R. E., Mirin, S. M., Davies, M., Valentine, N., and Rawlins, M. (1974). Interpersonal behavior in a small group setting during the heroin addiction cycle. Paper presented at the 127th Annual Meeting of the American Psychiatric Association, Detroit.

Chessick, R. D. (1960). The "pharmacogenic orgasm" in the drug addict. *Archives of General Psychiatry* 3:545–556.

Cohen, S. (1969). *The Drug Dilemma.* New York: McGraw-Hill.

Eidelberg, E. (1975). Acute effects of ethanol and opiates on the nervous system. In *Research Advances in Alcohol and Drug Problems,* Vol. 2, eds. R. J. Gibbons et al., pp. 147-176. New York: John Wiley and Sons.

Feldman, H.W. (1970). Ideological supports to becoming and remaining a heroin addict. *Drug Dependence* March:3-11.

Fiddle, S. (1967). *Portraits from a Shooting Gallery.* New York: Harper and Row.

Fry, Lincoln J. (1985). Drug abuse and crime in a Swedish birth cohort. *British Journal of Criminology* 25:46-59.

Gebhard, P. H. (1972). A comparison of white-black offender groups. In *Sexual Behavior: Social, Clinical, and Legal Aspects,* eds. H. Resnick and M. Wolfgang, pp. 89-130. Boston: Little, Brown.

Gould, L. C., and Kleber, H. D. (1974). Changing patterns of multiple drug use among applicants in a multimodality drug treatment program. *Archives of General Psychiatry* 31:408-413.

Halleck, S. L. (1967). *Psychiatry and the Dilemmas of Crime.* New York: Harper and Row.

Hendin, H. (1975). *The Age of Sensation.* New York: Norton.

Hesse, E. (1964). *Narcotics and Drug Addiction.* New York: Philosophical Library.

Hoffman, F. G. (1975). *A Handbook on Drug and Alcohol Abuse: The Biomedical Aspects.* New York: Oxford University Press.

Irwin, S. (1970). *Drugs of Abuse: An Introduction to Their Actions and Potential Hazards.* Beloit, WI: Student Association for the Study of Hallucinogens.

James, I., and D'Organ, P. (1970). Patterns of delinquency among British heroin addicts. *Bulletin on Narcotics* 22:13-19.

Kaplan, J. (1983). *The Hardest Drug.* Chicago: University of Chicago Press.

Kolb, L. (1925). Drug addiction in its relation to crime. *Mental Hygiene* 9:74-89.

Kolb, L. (1962). *Drug Addiction.* Springfield, IL: Charles C. Thomas.

Kramer, J. D. (1969). New directions in the management of opiate dependence. *New Physician* 18:203-210.

Lerner, A. M., and Oerther, F. J. (1967). Recent trends in substance abuse. *International Journal of the Addictions* 2:312-327 (Reprinted by courtesy of Marcel Dekker, Inc.).

Lidz, C. W., Lewis, S. H., Crane, L. E., and Gould, L. C. (1975). Heroin maintenance and heroin control. *International Journal of the Addictions* 10:35-72 (Reprinted by courtesy of Marcel Dekker, Inc.).

Lindesmith, A. R. (1965). Problems in the social psychology of addiction. In *Narcotics,* eds. D. M. Wilner and G. G. Kassebaum, pp. 118-139. New York: McGraw-Hill.

——— (1968). *Addiction and Opiates.* Chicago: Aldine.

Ling, W., Holmes, E. D., Post, G. R., and Litaker, M. B. (1973). A systematic psychiatric study of the heroin addicts. In Proceedings of the 5th National Conference on Methadone Treatment, Vol. 1, pp. 429–432. New York: National Association for the Prevention of Addiction to Narcotics.

Lingeman, R. R. (1974). *Drugs from A to Z: A Dictionary,* 2nd ed. New York: McGraw-Hill.

Long, R. E., and Penna, R. P. (1968). Drugs of abuse. *Journal of the American Pharmaceutical Association* January:12–27.

Louria, D. B. (1967). Cool talk about hot drugs. *The New York Times Magazine* August 6.

Maurer, D. W., and Vogel, V. H. (1967). *Narcotics and Narcotic Addiction,* 3rd ed. Springfield, IL: Charles C. Thomas.

National Commission on Marihuana and Drug Abuse. (1973). *Drug Use in America: Problem in Perspective.* Second Report of the National Commission on Marihuana and Drug Abuse. Washington, D.C.: Government Printing Office.

Nyswander, M. (1956). *The Drug Addict as a Patient.* New York: Grune and Stratton.

——— (1974). Drug addiction. In *American Handbook of Psychiatry,* Vol. 3, eds. S. Arieti and E. B. Brady, pp. 393–403. New York: Basic Books.

Pierce, J.I. (1969). Delinquency and heroin addiction in Britain. *British Journal of Criminology* 9:108–124.

Rado, S. (1933). The psychoanalysis of pharmacothymia (drug addiction). *Psychoanalytic Quarterly* 2:1–23.

Ray, O. S. (1972). *Drugs, Society, and Human Behavior.* Saint Louis: C. V. Mosby.

Redlich, F. C., and Freedman, D. X. (1966). *The Theory and Practice of Psychiatry.* New York: Basic Books.

Reed, T. (1980). Challenging some "common wisdom" on drug abuse. *The International Journal of the Addictions* 15:359–373.

Savitt, R. A. (1963). Psychoanalytic studies on addiction: ego structure in narcotic addiction. *Psychoanalytic Quarterly* 32:43–57.

Scher, J. (1966). Patterns and profiles of addiction and drug abuse. *Archives of General Psychiatry* 15:539–551.

Smith, Kline, and French Laboratories (1967). *Drug Abuse: Escape to Nowhere.* Philadelphia: Smith, Kline and French Laboratories.

Sutter, A. G. (1969). Worlds of drug use on the street scene. In *Delinquency, Crime, and Social Process,* eds. D. Cressey and D. A. Ward, pp. 802–829. New York: Harper and Row.

Task Force on Narcotics and Drug Abuse. (1967). *Narcotics and Drug Abuse.* Report to the President's Commission on Law Enforcement and Administration of Justice. Washington, D.C.: Government Printing Office.

Taylor, P. L., and Albright, W. J. (1981). Nondrug criminal behavior and heroin use. *The International Journal of Addictions* 16:683–696.

Tinklenberg, J. R., and Stillman, R. C. (1970). Drug use and violence. In *Violence and the Struggle for Existence,* eds. D. N. Daniels et al., pp. 327–365. Boston: Little, Brown.

Wallis, F. A. (1926). The curse of civilization. In *Narcotic Education,* ed. H. S. Middlemiss, pp. 145–158. Washington, D.C.: H. S. Middlemiss.

Washington Post (3/17/76). "Epidemic" of heroin continuing.

Weppner, R. S. (1971). "Cheap kicks": codeine cough syrup abusers and their social characteristics. *International Journal of the Addictions* 6:647–660 (Reprinted by courtesy of Marcel Dekker, Inc.).

Wikler, A. (1967). Personality disorders. III: sociopathic type: the addictions. In *Comprehensive Textbook of Psychiatry,* eds. A. M. Freedman and H. I. Kaplan, pp. 989–1003. Baltimore: Williams and Wilkins.

Wikler, A., and Rasor, R. (1953). Psychiatric aspects of drug addiction. *American Journal of Medicine* 14:566–570.

Williams, J. B. (1974). *Narcotics and Drug Dependence.* Beverly Hills, CA: Glencoe Press.

Wilson, J. Q. (1983). *Thinking About Crime.* New York: Basic Books.

Zimmering, P., Toolan, J., Renate, S., and Wortis, S. B. (1951). Heroin addiction in adolescent boys. *Journal of Nervous and Mental Disease* 114:19–34.

COCAINE

Altshuler, H. L, and Burch, N. R. (1976). Cocaine dependence: psychogenic and physiological substrates. In *Cocaine: Chemical, Biological, Clinical, Social and Treatment Approaches,* ed. S. J. Mule, pp. 135–146. Cleveland: CRC Press.

Ashley, R. (1975). *Cocaine: Its History, Uses and Effects.* New York: St. Martin's Press.

Bewley, T. (1965). Heroin and cocaine, *Lancet* April 10:808–810.

Brecher, E. M., and the editors of *Consumer Reports.* (1972). *Licit and Illicit Drugs.* Boston: Little, Brown.

Carr, R. R., and Meyers, E. J. (1980). Marijuana and cocaine: the process of change in drug policy. In The Drug Abuse Council. *The Facts about "Drug Abuse"* pp. 153–189. New York: Free Press.

Eddy, N. B., Halbach, H., Isbell, H., and Seevers, M. H. (1971). Drug dependence: its significance and characteristics. In *Drug Dependence and Abuse Resource Book,* eds. P. F. Healy and J. P. Marak, pp. 377–380. Chicago: National District Attorneys Association.

Eiswirth, N. A., Smith, D. E., and Wesson, D. R. (1972). Current perspectives on cocaine use in America. *Journal of Psychedelic Drugs* 5:153–157.

Ewing, J. A. (1967). Addictions II: non-narcotic addictive agents. In *Comprehensive Textbook of Psychiatry,* eds. A. N. Freedman and H. S. Kaplan, pp. 1003–1011. Baltimore: Williams and Wilkins.

Ferguson, R. W. (1975). *Drug Abuse Control.* Boston: Holbrook Press.

Freud, S. (1970). On the general effects of cocaine. Reprinted in *Drug Dependence* October:15–17.

Gay, G. R., Sheppard, D. W., Inaba, D. S., and Newmeyer, J. A. (1973). An old girl: flyin' low, dyin' slow, blinded by snow: cocaine in perspective. *International Journal of the Addictions* 8:1027–1042 (Reprinted by courtesy of Marcel Dekker, Inc.).

Holbrook, J. M. (1983). CNS stimulants. In G. Bennett, G. Vourakis, and D. S. Woolf. *Substance Abuse,* pp. 57–69. NY: Wiley.

Grinspoon, L., and Bakalar, J. B. (1976). *Cocaine: A Drug and Its Social Evolution.* New York: Basic Books.

Julien, R. M. (1978). *A Primer of Drug Action.* San Francisco: W. H. Freedman and Co.

Kiev, A. (1975). *The Drug Epidemic.* New York: Free Press.

Kolb, L. (1925). Drug addiction in its relation to crime. *Mental Hygiene* 9:74–89.

Maurer, D. W., and Vogel, V. H. (1967). *Narcotics and Narcotic Addiction,* 3rd ed. Springfield, IL: Charles C. Thomas.

Millman, R. B. (1982). Adverse effects of cocaine. *Hospital & Community Psychiatry* 33:p. 804.

National Clearinghouse for Drug Abuse Information (1972). Cocaine. Report Series 11, no. 1. Washington, D.C.: Government Printing Office.

National Institute of Mental Health. (1971). Stimulants. Public Health Service Publication No. 2097. Washington, D.C.: Government Printing Office.

Olden, M. (1973). *Cocaine.* New York: Signet.

Phillips, J., and Wynne, R. D. (1976). Sociological aspects of cocaine use and abuse. In *Cocaine: Chemical, Biological, Clinical, Social and Treatment Aspects,* ed. S. J. Mule, pp. 231–241. Cleveland: CRC Press.

Post, R. M. (1975). Cocaine psychoses: a continuum model. *American Journal of Psychiatry* 132:225–231.

Redlich, F. C., and Freedman, D. X. (1966). *The Theory and Practice of Psychiatry.* New York: Basic Books.

Resnick, R. B., and Schuyten-Resnick, E. (1976). Clinical aspects of cocaine: assessment of cocaine abuse behavior in man. In *Cocaine: Chemical, Biological, Clinical, Social and Treatment Aspects,* ed. S. J. Mule, pp. 219–228. Cleveland: CRC Press.

Weil, A. T. (1975). The green and the white. *Journal of Psychedelic Drugs* 7:401–413.

Williams, J. B. (1974). *Narcotics and Drug Dependence.* Beverly Hills, CA: Glencoe Press.

AMPHETAMINES AND AMPHETAMINE-LIKE COMPOUNDS

Angrist, B. M., and Gershon, S. (1969). Amphetamine abuse in New York City 1966-1968. *Seminars in Psychiatry* 1:195-207.

Angrist, B. M., Schweitzer, J. W., Gershon, S., and Friedhoff, A. J. (1970). Mephentermine psychosis: misuse of the Wyamine Inhaler. *American Journal of Psychiatry* 126:1315-1317.

Bell, D. S., and Trethowan, W. H. (1961). Amphetamine addiction and disturbed sexuality. *Archives of General Psychiatry* 4:74-78.

Clement, W. R., Solursh, L. P., and Van Ast, W. (1970). Abuse of amphetamine and amphetamine-like drugs. *Psychological Reports* 26:343-354.

Cohen, S. (1969). *The Drug Dilemma.* New York: McGraw-Hill.

Connell, P. H. (1966). Clinical manifestations and treatment of amphetamine type of dependence. *Journal of the American Medical Association* 196:718-723.

Ellinwood, E. H. (1967). Amphetamine psychosis: I. description of the individuals and process. *Journal of Nervous and Mental Disease* 144: 273-283.

———(1968). Amphetamine psychosis: II. theoretical implications. *Journal of Neuropsychiatry* 4:45-54.

Ferguson, R. W. (1975). *Drug Abuse Control.* Boston: Holbrook Press.

Fort, J. (1971). Testimony before the Select Committee on Crime. 91st U.S. Congress. House of Representatives. *Amphetamines: Fourth Report by the Select Committee on Crime.* Washington, D.C.: Government Printing Office.

Girdano, D. D., and Girdano, D. A. (1976). *Drugs—A Factual Account.* 2nd ed. Reading, MA: Addison-Wesley.

Glatt, M. M. (1974). *A Guide to Addiction and Its Treatment.* New York: Halsted Press.

Greene, M. H., DuPont, R. L., and Rubenstein, R. M. (1973). Amphetamines in the District of Columbia. *Archives of General Psychiatry* 29:773-776.

Grinspoon, L., and Hedblom, P. (1975). *The Speed Culture.* Cambridge, MA: Harvard University Press.

Irwin, S. (1970). *Drugs of Abuse: An Introduction to Their Actions and Potential Hazards.* Beloit, WI: Student Association for the Study of Hallucinogens.

Kalant, O. J. (1973). *The Amphetamines: Toxicity & Addiction.* Toronto: University of Toronto Press.

Kiev, A. (1975). *The Drug Epidemic.* New York: The Free Press.

Long, R. E., and Penna, R. P. (1968). Drugs of abuse. *Journal of the American Pharmaceutical Association* January:12–27.

Milkman, H., and Frosch, W. (1977). The drug of choice. *Journal of Psychedelic Drugs* 9:11–24.

National Clearinghouse for Drug Abuse Information. (1970). *Answers to the Most Frequently Asked Questions about Drug Abuse.* Washington, D.C.: Government Printing Office.

National Institute of Mental Health. (1971). Stimulants. Public Health Service Publication No. 2097. Washington, D.C.: Government Printing Office.

Pittel, S. M., and Hafer, R. (1973). The transition to amphetamine abuse. In *Uppers and Downers,* eds. D. E. Smith and D. R. Wesson, pp. 62–75. Englewood Cliffs, NJ: Prentice Hall.

Ray, O. S. (1972). *Drugs, Society, and Human Behavior.* Saint Louis: C. V. Mosby.

Redlich, F. C., and Freedman D. X. (1966). *The Theory and Practice of Psychiatry.* New York: Basic Books.

Schofield, M. (1971). *The Strange Case of Pot.* Middlesex, England: Penguin Books.

Seevers, M. H. (1969). Psychopharmacological elements of drug dependence. In *Drug Dependence: A Guide for Physicians.* American Medical Association. Council on Mental Health, pp. 5–14. Chicago: American Medical Association.

Shick, J. F. E., Smith, D. E. and Wesson, D. R. (1973). An analysis of amphetamine toxicity and patterns of use. In *Uppers and Downers,* eds. D. E. Smith and D. R. Wesson, pp. 23–61. Englewood Cliffs, NJ: Prentice-Hall.

Tinklenberg, J. R., and Stillman, R. C. (1970). Drug use and violence. In *Violence and the Struggle for Existence,* eds. D. N. Daniels et al., pp. 327–365. Boston: Little, Brown.

Vista Hill Psychiatric Foundation. (1972). The abuse of amphetamine. *Drug Abuse and Alcoholism Newsletter,* February.

Wiley, R. F. (1971). Abuse of methylphenidate (Ritalin). *New England Journal of Medicine* 285:464.

Yatsu, F. M., Wesson, D. R., and Smith, D. E. (1975). Amphetamine abuse. In *Medical Aspects of Drug Abuse,* ed. R. W. Richter, pp. 50–56. Hagerstown, MD: Harper and Row.

SEDATIVE-HYPNOTICS

American Medical Association. Committee on Alcoholism and Addiction. (1965). Dependence on barbiturates and other sedative drugs. *Journal of the American Medical Association* 193:673–677.

Brecher, E. M., and the editors of *Consumer Reports.* (1972). *Licit and Illicit Drugs.* Boston: Little, Brown.

Cameron, J. (1973). Pretty poison. *The Washington Post/Potomac,* February 11.

Carroll, E. N. (1974). Psychopathology and sensation seeking in "downers," "speeders," and "trippers": a study of the relationship between personality and drug choice. Paper presented at the 82nd Annual Convention of the American Psychological Association, New Orleans.

Chambers, C. D. (1969). Barbiturate-sedative abuse: a study of prevalence among narcotic abusers. *International Journal of the Addictions* 4:45–57 (Reprinted by courtesy of Marcel Dekker, Inc.).

Ewing, J.A. (1967). Addictions II: non-narcotic addictive agents. In *Comprehensive Textbook of Psychiatry,* eds. A.M. Freedman and H.S. Kaplan, pp. 1003–1011. Baltimore: Williams and Wilkins.

Gerald, M. C., and Schwirian, P. M. (1973). Nonmedical use of methaqualone. *Archives of General Psychiatry* 28:627–631.

Hendin, H. (1975). *The Age of Sensation.* New York: Norton.

Hoenig, G. (1972). The danger of the down high. *The New York Times,* December 24.

Inaba, D. S., Gay, G. R., Newmeyer, J. A., and Whitehead, C. (1973). Methaqualone abuse. *Journal of the American Medical Association* 224:1505–1509.

Irwin, S. (1970). *Drugs of Abuse: An Introduction to Their Actions and Potential Hazards.* Beloit, WI: Student Association for the Study of Hallucinogens.

Kempton, R. J., and Kempton, T. (1973). Methaqualone abuse: an epidemic for the seventies. *Journal of Drug Education* 3:403–413.

Kiev, A. (1975). *The Drug Epidemic.* New York: The Free Press.

Long, R. E., and Penna, R. P. (1968). Drugs of abuse. *Journal of the American Pharmaceutical Association* January: 12–27.

Mitcheson, M. (1970). Polydrug abuse. In *ABC of Drug Addiction,* pp. 89–93. Bristol, England: John Wright and Sons.

National Commission on Marihuana and Drug Abuse. (1973). *Drug Use in America: Problem in Perspective.* Second Report of the National Commission on Marihuana and Drug Abuse. Washington, D.C.: Government Printing Office.

National Institute of Mental Health. (1969). The up and down drugs. Public Health Service Publication No. 1830. Washington, D.C.: Government Printing Office.

Pascarelli, E. F. (1973). Methaqualone abuse, the quiet epidemic. *Journal of the American Medical Association* 224:1512–1514.

Ray, O. S. (1972). *Drugs, Society, and Human Behavior.* Saint Louis: C. V. Mosby.

Raynes, A. E. (1973). The heroin and barbiturate epidemics in Boston. In *Proceedings of the 5th National Conference on Methodone Treatment,*

Vol. 2, pp. 995-1001. New York: National Association for the Prevention of Addiction to Narcotics.

Spotts, J. V., and Shontz, F. C. (1982). Ego development, dragon fights, and chronic drug abusers. *The International Journal of the Addictions* 17:945-976.

Swartzburg, M., Lieb, J., and Schwartz, A. H. (1973). Methaqualone withdrawal. *Archives of General Psychiatry* 29:46-47.

Tinklenberg, J. R., and Stillman, R. C. (1970). Drug use and violence. In *Violence and the Struggle for Existence,* eds. D. N. Daniels et al., pp. 327-3650. Boston: Little, Brown.

Tinklenberg, J. R., Murphy, P. L., Darley, C. F., Roth, W. T., and Kippell, B. S. (1974). Drug involvement in criminal assaults by adolescents. *Archives of General Psychiatry* 30:685-689.

U.S. Medicine (5/15/72). Barbiturates 'eclipse' heroin use, new drug culture seen emerging.

U.S. News & World Report (12/27/71). Drug abuse: now it's 'downers'.

Washington Post (5/14/72). Sopors: downs as a drug fad.

Wesson, D. R., and Smith, D. E. (1977). *Barbiturates: Their Use, Misuse, and Abuse.* New York: Human Sciences Press.

Woolf, D.S. (1983). CNS depressants: other sedative hypnotics. In *Substance Abuse,* eds. A. Bennett, C. Vourakis, and D. S. Woolf, pp. 39-56. New York: Wiley.

Zwerdling, D. (1972). Methaqualone: the 'safe' drug that isn't very. *Washington Post,* November 12.

VOLATILE SUBSTANCES

Ackerly, W., and Gibson, G. (1964). Lighter fluid sniffing. *American Journal of Psychiatry* 120:1056-1061.

Alex, T. (1968). Denver juvenile court glue-sniffing project. In *Inhalation of Glue Fumes and Other Substance Abuse Practice Among Adolescents,* Denver Juvenile Court, Conference Proceedings, pp. 96-103. Office of Juvenile Delinquency and Youth Development. Department of Health, Education, and Welfare. Washington, D.C.: Government Printing Office.

Allen, S. M. (1966). Glue-sniffing. *International Journal of the Addictions* 1:147-150 (Reprinted by courtesy of Marcel Dekker, Inc.).

Bass, M. (1970). Sudden sniffing death. *Journal of the American Medical Association* 212:2075-2079.

Clinger, O. W., and Johnson, N. (1951). Purposeful inhalation of gasoline vapors. *Psychoanalytic Quarterly* 25:557-567.

Cohen, S. (1969). *The Drug Dilemma.* New York: McGraw-Hill.

Ferguson, R. W. (1975). *Drug Abuse Control.* Boston: Holbrook Press.

Friedman, C. J., and Friedman, A. S. (1973). Drug abuse and delinquency. In Technical Papers of the Second Report of the National Commission on Marihuana and Drug Abuse. *Drug Use in America: Problem in Perspective* (appendix) pp. 398–484. Washington, D.C.: Government Printing Office.

Gioscia, V. (1968). Glue sniffing: exploratory hypotheses of the psychosocial dynamics of respiratory intrajection. In *Inhalation of Glue Fumes and Other Substance Abuse Practices Among Adolescents,* Denver Juvenile Court, Conference Proceedings, pp. 60–73. Office of Juvenile Delinquency and Youth Development. Department of Health, Education, and Welfare. Washington, D.C.: Government Printing Office.

Hahn, Paul H. (1978). *The Juvenile Offender and the Law.* Cincinnati: Anderson Publishing Co.

Hoffman, F. G. (1975). *A Handbook on Drug and Alcohol Abuse: The Biomedical Aspects.* New York: Oxford University Press.

Irwin, S. (1970). *Drugs of Abuse: An Introduction to their Actions and Potential Hazards.* Beloit, WI: Student Association for the Study of Hallucinogens.

Krug, D. C., Sokol, J., and Nylander, I. (1964). Inhalation of commercial solvents: a form of deviance among adolescents. In *Drug Addiction in Youth,* ed. E. Harms, pp. 36–450. Oxford, England: Pergamon Press.

Lewis, J. D., Moritz, D., and Mellis, L. P. (1981). Long-term toluene abuse. *American Journal of Psychiatry* 138:368–370.

Long, R. E., and Penna, R. P. (1968). Drugs of abuse. *Journal of the American Pharmaceutical Association* January: 12–27.

Massengale, O. N., Glasser, H. H., LeLievre, R. E., Dodds, J. B., and Klock, M. E. (1963). Physical and psychologic factors in glue sniffing. *New England Journal of Medicine* 269:1340–1344.

National Commission on Marihuana and Drug Abuse (1973). *Drug Use in America: Problem in Perspective.* Second Report of the National Commission on Marihuana and Drug Abuse. Washington, D.C.: Government Printing Office.

Preble, E., and Laury, G. (1967). Plastic cement: the ten cent hallucinogen. *International Journal of the Addictions* 2:271–281 (Reprinted by courtesy of Marcel Dekker, Inc.).

Rubin, T., and Babbs, J. (1970). The glue sniffer. *Federal Probation* 34:23–28.

Schroeder, Richard C. (1980). *The Politics of Drugs.* Washington, D.C.: Congressional Quarterly Press.

Tolan, E. J., and Lingl, F. A. (1964). "Model psychosis" produced by inhalation of gasoline fumes. *American Journal of Psychiatry* 120:757–761.

Washington Post (7/16/76). Costly euphoria.

Wilde, C. (1975). Aerosol metallic paints: deliberate inhalation: a study of inhalation and/or ingestion of copper and zinc particles. *International Journal of the Addictions* 10:127–134 (Reprinted by courtesy of Marcel Dekker, Inc.).

Williams, J. B., ed. (1967). *Narcotics and Hallucinogens: A Handbook*, rev. ed. Beverly Hills, CA: Glencoe Press.

Wilson, R. (1968). Workshop D (report). In *Inhalation of Glue Fumes and Other Substance Abuse Practices Among Adolescents*, Denver Juvenile Court, Conference Proceedings, pp. 136–138. Office of Juvenile Delinquency and Youth Development. Department of Health, Education, and Welfare. Washington, D.C.: Government Printing Office.

MARIJUANA

Addiction Research Foundation (1983). *Cannabis: Health Risks*. Toronto: ARF Books.

Allentuck, S., and Bowman, K. M. (1942). The psychiatric aspects of marijuana intoxication. *American Journal of Psychiatry* 99:248–251.

American Academy of Pediatrics Committee on Drugs (1975). Effects of marijuana on man. *Pediatrics* 56:135–142.

Apsler, R. (1978). Untangling the conceptual jungle of drug abuse. *Contemporary Drug Problems* 7:55–80.

Ausubel, D. P. (1958). *Drug Addiction*. New York: Random House.

Balis, G. U. (1974). The use of psychotomimetic and related consciousness-altering drugs. In *American Handbook of Psychiatry*, Vol 3, eds. S. Arieti and E. B. Brody, pp. 404–446. New York: Basic Books.

Ball, J. C., Chambers, C. D., and Ball, M. J. (1968). The association of marijuana smoking with opiate addiction in the United States. *Journal of Criminal Law, Criminology and Police Science* 59:171–182.

Barnes, H. E. (1939). *Society in Transition*. New York: Prentice-Hall

Baudelaire, C. An excerpt from The Seraphic Theatre. In *The Marijuana Papers (1966)*, ed. D. Solomon, pp. 136–146. Indianapolis: Bobbs-Merrill.

Bejerot, N. (1972). *Addiction: An Artificially Induced Drive*. Springfield, IL: Charles C. Thomas.

Berke, J., and Herton, C. (1974). *The Cannabis Experience*. London: Peter Owen.

Bloomquist, E. R. (1971). *Marijuana: The Second Trip*. Beverly Hills, CA: Glencoe Press.

Brown, T. T. (1961). *The Enigma of Drug Addiction*. Springfield, IL: Charles C. Thomas.

Chappel, P. A. (1966). Cannabis — a toxic and dangerous substance — a study of eight takers. *British Journal of Addiction* 61:269–282.

Charen, S., and Perelman, L. (1946). Personality studies of marijuana addicts. *American Journal of Psychiatry* 102:674-682.

Chopra, G. S. (1969). Man and Marijuana. *International Journal of the Addictions* 4:215-247 (Reprinted by courtesy of Marcel Dekker, Inc.).

Cohen, S. (1964). *The Beyond Within: The LSD Story.* New York: Atheneum.

De Ropp, R. S. (1968). *The Master Game.* New York: Dell.

Eddy, N. B., Halbach, H., Isbell, H., and Seevers, M. A. (1971). Drug dependence: its significance and characteristics. In *Drug Dependence and Abuse Resource Book,* eds P. F. Healy and J. P. Manak, pp. 377-380. Chicago: National District Attorneys Association.

Ferguson, R. W. (1975). *Drug Abuse Control.* Boston: Holbrook Press.

Gaskill, H. S. (1945). Marijuana, an intoxicant. *American Journal of Psychiatry* 102:202-204.

Gomila, F. R., and Lambou, M. C. (1938). Status of the marijuana vice in the United States. In *Marijuana: America's New Drug Problem,* ed. R. P. Walton, pp. 27-39. Philadelphia: J.B. Lippincott.

Goode, E. (1969). Marijuana and sex. *Evergreen* 66:19-20.

——— (1972). Drug use and sexual activity on a college campus. *American Journal of Psychiatry* 128:1272-1276.

——— (1974). Marijuana use and the progression to dangerous drugs. In *Marijuana: Effects on Human Behavior,* ed. L. L. Miller, pp. 303-338. New York: Academic Press.

Grinspoon, Lester (1977). *Marihuana Reconsidered.* Cambridge, MA: Harvard University Press.

Hahn, Paul H. (1978). *The Juvenile Offender and the Law.* Cincinnati: Anderson Publishing Co.

Halikas, J.A . (1974). Marijuana use and psychiatric illness. In *Marijuana: Effects on Human Behavior,* ed. L. L. Miller, pp. 265-302. New York: Academic Press.

Hendin, H. (1975). *The Age of Sensation.* New York: Norton.

Institute of Medicine (1982). *Marijuana and Health.* Washington, D.C.: National Academy Press.

Irwin, S. (1970). *Drugs of Abuse: An Introduction to their Actions and Potential Hazards.* Beloit, WI: Student Association for the Study of Hallucinogens.

Jones, H. B. (1971). A report on drug abuse in the armed forces in Viet Nam. Berkeley, CA: University of California (November 15), Unpublished.

Kandel, D. (1984). Marijuana users in young adulthood. *Archives of General Psychiatry* 41: 200-209.

Kaplan, J. (1970). *Marijuana — The New Prohibition.* New York: World Publishing.

Kiev, A. (1975). *The Drug Epidemic.* New York: Free Press.

Kolansky, H., and Moore, W. T. (1971). Effects of marijuana on adolescents and young adults. *Journal of the American Medical Association* 216: 486–492.

Kolb, L. (1962). *Drug Addiction.* Springfield, IL: Charles C. Thomas.

Lewin, L. (1964). *Phantastica, Narcotics and Stimulating Drugs.* New York: E. P. Dutton.

Lingeman, R. R. (1974). *Drugs from A to Z: A Dictionary,* 2nd ed. New York: McGraw-Hill.

Long, R. E., and Penna, R. P. (1968). Drugs of abuse. *Journal of the American Pharmaceutical Association* January: 12–27.

Macdonald, J.M. (1976). *Psychiatry and the Criminal,* 3rd ed. Springfield, IL: Charles C. Thomas.

McGlothlin, W. H., and West, L. (1968). The marijuana problem: an overview. *American Journal of Psychiatry* 125:370–378.

McMorris, S. C. (1966). What price euphoria: the case against marijuana. *Medio-Legal Journal* 34:74–79.

Maurer, D. W. and Vogel, V. H. (1967). *Narcotics and Narcotic Addiction,* 3rd ed. Springfield, IL: Charles C. Thomas.

Nahas, G. G. (1973). *Marijuana—Deceptive Weed.* New York: Raven Press.

National Commission on Marihuana and Drug Abuse. (1972). *Marihuana: A Signal of Misunderstanding.* First Report of the National Commission on Marihuana and Drug Abuse. Washington, D.C.: Government Printing Office.

National Institute of Mental Health. (1971). Marihuana. Public Health Service Publication No. 1829. Washington, D.C.: Government Printing Office.

National Institute on Drug Abuse. (1976). *Marihuana and Health.* Fifth Annual Report to the U.S. Congress from the Secretary of Health, Education, and Welfare. DHEW Publication No. (ADM) 76–314. Washington, D.C.: Government Printing Office.

Opler, M. K. (1972). Sex mores and social conceptions of deviance. In *Sexual Behavior: Social, Clinical, and Legal Aspects,* eds. H. Resnick and M. Wolfgang, pp. 21–40. Boston: Little, Brown.

Pillard, R. C. (1970). Marijuana. *New England Journal of Medicine* 283: 294–303.

Ray, O. (1978). *Drugs, Society, and Human Behavior* St. Louis: C.V. Mosby Co.

Robins, L. N., Darvish, H. S., and Murphy, G. E. (1970). The long-term outcome for adolescent drug users: a follow-up study of 76 users and 146 nonusers. In *The Psychopathology of Adolescence,* eds. J. Zubin and A. M. Freedman, pp. 159–178. New York: Grune and Stratton.

Rubin, V., and Comitas, I. (1976). *Ganja in Jamaica.* Garden City, NY: Doubleday.

Schofield, M. (1971). *The Strange Case of Pot.* Middlesex, England; Penguin Books.

Schwartz, R. H. (1984). Marijuana: a crude drug with a spectrum of underappreciated toxicity. *Pediatrics* 83:455–458.

Simmons, J. L. ed. (1967). *Marijuana: Myths and Realities.* North Hollywood, CA: Brandon House.

Snyder, S. H. (1971). *Uses of Marijuana.* New York: Oxford University Press.

Solomon, D. *The Marijuana Papers,* pp. 136–146. Indianapolis: Bobbs-Merrill.

Szymanski, H. V. (1981). Prolonged depersonalization after marijuana use. *American Journal of Psychiatry* 138:231–233.

Talbott, J. A., and Teague, J. W. (1969). Marijuana psychosis. *Journal of the American Medical Association* 210:299–302.

Tinklenberg, J. R. (1974). Marijuana and human aggression. In *Marijuana: Effects on Human Behavior,* ed. L. L. Miller, pp. 339–357. New York: Academic Press.

Weil, A. T. (1972). *The Natural Mind: A New Way of Looking at Drugs and the Higher Consciousness.* Boston: Houghton Mifflin.

——— (1973). Toxic reactions to marijuana. In *Management of Adolescent Drug Misuse: Clinical, Psychological and Legal Perspectives,* ed. J. R. Ganage, pp. 14–23. Beloit, WI: Student Association for the Study of Hallucinogens.

Williams, J. B., ed. (1967). *Narcotics and Hallucinogens: A Handbook,* rev. ed. Beverly Hills, CA: Glencoe Press.

Winick, C. (1971). Marijuana use by young people. In *Drug Dependence and Abuse Resource Book,* eds. P. F. Healy and J. P. Manak, pp. 232–238. Chicago: National District Attorneys Association.

Wolff, P. (1949). *Marijuana in Latin America: The Threat It Constitutes.* Washington, D.C.: Linacre Press.

Zinberg, N. (1984). *Drug, Set, and Setting.* New Haven: Yale University Press.

HALLUCINOGENS, OR PSYCHOTOMIMETIC DRUGS

Balis, G.U. (1974). The use of psychotomimetic and related consciousness-altering drugs. In *American Handbook of Psychiatry,* Vol. 3, eds., S. Arieti and E. B. Brody, pp. 404–446. New York: Basic Books.

Barter, J. T., and Reite, M. (1969). Crime and LSD: the insanity plea. *American Journal of Psychiatry* 126:531–537.

Berger, F. M., and Potterfield, D. J. (1969). Drug abuse and society. In *Drugs and Youth: Proceedings of the Rutgers Symposium on Drug Abuse,* eds. J. R. Wittenborn et al., pp. 37–43. Springfield, IL: Charles C. Thomas.

Blaine, G. B. (1966). *Youth and the Hazards of Affluence.* New York: Harper and Row.

Burns, R. S. (1978). Causes of phencyclidine-related deaths. *Clinical Toxicology* 12:463–481.

Cattell, J. P. (1954). The influence of mescaline on psychodynamic material. *Journal of Nervous and Mental Disease* 119:233–244.

Cohen, S. (1969). *The Drug Dilemma.* New York: McGraw-Hill.

Committee on Alcoholism and Drug Dependence. American Medical Association. (1969). Dependence on LSD and other drugs. In *Drug Dependence: A Guide for Physicians,* American Medical Association. Council on Mental Health, pp. 124–132. Chicago: American Medical Association.

Davis, B. (1982). The PCP epidemic: a critical review. *The International Journal of the Addictions* 17:1137–1155.

De Ropp, R. S. (1957). *Drugs and the Mind.* New York: St. Martin's Press.

Domino, E. F. (1975). The hallucinogens. In *Medical Aspects of Drug Abuse,* ed. R. W. Richter, pp. 3–15. Hagerstown, MD: Harper and Row.

Drug Enforcement Administration (1977). DEA PCP analysis 1975–1976 (Statistical Report). Washington, D.C.: Drug Enforcement Administration.

Fauman, M. A., and Fauman, B. J. (1979). Violence associated with phencyclidine abuse. *American Journal of Psychiatry* 136:1584–1586.

Fink, P. J., Goldman, M., and Lyons, I. (1967). Recent trends in substance abuse. *International Journal of the Addictions* 2:143–151 (Reprinted by courtesy of Marcel Dekker, Inc.).

Fisher, D. D. (1968). LSD for science and kicks. In *Mind Drugs,* ed. M. O. Hyde, pp. 66–81. New York: McGraw-Hill.

Freedman, A. M. (1967). Drugs and sexual behavior. *Medical Aspects of Human Sexuality* November: pp. 25–31.

Gioscia, V. (1969). LSD subcultures: acidoxy versus orthodoxy. *American Journal of Orthopsychiatry* 39:428–436.

Girdano, D. D., and Girdano, A. (1976). *Drugs – A Factual Account,* 2nd ed. Reading, MA: Addison-Wesley.

Glass, G. S., and Bowers, M. N. (1970). Chronic psychosis associated with long-term psychotomimetic drug abuse. *Archives of General Psychiatry* 23:97–103.

Guarner, E. (1966). Psychodynamic aspects of drug experience. *British Journal of Medical Psychology* 39:157–162.

Hafen, B.Q. (1973). Use of nutmeg as an intoxicant. In *Drug Abuse,* ed. B. Q. Hafen, pp. 394–404. Provo, UT: Brigham Young University Press.

Hekimian, L. J., and Gershon, S. (1968). Characteristics of drug abusers admitted to a psychiatric hospital. *Journal of the American Medical Association* 205:75–80.

Helig, S. M., Diller, J., and Nelson, F. L. (1982). A study of 44 PCP-related deaths. *The International Journal of the Addictions* 17:1175-1184.

Hoffman, F. G. (1975). *A Handbook on Drug and Alcohol Abuse: The Biomedical Aspects.* New York: Oxford University Press.

Holbrook, John M. (1983). Hallucinogens. In *Substance Abuse,* eds. G. Bennett, D. Vourakis, and D. S. Woolf, pp. 86-101. New York: Wiley.

Huxley, A. (1954). *The Doors of Perception.* New York: Harper.

Irwin, S. (1970). *Drugs of Abuse: An Introduction to their Actions and Potential Hazards.* Beloit, WI: Student Association for the Study of Hallucinogens.

Julien, R. M. (1978). *A Primer of Drug Action.* San Francisco: W.H. Freeman and Co.

Kiev, A. (1975). *The Drug Epidemic.* New York: Free Press.

Klepfisz, A., and Racy, J. (1973). Homicide and LSD. *Journal of the American Medical Association* 223:429-430.

Klüver, H. (1926). Mescal visions and eidetic vision. *American Journal of Psychology* 37:502-515.

Leary, T. Litwin, G. H., Metzner, R. (1963). Reactions to psilocybin administered in a supportive environment. *Journal of Nervous and Mental Disease,* 137:561-573.

Leech, K. (1970). The drug scene and the Christian community. In *ABC of Drug Addiction,* pp. 37-40. Bristol, England: John Wright and Sons.

Long, R. E., and Penna, R. P. (1968). Drugs of abuse. *Journal of the American Pharmaceutical Association,* January: pp. 12-27.

Ludwig, A. M., and Levine, J. (1966). The clinical effects of psychedelic agents. *Clinical Medicine* 73:12-24.

Marshall, C. R., and Wells, T. (1937). An enquiry into the causes of mescal vision. *Journal of Neurology and Psychopathology* 17:289-304.

McGlothlin, W. H. (1973). *Amphetamines, Barbiturates and Hallucinogens: An Analysis of Use, Distribution and Control.* Washington, D.C.: Government Printing Office.

McGlothlin, W. H., and Arnold, D. O. (1971). LSD revisited, *Archives of General Psychiatry* 24: 35-49.

National Clearinghouse for Drug Abuse Information. (1973). Mescaline. Report Series 15, no. 1. Rockville, MD: Alcohol, Drug Abuse, and Mental Health Administration.

——— (1973). Psilocybin. Report Series 16, no. 1. Rockville, MD: Alcohol, Drug Abuse, and Mental Health Administration.

National Institute of Mental Health. (1971). LSD. Public Health Service Publication No. 1828. Washington, D.C.: Government Printing Office.

National Observer (11/20/71). A father's story of his LSD-crazed son.

Pollard, J. C., Uhr, L., and Stern. E. (1965). *Drugs and Phantasy.* Boston: Little, Brown.

Psychiatric Progress (1966). Management of psychotic episodes in users of LSD posing new problems; identification seen difficult. September-October.

Ray, O. S. (1978). *Drugs, Society, and Human Behavior.* Saint Louis: C. V. Mosby.

Reich, P., and Hepps, R. (1972). Homicide during a psychosis induced by LSD. *Journal of the American Medical Association* 219:869–871.

Rinkel, M., Atwell, C. R., DiMascio, A., and Brown, J. (1960). Experimental psychiatry. V. psilocybin, a new psychotogenic drug. *New England Journal of Medicine* 262: 295–297.

Rynearson, R. R., Wilson, M. R., Jr., and Bickford, R. G. (1968). Psilocybin-induced changes in psychologic function, electroencephalogram, and light-evoked potentials in human subjects. *Mayo Clinic Proceedings* 43:191–204.

Scher, J. (1966). Patterns and profiles of addiction and drug abuse. *Archives of General Psychiatry* 15:539–551.

Schroeder, Richard, C. (1980). *The Politics of Drugs.* Washington, D.C.: Congress Quarterly Press.

Siegel, R. K. (1973). Hallucinogens and perceptual changes. In *Drug Abuse,* ed. B. Q. Hafen, pp. 323–329. Provo, UT: Brigham Young University Press.

Smith, P. B. (1959). A Sunday with mescaline. *Bulletin of the Menninger Clinic* 23:20–27.

Terrill, J. (1964). The nature of the LSD experience. In *LSD: The Consciousness-Expanding Drug,* ed. D. Solomon, pp. 175–182. New York: G. P. Putman's Sons.

Thale, T., Gabrio, B. W., Salomon, K. (1950). Hallucination and imagery induced by mescaline. *American Journal of Psychiatry* 106:686–691.

Wells, B. (1974). *Psychedelic Drugs.* Baltimore: Penguin Books.

Williams, J. B. (1974). *Narcotics and Drug Dependence.* Beverly Hills, CA: Glencoe Press.

Wright, H. H. (1980). Violence and PCP abuse. *American Journal of Psychiatry* 137:752–753.

POLYDRUG USE

Chambers, C. D., Moffett, A. D., and Cuskey, W. R. (1971). Five patterns of Darvon abuse. *International Journal of the Addictions* 6:173–189 (Reprinted by courtesy of Marcel Dekker, Inc.).

Chessick, R. D. (1960). The "pharmacogenic orgasm" in the drug addict. *Archives of General Psychiatry* 3:545–556.

Ewing, J. A. (1967). Addictions II: non-narcotic addictive agents. In *Comprehensive Textbook of Psychiatry,* eds. A. M. Freedman and H. S. Kaplan, pp. 1003–1011. Baltimore: Williams and Wilkins.

Ferguson, R. W. (1975). *Drug Abuse Control.* Boston: Holbrook Press.

Forrest, J. A. H., and Tarala, R. A. (1973). Abuse of drugs "for kicks": a review of 252 admissions. *British Medical Journal* 4:136–139.

Frosch, W. A. (1968). Physical and mental effects of LSD. *New York Medicine* 24:424–430.

Gould, L. C., Berberian, R. M., Kasl, S. V., Thompson, W. D., and Kleber, H. D. (1977). Sequential patterns of multiple-drug use among high school students. *Archives of General Psychiatry* 34:216–222.

Hamburger, E. (1964). Barbiturate use in narcotic addicts. *Journal of the American Medical Association* 189:366–368.

Hoffman, F. G. (1975). *A Handbook on Drug and Alcohol Abuse: The Biomedical Aspects.* New York: Oxford University Press.

Johnston, L. (1973). *Drugs and American Youth.* Ann Arbor, MI: Institute for Social Research.

McGlothlin, W. H. (1975). Drug use and abuse. In *Annual Review of Psychology,* Vo. 26, eds. M. R. Rosenzweig, and L. W. Porter, pp. 45–64. Palo Alto, CA: Annual Review.

Merry, J. (1967). Glue sniffing and heroin abuse. *British Medical Journal* 2:360.

Milby, J. B. (1981). *Addictive Behavior and Its Treatment.* New York: Springer Publishing Co.

Mitcheson, M., Haeks, D., Davidson, J, Hitchens, L., and Malone, S. (1970). Sedative abuse by heroin addicts. *Lancet,* March 21: 606–607.

National Clearinghouse for Drug Abuse Information (1972). Cocaine. Report Series 11, no. 1. Washington, D.C.: Government Printing Office.

New York State Office of Drug Abuse Services (1975). A survey of substance abuse among junior and senior high school students in New York State. Report no. 1: prevalence of drug and alcohol use. New York State Office of Drug Abuse Services.

Scher, J. (1966). Patterns and profiles of addiction and drug abuse. *Archives of General Psychiatry* 15:539–551.

Williams, J. B. (1974). *Narcotics and Drug Dependence.* Beverly Hills, CA: Glencoe Press.

Woody, G., O'Brien, C. P., and Greenstein, R. (1975). Misuse and abuse of diazepam: an increasingly common medical problem. *International Journal of the Addictions* 10:843–848 (Reprinted by courtesy of Marcel Dekker, Inc.).

ALCOHOL

Bacon, S. D. (1962). Alcohol, alcoholism, and crime: an overview. In *Alcohol, Alcoholism and Crime,* eds. D. W. Haughey and N. A. Neiberg, pp. 5–27. Proceedings of the Conference on Alcohol, Alcoholism and

Crime. Chatham, MA.

Banay, R. S. (1942). Alcoholism and crime. *Quarterly Journal of Studies on Alcohol* 2:686-716.

Berry, R. E., and Boland, J. P. (1977). *The Economic Cost of Alcohol Abuse.* New York: Free Press.

Blacker, E., Demone, H. W., and Freeman, H. E. (1965). Drinking behavior of delinquent boys. *Quarterly Journal of Studies on Alcohol* 26:223-237.

Blane, H. T. (1968). *The Personality of the Alcoholic.* New York: Harper and Row.

Brecher, E. M., and the editors of *Consumer Reports* (1972). *Licit and Illicit Drugs.* Boston: Little, Brown.

Denver High Impact Anti-Crime Program (1974). Characteristics and recidivism of adult felony offenders in Denver. Report of the Denver High Impact Anti-Crime Program. Denver, CO: City and County of Denver.

Ferguson, R. W. (1975). *Drug Abuse Control.* Boston: Holbrook Press.

Ferracuti, F. (1972). Incest between father and daughter. In *Sexual Behavior: Social, Clinical, and Legal Aspects,* eds. H. Resnick and M. Wolfgang, pp. 169-183. Boston: Little, Brown.

Fort, J. (1968). LSD and the mind-altering drug (M.A.D.) world. In *The Problems and Prospects of LSD,* ed. J. T. Ungerleider, pp. 3-21. Springfield, IL: Charles C Thomas.

Gebhard, P. H., Gagnon, J. H., Pomeroy, W. B., and Christenson, C. V. (1967). *Sex Offenders: An Analysis of Types.* New York: Bantam.

Goodwin, D. W., Crane, J. B., and Guze, S. B. (1971). Felons who drink: an eight year follow-up. *Quarterly Journal of Studies on Alcohol* 32:136-147.

Greene, B. T. (1981). An examination of the relationship between crime and substance abuse use in drug/alcohol treatment population. *The International Journal of the Addictions* 16:627-645.

Guze, S. B., and Cantwell, D. P. (1965). Alcoholism, parole observations and criminal recidivism: a study of 116 parolees. *American Journal of Psychiatry* 122:436-439.

Guze, S. B., Wolfgram, E. D., McKinney, J. K., and Cantwell, D. P. (1968). Delinquency, social maladjustment, and crime: the role of alcoholism. *Diseases of the Nervous System* 29:238-243.

Haughey, D. W., and Neiberg, N. A. (1962). Summary of group discussions. In *Alcohol, Alcoholism and Crime,* eds. D. W. Haughey and N. A. Neiberg, pp. 98-115. Proceedings of the Conference on Alcohol, Alcoholism and Crime. Chatham, MA.

Hoffman, F. G. (1975). *A Handbook on Drug and Alcohol Abuse: The Biomedical Aspects.* New York: Oxford University Press.

Kaplan, J. (1984). Alcohol, law enforcement and criminal justice. In The American Assembly. *Alcoholism and Related Problems* pp. 78-90. Englewood Cliffs, NJ: Prentice-Hall.

MacDonald, J. M. (1961). *The Murderer and His Victim*. Springfield, IL: Charles C. Thomas.

MacKay, J. R. (1962). Drinking and delinquency. In *Alcohol, Alcoholism and Crime*, eds. D. W. Haughey and N. A. Neiberg, pp. 46–57. Proceedings of the Conference on Alcohol, Alcoholism and Crime. Chatham, MA.

McClelland, D. C. (1971). The power of positive drinking. *Psychology Today*, January, Vol. 5: pp. 77ff.

McPeek, F. W. (1944). Youth, alcohol, and delinquency. *Quarterly Journal of Studies on Alcohol* 4:568–579.

National Commission on Marihuana and Drug Abuse (1973). *Drug Use in America: Problem in Perspective*. Second Report of the National Commission on Marihuana and Drug Abuse. Washington, D.C.: Government Printing Office.

Plaut, T. F. A. (1962). Summary of conference. In *Alcohol, Alcoholism and Crime*, eds. D. W. Haughey and N. A. Neiberg, pp. 116–124. Proceedings of the Conference on Alcohol, Alcoholism and Crime. Chatham, MA.

Quimby, F. H. (1970). Little known facts about the psychoactive drugs (Part I — alcohol). Multilith from Science Policy Research Division, Congressional Reference Service, Library of Congress, Washington, D.C.

Rada, R. T. (1975). Alcoholism and forcible rape. *American Journal of Psychiatry* 132:444–446.

Shakespeare, W. *The Tragedy of Macbeth*. Signet Classic Shakespeare Series, ed. S. Barnet. (1963) New York: New American Library.

Taylor, S. P., and Gammon, C. B. (1976). Aggressive behavior of intoxicated subjects. *Journal of Studies on Alcohol* 37:917–930.

Tinklenberg, J. (1973). Drugs and crime. In Technical Papers of the Second Report of the National Commission on Marihuana and Drug Abuse. *Drug Use in America: Problem in Perspective* (appendix), pp. 242–299. Washington, D.C.: Government Printing Office.

Tinklenberg, J., and Stillman, R. C. (1970). Drug use and violence. In *Violence and the Struggle for Existence*, eds. D. N. Daniels et al., pp. 327–365. Boston: Little, Brown.

Voss, H. L., and Hepburn, J. R. (1968). Patterns in criminal homicide in Chicago. *Journal of Criminal Law, Criminology and Police Science* 59:499–508.

Washington Post (2/25/73). Alcohol.

Wolfgang, M. E. (1958). *Patterns in Criminal Homicide*. Philadelphia: University of Pennsylvania Press.

Wolfgang, M. E., and Strohm, R. B. (1956). The relationship between alcohol and criminal homicide. *Quarterly Journal of Studies on Alcohol* 17:411–425.

Chapter 3

The Drug-Using
Criminal's Way of Life

IN THIS SECTION, we present a profile of the drug-using criminal before he involved himself with drugs. His drug use may have begun at virtually any time — before adolescence, during adolescence, in young adulthood, or later. It is important that the reader have a clear concept of the kind of person the criminal was before using drugs, irrespective of when that occurred. The reader then will recognize that the basic problem was the predrug personality of the user, not the drug use per se. The type of person being discussed here was first a criminal, only later a drug user.

THE CHILDHOOD OF THE POTENTIAL
DRUG-USING CRIMINAL: AN OVERVIEW

At an early age, future drug user and the nonuser choose to seek excitement through engaging in forbidden activities. As a child, regardless of family background or parental attitudes, the future criminal departs from the expected, engaging in behavior considered unacceptable by his parents and society while attempting to preserve the comforts of home life. As long as the family members tolerate his deviance, he is satisfied. When they object, he rebels. Lying and deception become a way of life. He demands that others trust him, but he continually betrays them. He pursues what he wants, regardless of the adverse effects on others. In his secretiveness he establishes a life of his own, so private that his parents complain of a painful "communication gap," which they cannot bridge. He baffles his family because his violating patterns are in opposition to their values and standards of acceptable conduct.

In the neighborhood the criminal, as a child, rejects his more responsible peers to seek association with irresponsible youngsters who are engaging in

This chapter is a condensation of material presented in Chapter 3 of Volume I.

activities that he considers exciting. He admires and strives to emulate them. He regards those who are more conventional in their choices of friends and interests as "squares"; he thinks that they are boring and stupid. Very early he drops out from the mainstream of society.

School is irrelevant; it does not provide him with excitement. Nevertheless, as he grows older, he continues in school for he knows that dropping out will result in others being more watchful of him. He demands modification of school requirements, asks for exemptions, devises shortcuts, cheats, plagiarizes, and blames others when he is held accountable. He may pursue excitement in the classroom by being disruptive and is labeled a "behavior problem." Or he may refuse to work at all and be retained or placed in special education classes. However, the criminal child is bright and generally able to fulfill the requirements easily. He may choose to do enough work to progress steadily through the grades, thus avoiding confrontations with the family. He may receive good marks but fails to gain an education. Maintaining a satisfactory academic record offers a respectability that makes it easier for him to commit offenses and remain above suspicion. Only when his behavior becomes utterly intolerable is he expelled.

At home this child rejects, defers, and defaults on household chores. To keep his parents from pressuring him and to keep them in the dark as to his objectives, he occasionally satisfies their requirements. Even if he leaves school and works, the same patterns generally continue. The criminal has high potential and often considerable talent. He has the same attitudes toward work as toward school. Some criminals refuse to work. Some comply in a token manner, although with disinterest and scorn. Some work only when it makes possible the attainment of a larger criminal objective. Some value a job mainly to pursue power and control and demand recognition for relatively minor accomplishments. Some blatantly use work as an arena for crime and to pilfer, bribe, embezzle, and establish sexual liaisons. Jobs are a potential cover for all criminals who work because society is apt to regard a man as responsible simply because he is employed. Like going to school, holding a job provides the criminal with a superficial aura of responsibility.

In all our cases there was an enormous amount of early sexual thinking and, in most, substantial early sexual activity (before the age of ten). In childhood the sensual aspects of sex are minimal; the thrill of doing the forbidden outweighs sensual gratification. As a youth the criminal propositions, coerces, and in other ways exploits males and females for sexual conquest, usually showing little selectivity in his choice of partners. Availability is an important factor, but when partners are not readily available in his immediate environment, the criminal youth seeks them elsewhere. Basically his sexual conquest is like any other criminal enterprise. He approaches a prospective partner just as an older criminal approaches a bank, with lying, scheming and an exploitative modus operandi. In adolescence, his sexual patterns may include voyeurism, exhibitionism, homosexuality, child molestation, intimidation, and coercion. Some criminals object to particular forms of sexual activity, but, whatever their preferences, the sex is exploitative, not an integral part of a love relationship. The partner has no rights. The criminal acts as though he owns whomever he decides to exploit. He behaves the same way toward steady girlfriends and, when he marries, he functions toward his wife as he has with associates on the street. He requires his wife to be faithful, despite his lack of concern and tenderness and his inevitable infidelity. He insists on his right to have sex with whomever he chooses. He has no concept of love, interdependence, trust, putting himself in another's place, or openness.

Despite his many violations, each criminal believes himself to be inherently a good person, not a criminal. He readily points out that he gives money to charity, is fond of babies, has compassion for the infirm and elderly, and loves animals. He may enjoy good music, read philosophy, or write poetry. Although some criminals reject organized religion, nearly all retain a belief in a God. In their assessment of themselves, it is these features that they hang onto. Ignored is the fact that they injure others by their many violations and that they break the hearts of responsible people who care about them.

The 52 thinking errors of criminals described in Volume I are present in both drug users and nonusers.* We pointed out that the criminal is very fearful. To commit crimes, he must cut off both the external deterrents (the fears of getting caught and of being injured) and the internal deterrents (conscience). He is a predator who pursues power and control for his own sake. He has never learned to function interdependently, but demands to be recognized as "the unique number one" person in whatever he does. He uses a battery of tactics to make fools out of others. When he does not get his way, he is put down and angry. He is then all the more relentless in pursuing his objective by stealth or force. He neither cares nor knows how to make responsible decisions. Except for planning "scores" in crime, he fails to think long range; he prejudges, and he does not seek facts. These are a few of the thinking errors present in all criminals.

This is a basic overview of the kind of person the criminal is long before he becomes involved with drugs.† Before he uses his first drug, he commits many crimes. The number and seriousness of the crimes in the property, assault, and sex categories expand as he grows older. He becomes more and more confident that he can get away with violations because he is rarely detected, despite a growing number of offenses. If he is caught as a youngster, the penalties are minimal unless he already has amassed a police record of serious crimes.

*The reader is referred to Volume I for full development of these errors.

†Thus far we have been unable to predict which criminals will become drug users. We believe that further study will make such a determination possible.

THE DRUG USER AND HIS FAMILY

The user's contention that his resorting to drugs was part of a family pattern is generally only one of his many accountability lies. Most parents of our drug users were, and are, responsible people. In no family were both parents illegal drug users; in fact, in only one instance was one parent a drug user. In a few families one parent was an excessive drinker, but not a chronic alcoholic. In all instances parents actively opposed drug use.

Most of the drug users' siblings and other relatives were responsible individuals. Not only were they nonusers of drugs, but they did whatever they could to prevent any member of the family from any kind of irresponsible action. If more than one child in a family used drugs, there were others who did not. Just as the criminal nonuser intimidated his family, so did the criminal user. The latter expected that other family members would not reveal his activities and would cover for him if it appeared that he was about to get into trouble.

> The S family had two sons, P and D. The younger, P, was responsible, truthful, worked hard in school, and associated with others like himself. D wanted to play both sides of the street. He usually appeared cooperative and considerate of his family. Yet when his parents were not home, he invited his friends in to drink and smoke marijuana. Unknown to his parents, D was frequently truant from school, during which time he was shoplifting and engaging in sexual activity. D's objective was to preserve the comforts of home and to retain its privileges. He warned P that if he ever revealed anything to their parents about the drinking and drugs, he would "break his neck." As P learned more and more of what was happening, he was in a dilemma. Not at all interested in participating in D's activities, he finally decided that their parents should be informed, for he feared for his brother. Furthermore, he was increasingly afraid of his brother, who missed no occasion to taunt and ridicule him as a coward and a "square" and to threaten him.

Generally, it appears that the responsible sibling has been fearful of interfering with a brother's or sister's drug use even when he has wanted to intervene to help the user avoid serious trouble. The user has maintained the same exploitative stance toward his family as has the criminal who is a nonuser. He has expected family members to provide him with money with no questions asked. When money is given to him for a legitimate purpose, he often secretly uses it for drugs. When queried about expenditures, he has lied. He has expected to be permitted to go where he wished and do what he wanted without interference. If he got into trouble, he demanded to be bailed out.

When the user's parents were first informed (usually by a neighbor or the school) that their child was suspected of drug use, most were incredulous.* They had not detected any signs of drug use and certainly had no proof of it. It took hard evidence such as the discovery of drugs in their youngster's room to convince them. An example of parental resistance is evident in this description of an interview.

> We spent twenty hours interviewing D, a sixteen-year-old drug user. He was referred to us by a guidance counselor, who knew that D was not only failing in school but also using drugs. In our meetings with D, he acknowledged that he was a liar, thief, drug user, and seller of drugs. He boasted that his way of dealing with the world was to exploit and cheat people. Despite his many violations and the fact that he regarded himself as a gang leader in the Al Capone style, D considered himself at heart a decent person, not a criminal.

> At the suggestion of the school counselor who knew of our work, D's parents had consented to have their son evaluated by us. After we interviewed D, his parents requested a meeting with us at which D was also present. During this interview, it became quite evident that D's parents knew nothing about his drug abuse. His father and mother knew only that D was an underachiever in school. D did not want to reveal fully why his guidance counselor had referred him to us. In his parents' presence, D responded to our questioning with an array of tactics that effectively obscured disclosure. For the most part, he was silent, but responded to occasional questions with "I don't know," "maybe," "not extensively," "perhaps," and was in other ways calculatingly vague.

> D's father stated that D posed no problem at home. He reported that D was relatively placid and spent much time watching television. He said that D was musically talented and was doing well in this field. He surmised that D's problems might be due to being the youngest of several children and to his being led astray by undesirable associates. D's father thought that we would provide assistance in coping with D's scholastic underachievement, that and nothing else.

---

*Fiddle (1967, p. 109) cited a phenomenon that we have observed many times. The parents, especially the mother, do not want to acknowledge even to themselves that their child is a drug user. Fiddle quoted a user as saying: "She had to know that there was somethin' wrong, but, you know, they say that mothers never want to admit to themselves that their angel is doin' somethin' wrong. That their son is a good boy. He wouldn't do nothin' wrong, you know?"

D's mother said that her son's problems might be more serious than poor school performance, but she was puzzled as to what those problems were. She stated that D had stolen eight dollars worth of gum at the age of eight and that he had periodically boasted of swindling other youngsters in gambling at cards.

D's sullenness and silence, coupled with the guidance counselor's nonspecific statements that D had serious problems, suggested that D really was in need of outside help. Yet D's parents resisted this suggestion. D's father was especially stubborn in this regard. He abruptly said, "All right, let's rule out drugs." Unknown to his parents, D was selling drugs at the time, as well as using them, but would neither agree nor disagree with ruling out drugs. At this point D's mother commented that nothing D did would surprise her.

By the end of the interview, D's father (and to a lesser degree his mother) still had not faced the fact that D's problems were more extensive than poor schoolwork. They did agree that it might be a good idea for D to enter our program. D did so, but later dropped out. At no time during our contact with D did his parents have an accurate picture of the extent of his irresponsibility.

The user, instead of becoming defensive when his criminality is revealed, responds with a counteroffensive. He claims that drugs will not hurt him; they are his "affair." His parents and society are hypocrites if they criticize his drug use while they have their cocktails. In fact, liquor is more harmful than drugs. Unjust laws should be changed. Besides, "Everyone's doing it." He berates his parents, "You don't know anything because you never used drugs." He excuses himself, saying, "It's all right as long as no one suffers." Finally he declares his independence from his parents, averring that his life is his own and that he will do with it as he pleases.

Once parents are convinced that their youngster is using drugs, they are at a loss of what to do. They may differ with each other in their perception of the seriousness of drug use. If they believe that marijuana is the only drug used, they may countenance it because they have become convinced that "everybody does it" or because they have been persuaded by arguments that marijuana is less harmful than alcohol. Usually, they agree that some action must be taken, but they may differ as to how to deal with the child. Should they search his room for drugs? Should the child be sent to a different school? Should privileges be curtailed? Should they monitor their child's time and associates more strictly? Disagreements between parents on these and other issues are exploited by the drug user. He plays one parent against the other, capitalizing on their inconsistencies and disagreements. He then attributes his drug use to family dissension that either he created or exacerbated.

The family exerts maximal effort to help the youngster resolve his "problem." The major obstacle is that although the parents view it as a problem, the youngster does not. To him, his only problem is that he has been found out.

Most parents assiduously try to do all they can — partly out of genuine love and obligation but also because of fear of more serious difficulties.

The discovery of their offspring's drug use jolts parents into a self-examination. Their immediate assumption is that they have failed as parents. Mothers and fathers, who believe that they knew their child, castigate themselves for lacking sensitivity and perceptiveness. Retrospectively, they can see earlier indications of drug use, and they blame themselves for not having done something sooner. There is a terrifying helplessness, and fear sets in. Most parents react initially by drawing in the reins and supervising the youth more closely in an attempt to hold him accountable for how he spends time, where he spends money, what he does at school, and whom he chooses as friends. If the parents surmise that their child has been corrupted by his contemporaries, they attempt to limit his association with those whom they think have exerted a detrimental influence.

Many parents turn to outside sources for help. They consult guidance counselors, pastors, and personnel at community clinics, or even seek expensive private care that they can ill afford. In trying to help their child, money is not a consideration. Already blaming themselves, parents often find that the clinicians whom they consult regard them as a "cause" of the problem.* But often they are accused of being too prohibitive, too indulgent, or indifferent. They are often told that they are at fault for not communicating with the youngster, despite the fact that the user is more responsible for the "communication gap" than is the family. The child's delinquencies are viewed as an outgrowth of conflicts between the parents or even as a consequence of the parents' unconscious needs and wishes.† In some therapeutic groups parents endure confrontations with such allegations because they believe that the

---

*See the section on family therapy in the literature review of Chapter 7.

†An exception to the tendency to blame parents is a set of observations by Alexander and Dibb (1975, p. 509) made during the course of family therapy. These writers commented on the drug users' parents' stability and dedication to family life: "We have not found fathers in two-parent families to be weak or isolated as many other investigators have. . . . The fathers in our families were all respectable by community standards." In contrast, the drug users nagged parents to get what they wanted, accused them of not caring, threatened to leave home, and threatened self-destructive behavior, while continuing to be totally irresponsible at home and elsewhere.

therapist has expert knowledge. Baffled or intimidated, they either gullibly or reluctantly accept many statements about themselves that earlier they would not have believed.*

Parents learn that instead of cooperating in counseling or psychotherapy, the drug user thwarts their efforts to help. When recommended measures fail, desperate parents adopt sterner measures. They threaten, but seldom are able to implement successfully their threats. Some enroll the drug user in a private or residential school, hoping that he will be removed from the environment where drugs are available and where drug users congregate. Invariably the user finds the same kinds of groups in his new school. Some parents threaten to throw the child out of the home if he is of age, but they rarely do it. It is more likely that the drug user will run away or leave on his own. Often there is already a long history of running away. If there have been repeated offenses, parents may threaten to turn their child over to legal authorities. Some do press charges, whereas others wait for the youngster to get into trouble on his own. While hoping that the police and courts will have some impact on their child, the parents nevertheless exert effort and spend money to prevent his confinement. Even when a child has left home or has been confined, his parents almost always welcome him back to the family.

When the drug user is first confronted by his parents after they discover his drug use, he reacts characteristically with a barrage of denials and countercharges. If he is caught redhanded, whatever his outward stance, further violation is not long deterred; the lesson is to be more careful the next time. The drug user may decide that mollifying his parents is preferable to defiance. Thus, he assumes a more cooperative attitude and fulfills minimal requirements, such as improving his grades at school and doing a few chores at home. But this does not last. Another ploy is psychological warfare in which he exploits his parents' self-blame and guilt by threatening them with dire consequences, such as harming himself or running away from home. We know of instances in which youngsters inflicted superficial cuts on their arms when their parents discovered their drug use.

Whatever his parents' position and whatever his response, eventually the youngster returns to drugs. However, he is more careful as to when and where he uses them. If he increases his participation in family life, he simultaneously lives in the drug world outside home.

When he becomes an adult, the drug user is in contact with immediate family, relatives, neighbors, and friends who take an active interest in him and who believe his irresponsibility is attributable solely to drugs. Although gen-

---

*An example of a parent being so intimidated that he covered for his drug-using daughter was reported by Bartlett (1975, p. 273): "It's better for Debby to steal from the family than other people. When she takes it from her brothers, I pay it back to them. Sometimes she doesn't even know."

uinely fond of such well-intentioned people, he exploits them for his purposes.

> D was intimately involved with a responsible woman who was very much concerned about him and ever loyal. For years she tried to convince him to give up drugs. When D was confined for a crime, she visited him and continued urging him to change and stop using drugs. After he was released from confinement, she mothered him and gave him money when he needed it. Her gratification came from the sexual relationship and a belief that she could make a difference in D's life and redeem him. Finally realizing that she was getting nowhere, she gave D the choice of either living responsibly or losing her. Once D understood that he could no longer use her, they separated.

Even when the drug user is the head of his own family, the patterns described above are operative just as they were when he was a child in his own home. His life is a fraud, and he plays both sides of the street. As he did with his parents, he demands that his wife provide him with a comfortable home, take care of their children, and manage the home responsibly and efficiently. He professes concern for his family and endeavors to maintain a facade of responsibility. In fact, his irresponsibility is incompatible with seeing to the welfare of the family. Repeatedly he promises to stop using drugs and change, but his promises are regularly broken, whether under the influence of drugs or not.

In the home he lies by commission and omission, he is irritable when he does not have his way, and seeking criminal excitement, he concocts a variety of reasons to be out of the house. Consequently he contributes little, if anything, to family life, but insists that everything be done to accommodate him. Some of the money that should be used for family purposes he diverts to irresponsible activities, including drug use. He is promiscuous and has no sustained loyalty to his wife and children.

> We received a call from D at 10 P.M. In the background we heard his wife screaming. D complained that his wife had accused him of using drugs, which he denied. (Actually, we knew of his continuing drug use.) His wife stated that D came home without his check on payday. His excuse was that he had had expenditures of thirty dollars and that he had mailed her the rest of the money in a bank-by-mail envelope. Obviously this made no sense. D would not cash the check and send the balance of the cash through the mail.

D turned this episode around to berate his wife for not trusting him. His lying occurred day in and day out. D's one redeeming feature seemed to be the fact that he was working; but even at work he was misappropriating funds.

The general patterns of thought and action are basically the same before and after the beginning of drug use. With drug use the person is even more irresponsible and inflicts greater injury on his family. Unfortunately the family and society, almost universally, focus on drugs as the cause of the user's antisocial behavior, whereas the truth is that the havoc raised by the user is not solely the result of drug use. The more appropriate focus is the predrug personality. What was the person like before he used drugs? What did he want out of life? In subsequent chapters we shall show that drugs only made it easier for him to achieve his criminal objectives.

THE DRUG USER'S NEIGHBORHOOD AND ASSOCIATES

Had we uncritically accepted the views of the drug user and of those who regard social influences as crucial determinants of human development, we would have been blinded to the facts. Our research confirms the view of Matza (1964), who observed that the preponderant forces in any neighborhood, affluent or blighted, exert influence on its residents to become responsible citizens. Neighbors, schools, churches, social clubs, and community programs — all aim to develop responsible citizens. But in justifying his drug use, the user not only claims that everyone in his neighborhood uses drugs but also exaggerates the extent of that use. Fearful citizens in a community, alarmed over a problem like drug use, also magnify its prevalence. In any given area, criminals who are regular drug users constitute a minority of the population. Of course, small clusters do exist. A number of these groups, congregating in any particular location, is termed a *drug subculture*.

Drugs used to be available almost exclusively in the inner city, and suburbanites had to go there to procure them. Now drugs are widely available in the suburbs.* In rural areas they are less visible and more difficult to obtain.†

It is widely believed that youths are enticed into drug use. We have found that this is not so. Rather, whoever wants drugs seeks them on his own initiative. The criminal youngster gravitates toward a group that he considers elite because its members are older, use drugs, and are involved in illicit activities. He scorns his more conventional peers. However, he is likely to maintain ties with them mainly for the sake of appearance and perhaps because of a commonality of particular interests.

*The newspapers are filled with accounts of arrests for drug use, sales, and even manufacture in suburban areas.

†An analogy is prostitution. Sections of large cities are well-known "red light districts" where prostitution flourishes. Suburbanites in search of a prostitute go there. The point is that the person who wants something learns where to find it.

The dispenser of drugs is cautious about whom he talks to and what he talks about. He neither displays his wares nor jeopardizes himself by approaching a stranger. Rather, he must be convinced directly or through a second party that the seeker of drugs is reliable and not an informant. Unless the new user convinces the purveyor of drugs of his reliability, he may be ignored or rebuffed.

The would-be user learns the style of communication of the user. He dresses a particular way, uses street language, and talks with sophistication about drugs, the chief topics of conversation being the availability and advantages of different drugs and how to avoid detection at home, at school, and by the law. Also discussed are a variety of means of pursuing criminal excitement. The neophyte may be required to find a user who will assure other users that he is reliable. He then has to convince them that he is not "chicken." One user recalled that at the age of twelve he drank a six-pack of beer to show that he had "heart" or courage. This test stamina gave him an entrance to a group of older youngsters who drank and not long after began to use other drugs. Youths who have made known their interest are invited to "beer and dope" parties or "pill parties," where the talk is of cars, motorcycles, sex, and, of course, drugs. Some have to be "trained" in the use of specific drugs. Nonsmokers have to be shown how to smoke. Others are taught how to "snort" a drug.

> D wanted to demonstrate to the members of a particular group that he was not "chicken" or "square." He was a better pool player than they, but this status did not mean much to him. So he asked one of the fellows to teach him to snort heroin. After his first experience, he was nauseated and vomited. He was instructed to use the drug a few times so that he would overcome this effect. Every two or three days, D used heroin. Then he began "nodding," which was for him a strange experience. Finally he overcame the initial unpleasant effects and began to get something out of it. Now he was accepted by this group, which he regarded as superior. The members were engaged in activities that he wanted to be part of — mostly crimes more serious than those in which he had participated before using drugs.

When a criminal is apprehended for drug use or possession, others assume that he was a victim of enticement or persuasion. Taking advantage of this, he then blames others for corrupting him. Obviously he has obtained the drug from a person already involved in the drug world. In any community — in the immediate neighborhood, on a playground, at school, in a pool hall, or on a street corner — he can find other drug users. Users perceive cues that enable them to identify one another within a very short time. In every case it has been the neophyte who has gone to drugs; drugs have not been forced on him.

As we have pointed out, the user has already violated the expectations of parents and the laws of society. Drug use in and of itself is another violation that provides criminal excitement.

It is commonly believed that the new user is ignorant of the effects of drugs. In fact, having chosen his associates from within the drug world, he has already learned a great deal about the subject. He knows about the adverse effects and about which drugs are "addicting." In addition to acquiring the street lore about drugs, he is likely to have read about them. By the time he uses his first drug, he knows the risks and has had many warnings. But like all criminals he believes that what may apply to others does not apply to him. He is certain that the advantages are many and that the disadvantages can be avoided.*

> "Who cares about the danger when there is a chance to be bigger than you are! To feel that you are in command and that nothing can stop you!"

> "No. I was not forced by anyone or induced by anyone to take drugs. In fact, I was warned to stay away from drugs as being bad for me. But I wanted to be like others. So I eventually took drugs to prove myself before I was accepted."

In addition to learning about drug effects, a user becomes acquainted with legal aspects of controlled-substance use, such as search-and-seizure laws. He learns which people are relatively safe to associate with and which areas are heavily policed. However, the greatest knowledge is derived through actual experiences with using drugs. He discovers that the "high" has more to it than "feeling great."† Fears are eliminated, and he is able to do things that he formerly was afraid to do. His sexual interest and capacity are increased. These advantages far outweigh the legal and medical risks.

Some drug users are afraid of the needle and snort, rather than inject, drugs. Others request associates to inject them until they learn to do it themselves.

> D, a user who did not inject drugs, met a man when he was in confinement who had sold heroin on the street. D decided that he wanted to learn to inject when he got out. Upon his release, he gravitated to an area where he knew heroin was available. Still, he was afraid to inject the drug be-

---

*Millman and Khuri (1973, p. 153) observed: "Most of the kids have seen the horrible effects heroin has had on someone else; none of them considers this a real possibility for himself."

†We shall develop material on the "high" in the next chapter.

cause of a longstanding fear of needles and blood. Several times he backed out of injecting heroin because of fear. When he was accused of being "chicken" by members of the crowd that he was hanging around with, he could not tolerate it. Finally he consented to permit someone to inject the drug into him. From then on, he injected himself.

A striking feature is that an informed new user, despite personal knowledge of users who became "addicted," is certain that he is the unique exception and that he will not get "hooked." To insure this, he becomes a polydrug user who indiscriminately searches for a higher "high." Youths have reported that they take anything offered at "pill parties." In this indiscriminate search, some do become physically dependent.

As they become more experienced, drug-using criminals sell drugs as well as consume them. This occurs even in early adolescence on a low level. Very few push large amounts of drugs on the street. Rather, they obtain small quantities and make sales to friends. Compensation may be in the form of more drugs, money, or having others in debt to them. However, the primary excitement is in the sale itself. Some users derive even greater excitement by arranging a drug sale between two people but never personally handling money or drugs during the transaction.

The drug user's associates include nonusers. The responsible youths break away, but the irresponsible continue to share common interests, with or without drugs. The user excludes the responsible person when he suspects that the latter represents a threat as an informer. Conversely the responsible youths exclude a drug user if they fear that they are being jeopardized by his activities.

Criminals who use drugs early in life and some who begin drug use later find it expedient to maintain ties to the responsible world and to participate in responsible activities. To an extent, they avoid suspicion because of some of their relationships. Their other life in the drug world is comprised of entirely different associates and activities. Responsible contacts are exploited as the user cons them into doing things for him, especially when he is in trouble. In contrast, some drug users scorn any relationships with responsible people. Although active and sociable in the drug world, they remain secretive and aloof in the company of responsible people.

Very few users are totally private in their drug use. It is common for two or three drug-using friends to get together. The fabled, prolonged, large drug orgies do occur, but accounts of them are exaggerated with respect to their frequency and what happens.

To recapitulate, neighborhoods — especially those that are blighted — have been striving to reduce or eliminate the drug problem. Educational campaigns that include community efforts and massive publicity in school and church programs have warned of the dangers of drug use.* Drug use is condemned, but the user is not. More often than not, he is pitied and viewed as a victim. Perceiving this, the user has disdain for the very people who go out of their way to assist him. Although community pressures to function responsibly are great, the drug user continues to live the life he has chosen, but he is even more secretive, discreet, and cunning.

THE DRUG USER AT SCHOOL

The older drug users in our study have reported that their involvement with drugs was slight during their elementary school years. Even now, although drug use has become more widespread and begins at an earlier age, there is relatively little of it among elementary-school children. Some do experiment with liquor, with inhalation of volatile substances (e.g., glue sniffing), and in some instances, with marijuana. An expansion of the earlier violating patterns, previously discussed, characteristically occurs during the junior-high-school years, and drug use generally begins at this time. At school, as in his neighborhood, the youngster who is interested in drugs quickly spots others who share that interest.

The young user pursues his irresponsible objectives while endeavoring to avoid "hassles" with teachers and school officials.† Most find that the best policy is to fulfill at least the minimal requirements of the school, and they accomplish this easily, but not always honestly. Many are capable enough to complete required work in class and rarely study elsewhere. They are constantly told by teachers, counselors, and especially parents that they have higher potential and can do better. When under pressure, some bring their grades up not for educational purposes, but to make life easier for themselves.‡ The ensuing reduction in pressure permits them to continue their irresponsible behavior.

For some drug users, their desire for criminal excitement in later school years outweighs the perceived advantages of remaining in school, and they drop out. Many still prefer to stay. Although irresponsible and still using drugs, they know that it is easier to continue in school than to hold a job and be subjected to other social pressures.

*See Chapter 7, in which we describe community prevention and treatment programs.

†The criminal as a child in school is extensively described in Chapter 3 of Volume I.

‡Levy (1968, p. 52) observed the following with respect to teenage drug users' attitudes toward school: "Cheating, submitting someone else's term paper, cutting classes, and only worrying about passing were usual occurrences. . . . Functioning far below potential, as reported by high school records and psychological reports, was usual. In fact several flaunt[ed] this fact and said they were 'sick and tired of being told the test showed they could be better if they tried.' "

When these youngsters do satisfactory work in school, it is because of their high native ability or the school's low standards. The family and community regard continuing in school as the primary indicator of a youngster's responsibility, just as work is considered a barometer of responsibility later in life. Should he get into a jam, a creditable performance at school is perhaps the best insurance to the user that he will still be viewed in a relatively benign light and be given the benefit of the doubt.

Whether a youth actually uses drugs on the school grounds depends, to a great extent, on the school's attitude. If the authorities ignore drug use, then drugs will be used at school — on the playground, in lavatories, at school functions, and even between classes. Such use is reported to have diminished or disappeared in schools that have cracked down against drug use by searching lockers, hiring undercover policemen, and imposing major penalties.

Drugs Cause Suspension of 400 Pupils

A "drastic" suspension policy enacted last fall to punish drug offenders in Prince George's County schools has led to 400 student suspensions in six months and incidents of drug-related violence appear to have stopped, according to a report released yesterday. (*Washington Post* 6/25/76)

Although drugs may not be used at school, school is the arena for talking and planning and, if surveillance is not too great, making sales.

Some drug users are blatant "hellraisers" in school.

Before using drugs, D was expelled from the third grade. He disrupted the class to such an extent that the school could do nothing with him. His parents sought psychiatric evaluation for him. The boy was diagnosed as hyperactive and placed on medication. His violations continued but were excused because of the diagnosis. Later developments indicated that he was misdiagnosed. (The diagnosis of hyperactivity is often given to youngsters whom adults cannot control.) D's own view was, "My hyperactivity was a problem to others, but not to me." In mid-adolescence D was arrested three times while a heavy user of drugs. In a special school he had been promoted from grade to grade because of his teachers' belief that retaining him in a grade would only further his delinquency.

Like this youngster some drug users pose severe behavior problems. However, most are far less obstreperous. They succeed in conning the system, which they exploit to their advantage. They know that if they present a facade of interest and compliance, they will get away with drug use and other violations more readily.

In college it is easy for the user to find clusters of other users. When he is away from home and few restrictions are imposed by the college, drugs increasingly become part of his life. A minority restricts its drug use to marijuana. Most consume, in addition, a substantial amount of liquor and various pills, such as amphetamines and sedative-hypnotics. Occasionally these drugs are used in combination; more frequently, one type is used at a time. College users are apt to shy away from injectable substances, although their use is by no means uncommon.

With greater drug use and other violations, school performance inevitably deteriorates. Some students come to class boasting, often in exaggerated fashion, that they are "stoned" and "out of it." Actually they are very much in contact with what is going on around them, and if they are called on and are acquainted with the material, they respond appropriately (although usually inadequately). The collegiate drug user may do very little work, but his grade point average may not reflect how little he has learned. He loads things in his favor by electing subjects that require relatively little discipline and organization and taking courses in which the curriculum is unstructured and grading is reputed to be lenient. He may request or be assigned by chance to instructors not much older than he, some of whom are not opposed to drug use or who are drug users themselves. It is with required intensive courses calling for self-discipline that the drug user has the greatest difficulty. Performance is poor in foreign-language classes, which demand prolonged concentration, memorization, and regular drill. He also does poorly in science and mathematics, which require careful reading, methodical study of detail, and precision in problem solving.

The "drug scene" in the college community consists of more than a "counterculture" group that is critical of the establishment, embraces a particular kind of music, dresses and speaks in a particular way, or uses drugs. Certainly the excitement in talking about, procuring, and using drugs is central. But drug use is concurrent with other criminal patterns. In our study of dropouts from a major midwestern university, we found that those who were drug users were involved in a variety of violating patterns — stealing, vandalizing, assaulting, exploitative sex, cheating, and general exploitation of one another.* These competing excitements assume increasing importance in the user's daily life. Some drug users find it harder to slide by in college than in earlier school careers. They are not automatically given passing grades in courses on the basis of high potential, but find themselves subject to administrative action because of poor performance. They accumulate a list of "incompletes" for papers not written and examinations not taken. Worried instructors and deans call them to account. Finally some decide that staying in school is just not worthwhile. Nothing at college can compete with

*Samenow, Stanton E. *The College Dropout: A Study in Self-Definition.* Unpublished doctoral dissertation. The University of Michigan, Ann Arbor 1968.

the other excitements. "School was a waste of time. It wasn't at all what I was interested in. I was committing myself to other things. I was fed up with the whole thing. I quit the fraternity, quit school, and broke up with my fiancée. . . . I didn't know what I was going to do. . . . I just quit. I just walked out."

Others do not drop out, but hang on and manage to get by. Thus they retain financial support by their parents, they avoid having to get a job, and they need not explain to others what they are doing with their lives. Some leave, but return a year or two later, having decided to acquire a degree and further use the system to their advantage.

Whether they remain in school or not, drug-using criminals live disorganized lives in which there is a great deal of sickness, accident-proneness, and, at times, suicidal thinking. They neglect their health and experience severe mood reversals. Poor health, extreme fluctuations in emotional state, and general disorganization are often made worse because of poor judgment under drugs.

The drug user is not a "rebel against authority" or angry at the system as long as he can do what he wants without obstruction. As he views it, a good teacher is like a "good cop": he ignores violations and leaves the user alone. The user "rebels" only when he is pressured into doing what he does not want to do or when he is held accountable for poor achievement or breaking rules. As long as others do not interfere with him, he cooperates.

Schools are alarmed when these intelligent and potentially creative students are uninterested in academic performance and find their excitement in illicit activities. Some school administrators ignore drug use for fear that making an issue of it will result in more trouble from both users and parents. They are reluctant to assume the role of policeman or to invite unpleasant confrontations. Blatant and repetitious drug use makes it imperative that the school act. Then someone in the administration, often a counselor, calls the user to account but seldom does more than admonish him. When the student is a repeat offender, parents are notified. Counseling staffs are limited in resources, and long-term counseling seldom is available. Many counselors have neither the time nor the training for working with drug-using antisocial adolescents. When undertaken, such counseling is usually without discernible benefit. Furthermore, confidentiality limits what a counselor can communicate to others to insure some sort of external leverage for change.

Like parents, schools at all levels have blamed themselves for failing the student who turns to drugs. But, try as they may, there is little that they can provide that can compete with drugs for excitement. The drug user latches on to criticisms of teachers, curriculum, and facilities and uses these as excuses for his drug use and lack of scholastic achievement. Many parents, teachers, and administrators have failed to recognize this as a tactic by which he absolves himself of responsibility. Other students have complaints about their schools, but they do not use drugs. They attempt to overcome problems because they are intent on pursuing an education.

The final recourse is suspension or expulsion of the drug-using student, a measure the school is reluctant to take for several reasons: it has to face the wrath of parents, it has to contend with ever-present community opposition to having these youngsters on the street and, finally, it knows that although suspension or expulsion is expedient for the school, this course poses no solution to the drug use problem.

Some school systems concentrate on preventive efforts. Physical education, courses in family living and sex education, classes in physical and mental hygiene, and drug education are provided. To appeal to diverse abilities and interests, schools have liberalized regulations, offered more elective programs, and beefed up extracurricular opportunities. These measures are designed to educate, to deter drug use, and to provide attractive alternatives to drug use.* But they have been of no avail because such offerings cannot compete with the "high" of drug use and other violations.

Stricter student supervision and a tough antidrug attitude does deter some drug use. This does not mean that the user mends his ways, but rather that he becomes more circumspect about infractions and seeks his criminal excitement off the school grounds. Efforts to interest the drug user in academic work or to attract him to extracurricular activities may succeed temporarily, especially if the drug user wants to impress others and avoid suspicion or if he wants to be a "big shot." But they by no means substitute for life in the drug world. In short, no school offering can sustain his interest. His interests are incompatible with the school's purposes. As one youthful drug user stated, "School is not useful for the life I am planning on leading."

THE DRUG USER AT WORK

The employment patterns characteristic of the drug user and the criminal nonuser are basically the same.† Attitudes include total opposition to work and holding a job only when absolutely necessary (such as when fulfilling probation or parole requirements); half-heartedly holding a job as part of a facade of responsibility; working, but with a search primarily for self-aggrandizement (invariably at the expense of others); and working because it affords an opportunity to continue criminal activities.

Some drug users are under the influence of drugs before and during work. "Stoned" upon arrival at work, they often reload on drugs throughout the

*For some specifics about drug education in the schools, see the literature review of Chapter 7.

†See Chapter 3 of Volume I.

day.* Drugs may be tucked away in the car, locker, desk, or on their person. Some leave the job to meet their connection either on business premises or elsewhere. Most drug users are totally secretive, but some do share drug information with selected fellow employees. Some act at work as they have in their neighborhoods, schools, and social groups. They seek cues to identify other drug users among their co-workers and usually are quickly successful at spotting them. When they gain the confidence of other drug-using employees, they in turn may become drug "connections."

Many drug users are capable and talented; they easily fulfill minimal requirements that satisfy employers.† That the drug user is functioning below his potential is not recognized. As long as he does his job and no one complains about him, he escapes detection. A marked decline in job performance, however, may result in steps being taken to hold him accountable. Frequent tardiness, time away from the job, inconsistent and unpredictable quality of work, laziness, lack of interest, absenteeism, irritability, and concurrent criminality—lying, stealing, fighting, or sexual impropriety—raise questions. So does excessive time spent in making personal phone calls or in receiving visitors who are not related to business. Carelessness, poor decision making, mistakes, and accidents are causes for concern by his superiors.

When held accountable, some drug users claim that under drugs they are more productive and creative. However, drugs distort their evaluation of themselves, so they ignore both the deterioration in their performance and others' assessments of them.

> D had remained off drugs for several months. Then he resumed sporadic use. At his job he was regarded as an efficient waiter. In addition, because he had many talents, he was assigned such projects as construction of shelves and furniture finishing and repair. D increased his drug use and believed that he was still doing a competent job. Even though he was under the influence of drugs at work, others did not suspect this. However, as a consequence of his drug-altered state of mind, his boredom and irritability increased markedly. Bus boys began to complain that D was underpaying them from his tips. A hostess was unhappy with his rudeness to her. Others were inconvenienced when projects assigned to D

*A union steward at an automobile plant reported the visibility of drug use on the job site: "In the plant, snorting [taking cocaine or heroin like snuff] is almost socially acceptable. You can stand on the line and see it, although it's in the bathroom where it happens mostly" (*Washington Post* 4/10/72).

†Nelson *et al.* (1975, p. 601) pointed out that the staff at a Job Corps center characterized the drug-using members as "on the whole brighter and more competent than the general center population."

were not completed. Problems multiplied to the point where the manager fired him. The management never realized that D was a drug user.

It is remarkable that with so many signs pointing to drug use, so few users are suspected of it. When productivity or efficiency are obviously deteriorating, it is assumed that the employee has financial problems or domestic difficulties. The user who is called in by the boss for discussion of his shortcomings may actually be on drugs at the time or have drugs on his person. Yet the subject of drugs does not arise. Only if his performance is extremely detrimental to the company or agency is his employment terminated, usually without discovery of his involvement with drugs. Should an employer learn that an employee is using drugs, his first reaction may be one of compassion. Rather than punish the worker, some employers want to help him because they regard drug use as an illness, not a crime. The drug user may be retained if he promises to seek help, and he is referred to a drug treatment program. Users, for example, are enrolled in methadone programs and retain their jobs. Some institutions and businesses have established treatment programs of their own. An employer who discovers that an employee is using drugs may fire him if he fears that the user's continued presence will endanger other people, as when a drug-using employee operates heavy machinery or drives company vehicles. However, there are employers who will terminate an employee at the first suggestion that he is a drug user—even if conclusive evidence is lacking.

Some employers accept the conventional belief that drug use results from adverse environmental conditions. Because work constitutes a large part of an employee's daily environment, they think that conditions at work may be at the heart of the adversity that the employee is facing. In its "personal report," the Research Institute of America (1974) urged that executives "consider the job as a possible cause of the problem":

> It's important to take a new look at the drug user and his job. Perhaps he is not able to cope with it; the responsibility may be too great, or the workload too heavy. Indirectly, you—and the position you put him in—may be contributing to his drug problem. . . . Condemning the drug user is useless and cruel—and a potential waste of human resources. If those resources are to be salvaged, you, the manager, will have to supply understanding and help.

Accepting the premise that specific job conditions contribute to the employee's use of drugs, executives have altered working conditions for the better, but not for the correct reason.

A comparable attitude toward drug users has been assumed by parents, educators, and others in the community, resulting in the user immediately adopting the excuses others put forth for him. The drug user is practiced in exploiting those who show compassion. He persists in his drug use, all the while assailing the very people and institutions that have tried to help him.

THE DRUG USER IN THE MILITARY

We have studied and worked with men who used drugs before, during, and after military service. Our observations reported here are necessarily dated. Policies toward drug use in the military change from time to time. But our focus is on how the criminal operates, not the military policy.*

During the Korean conflict, there was considerable drug use in the military, but at the time it was not publicly recognized as a significant problem. During the 1960s and 1970s drug use became increasingly prevalent and emerged as a central social issue. Drug use has perhaps been more striking in the military than in other segments of society because of the service insistence on loyalty, discipline, and obedience. While consulting with service personnel on drug use in the 1960s, we were surprised that the command had overestimated the incidence of the problem. This paralleled the alarm and exaggeration in civilian society. At that time we suggested that a more accurate study of the situation would reveal that heavy drug use was limited to a small minority of users who were having an inordinate impact on military life. The extent of the problem was similar to that experienced in the rest of society.

A few of the drug users in our study were disqualified from military service because of drug use. Some, in poor physical condition, showed indications of drug use, such as needle tracks. Some evaded the draft by inventing or exaggerating the extent of their drug use. Some used drugs before the physical examination, then displayed such disorganized behavior that it resulted in their disqualification. Some draft evaders who presented letters from counselors or other mental health practitioners attesting to their drug use were deemed unsuitable for military service.

Many drug users, however, were eager to be in the service and enlisted voluntarily.† Others welcomed the draft. This was their opportunity to end their troubles at home and avoid arrest for crimes committed and for which they

---

*The reader is reminded that military policies have changed frequently. The experiences with drug users that we describe have occurred at various times and do not necessarily reflect the current situation.

†According to Dr. Richard S. Wilbur, former Assistant Secretary of Defense for Health and Environment, despite the fact that the Vietnam-era Army consisted primarily of draftees, 62 percent of the drug users in a Pentagon-funded study were enlistees (*Washington Post* 4/24/73).

thought arrest might be imminent.* The excitement of being heroes in combat appealed to many. Several hoped that joining the military would help them to end their drug patterns. Whatever their reasons for entering the service, they successfully concealed their drug use.

The drug users in our study had used drugs before they entered the service and continued to do so after discharge.† Despite their claims, no adverse condition of military life caused them to turn to drugs. Because of the easy availability of drugs, some users began to use controlled substances that they had not used at home. This was particularly true overseas, where drugs were not only more readily available but also less expensive and more potent.

Drugs were more likely to be used on base than in combat.‡ Many drug-related offenses were committed when a dearth of combat action resulted in boredom. An Army captain described drug users' violations to us:

> Captain Y said that the concept of working as a team broke down when drug users were involved. They asserted their authority belligerently and were irresponsible on the job. The captain observed among unit members considerable fighting that he did not see when drugs were not readily available. He stated that there was stealing, vandalism, and assaults by drug users as well as numerous absences without official leave (A.W.O.L.). The captain described incidents of "fragging," in which men on drugs threw grenades into officers' tents. Captain Y asserted that there was less drug use in combat than on base because most soldiers did not want someone under the influence of drugs responsible for protecting them from the enemy. Consequently, peer pressure was exerted on users to reduce drug use.

Drugs were used in combat, however. On drugs some soldiers had the courage to do what they otherwise were afraid to do.§ Drugs were a precipitating

---

*Greden et al. (1974, p. 81) said of heroin users in the service: "When compared with non-users, a much higher percentage reported conflicts in civilian life with parents, school officials, and legal authorities. Their marital and job histories were dramatically chaotic. A number had entered the military to avoid jail."

†Robins (1973) reported substantial drug use before military service among those who were drug users in Vietnam.

‡A newspaper article on the Army's "struggle for survival" reported: "Drugs are a key factor in barracks crime, whether assaults or robberies. Few soldiers feel safe — either inside or outside their barracks" (*Washington Post* 9/12/71).

§In later chapters we shall describe in detail how the drug user relies on drugs to facilitate whatever he is seeking but is afraid to do without drugs.

factor in mutilations, homicides, and rapes, as well as in acts of bravery.*

Much drug use remained undetected. Needle marks were concealed by injecting drugs between the toes, in the armpits, under the scrotum, or in areas covered by body hair. To avoid detection, many soldiers preferred to snort or smoke drugs, rather than leave telltale marks. In addition, the availability of relatively pure drugs overseas lessened the necessity of injecting them. When urine tests were introduced at bases, drug users who knew in advance that they would have to participate prepared themselves.

Major M reported that drug users were buying urine from others. Because there was no surveillance when they submitted a urine sample, these users were able to substitute the purchased urine for their own. Major M commented that a group of users had a laugh when one man unknowingly bought urine that produced a positive test result. At one of the testing stations a technician in league with the users assured them that he would conceal positive results, thus making any other form of subterfuge unnecessary. Many users simply stopped drug use during the period in which they expected to be tested.

Situations arose in which drug users became disenchanted with military life. Instead of the excitement that they had anticipated, they found that life consisted of being ordered around and doing assigned tasks that involved interminable drudgery and intolerable boredom. Fed up and wanting to get out, they revealed their drug use. In some cases, doing so resulted in their avoiding combat and precipitated a return to the United States.

When drug use was discovered by the command, it was at times overlooked if the soldier was considered brave and loyal to his unit.

D and other soldiers were commended for heroic action during a major battle overseas. With the fight over, D and his comrades took command of a brewery and got "roaring drunk." They then tried to take over another building and began firing. It turned out that American soldiers were inside, but they escaped unharmed. No disciplinary action was taken against the obviously intoxicated soldiers because they had been so valiant in their earlier assignment.

---

*A former Veterans Administration psychiatrist, Dr. Myron Feld, was quoted as saying that the Mylai (Vietnam) massacre of civilians may have been caused by American soldiers on drugs (*Washington Post* 5/11/70). According to a report in the *Washington Star* (6/21/71), a Medal of Honor winner stated that he was "stoned" on marijuana when he staved off two attacks of Viet Cong soldiers.

When the command was faced with a soldier's poor performance (whether or not he used drugs), it sometimes assigned him to disagreeable tasks or extra duty or reduced him in rank. In some instances, when a user was more trouble than he was worth, he was prosecuted and given a dishonorable discharge or a discharge without honor. In accordance with civilian practice, however, the military for the most part tended to regard drug users as psychologically disturbed rather than criminal. They were offered treatment, not punishment.* Some officers have believed, as have many civilian employers, the drug users' claims that their immediate living and working conditions are partially responsible for their drug use. One Army officer stated that users are victims of despair bred by conditions of serving what he called "the green machine" (the Army). Such beliefs have led the command to offer an "amnesty program" in which the user was withdrawn from drugs and returned to his outfit. When the military has decided to have a user leave the service, it has offered to extend his tour of duty for a month, so that he could be detoxified and later enrolled in a rehabilitation program at a Veterans Administration hospital. When very few volunteers took advantage of such programs, the military made participation mandatory. Users then received honorable discharges with the advantage of retaining V.A. benefits. Our findings indicate only token participation by drug users.† Those who have been in such programs used drugs during the course of the program and thereafter.‡

The military now tries to deter drug use by better methods of detection. Barracks are routinely searched. Urine tests are conducted at random and without advance notice. At some installations, personnel have been rewarded for turning in a user or pusher.

The military also engages in preventive efforts. Screening of enlistees is more thorough. Drug information campaigns are directed at both troops and officers. In addition, sports programs, service clubs, and social functions are organized on the base in the hope that they will serve as attractive alternatives

---

U.S. Medicine (2/1/73) noted that in fiscal 1971 the Pentagon spent $400,000 for treatment and rehabilitation of drug users, compared with $62.6 million in fiscal 1973.

†A V.A. spokesman was quoted as stating that the commitment to rehabilitation by drug users assigned there is minimal, and all the V.A. can do is "give positive indications of a desire to help" (*U.S. Medicine* 9/15/72). With the establishment of drug-treatment centers at V.A. hospitals, there has been a significant increase in drug use on the premises. The problem was said to have been the most severe in hospitals where large numbers of veterans were being treated (*Washington Star* 9/30/71).

‡*U.S. Medicine* (6/15/73) reported: "A study of 39 Vietnam veteran heroin addicts in New York City has found that about 90 per cent are either still addicted, in jail or in trouble with the law."

to drug use.* Our study indicates that these measures have not had a lasting influence upon the criminal who is a drug user.

ACQUISITION AND DISTRIBUTION OF DRUGS

The picture of drug sales conjures up images of street pushers looking for trade, enticing or perhaps coercing people into using drugs.† Many sales of drugs, however, do not occur through pushers.‡ In junior or senior high school when a student sells a small amount of marijuana to a friend, he is a seller, to be sure, but not a pusher. In such a transaction neither seller nor buyer considers the seller a drug pusher.

A seller who vends drugs on a much broader scale is termed a *pusher*. (This designation usually is applied to sellers of heroin). When a pusher gets others to sell for him, he becomes a *dealer*. The pusher is not apt to be physically dependent on drugs. He may use alcohol, marijuana, and occasionally pills of various types, but he generally avoids controlled substances that are known as "addictive." Business is business, and he tries to maintain a reputation for reliability. The rare pusher who is a heavy drug user is notoriously unreliable. He fails to show up when he promises, and his chances of arrest are greater than those of a less heavy drug user.

A pusher does not attempt to entice, persuade, or coerce anyone into using drugs. To avoid unnecessary risk, he is cautious about his customers. He operates in locations that known drug users frequent. Often he sets up an apartment away from the drug area where he lives with a woman who sells his drugs. He is attuned to the slightest cues and becomes skilled in identifying a drug user without a direct approach. He waits for the interested party to come to him. Before a sale he may ask reliable drug purchasers to vouch for a new customer. More frequently, however, a user already regarded as reliable

---

*Recently, DuPont (1984) has praised "effective action" taken by the military against drug abuse:

> After years of inaction, the military – led by the Navy – got moving in 1981. . . . The principal enforcement technique was a program of regular, random urine testing for drug use, with strict, clearly defined punishment for those caught having illicit drugs in their bodies. This program was coupled with a powerful and broadly based education campaign. (p. 309)

†In this account we do not purport to describe fully the complex network of production, distribution, and sales in the illicit drug market. Rather, these are observations that reflect the experience of drug-using criminals in our study.

‡The *Washington Post* (9/5/76) reported that one study found that only 7 of 100 heroin addicts were introduced to heroin by a pusher, the others finding sources of the drug among friends, relatives, and acquaintances.

by the seller introduces a new customer. Such precautions are necessary because of the high incidence of informers and undercover agents.

Suspicion of informers being present is pervasive among both users and pushers. This is not paranoia, but realistic fear. The drug user who is not suspicious is foolish. It is known that the police recruit drug users to act as informants. An official of the Drug Enforcement Administration (see Allen 1976) observed that, "if you went through 1,000 drug arrests, you'd find an informant in 95 percent of them." A considerable number of informants are drug pushers who "snitch" readily if it is necessary to save their own skins. On the street such informants may not be shunned or despised. Users and pushers know that no one in the drug world can be trusted and that each person will do what he must to reduce his own jeopardy.

Some sellers, fearful of arrest or other consequences, do use drugs to fortify their courage. However, when a seller is on drugs, he is superoptimistic and therefore less careful in his assessment of people and imprudent in decision making, thus increasing the risk of apprehension. Having cut off fear, he is absolutely certain at the time that he will conduct his transaction successfully and not be apprehended (see Chapter 6 of Volume I). Indeed, for the fearful pusher, drugs are necessary to achieve this state of superoptimism.

When the drug seller makes a sale, he views himself as providing the buyer the means to alter a mood, and nothing else, even though he knows that under drugs the user will more readily commit any kind of crime. This realization, however, does not result in any concern that either the user or the user's victim might be injured. The fact that he is violating the law in selling controlled and dangerous substances is of little significance to him at the time. His focus is his self-interest; he is doing his "job," and the consequences are the user's problem. Overriding all else is the excitement and sense of power that he derives from every sale.

Thinking about drugs, talking about drugs, and obtaining drugs are all exciting to users. They report that depression, boredom, uncomfortable physical symptoms, and other unpleasant states have been relieved by the excitement of merely thinking about drugs. Greater relief occurs once the decision is made to acquire drugs. The excitement mounts when the user reaches the drug area and discusses the availability and quality of drugs with other users. At this point, subjectively, his physical and psychological condition improve markedly, even before he has introduced the drug into his body. The excitement heightens at each stage until he purchases the drug and experiences the "high voltage" of the drug effects.

When procuring drugs, the user is commonly suggestible and indiscriminate. Consequently, he can be "burned" (deceived) by being sold diluted or contaminated drugs. Many purchases contain minuscule amounts of the drug and a substantial amount of other substances, such as baking soda, quinine, cornstarch, sugar, and flour. More toxic contaminants are formaldehyde and strychnine.

Drug users with ample funds may obtain far more of the drug than they can use. Just as they often give away the proceeds of their crimes (e.g., stolen merchandise) to show their success, so drug users boast of their success in garnering a large supply of drugs and then they proceed to give them to others.

Some users gain access to medical facilities as a source of drugs by theft. Another method is by faking a physical illness or disability or exaggerating the seriousness and duration of a known illness. By doing this, they obtain prescriptions for controlled substances. One user convinced a physician that he had narcolepsy. Thereafter, by carrying a card certifying his condition, he was able to keep himself supplied with large amounts of Desoxyn, an amphetamine that he both used and sold. Users learn which doctors are reputed to prescribe barbiturates or opiates without careful examination or much curiosity. They also learn which pharmacies are lax about checking prescription refills.

Our drug users have stolen prescription pads from medical offices and forged their own prescriptions.

> D waited two to three weeks between forging and having each prescription filled. Furthermore, he was careful not to go to the same drug store twice. He was well aware that only the user who forges many prescriptions in a short period and has them filled in the same place is likely to get caught. D was never apprehended.

If drugs are scarce on the streets, users may elect to enroll in a treatment program to obtain methadone (for a drug effect)* or to visit a physician, feigning an illness for which they are prescribed a drug that they then use or sell to others. When drugs are scarce, a "panic" on the streets exists, and users often obtain prescriptions for codeine or for cough medicines and other preparations fortified with codeine. In virtually all cases, the user remains within his own community, where he knows the drug sources, where others know him, and where he experiences comparative security in the company of his associates.†

---

*Methadone, a synthetic opiate, will be discussed in Chapter 7.

†Brown (1961, p. 318) observed: "The addict apparently is tied to the community in which he dwells and will not take the chance of making new connections in strange places, unknown by pushers and other addicts. He feels 'safer' and more certain of procuring his vital dope in familiar surroundings."

ANTISOCIAL PATTERNS

Before they began using drugs, the men in our study made a series of irresponsible choices that resulted in a criminal way of life. Ignoring the expectations of responsible people, they pursued criminal excitement through conning, stealth, or violence. Property crimes — such as shoplifting, breaking and entry, vandalism, and misappropriation of money — occurred in all cases. Exploitative sexual improprieties run throughout most histories of drug abuse. Assaults are also part of the user's history, in thinking if not in action. Lying by omission and commission is essential to the life that he has chosen.

Drugs facilitate an enormous expansion of all these violating patterns. The process by which drugs alter patterns of thought and action will be developed in Chapter 5. In the present section we shall present a perspective of the magnitude of the crimes the criminal commits — the seriousness and number increasing with drug use.

The criminal as a user commits far more thefts than he did before he began using drugs. Even if he has a vast wardrobe, an expensive apartment, and a luxury-model car, he still commits numerous thefts, becoming under drugs ever more audacious, taking greater risks. As we pointed out in Volume I, the criminal steals primarily for the excitement. This overrides the monetary value of his haul, which is merely an index of how successful he is. The user on drugs wants the excitement of bigger crimes and conceives of "big scores" that will yield proceeds far in excess of what is necessary for his drug needs. No matter how much money he acquires, the user pursues ever bigger conquests.

> D sporadically used drugs and was receiving nearly $15,000 a week in narcotic sales. He had so much money that he did not know what to do with it, but he wanted greater excitement. So he committed four armed robberies at nearby bars, each of which he knew in advance could yield no more than $900. It was in the last of these that he was apprehended and charged with all the others.

In the daily grind* a user commits thousands of thefts.

> D broke into two or three apartments a day, a minimum of 600 per year. Daily he entered seven or more stores, stealing a half-dozen items per store, or about 14,000 separate thefts a year. At the age of forty he had been arrested only once for property crimes. D had committed hundreds of sexual crimes but again had been apprehended only once.

*Chapter 3 of Volume I describes the "daily grind" and introduces the concept of crime as "work."

When the user has had a run of "bad luck" at theft or is deeply indebted to others for drugs supplied to him, his first priority is to get money to acquire drugs, whether or not he is physically dependent on them. Even then his main objective is to steal more than is necessary to satisfy his drug requirements. At no time does he steal solely to support his drug usage, but rather he does so for the impetus the drug will give him to commit more thefts and crimes of other types.

On drugs, users not only steal property but destroy it. It is especially true that youths, when on drugs, set fires, deface property, smash windows and lights, vandalize vehicles, ransack buildings, and destroy whatever is in their path. They are far more brazen in this when fortified by drugs than when they are not on drugs, and they vandalize, usually not out of anger at the property owners but mainly for the excitement.

Violence is more frequent when the user is on drugs. He is more irritable, anger is close to the surface, and if put down, he is more likely to react explosively. As one man put it, "on drugs, I am afraid of nothing." Drug-using youths intimidate fellow students at school, extorting money and property and beating them if they do not comply with demands. Whereas the user may basically have been afraid to assault anyone, with drugs anything is possible. Acts thought of without drugs may have been rejected, but with drugs in him the user commits them. The drug user who is afraid to carry and use weapons is less afraid of doing so when he is on drugs.

> D got into an argument with his brother-in-law, who owed him money for drugs. The scope of the argument widened to his brother-in-law's misuse of D's sister and the sister's children. Many grievances unrelated to the monetary aspect were brought in. D was heavily under the influence of drugs during the argument. He grabbed a nearby gun and shot his brother-in-law twice; he had sufficient control to aim for and shoot him in the legs. Although D was jailed for forty-eight hours, the family decided not to press charges, and D was released.

D acknowledged to us that, without drugs, he would have been afraid to shoot his brother-in-law.

The drug user discovers that drugs expand sexual thinking and enhance his sexual performance. A portion of this thinking invariably results in action, and sexual violations greatly increase. We have studied drug users who committed numerous rapes while on drugs but were too fearful to do so without drugs. Other sexual patterns (depending on user preference) that occur under the influence of drugs are voyeurism, exhibitionism, obscene phone calls, child molestation, and homosexual prostitution.

The user is a more facile liar when on drugs, and his lies are more extreme.

In fact, when off drugs, users are often amazed at the fantastic lies they had concocted and even more amazed that others believed them.

Not all drug users commit all types of offenses. Each has his preferences. Even if he has not committed a particular type of crime, he has thought about many forms of property, sexual, and assaultive crimes. The fact that such thinking is accelerated by drugs signifies that anything is possible, given the appropriate circumstances.

It is widely believed that an insatiable, virtually compulsive desire for drugs forces the user into crime simply because he could not otherwise afford drugs. This misconception is based on a lack of understanding of the criminal's thinking. It is true that criminals steal to obtain money for drugs. But critical to the issue is what they want the drugs for. On drugs, they have the "nerve" to commit bigger and more daring crimes. Consequently, on drugs, they do in fact commit huge numbers of crimes in the property, sex, and assault categories that otherwise they would not.

THE DRUG USER IN CONFINEMENT

When arrested for a drug offense, the drug user presents himself to others as a victim of an illness for which he desperately needs treatment. If he convinces others that he needs help rather than imprisonment,* he then travels the psychiatric, rather than the correctional, route. If he is arrested for a property crime, others assume that his motivation was to obtain money to support his drug use. If commission of another type of crime (assaultive or sexual) is involved, it is frequently assumed that he "lost control" because of drugs. In all cases, his crime is attributed to drugs, not to his criminal personality. This view of drugs as the primary cause of crime is pervasive.

In some quarters dependence on drugs has been regarded as a mental illness, and this view has been reinforced by court decisions.

Ruling on Addiction as Illness is Slated
The D.C. Court of Appeals in a 2-1 decision today ruled that drug addiction is an illness and persons accused of possessing narcotics for their own use are not criminally responsible if they can prove they are drug addicts. . . . [The majority wrote,] "It seems clear that . . . to punish an individual for an act that was not the product of his free will may be a violation of the constitutional guarantee of due process of law" (*Washington Star* 2/27/73).

---

*In Chapter 6 of Volume I we described in detail how the criminal reasons and behaves in accountability situations.

The criminal exaggerates the extent of his drug use if he knows that once he is released from a treatment facility, he will have to serve backup time for violation of probation or parole or for other crimes for which he has been convicted. He counts on the court's regarding drugs as the culprit in his life and consequently deciding that further confinement amounts only to punishment. He expects to be remanded to a treatment program as the final disposition of his case.

In confinement the drug user functions as he has elsewhere. Drug users find each other in prisons or psychiatric units just as easily as they do in the community, at school, and at work. If they socialize, their regular topics of conversation are sex, crime, drugs, and, of course, release from confinement. Some users avoid such associations and conversation. Remaining more to themselves, they try to convey to the staff that they are through with their old life; this is a con job. Others may be in a transient, but nevertheless genuine, phase of self-disgust and be sincere about change. Still others want to change, but only to the extent of giving up drugs, because drugs expose them to risks in crime and they believe that they could learn to become more effective criminals without drugs.*

Some users who abstain from drugs in confinement anticipate drug use after release. They abstain mainly because their desire to get out overrides their desire for drugs. Some arrange a drug "connection" while they are in the institution. Under conditions of privileged communication, users have informed us of their plans to resume drug activity after release, specifying which drugs they propose to use and which they expect to discontinue.

When confined, if the user wants drugs, he can usually obtain them. It is difficult, but by no means impossible, to do so in maximum security, where surveillance is constant. When a few resourceful people acquire drugs, a network for distribution is established within an institution. From time to time, extensive drug rings operate. One man controlled an elaborate drug operation in the maximum security unit of a hospital's forensic division:

> C, a criminal, but a nonuser of drugs, found a drug-using nursing assistant (N.A.) in maximum security who did a small favor for him by making a phone call. The N.A. was marked as a "sucker" and as a likely accomplice in C's scheme because he did the favor. C asked the N.A. to bring in a pint of brandy (contraband). With money given him by his family, C paid for the brandy and generously tipped the N.A. C then asked the N.A. to deliver a package to him, for which the N.A. would be paid $15.

---

*The user may be sincere about total change or about giving up drugs when he is confined. He may also be sincere in such intentions as he is about to be released from confinement. However, as we have pointed out so often, there is a difference between sincere intention and translating intention into lasting behavior changes. The drug user's sincerity does not last.

The N.A. complied after being assured that the package included no weapons. By this time the N.A. was fairly certain that the parcel contained drugs. Knowing that C had plenty of money, the N.A. then filled out an IOU for a loan from C. Subsequent loans were made, with C charging interest at the rate of 25 percent per week. C did not call for payment, and the debt mounted. C offered to reduce the debt if the N.A. would take greater risks by bringing in more parcels. The N.A. consented, and the drug trafficking increased.

In the privacy of his room, C cut and packaged the drugs in capsules. With the N.A. obligated, C was in a position to have numerous favors granted. The N.A. had virtually become C's accomplice. The N.A. was paid to distribute the drugs to particular patients. C then had these patients distribute the drugs and collect the money. The N.A. became less important as an intermediary when C was transferred to minimum security. There he relied mainly on other patients to distribute drugs for him. C kept the N.A. available, however, in case his other distributors backed out or double-crossed him. A nonuser of drugs, C was taking in at least $700 a week. When he left the institution to return to the community, two independent operators took over his drug-selling business.

In this situation it was possible for a violent criminal (who had contempt for drug users) to earn thousands of dollars a month and experience the triumph of running a successful drug operation in maximum security.

Drug rings operate through similar collusions of inmates with personnel in many correctional institutions and maximum-security hospitals. Although most personnel vigorously oppose drug rings, there are some staff members available to collaborate, thereby making a ring operative. It is all too common for a few staff members to bring in contraband of various types to sell at a considerable profit.* In those hospitals where controls are lax, it is by such collusion that medical supplies are diverted to improper use. Morphine and its derivatives, Doriden, barbiturates, and chloral hydrate find their way into inmates' hands.

Patients in psychiatric or prison hospitals obtain drugs by conning the doctors. A cough may be so exaggerated that a preparation containing codeine is prescribed for the drug user. A minor injury may be capitalized on so that the patient receives an opiate as a painkiller. A claim of insomnia may result in his being given a soporific.

The vast majority of staff members do not participate in drug sales or distribution, but some who do know of such activities turn their backs unless the offenses are too blatant. Personnel are almost immune from penalty. They

*For more on this, see Chapter 11 of Volume II.

are not searched or even suspected of harboring contraband as they report each day for duty. Nor do drug-using inmates or even responsible personnel inform on them. The latter do not inform because they believe that nothing will come of it. Both inmates and personnel know that to incriminate a staff member requires overwhelming evidence, which is rarely obtainable.

Visitors are still another source of drugs. Drugs are baked into cookies and other foods. A drop of hallucinogen is placed on the back of a postage stamp; all the user needs to do is lick the stamp to get some drug effect. Drugs are sprinkled over food, but are invisible or appear as powdery sugar (e.g., on hard candy). One method of importing drugs is to cut out the core of an apple, insert the drug, and carefully seal the apple together. Drugs placed in condoms are transmitted through kissing.

Institutional shakedowns often reveal hidden drugs and paraphernalia. If warned of a drug bust, however, the user quickly disposes of the evidence by ingesting the drug, throwing it out the window, or flushing it down the toilet. In a shakedown when there is no warning, paraphernalia are found by the staff.

In minimum security it is much easier to obtain drugs and bring them into the institution. The user takes advantage of programs that permit him the freedom of the grounds or of spending the day in the city on work-release or study programs. He uses such opportunities to buy and use drugs and to bring them back to the institution, where distribution is easy.* Some, more wary, restrict their drug use to places outside the institution.

> For several weeks D had permission to leave the hospital grounds to look for a job. On that pretext he was in the community daily, using drugs and committing numerous crimes. The hospital was a haven where he had a bed and meals. Being on the hospital rolls, he was immune if apprehended in a crime because he would be regarded as mentally ill and thus not responsible.

In facilities where surveillance and enforcement of regulations are lax, relatively little risk is involved in bringing drugs back to the residential unit.

> On a minimum security forensic hospital ward it was common for those with ground and community privileges to bring liquor onto the wards. After bottles were discovered lying around, the patients concealed liquor

---

*Chapter 2 of Volume II offers some material on the abuse of work-release and similar programs. An item in the *Washington Star* (9/16/76) exemplified the abuses being reported: "The arrest [of two inmates] . . . is part of an ongoing investigation into abuses of D.C. Corrections furlough programs. Abuses, police said, center around drug dealing and inmates thought to be taking drugs from the city into the D.C. Corrections complex in southern Fairfax County."

in soft drink cans. Some guards at the gate voiced no objection to patients' drinking but advised that drinking be done off the grounds. Some ward administrators continued to tolerate liquor use because they regarded it as less serious than drug use.

On probation or parole, the drug-using criminal functions much as he has in the past. The probation or parole officer (P.O.), burdened with a large caseload, and provided that no further crime requires his attention, has perhaps only half an hour each month (or at best every couple of weeks) to see his client. The criminal is asked to provide evidence that he is working, and the officer may make a home visit to check on his client's living situation. The drug user's stance toward his P.O. is to reveal as little as possible, knowing full well that the P.O. does not have much time to check on him. Some probation and parole officers insist that their clients submit to urinalysis tests, but most users believe that nothing serious will happen if a test result is positive. They expect only a warning and to still retain their freedom. More often than not, they are correct. It is unlikely that probation or parole will be revoked simply for drug use unless it is persistent and coupled with other violations. The fact is that the drug-using criminal is at best only temporarily affected by the surveillance that he is subjected to by the criminal justice system either in the institution or the community.

BIBLIOGRAPHY

Alexander, B. K., and Dibb, G. S. (1975). Opiate addicts and their parents. *Family Process* 14:499–514.

Allen, H. (1976). The informers. *Washington Post/Potomac,* August 1.

Bartlett, D. (1975). The use of multiple family groups with adolescent drug addicts. In *The Adolescent in Group and Family Therapy,* ed. M. Sugar, pp. 262–282. New York: Brunner-Mazel.

Brown, T. T. (1961). *The Enigma of Drug Addiction.* Springfield, IL: Charles C. Thomas.

DuPont, R. L. (1984). *Getting Tough on Gateway Drugs.* Washington, DC: American Psychiatric Press.

Fiddle, S. (1967). *Portraits from a Shooting Gallery.* New York: Harper and Row.

Greden, J. F., Morgan, W. M., and Frankel, S. I. (1974). The changing drug scene: 1970–1972. *American Journal of Psychiatry* 131:77–81.

Levy, N. (1968). The use of drugs by teenagers for sanctuary and illusion. *American Journal of Psychoanalysis* 28:48–59.

Matza, D. (1964). *Delinquency and Drift.* New York: John Wiley.

Millman, R. B., and Khuri, E. T. (1973). Drug abuse and the need for alternatives. In *Current Issues in Adolescent Psychiatry,* ed. J. C. Schoolar, pp. 148-157. New York: Brunner-Mazel.

Nelson, S. H. et al. (1975). Manpower training as an alternative to disadvantaged adolescent drug misuse. *American Journal of Public Health* 65:599-603.

Research Institute of America. (1974). Personal Report for the Executive. New York: Research Institute of America.

Robins, L. N. (1973). *A Follow-up of Vietnam Drug Users.* Interim final report. Washington, D.C.: Special Action Office for Drug Abuse Prevention.

U.S. Medicine. (9/15/72). Few vets contest drug-use ousters.

——— (2/1/73). DOD [Department of Defense] still concerned about GI drug abuse.

——— (6/15/73). Addicted veterans fail to kick drug habit.

Washington Post. (5/11/70). Doctor blames marijuana for needless killings.

——— (9/12/71). The U.S. Army: a battle for survival.

——— (4/10/72). Drugs on the assembly line.

——— (4/24/73). GI drug use figure raised, but few are still addicted.

——— (6/25/76). Drugs cause suspension of 400 pupils.

——— (9/5/76). Deaths, addiction on increase as heroin use spreads in city.

Washington Star. (6/21/71). He won medal of honor "stoned."

——— (9/30/71). V.A. hospital directors find drug abuses are growing.

——— (2/27/73). Ruling on addiction as illness is slated.

——— (9/16/76). Lorton inmates on furlough arrested in drug operation.

Chapter 4

Toward a Conceptual Understanding: The High, the Nod, the Rush, Craving, and Addiction

IN CHAPTER 2, we examined reports of the effects of drugs on human behavior. A major shortcoming of the professional literature is a lack of agreement on definitions of some of the important concepts discussed. Authors sometimes assume that commonly used terms are well understood by everyone. To avoid the confusion that ensues from such an assumption, we shall discuss at length five terms that are important for a clear understanding of drug effects: the *high,* the *nod,* the *rush, craving,* and *addiction.*

In the initial stages of our investigation, it was difficult to pin down what the drug-using criminals in our study meant when they used these terms. Our questions elicited vague, simplistic, and sometimes misleading statements from the users, who often disagreed among themselves as to the meanings of these words. When we acknowledged that we lacked a precise understanding of particular terms, the drug users indicated that we were ignorant for not understanding what "everyone knows." They either considered us not worth bothering with or as needing enlightenment. In the latter case they quickly took control and told us what they thought we wanted to hear. They related just enough to lead us to believe that we were learning something, but they never provided the detailed information we were seeking. Instead, they used interviews with us to air their justifications for drug use.

Through persistent work with criminal drug users over a sixteen-year period in which we guaranteed privileged communication and exercised no administrative authority, we gradually learned what the thinking and action patterns are in the *high,* the *nod,* the *rush, craving,* and *addiction.* As we altered our interviewing methods and our format for change, we became more knowledgeable. Having learned what the users' thinking patterns were in those states, we presented new participants in our study with our understanding of their terms, demonstrating that we were, in fact, knowledgeable and ready to probe further. This approach enabled us to discuss with the user his thinking before he had the opportunity to divert us with descriptions of his feelings (which he used to justify his behavior). As we probed, the drug users themselves became interested in clarifying concepts, especially when they were in small groups and could debate one another. In all interviews we checked and rechecked our information, discarding what could not be substantiated and using and clarifying what was confirmed by new participants.

The concepts set forth in this chapter will provide a frame of reference for succeeding chapters on the role of drugs in the drug-using criminal's life and on the ways in which drugs alter his thinking patterns.

THE HIGH

The term *high* is so frequently used that it is now part of the daily vernacular. It is one of many terms that, although vague, is assumed to be precise and clear. It denotes a state of mind that is both pleasurable and desirable. Its meaning used to be restricted to an effect of alcohol or other drugs. Now the word is used much more broadly, and one hears of being high in spiritual experiences, love relationships, poetry, music, and other fields.

The professional literature usually refers to a drug-induced elevation of mood that attends the user's attempts to find relief from anxiety, depression, or unfavorable circumstances of life. Euphoria is perhaps the word most commonly used to describe the high state (e.g., Wald and Hutt 1972, Scher 1966). It has been asserted that when a drug user is high, psychic conflicts are allayed (Mayor's Committee 1944) and he has "a heightened sense of well-being" (De Long, 1972). Weil (1972) has made the point that a person can attain a "pure," or drugless, high through such experiences as meditation. As he uses it, the term refers to "prominent periods of euphoria." The more one reads the literature, the more one is struck by the lack of a clear conceptualization of the high. The state of being high is usually an incidental topic and generally refers only to a mood effect.

One reason for the vagueness as to the meaning of high is that the drug users themselves are neither clear nor specific about their own states of mind. They use high to refer to any drug effect that is pleasing. Not only do they use the term loosely, but they also use it in contradictory ways. Some consider themselves high when a drug induces sleep. Some refer only to calmness and tranquility, clearly not euphoria. High has been used to refer to a spiritual or monastic state and to virtually any other mental state that is not depressive. A few drug users have spoken of being high at a time when they regarded suicide as solving all problems.

When one asks a drug user what he means by high the response is a quizzical look followed by a declaration that everyone knows what being high is—

"you feel great." When we pressed for elaboration of that statement, we were regarded as stupid for even asking. If we did not know that, we were not worth talking to unless the user could become our teacher and then exploit us for his own purposes. The other type of response was for him to feed us what he thought we already believed and at the same time justify his drug use. He explained the high as relief from fear, depression, and physical distress.

Having found that it was counterproductive to focus on feelings, we gradually learned what thinking patterns are operative in the criminal, regardless of whether he is on drugs. As we improved our interviewing techniques (described in Volume II), we no longer were perceived as being on a fishing expedition. Instead we were bringing to a discussion of the high our knowledge of criminal thinking patterns (described in Volume I). New interviewing techniques and our presentation of the drug user's cognitive processes resulted in the drug user's making what in other settings would be self-incriminating disclosures about thinking processes in the high. We were then able to conceptualize the high as a mental state.

Criminal drug users and criminals who do not use drugs have described phenomena similarly in speaking of the high. The nonuser experiences a natural high in his pursuit of conquests. His mind races with ideas that enhance his power and control in both arrestable and nonarrestable enterprises. A high is experienced most intensely from thinking about, discussing or actually doing the forbidden. The nonuser has total control over his thinking processes. Deterrents are eliminated, and he is superoptimistic about achieving his objectives, whatever they may be. He terminates his high whenever he wishes. On the other hand, without drugs, some criminals are not able to achieve such a high, except in a feeble and short-lived manner that is unsatisfactory to them. With the aid of a drug, however, they are able to reach a high of greater impact.*

The high is rarely assessable in the drug-using criminal's overt behavior or in the intensity of his visible expression of a mood. Only by knowing the user's thinking patterns before, during, and after drug use can an observer possibly comprehend the full impact of the high. Some of his thinking is reflected in his talk and criminal operations, but nowhere near the totality of it. His behavior may appear innocuous while he is planning a crime. He may seem somnolent while his mind is racing with exciting fantasy. He may appear jovial but be inwardly angry. The user's increased velocity of thinking, his cutoff of fears, and the expansion of his thinking of power and control are not observable. The behavior contemplated by the user when the high is

---

*The components of the natural high and the drug-induced high are identical. To avoid repetition, we shall describe only the high of the drug user, with the analysis consisting of a discussion of his thinking in that mental state.

sometimes so extreme that, were it known, he would undoubtedly be labeled "psychotic" by a psychiatric examiner.

The high is a state of excitement, not necessarily one of happiness or euphoria. When euphoria is present, it is expressed as a sweeping aside of inhibitions and a heightened sense of power. The quality of thinking is best characterized in a statement of one user on drugs: "I feel ten feet tall." When we use that phraseology in interviewing drug users, they indicate immediate comprehension of what we are talking about and are more responsive than when we speak of happiness or euphoria.

On drugs the user has an expanded idea of his own capacity. He is without fear; he can do anything and everything, and there is nothing to stand in his way.* As one criminal put it, "I wanted a traffic light state where the green light was constant." By this he meant that on drugs (his particular choice was LSD) he was all-powerful and nothing impeded his thought or action. This state of mind has been expressed in a variety of ways, all of which emphasize the "ten feet tall" or power aspect.

> "I felt that I had it made. I thought that the world was my oyster. Nobody could touch me."

> "When I'm under the effect of LSD-25, I can do anything I want. Reality doesn't exist. Time and space are not in control of me. I can do and be where I choose to be. Nothing can contain me."

On drugs the user is immune to criticism; he does not "give a damn" and is less affected by what others say and do than when he is off drugs. "I turn off my attention and start thinking about something else . . . I ignore the things going on around me."

When he is high on drugs, the user's view of himself as a person and of his place in the world changes. Without the excitement of the high he is a nothing;† the world is boring, and he experiences a sense of tedium that he chooses not to endure. With drugs not only is he somebody, but he is the center of the universe. Drugs elevate him to the greatest heights, where his thinking renders certain what before was only in the realm of the possible.

In the high the user is in control of himself, despite his assertions that he is "stoned" or "bombed." These colloquial expressions actually signify that he is sufficiently high to derive an exciting impact from the altered mental state.

---

*Little and Pearson (1966, p. 555) described the frame of mind of the addict: "When I take the drug, I am not afraid of anyone or anything." However, this was interpreted by the authors within a psychoanalytic framework.

†For a discussion of the "zero state," see Chapter 4 of Volume I.

They are badges of belonging to groups whose members competitively exaggerate the effect of their drug experiences to build themselves up. More important, however, in claiming to have been "stoned" or "bombed" the user has a ready excuse if he is held accountable. The implication of such an excuse is that he was not in control of himself because he was on drugs. One young man told his professor, "You can't ask me that question when I'm stoned." Actually the user makes choices all along the line. Depending in part on availability, he chooses a particular drug to attain the high that he wants. In that mental state, he is still in control of his thinking and action. "I always controlled my trips. I knew exactly what I was doing. To take a trip requires a certain amount of professional competence. I was in another world. A world of my own."

Acceleration in thinking is a definitive feature of the high.* No matter what drug is used, the speed of thinking increases, but physical activity may slow, except when cocaine or amphetamines are used.† When the user is satisfied solely with the altered thinking state, he appears inert (see the following section on the "nod"). How physically active he wants to be remains his decision.

The high, satisfactory as it seems at the time, is eventually evaluated as insufficient. The user seeks the highest high, and this is important in his deciding which drug or drugs to use. The search for the highest high is the significant factor in using a larger quantity of a drug or different drugs concurrently or sequentially. The user's thinking is similar to that of a person with a headache who believes that if one aspirin will alleviate a headache, two will do the job twice as fast. Despite the user's knowledge of the perils of mixing drugs, he does this repeatedly in his search for the highest high. Regardless of unfavorable experiences, he persists with new combinations to achieve the "ten feet tall" effect.

In the following chapter we shall turn our attention to the high in crime, and our focus will be on drugs as facilitators of crime. Throughout Volumes I and II we have stressed that the criminal (drug user and nonuser) pursues power and control in nonarrestable activities, as well as arrestable activities.‡ With drugs he can have a "higher" high in thought, talk, and action when seeking power in a nonarrestable manner.

When high the user views himself as a totally unique person — superior to

---

*We found only one writer who referred to the increase in the speed of thinking: Rosenberg (1975, p. 155) stated that, "during a marijuana high, one experiences a rapid flow of thoughts and associations." However, there was no elaboration as to the substance of the thinking.

†It should be noted that a very large dose of a drug may induce sleep or render a user unconscious.

‡See Chapter 7 of Volume I for a discussion of the criminal's nonarrestable phases.

others, able to outwit them, and more knowledgeable than they.* In his thoughts and deeds, he makes fools of them.

> D had managed to obtain a hallucinogenic drug while confined in a psychiatric hospital. A nursing assistant asked him to do some typing. He received a charge out of the fact that he was sitting right in the ward administrator's office, high on drugs, but the ward personnel were "too stupid" to realize it. Furthermore, the kick was even greater because he had managed to outwit the surveillance of maximum security and acquire the drug.

On drugs, the user either tries to control people in his immediate environment or withdraws into fantasy. He may listen quietly to music, but under the influence of drugs his experience is more than an enhanced appreciation of music. (The user sees himself as having a knowledge and understanding of music vastly superior to others.) Music provides background for a mind racing with exciting thoughts. He enters a drug-induced reality, thinking of himself as "Mr. Big" and as an expert on everything. When the drug wears off, he has difficulty remembering what music he has listened to. If he hears the music on a tape when off drugs, he regards his reaction under drugs as silly.

Some users become very outgoing, especially at a party. They become loud and boisterous, saying and doing things that might appear out of character to a casual observer. Their objective is to be the center of attention. When high they may be brazen enough to attempt to counsel or instruct others whether they are at home, in school, on a job, or at a party.

On drugs, the user may derive as much of a high from religious fervor as he does from crime. Drug users, on or off drugs, have participated in a variety of religious movements. In the few with a psychotic predisposition, drugs unleash psychotic phenomena that have a power component. In a psychotic phase such a user fights the battle of good and evil as God's appointed agent. At all times he retains the capacity to make choices, including how to conceal the psychosis.†

Thinking about suicide has occurred in states that the user has termed high. All our criminals, drug users as well as nonusers, have at one time or another had suicidal thinking. If such thinking is present before drug use, it may become markedly intensified while they are on drugs. Despair is not limited to the user's view of himself but extends to life in general. A high occurs as the user thinks about his occupying an exalted place in the order of things. He regards himself as too good to continue in this life and sees no reason to stay in

---

*For a discussion of the criminal's view of himself as unique, see Chapter 4 of Volume I.

†For a discussion of psychotic phases in criminals, see Chapter 7 of Volume I.

this world. The world offers him nothing; it prevents him from being what he knows he can be. He is not appreciated, and he will not tolerate life as it is. Under the influence of drugs this grandiose thinking increases and is accompanied by irritability toward everyone. Without drugs the user occasionally has feeble thoughts of suicide, but his fears of injury and death are intense; consequently, the likelihood of self-destruction is not great. With drugs such fears are lessened, and this increases the likelihood of an actual suicide attempt.

The duration of the high depends on several factors. To a great extent it is a function of the user's expectations. Users are so suggestible that at times they report an intense high from substances that turn out to contain either no drug or very little drug.* A significant factor in estimating the duration of the high is the method of measuring it. Many users consider the high to consist only of the peak effect. Thus, although the drug effect may last for hours, a user may regard the high as lasting for only a small fraction of that period. Less subjective variables that determine the duration of the high include the type of drug (or combination of drugs) used, the quality of the drugs, the dosage, and the user's drug tolerance.

In the professional literature there is frequent emphasis upon alterations in visual and auditory acuity, taste and touch sensitivity, and time and space perception. Our drug users have reported all these, but they have acknowledged that they would not go to the trouble and expose themselves to the risks that drug use entails merely to achieve perceptual alterations. The much-touted sensory effects tell only half the story of the high. The other half — the more significant half from the standpoint of society — is the "ten feet tall" aspect that results in power seeking and injury to others. It is noteworthy that even in discussions of their experiences with others a power component is present. Each drug user believes that his experiences are unique — not duplicated by others — even though his buddies may tell of comparable sensations and perceptions.

The high is, in fact, a far cry from the nebulous expressions of users and from the formulations of those who have referred to the high in the literature. To limit the description of the high to sensory or perceptual alterations, to observable behavior, or to feelings that the users stress is to miss the data of cognition. The concept of the high that we have set forth extends far beyond the conventional idea that the high provides relief from anxiety, depression, low self-esteem, or environmental adversity. The germane question is: What sort of anxiety, depression, or low self-esteem is the drug user experiencing, and what is wrong with his environment? We have found that he handles parental loss, the loss of a job, and other adversities with far less anx-

---

*The extent of the suggestibility is indicated by a user's beginning his high when he reads the label on a bottle containing codeine.

iety and depression than most responsible people experience. The main factor in seeking a high is that the drug user is dissatisfied with what he considers the banal nature of existence. The antidote for his dissatisfaction is the excitement of violation. Drug use facilitates this excitement.

THE NOD

The *nod* has been described as a phenomenon that accompanies the use of opiates in which the user is drowsy and has little awareness of events outside himself.* The serenity, tranquility, and drowsiness of the nod are the features that are apparent to an observer and therefore are cited most frequently in the literature. Descriptions of the nod refer mostly to the degree of awareness. Fiddle (1967, p. 36) determined three degrees of awareness in the nod: "true oblivion," or a loss of touch with reality; a vague awareness of internal processes and events in the outside world; and fitful wakefulness and sleep.

That scant attention has been paid to the content of the thinking in this mental state is understandable. It is difficult to gain access to that material because if a drug user fully disclosed this thinking during the nod, he would admit to thoughts that would be self-incriminating. When held accountable, the user speaks vaguely about innocuous qualities of the nod that are already fairly well known. Because interviewers are led to believe that the nodding drug user is in a sleeplike state, the user's thinking is not a subject of inquiry; it seems pointless to try to examine the thinking of someone who is somnolent.

We have probed the thinking of drug users while they were nodding in our office. We have also received numerous retrospective reports of the mental contents of that state. We were surprised to find that the nod is quite the opposite of what it appears to be. The nodding drug user appears immobile, drowsy, and indeed almost asleep. But this does not reflect his mental state; in the nod, his mind is racing. His speech and concentration may be impaired because his attention is not wholly absorbed by external events, but rather is divided between the reality in front of him and his own thoughts. Although the user may slur his words and appear inattentive, his thinking is razor sharp.

The nod is the part of the high that is limited to thinking. It does not pertain to talk and action. It is a state in which the drug user fantasizes future criminal activities or power thrusts in nonarrestable enterprises and relives in his mind incidents that were exciting. The nod has been described as a phenomenon associated mainly with heroin. However, drug users in our study

*Tylden (1970) said that to be "on the nod" is "to be sleepy after taking a drug."

assert that they go on the nod with virtually any drug — marijuana, cocaine, amphetamines, sedative-hypnotics, or the so-called hallucinogenic drugs. The nod also occurs with other opiates, including methadone. In addition, just as there is a "natural high," so there is a "natural nod." A drug user does not require drugs for fantasy. However, without drugs the natural nod is not as intense or prolonged. With drugs the mind ranges over more extreme criminal enterprises.

In the nod, there is an acceleration of thinking that is exciting to the user. Fantasies are more intense, rapid, and expansive. The mind devises more daring and complex schemes. These may be in the category of property, sex, or assault crimes, or may focus on attaining the zenith of power in non-arrestable activities. The nod prepares the way for action in that fears are eliminated, deterrents are cut off, and the user believes that nothing stands in his way. Thus it can accurately be said that the "heart" for a crime develops in the nod. If no particular action is contemplated at the time, the criminal thinking becomes more extensive, and the user is satisfied with that for the time being. How active he wants to be is his choice, unless he has had such a large dose of a drug that he is physically incapacitated. It is his decision whether to act or continue nodding. There is excitement in both.

> While a passenger in a car on the way to commit a crime, D was nodding. When he arrived at the scene and it was time to get out of the car, he snapped out of the nod and proceeded into the action of the crime.

Here the element of choice was clear. Drug users have told us that they could pull out of a nod at any time in order to act.

That the nod is characterized by considerable sensitivity to the environment is evident in the drug user's quick response to danger. One user of heroin asserted that in the nod "I am aware of everything." By this he meant that he was not totally preoccupied by his own thoughts, but was alert to his surroundings. If there were a rap on the door, he could be quick to act in his own best interest.*

In short, the drug user determines when and where to nod and whether to prolong the nod or interrupt it for something more exciting or important.

THE RUSH

Rush, like *high,* is a term that drug users employ in a variety of ways which they assume others understand. "Rush," "thrill," "hit," "kick," "flash," and "splash" are all synonymous and supposedly self-explanatory.

---

*Fiddle (1967, p. 35) pointed out that the nodding drug user is "easily irritated into angry awareness."

In the professional literature, the rush is defined mainly as a physical effect that immediately follows the injection of a drug. Long and Penna (1968) described the rush as "a feeling of warmth and a tingling sensation in the abdomen similar to orgasm." Ray (1972, p. 202) called it "similar to a whole body orgasm."

Users have reported to us that the injection of heroin or amphetamines is followed immediately by a gastrointestinal relaxation, a tingling sensation, and a suffusion of warmth arising from the abdomen and "hitting" the face. The intensity and speed of the physical effect depend on the amount of drug used and the speed of injection. At most, the sensations last a few minutes. The user who injects approximately the same dose several times a day over a period of time develops a tolerance to the drug's effects; he no longer experiences a rush from that dose and progressively requires more of the drug to achieve the effect he wants. Some users assert almost wistfully that their first rush was incomparable. With later injections of drugs, they seek to recapture the impact of that initial experience.

The physical aspect of the rush results from the presence of adulterants in the drug, such as quinine in opiates or camphor in amphetamines. There is no rush when a drug like cocaine or morphine is used in pure form. When the adulterant is filtered out, the physical rush effect is minimal.* The neophyte user may believe that the physical sensations of the rush constitute the entire desired drug effect, but a more sophisticated user knows that there is more to the drug experience. If a high does not follow the physical effect, he quickly realizes what has happened. He has been "burned"—i.e., sold a substance that contains almost all adulterants and little or none of the expected drug.

> D stated that a dealer had sold him and three friends drugs that had no heroin. They all experienced the effect of the quinine—a tingling sensation and ringing in the ears. This was initially exciting because they were eagerly anticipating the high that was to follow. One man referred to the initial rush as "beautiful." However, their enthusiasm quickly changed to anger because they did not experience the altered state of mind or high that they were seeking. Consequently they set off to even the score with the drug dealer.

The user does not take risks or go to a great deal of trouble to experience a physical effect only. The physical aspect of the rush only signals the user that the drug is in his system. Of far more significance in the rush is the thinking that follows injection of the drug. This is the same kind of thinking that is

*De Long (1972, p. 107) pointed out that some users of stimulants prefer methamphetamine that is impure "because of the belief that the impurities cause a faster, more intense rush."

part of the high and the nod. The cognitive component of the rush is not described in the literature.* The physical effect is only a harbinger of an altered state of thinking. The rush also involves an intense and abrupt alteration in thinking—an increase in alertness and velocity of thinking and a shift in the quality of thinking so that greater excitement is generated. This occurs when opiates or amphetamines are injected along with adulterants. There is no rush with LSD, which is ingested and enters the bloodstream more slowly. The physical effect anticipates the excitement of thinking and action related to crime, sex, nonarrestable power plays, sometimes a religious experience, and in a few cases removing oneself from this unsatisfactory world.

Just as there is a natural high, so there can be a natural rush. The rush is a result of a mental set. If a drug user anticipates excitement, even though he does not use a drug at the time, there may be a rapid acceleration in his thinking, although less intense and shorter than if he were using drugs. The criminal nonuser does not require drugs for a rush. More readily able to cut off fear, he experiences a natural rush whenever his mind embraces a variety of exciting criminal possibilities. His drug-using counterpart does not even entertain many of these ideas without using a drug to remove restraints to such thinking.

The rush is sometimes seen as opposite to the nod. That is, the amphetamine rush produces alertness, while an opiate-induced nod is characterized by drowsiness. The contrast is between observable behaviors. However, with both types of drugs, the velocity and quality of thinking are the same. Although the heroin user on the nod may appear drowsy, his mind is racing with criminal thinking, and he is extremely alert to his environment. The amphetamine user is physically more active, but the content of his thinking may be no different from that of the opiate user.

CRAVING

The term *craving* is seldom defined explicitly in the drug literature. It is usually discussed in the context of a person's reaction to withdrawal from a drug on which he has been physically or psychologically dependent. It is said that a user craves a drug because it will provide relief from the discomfort of withdrawal. The desire for a drug under such circumstances has been called "uncontrollable" (Hesse 1946, p. 14). Taking a different view, Chein (1958, p. 148) observed that craving may exist without physical dependence. Chein et al. (1964) asserted that something beyond the elimination of bodily tensions is involved in craving: "[There is] a powerful drive for the drug inde-

---

*Gorodetzky and Christian (1970) referred to the amphetamine rush as "a state of intense physical and mental pleasure," but they did not explain what the "mental" aspect is.

pendent of the degree to which the drug has insinuated itself into the physiological workings of the body" (p. 6). Chein et al. stated explicitly that what is craved is not simply the drug itself but rather the drug's chief effect — the high. "The full-blown addict is not content with a maintenance dose that will prevent the withdrawal syndrome. He craves the experience of the 'high' and will go to great lengths to achieve it" (p. 26).

Through our phenomenologic approach to the drug user's thinking, we have determined that craving is indeed a phenomenon distinct from the physical aspects of drug dependence. The user seeks relief primarily of mental misery, rather than physical misery, although he may also experience the latter. Craving occurs when he is bored, tense, full of self-pity, and in a state of despair because life appears to offer him nothing. Without criminal excitement the drug user perceives himself as a nobody and life as not worth living. He wants to eliminate this agonizing state of mind and achieve a more agreeable homeostasis.

Responsible people crave things, too — like chocolate. Consequences of eating large amounts of chocolate may be obesity and cavities. But the craving for chocolate does not result in injuring others. *The primary factor in craving drugs is the desire to do the forbidden.* The desire for drugs and the desire for action go hand in hand. The user craves the excitement of a "big score" in crime, of a sexual conquest, or of involvement in some other form of activity that will provide him with a buildup in which he will emerge on top.

With a drug in him, the user finds that life has fewer restraints and that new possibilities open up. His thinking and action expand into a criminal world from which he was at least partially deterred by conscience and the fear of getting caught. He is Mr. Big, the unique number-one person, free to pursue his objectives, whether it be through crime or nonarrestable power maneuvers.

Craving sometimes results in such physical manifestations as tension in the arm favored for injection. Users who abstain for a long time from drugs on which they were physically dependent occasionally experience physical symptoms identical to those of withdrawal. Later if they justify their reversion to drug use, they contend that these symptoms, psychosomatic in origin, were a "call" to drugs — i.e., they compelled him to seek drugs for relief. However, users also crave drugs whose discontinuance does not result in withdrawal-like symptoms. For example, they crave marijuana. This is not because of a physical dependence on it, but because that drug is available and they want something to alter their thinking and provide an antidote to an otherwise dull, plodding, wearisome, and to them, intolerable existence.

Craving is not attributable to a compulsion or lack of control. The user makes choices in determining what kind of life he wants to live. Craving occurs (with or without physical concomitants) whenever life is unsatisfactory—i.e., whenever there is a dearth of criminal excitement.

The user craves continuation of the exciting state of mind that drugs facilitate, and so he finds it unnatural not to have a drug in his system. In his view drugs are a necessity of life, as essential as food or clothing. Being without drugs is like functioning without a vital body organ. Even when the extreme user reaches middle age and drugs have less effect than before, he continues to use some type of mind-altering substance, usually alcohol. One user commented that without drugs his mind and body were "not right," and he could not think well. He maintained that his thinking was more precise with drugs than without them. Furthermore, life seemed to hold more promise. For the extreme drug user, the increased speed and altered quality of thinking are "natural." He craves what is for him a natural (or preferable) state.

ADDICTION

We stated in Chapter 2 that we do not use the term *addiction* in presenting our own findings because it has been and still is used so loosely that it has no substantive meaning. More than two decades ago, the Ad Hoc Panel on Drug Abuse (1962, p. 276) asserted: "The term addiction has such a multiplicity of meanings that even its most important connotation, habitual use, may no longer be associated with it."

In the professional literature, physical dependence is regarded as the hallmark of addiction. This is a reference to the biochemical adaptation that occurs in the nervous system as the drug is used. The addict requires steadily larger doses of the drug to produce the desired effect, a phenomenon known as "tolerance." According to the literature, the critical factor in determining if a user is addicted is whether he experiences withdrawal symptoms on discontinuance of the drug.* A variety of physical effects attends withdrawal from opiates, including yawning, tearing, pupillary dilatation, sweating, abdominal cramps, muscle aches, hot and cold flashes, goose bumps, itching skin, increased blood pressure, increased temperature, increased blood sugar, hemoconcentration, panting, loss of appetite, insomnia, weight loss, spontaneous ejaculation and orgasm, muscle tremors, diarrhea, vomiting, fever, and hyperactivity. Effects of barbiturate withdrawal include restlessness, anxiety, tremulousness, weakness, nausea, cramps, and psychosis with hallucination and disorientation; such withdrawal may constitute a life-threatening situation with convulsive seizures and delirium. Characteristic of the amphetamine withdrawal syndrome are decreased activity, exhaustion, sleep disturbance, and severe depression.

---

*Ray (1972, p. 201) observed that the term *addiction* is "restricted to those conditions where physiological symptoms occur when the regular use of the drug is discontinued."

The concept of psychologic dependence holds that a person persists in the use of drugs when drugs are not necessary to relieve physical symptoms. That is, the user wants drugs even though he has been detoxified (drugs are no longer in his system), and he has no physical manifestations of withdrawal. "Craving" or the desire for a high (usually expressed as a mood alteration) is the core of psychologic dependence.

A common belief is that the physically dependent user is almost helpless once he is addicted. Van Kaam (1968, p. 54) made that point discussing the derivation of the term *addiction*.

> The term addiction comes from the Latin *ad dicere* which means to give oneself up or over. The emphasis on surrender, on giving up . . . seems to be related more to the passive than to the active dimension of man's life . . . The passive constituent is so overwhelmingly strong in the addictive personality that no room is left for the mastering dimension.

It is widely held that addiction is both a compulsion and a disease which hold the drug user helplessly in their grip. In sharp contrast we consistently have found that discontinuation of drug use is well within the user's choice, never a matter of compulsion. The user chooses a particular life-style. He uses drugs for specific purposes, which he can change or modify as circumstances warrant. Psychologic dependence results from a series of choices to achieve and prolong an altered state of mind. Psychologic dependence is the continuing desire for what drugs will facilitate—criminal excitement in the form of thought, talk, and action. Drugs are "psychedelic" in that they expand the user's horizons so that he is "ten feet tall." The desire to be on top of the world is a far more significant contributor to the user's dependence on drugs than is the desire to avoid the symptoms of withdrawal.

> While in confinement D asserted that when he was released, he would remain off heroin. He did this for a while but then started to use the drug again. D once again decided to get rid of the "monkey" on his back. Within several days he had gone through withdrawal. Later he reported to us that the physical symptoms of withdrawal were far less objectionable than was his mental state off drugs.

In other words, it was not the chills, diarrhea, or other symptoms that mattered. What was repugnant to D was the dull, constraining life without heroin. Off drugs he lacked the "heart" or courage for some of the more exciting, risky adventures in which he had engaged while on drugs and which made life worthwhile.

One might think that the user exercises little choice in the matter, because he becomes physically dependent despite intentions not to.* Initially, each user is certain that he is in control. He knows that others have become dependent on drugs, but is positive this will not happen to him. Then, as one man put it, "I used one pill and got a kick. The next day, two pills. Then three to get the same kick." Even though he was using increasingly larger doses of a drug, this person never considered himself "addicted." This is true generally of users who become physically dependent on drugs. Each user retains the belief that he can make the present shot or pill his last. The fact is that he does retain the capacity to make such a choice and follow through on it. He only pleads that he is helpless and impaired by his addiction when he is held accountable by others. If the user is apprehended for a crime, he uses addiction as a defense to plead diminished responsibility. He is sometimes successful in convincing others that because he was addicted to drugs at the time, he was not responsible for his actions.

If the user has reason to remain off drugs for a while, he does so. The fear of withdrawal does not compel him to use them. He chooses to forgo drugs and suffer through withdrawal in order to pursue his objectives. Some drug users go through withdrawal to reduce the size of their habits. They want to attain a high, but on lower doses and at less cost. Another reason is to please an irate spouse or dissatisfied employer. The drug user is not a loyal family man or devoted worker, but he may regard it as advantageous to be off drugs for a while so that he can preserve an aura of respectability that a stable home and a job provide. Users also stop using drugs because on high doses their sexual performance is impaired. Some withdraw on their own, whereas others voluntarily enter detoxification programs "to get my sex back," as several put it. A minority go through withdrawal because they fear that drugs will impede rather than help them in the commission of a crime. This is particularly true if they have been reckless enough on drugs in the past to get caught or are on such large doses that they experience a loss of agility.† Users become weary of the hassles and risks that acquiring and using drugs entail. One man withdrew from drugs because, as he said, "I was sick and tired of being sick and tired." Whatever the reason, a sufficiently important objective overrides the distress of going through withdrawal. Rather than constituting an agonizing ordeal, withdrawal is experienced as a relatively small inconvenience.

*This phenomenon is frequently mentioned in the drug literature. For example: "They report, no doubt truthfully, that they started off as occasional users. They did not intend to become addicted; indeed, they were confident that they would escape addiction by using the drug only on occasion. Then the kind of occasions on which they used heroin became more numerous, and the intervals shorter. After weeks or months of increasing use, daily use began — and soon thereafter the casual user became an addict." (Brecher et al. 1972, p. 15)

†If they later contemplate major crimes or sexual conquests, they return to drugs for "heart" or courage.

D flew to Bermuda to participate in a criminal enterprise. He perceived that in the particular situation, it was to his advantage to be off drugs. Although heavily dependent on heroin, D resolved to go "cold turkey." With his mind resolutely set on achieving specific criminal objectives, he hardly noticed the mild withdrawal symptoms that ensued.

Over and over, our drug users indicated that the seriousness of withdrawal has been greatly exaggerated.* In the last few decades the quality of drugs has been extremely poor. Withdrawal from heavily adulterated preparations of drugs has been fairly easy, with symptoms resembling a mild case of the flu. It is a matter of a person's choice as to how he reacts.

D traveled to a vacation spot far from home. In his eagerness to get there, he left without his drug supply and paraphernalia. It was of paramount importance that the others in the group not know that he was on drugs. He directed his thinking and action away from his symptoms and consequently hardly noticed them.

A powerful determinant of the severity of withdrawal symptoms is the user's mental set. Having observed others withdraw and having heard a great deal about withdrawal, he has developed expectations. A suggestible individual anyway, he is readily psychologically programmed. His experiences, therefore, correspond both to what he has been led to believe and what he has observed.

Drug users are intolerant of any distress, whether physical or psychologic. In the presence of someone who could alleviate their discomfort, they dramatize even the slightest ache. They are eager to obtain pills or find any other solution that appears to promise immediate relief. They may turn to another class of drug.

D was experiencing withdrawal symptoms at home as he attempted to prove to his wife that he was going to stop using heroin. He took aspirin for a headache and went to bed with a hot-water bottle to relieve his cramps. When his wife left the house, D found a bottle with several ounces of whiskey remaining. He consumed this instantly and for a while felt better.

*Our findings concur with the observations of Weil (1972, p. 42): "I have never seen a withdrawal reaction from heroin that came anywhere near the stereotype promulgated by Hollywood. . . . In a supportive setting, with proper suggestion, a heroin addict can withdraw without medication other than aspirin and have little more discomfort than that of a moderate cold." Farber (1968, p. 6) put it this way: "Even the well publicized and allegedly extreme agonies of heroin withdrawal have been disputed by the Lazaruses who came back. [A Synanon member remarked]: 'Kicking the habit is easy. It's not like that Frank Sinatra movie, crawling all over the walls. Sure, it's tough for a couple of days, but it's more like getting over a bad cold.' "

If confined, users go to sick call and request prescriptions for anything that will diminish the symptoms.* If a doctor or other person in authority does not accede to their demands, they try to place that person on the defensive, casting him in the role of the inhumane caretaker. Yet if they are in a situation where they do not want to be perceived as weak, they endure the symptoms and maintain their composure in order to show that they are tough and can take it.

The drug user knows that he can stop drug use if it is important enough to him. Until that time, however, he utilizes withdrawal manifestations as justification for his continuing use of drugs. It is true that, for him, life without drugs is insufferable. However, his gastrointestinal disturbance, muscle aches, or other physical symptoms are by no means the entire basis for wanting more drugs. More significant are his self-pity and anger at being deprived of the criminal excitement that drugs facilitate. And so he convinces others that dire consequences will ensue if he does not have drugs. In fact, he does this so often and so successfully that he may talk himself into half-believing it. There is a parallel in the employee who dislikes work and one day wakes up with a sore throat. The sore throat does not incapacitate him from going to work, but he uses it to avoid what he dislikes. He may even begin to believe that his sore throat is more disabling than it is.

The mental attitude is all-important. If a user is determined to abstain from drugs — if he decides, for whatever reason, that drugs are "poison" — then the physical distress that he experiences on discontinuing them is relatively minor and endurable. If, however, he still wants drugs, but is coerced by external circumstances to go through withdrawal, the same physical distress seems unbearable. If life without drugs is regarded as meaningless and if without drugs he views himself as a nothing, then withdrawal seems excruciating. Therefore if he returns to drugs, it is not because he is persuaded by others or experiences an uncontrollable, physical urge. The user's "addiction" is to the pursuit of criminal excitement — that which will make life worth living. What the user abhors in withdrawal is not the physical discomfort, but his mind's returning to its natural state to face a tedious existence, a world with restraints and without excitement — a life devoid of meaning.

PSYCHOSOMATIC WITHDRAWAL-LIKE SYMPTOMS

In the discussion of craving we said that users experience physical symptoms resembling those of withdrawal even long after they cease to be physically dependent on drugs. These symptoms are psychosomatic and are triggered by a variety of events.†

---

*A dentist observed that addict inmates in prison attend sick calls more frequently than do nonaddict inmates (*U.S. Medicine* 6/15/74).

†Brecher et al. (1972, p. 68) observed that some people believe that this phenomenon is organically based — that it is "a direct effect of the opiate molecule on the nervous system."

If a user is confined and desires drugs, the typical symptoms of withdrawal appear even if he has been previously detoxified. Although he has had no drugs, he is afflicted with diarrhea, muscle aches, weakness, or a variety of other withdrawal-like discomforts. Describing his experience, a former inmate reflected, "I felt as if I were on narcotics and needed another fix." A user may experience similar distress as he anticipates his discharge from confinement and a return to street life. One inmate had been abstinent from drugs for five years, but three days before his release from jail, he had a runny nose, tearing eyes, itching skin, stomach pains, and muscle aches. If this does not occur in confinement, it is likely to do so shortly thereafter. Many users have reported that with the onslaught of psychosomatic symptoms, their resolutions to stay off drugs crumble.

> D had been in confinement and had had no drugs for a year. The day he was released, he rode the bus to his old neighborhood. As he neared his stop, he became physically ill, experiencing the familiar symptoms of withdrawal. Once he was in the city, the first person he contacted was an associate who he knew would have drugs. Within a few hours of his release from jail, he had obtained heroin.

These symptoms may also occur when a "panic" in the streets over the unavailability of drugs ends, and the user discovers that drugs are again available. The symptoms also appear after he has stopped using drugs because of their poor quality, and he learns that more potent drugs can be acquired. Numerous other environmental cues prompt these withdrawal-like symptoms — meeting a drug-using friend, passing a "shooting gallery" where he knows drugs are used, listening to music that reminds him of a time or place of drug use, and watching a movie or television program or reading a book whose contents refer to drugs, crime, sex, or the exercise of power in other arenas.* A particular time of the year or time of day may stimulate memories that serve as cues to elicit the familiar symptoms.†

That the psychosomatic symptoms correspond to withdrawal symptoms is hardly surprising. Throughout his drug-using life, the user has experienced them as physical consequences of withdrawal. As is true of all psychosomatic

---

*Fiddle (1967, p. 50) pointed out that the smell of a burnt match may induce the symptoms because the addict burns heroin before injecting it.

†Many writers have used learning-theory concepts to describe this conditioning process. Crowley (1972) pointed out that "a whole series of previously neutral objects or events may develop reinforcement characteristics through association with a primary reinforcer." Wikler (1953, p. 46) attributed relapse after cure in part to this strong behavioral conditioning. He also observed that physically dependent users who return to a drug-using environment experience physical symptoms even after weeks or months of withdrawal.

symptoms, these symptoms, although psychologic in origin, are real. The user does experience the gastrointestinal distress, shortness of breath, and other manifestations of a withdrawal reaction.

The symptoms occur when the drug user is restraining himself from drug use and from other violations that drugs have facilitated. It is the lack of excitement that he reacts to in a physical manner.

> D had not used heroin or other drugs in several months. It had been a dull period of self-imposed abstinence. During that time he met a young woman at work who was a heroin user. He began to think about dating her, and as he did so, his mind went to drugs and sex. He temporarily vetoed the idea of dating her because he realized that to do so would increase the temptation to use drugs. As he was going through this debate, his nose began to run, his eyes teared, his skin itched, and his stomach became upset. Finally he said to himself, "The hell with it" and decided to purchase liquor and use the drugs that he surmised she would have available. Having made this choice, he felt better. There followed two days with the woman in which he drank, used heroin and marijuana, and had sex. He missed work both days and spent $140.

The itch for action automatically produces thinking about drugs. The user is not willing to assume the burdens of a responsible life. During a period of abstinence, he wearies of life's plodding pace, and the symptoms are likely to begin.

> At work D had a task that would have been challenging to a responsible person. He had been designated to outline a proposal for a complex project. Arriving at work, he discovered his problems compounded by the fact that a fellow employee had not prepared the relevant materials the day before. D had considerable difficulty structuring the outline. He grew impatient and began to doubt whether the proposal had any merit at all. As his impatience and apprehension mounted, he began to experience withdrawal-like symptoms. He wondered why he was bothering with the job at all. Was it worth it? Thinking about drugs ensued. Shortly thereafter, he left work and bought drugs.

D allowed himself to be defeated by the type of problem that responsible people in similar positions encounter every day and struggle to resolve. His automatic response to this situation was to abandon the project for something far more exciting. D had the knowledge to resolve this dilemma. He was a bright, resourceful employee who was capable of evaluating, organizing and presenting a complex proposal. His objection was to more than the task at hand. To live a life of going to work, struggling with obstacles, ironing out differences with others, spending time at home with his family, managing finances, and facing the other problems common to most people was not for him. Drugs not only offered escape from his monotonous existence but also held the promise of a world of exciting thought, talk, and action.

Withdrawal-like symptoms also occur when the user is suffering the consequences of being in a hole that he has dug for himself. When his irresponsibility is known to others and he is being closely watched, he may be temporarily restrained from the life that he prefers. Consequently he experiences the familiar symptoms that serve as a call to drugs. The same is true when he is temporarily deterred by conscience.

The very decision to obtain drugs produces a change in the user's mental and physical state. His entire demeanor changes. Boredom, despair, self-pity, anger, and fears are reduced because the user anticipates what drugs will do for him. Inertia and apathy give way to alertness and initiative. Speech changes. The user is more inclined to express himself in street language and is more brazen in the claims he makes and grandiose in the plans he announces. More important, his decision to obtain drugs greatly reduces the intensity of his physical symptoms.

> D stated that once he made a decision to pawn his watch to get money for drugs, he felt better physically. He then pawned the watch, purchased heroin, and committed a series of crimes.

> The more D thought about his aches and pains, the worse they became, and the more he thought about drugs. Finally he decided to send someone to buy drugs. Once he saw that person, obviously under the influence of drugs himself, coming toward him, the aches and pains vanished.

If the user is still physically dependent on a drug and is going through withdrawal, the same phenomenon occurs. Once he decides to acquire drugs, the symptoms disappear. Even if he chooses to go through withdrawal, the symptoms are not intense as long as he knows that drugs are available if he wants them. Whether a user is experiencing physical distress from actual withdrawal or from psychosomatic withdrawal-like symptoms, the most immediate remedy is not a tranquilizer or other prescribed treatment, but rather to set out in search of drugs that will give him a high. Each stage, from the time the decision to get drugs is made until the user has the drug in hand, provides mounting excitement and a reduction in mental or physical distress. Deciding how to get out of the house without arousing suspicion, approaching the drug area, walking through the neighborhood, meeting the seller, discussing the quality and price of the drug, and finally making the transaction all offer excitement that constitutes effective "treatment" for withdrawal-like symptoms.*

Among those who inject drugs, withdrawal symptoms or the psychosomatic aspects of craving are sometimes relieved through contact with a needle without a drug actually being injected. Relief occurs for some users when they watch someone else inject drugs or when they simply hold a needle in their hands. Some users report that they relax if they prick their skin and draw blood, even thought they do not experience a high. Others have relieved physical discomfort by injecting a nondrug substance. Sometimes they delude themselves into believing that they are getting enough of the old drug residue from used, unwashed paraphernalia to receive the desired effect. Actually all they may be injecting is an adulterant.

In the literature, reference is made to the "needle habit." In 1926 Cantala wrote: "I blame the syringe for at least fifty per cent of the number of addicts. The morphiomaniac has great love for the injection. It is not only for the pleasure the narcotic gives, but also for the joy the addict experiences in the act of injecting himself" (p. 238). Ray (1972) observed that the acts of preparing and injecting the drug become pleasurable themselves. He commented: "The ultimate is the addict who has a 'needle habit' and will insert the needle into a vein frequently even though he injects nothing" (p. 204). Some of our users report experiencing a high from the use of the needle alone. They pump blood back and forth in the syringe, but inject no drug. Users who have paraphernalia, but no drug, inject boiled water and get high. Some experience a high (and some a nod) upon injecting a pure adulterant, such as flour or quinine, when they are defrauded in a drug purchase. Without any drug in their systems, they experience the total effect.

We have repeatedly referred to drugs as "facilitators." In the next chapter we shall describe what they facilitate. The preceding material provides a frame of reference for that discussion.

BIBLIOGRAPHY

Ad Hoc Panel on Drug Abuse. (1962). Report to the White House conference on narcotic and drug abuse (Appendix 1). In *Proceedings: White House Conference on Narcotic and Drug Abuse,* pp. 271–308. Washington, DC: Government Printing Office.

Brecher, E. M., and the editors of *Consumer Reports.* (1972). *Licit and Illicit Drugs.* Boston: Little, Brown.

*Redlich and Freedman (1966, p. 731) observed: "One psychological factor to be considered is the powerful motive of 'hustling'; many addicts seem to value the search for illicit drugs and even prefer this highly absorbing chase to assured medical sources of supply."

Cantala, J. (1926). Opium, heroin, morphine: their kingdoms. In *Narcotic Education,* ed. H. S. Middlemiss, pp. 232-268. Washington, DC: H. S. Middlemiss.

Chein, I. (1958). The status of sociological and social psychological knowledge concerning narcotics. In *Narcotic Drug Addiction Problems,* ed. R. B. Livingston, pp. 146-158. Washington, DC: Government Printing Office.

Chein, I., Gerard, D. L., Lee, R. S., and Rosenfeld, E. (1964). *The Road to H: Narcotics, Delinquency and Social Policy.* New York: Basic Books.

Crowley, T. J. (1972). The reinforcers for drug abuse: why people take drugs. *Comprehensive Psychiatry* 13:51-62.

De Long, J. V. (1972). The drugs and their effects. In Drug Abuse Survey Project, *Dealing with Drug Abuse: Report to the Ford Foundation,* pp. 62-123. New York: Praeger.

Farber, L. H. (1968). Ours is the addicted society. *Review of Existential Psychology and Psychiatry* 8:5-16.

Fiddle, S. (1967). *Portraits from a Shooting Gallery.* New York: Harper and Row.

Gorodetzky, C. W., and Christian, S. T. (1970). *What You Should Know about Drugs.* New York: Harcourt, Brace, & Jovanovich.

Hesse, E. (1946). *Narcotics and Drug Addiction.* New York: Philosophical Library.

Little, R. B., and Pearson, M. M. (1966). The management of pathologic interdependency in drug addiction. *American Journal of Psychiatry* 123:554-560.

Long, R. E., and Penna, R. P. (1968). Drugs of abuse. *Journal of the American Pharmaceutical Association.* January 12-27.

Mayor's Committee on Marihuana. (1944). *The Marihuana Problem in the City of New York.* Lancaster, PA: Jacques Cattell.

Ray, O. S. (1972). *Drugs, Society, and Human Behavior.* St. Louis: C. V. Mosby.

Redlich, F. C., and Freedman, D. X. (1966). *The Theory and Practice of Psychiatry.* New York: Basic Books.

Rosenberg, P. (1975). The effects of mood altering drugs: pleasures and pitfalls. In *Fundamentals of Juvenile Criminal Behavior and Drug Abuse,* eds. R. E. Hardy and J. G. Cull, pp. 139-168. Springfield, IL: Charles C Thomas.

Scher, J. (1966). Patterns and predictions of addiction and drug abuse. Archives of General Psychiatry 15:539-551.

Tylden, E. (1970). ABC of drug addiction. In *ABC of Drug Addiction,* pp. 4-19. Bristol: John Wright.

U.S. Medicine. (6/15/74). Dentist finds atypical lesions among addicts.

Van Kaam, A. (1968). Addiction and existence. *Review of Existential Psychology and Psychiatry* 8:54–57.

Wald, P. M., and Hutt, P. B. (1973). The drug abuse survey project: summary of findings, conclusions, and recommendations. In Drug Abuse Survey Project, *Dealing with Drug Abuse: Report to the Ford Foundation,* pp. 3–62, New York: Praeger.

Weil, A. T. (1972). *The Natural Mind: A New Way of Looking at Drugs and the Higher Consciousness.* Boston: Houghton Mifflin.

Wikler, A. (1953). *Opiate Addiction: Psychological and Neurophysiological Aspects in Relation to Clinical Problems.* Springfield, IL: Charles C Thomas.

Chapter 5

Drugs as Facilitators

IN THE LAST CHAPTER, we discussed the "mind-expanding" feature of the high, the nod, and the rush. In this chapter, we deal with the direction in which thought, talk, and action expand as a result of drug use. Three themes are developed in this chapter:

1. Drugs facilitate the accomplishment of what the user wants;
2. Achievement of his objectives overrides the significance of what the user wants to escape;
3. The effects of particular drugs depend more on these objectives than on the properties of the drugs themselves.

Much emphasis has been placed on the use of drugs to escape adversity, whether it be external stress or internal conflict. The user's problems are mostly self-created. They result from his response to the responsibilities that he is asked to fulfill. Pressures from the responsible world become more and more difficult to ignore as he grows older. But he finds those pressures incompatible with his own objectives. The user finds intolerable adversity in the routine, tedious aspects of existence and seeks relief in doing the forbidden. Lying, blaming others, and offering a variety of excuses compound his problems. Another source of dissatisfaction may be present. Briefly when he is troubled by conscience or when he is unsuccessful in achieving power, the user views himself unfavorably.

Drugs do offer escape from the user's boredom with the routine and mundane, from the consequences of his irresponsibility, and from his occasionally negative view of himself. But more important than what he escapes is what he seeks. He searches for a more desirable state of mind. By going to something exciting, he automatically dispels boredom, fear, depression, and anger. At work he may find his job unchallenging and tedious. But on drugs he sees himself as a "big shot" who knows all the answers and who deserves to be in charge. Drugs provide him with the "ten-feet-tall" view of himself. The world is his oyster; his powers are unlimited.*

If one asks a criminal why he uses drugs, he responds in terms of euphoria or getting high. He certainly does not specify what he seeks as a result of using drugs. Wanting drugs is shorthand for desiring all that the drugs facilitate, whether it be to develop the "heart" for an armed robbery, an erection for prolonged sexual activity, or the daring to assault someone physically. A parallel is the heavy drinker who knows only that he wants a drink. He does not run through a list of what he wants from the alcohol. He drinks; the effects follow. The same is true of the drug user.

When the drug user is held accountable, he gives others a self-serving story. He emphasizes the escape theme by pouring forth a variety of sociologic and psychologic excuses: financial destitution, conflicts with parents, difficulties with a wife or girl friend, unfair treatment on the job, racial discrimination, physical disability, and so on. The user takes any condition of life that could conceivably be regarded as unfavorable and on the basis of it justifies his drug use and subsequent behavior. His accountability statements do not at all reflect his actual thinking on the street, where he has no need to justify drug use to himself or to others.

We found that a person might experience very different effects from the same drug on different occasions. We also found that different drugs had the same effect on a given individual. We were puzzled on both counts, until we shifted focus from the drug to what the user wanted before he used it. It is easy to be misled. The user describes what he seeks in terms of happiness, relaxation, and peace of mind. But the tranquility that the drug user claims to want is the "tranquility" of excitement. He is bored when things are going well from a responsible person's standpoint. The psychology of the "tranquility of excitement" is well captured in a statement of one user: "When I drive sixty miles per hour, I'm tense, but at ninety, how much I relax!"

Drug users resort to drugs to pursue various objectives. Not every user wants drugs to facilitate an actual crime. However, in our study of criminals who were drug users, we found that crime and sex were overwhelmingly what they were interested in. We shall describe here the potentiation of thought,

---

*McKee (1975, p. 590) is one of the few writers who chooses not to emphasize the escape theme and is explicit about the creation of a new reality. "To drug users, their behavior is not an 'escape from reality' or 'false reality.' Drug use and experience are simply a drug reality. . . . Their experiences are genuine, valid, and normal to them, whereas they may be symptoms of a social psychological pathology or illegality to the nonuser."

talk, and action along particular lines: crime, sex, criminal equivalents, monasticism and religiosity, suicide, and finally psychosis.

DRUGS AS FACILITATORS OF CRIME

THOUGHT

Our findings are based on studies of the flow of thinking before, during, and after drug use by criminals. In describing his drug experiences to responsible people, the user relates only thinking that does not incriminate him. One young man used to tell us that the chief effect of drugs for him was that he became carefree and appreciated music more than when he was not on drugs. Only after considerable probing did we determine that using drugs resulted in his developing plans for setting enormous fires and later carrying them out. Without drugs he had only fleeting thoughts of such crimes but was too fearful to act on them.

Drugs accelerate the velocity of thinking and have an impact on its direction, bringing out and accentuating what is already present in the user's thoughts.* Drugs enrich an already rich fantasy life. (In confinement, fantasy expanded by illicitly acquired drugs provides a partial substitute for action.) Generally, far too many ideas occur to the user for him to implement more than a small fraction.† Not only are the ideas that occur when under the influence of drugs too numerous, but some are truly so fantastic that they are not feasible. Thoughts about some offenses may be entertained, but the user may regard them as too repugnant to enact.

A critical difference between the criminal user and criminal nonuser lies in the way each deals with fears. The nonuser cuts off internal deterrents of conscience and external deterrents of fear of apprehension or injury. He can change instantly from gushy sentimentality to ruthless brutality or, as one nonuser put it, "from tears to ice." This is not the case with the criminal who frequently uses drugs. He is much more fearful and has difficulty cutting off fears of all types. On drugs, however, thinking is transformed, so the user's fears fade and he is confident that he can undertake anything successfully. Self-disgust and self-doubt disappear, at least long enough for him to pursue his current objectives. Conscience is disposed of, and the user entertains ideas that formerly were objectionable. He worries far less about injury and

---

*Our discussion in this chapter is in reference to the criminal who has had enough of a drug to achieve the desired effect but not such a heavy dose that he is stuporous.

†See Chapter 6 of Volume I for a description of the rapid flow of criminal ideas from which the criminal who does not use drugs selects the ones that he will enact.

apprehension and is willing to subject himself to greater risk.* Certainty of success is greatly increased as he thinks about pursuing his enterprises.

> D stated that he could not imagine himself committing a bank robbery without drugs. On drugs, however, he had planned a "big score" to the last detail. He knew the bank's business hours, when the manager arrived to open the bank, the time the vaults were opened, and when the tellers reported for duty. He was certain that he could execute the holdup by himself. He did not need anyone else's help.

An important change in the user's thinking when he is on drugs is the strengthening of his belief that he is totally in control of himself. Drugs transform his state of mind from "I am afraid of everything; I am afraid of life" to "I am afraid of nothing." If he is engaged in fantasy or "suspended in time" (as one user put it), he cares very little what is happening around him, so nothing makes him angry unless his fantasy is interrupted. The user experiences a heightened sense of control in that his view of himself as unique is heightened. One man, describing himself on drugs, stated that he was "like a tiger in a supermarket," an expression that captures his sense of separateness and distinctiveness, as well as the potential for violence.

Drugs do not change the makeup of the person, but they do allow him to expand on desires and ideas that are present, but unelaborated. Without drugs there has been considerable thinking about past and future crimes. On drugs the range of considerations expands, and there is greater excitement generated by the thinking. The state of mind is indicated in the following account.

> D reported that he had had numerous difficulties throughout the day at work. He was disturbed by people trooping in and out of his office. The air conditioning system malfunctioned. His wife slammed the receiver down during a telephone argument with him. Disgusted, bored, and angry, D left the office, went uptown, and smoked two marijuana cigarettes. Walking back toward the downtown area, he did not "give a damn" about anything. He walked against red lights and experienced a general sense of being in full control of the world. He passed a television store and thought about being a renowned interviewer who would put his guests on the spot. Then he started thinking about which passersby on the street might be vulnerable to a "con job." Strolling along, he eyed the

---

*This has been referred to in the literature as "false courage," but it is a concept that has had no elaboration in terms of the accompanying thinking processes. Wortis (1958, p. 178) said that, although opiates do not "directly incite" the drug user to violence, "they may diminish anxiety and supply a kind of *false willingness* for the addict to commit petty thievery" (italics ours).

girls and thought about which ones he could have in his stable as prostitutes so that he could live the life of a prosperous pimp. D then conceived of a scheme of embarrassing a prominent politician by luring him into a compromising sexual situation and then blackmailing him.

On drugs the user is beyond the problems of day-to-day living. There is the relaxation that comes with excitement. He conceives of violations, some of which are in the realm of possibility and others that he knows are preposterous. Fantasies are encouraged and savored. With drugs new possibilities arise, and new dimensions come to life. As one user commented, "Drugs added other rooms of thought to my life."

D reported that when he was on drugs, he had an exciting series of fantasies about hijacking an airplane. His idea was to hijack the airliner, have it flown to the state in which he had been incarcerated, and hold the passengers hostage in return for the release of his friends in prison, whom he referred to as the most vicious murderers that he knew. He would then exchange the hostages for free passage to Algeria for him and the other criminals.

TALK

Drugs expedite criminal thinking far more than they expedite criminal talk or action because talk and action obviously cannot possibly keep pace with the tremendous volume of thoughts. Yet it is in exciting talk that much criminal thinking finds an outlet. Criminal talk is exciting without drugs, but with drugs it is even more so. Through tremendous exaggeration the user tries to enhance his image. His language is supercharged, and he is even more boastful, brazen, and profane than usual. He not only boasts of what he has done in the past but also makes extravagant claims as to what he will accomplish in the future. If he is not speaking of violation *per se,* then he is referring to objectives that require violation.

A topic of nearly limitless fascination among drug users is drugs. They discuss where and how to acquire them. They talk over sources of supply, and speculate about informants and other risks. Conversations also revolve around the price of drugs and the purity of drugs, and there is an almost unending discussion of drug effects.

Without drugs the user tells lies, but it is harder for him to lie both to himself and to others because of his fear of being tripped up and sometimes because of his conscience. A lie told when he is drug-free is better thought out and therefore usually more credible than a lie told while he is on drugs. Off drugs, deterrence to telling outrageous lies is stronger. Furthermore, just the fact that a known user is reputed to be drug-free enhances his credibility. Some people assume that his being off drugs virtually ensures that he has become truthful.

On drugs there is a greater charge from lying, whether the purpose is to avoid revealing the truth, to get out of a jam, or simply to make a fool out of another person. As one criminal commented about his perception of the world while he was on drugs, "Why get anything legitimately if you can get it by conning?"

When a user is on drugs, with deterrents cut off, the frequency of lying increases and is often more imaginative. The user has supreme confidence that whatever he says will be believed. Although *he* is certain that the lies he tells are persuasive, they often are not. Although the quantity of lying increases, the lies become more absurd as well as transparent. Furthermore, on drugs he is likely to tell different people varying stories about the same matter. Then he forgets what he said to whom. After the criminal stops using drugs, he may recognize how patently absurd it was to lie brazenly to people who knew him so well.

Because drugs reduce conscience factors and external fears, barriers to the expression of anger are lower. On drugs the criminal is more inclined to become accusatory. Smoldering anger bursts forth. The user tells others off and verbally pushes people around. However, if he believes that expressing anger will interfere with achieving an objective, he can easily cut off the anger and suppress its expression. Drugs may appear to reduce anger when the criminal is off in fantasy and appears serene. However, if that thinking is interrupted, the anger quickly returns.

ACTION: COMMISSION OF CRIME

Drugs may be used to perfect a criminal scheme or to put into operation a scheme that was already thought through. The following situation is typical of drug use before and after a crime.

> Among his other crimes D had a history of setting fires. Arrested for arson as a youngster, D was known to the police and the fire department as a "fire bug." Consequently he was extremely fearful of being apprehended for any future fire that he was innocent of but that he was near. Despite his intention to cease fire setting, D had recurrent thoughts about setting a large fire. This thinking was deterred repeatedly over a five-month period, but it never disappeared. D had a large supply of a tranquilizer acquired through a doctor's prescription. At one time he was taking several of these a day. Having found that he could get high on the drug, D hoarded the tablets and had the prescription refilled several

times, lying about his need for it. Whenever he ingested a large dose of the drug, the thinking about fire-setting intensified. One day he thought about setting an enormous blaze at work. He realized that he might be an immediate suspect if the fire department and police were summoned. Yet the more he schemed and the more he thought about the fire while on drugs, the more remote the personal risk seemed. On the day when he set the fire, he had used a large amount of the drug in the afternoon. (By this time he was taking as many as fifteen pills a day.) D decided to set the fire at work and began checking out rooms to determine where the most spectacular blaze could be set. He was carrying out his duties at work normally, and no one noticed anything extraordinary in his demeanor or performance. By 4 P.M. he had selected the site. As the hours went by, he became increasingly certain that he had taken all precautions. In fact, he planned to be close to the scene to offer the firemen assistance. He thought that even if he were caught, there would be no tangible evidence, and he planned in some detail how he would handle an interrogation, never really believing that it would come to that. At 5:30 P.M. he set the fire.

Immediately after setting the fire, D experienced regret. He eradicated any remorse by using more of the drug and went home. Then he began thinking about setting another fire. Certain that whatever spot he chose would be safe, D set his next blaze at home. He was not charged with either fire, but later D developed a set of excuses in case he was apprehended. He would claim with respect to the first that he was driven to desperation by pressure, unfair treatment, and poor conditions at work. Yet D acknowledged to us that he had wanted to retain his job, had been given reasonable autonomy and authority, was well thought of by his supervisor, and was permitted to earn extra income by working overtime. His justification for the fire at home would have been anger at his parents, but D acknowledged to us that their treatment of him had nothing to do with the crime. He would have set the fire any place that he happened to be.

Our discussion in this chapter is applicable not only to arson but also to other crimes. The mental processes referred to are the same as those described in detail in Chapter 6 of Volume I. Our emphasis here is on the role of drugs as facilitators of thought and action patterns that result in crime.

Most users prefer to commit crimes without relying on drugs. With drugs there is a price to pay. There is the money, time, and energy spent locating a source and then making the purchase. There are risks of apprehension in purchasing, possessing, and using certain drugs. Then, there is the uncertainty as to the quality of what one has purchased and the physical risks that drug use entails. Users are also aware that drugs may reduce their efficiency and impair their judgment in crime. The criminal who uses drugs sporadically (the "chipper") uses them only for something major that he otherwise is too fearful to undertake.

ELIMINATION OF DETERRENTS

The two external deterrents to crime are the possibility of getting caught and the possibility of being injured or killed. One user noted, "Drugs knock off your caution." On drugs, the criminal has an inflated view of his proficiency and is certain that he can get away with whatever he has in mind. Sometimes his behavior approaches what would appear to an observer to be careless disregard. One user said that upon sighting a policeman near the scene of a crime that he was about to commit, his thinking was, "I know that I can get arrested, but I just don't give a damn." Actually the user does "give a damn," as demonstrated by his taking certain precautions (although they are often insufficient).

Conscience factors, or internal deterrents, are also eliminated by drug use. The values, ideals, and sentiments that the user professes are temporarily dispensed with. A particularly striking illustration of this occurs in the drug user who hears the "voice of conscience" in the form of a nonpsychotic hallucinatory deterrent. As we explained in Chapter 6 of Volume I, some criminals hear a voice addressing them momentarily when they are about to commit a crime. The voice is not a manifestation of psychosis, but a backlash of conscience urging the criminal to refrain from crime. The criminal remains in touch with reality. The voice assumes different forms, including that of a parent or a supernatural being. It is a deterrent emanating from conscience and is present more in the drug user than in the criminal nonuser. In fact, almost every one of our drug-using criminals has reported that he has heard such a voice. However, drugs weaken or totally knock out this internal deterrent.

> D said that whenever he was about to commit a crime, he heard a voice that was somewhere between a child's and a woman's voice. It said, "Don't do it. It's wrong." With drugs the voice was weaker, and he could more easily disregard it and proceed with the crime.

The drug user acknowledges that these voices are on the side of "good" and offer him guidance that he should heed. One man said that with drugs in him the voice vanished and he "lost a friend."

Once he has drugs in him, whatever fears remain give way to superoptimism. Drugs boost the user's sense of being in total control so that uncertainties of life fade. He regards himself as special—a person with the competence to succeed at anything. He is superoptimistic both about the success of any prospective criminal enterprise and about controlling his own drug use. He is equally certain that he will avoid apprehension for the possession or sale of drugs. The user understands the possibility that he might get caught someday for breaking the law. However, with drugs deterrents are eliminated, and scheming is facilitated so that he is certain that *this* time he will not get caught. With the user in this superoptimistic state the crime becomes a *fait accompli*. In his thinking he has already distributed the proceeds of the crime. His experience supports this thinking. He has used drugs in the past without being apprehended, and he has gotten away with many crimes.

The disadvantage resulting from superoptimism under drugs is that the user is so certain of success that he is less observant of the environment. He is not as vigilant in checking for evidence of surveillance as he otherwise might be. He may neglect to check out details of the security at the proposed site of the crime. Depending on how much of the drug he has had, the user may be superoptimistic to the point of being reckless.

> While using heroin, D became more and more audacious in his M.O. He had been stealing from the store where he was employed, but under drugs he began, in broad daylight, to carry out large bolts of cloth and put them into his car. Without drugs he would have been more discrete as to the time and means of his theft.

Another hazard of superoptimism on drugs is that the user may be less skillful in executing the crime because his judgment and coordination are impaired.

> D had had a series of arguments with his wife. On drugs he obtained a revolver and approached her, ready to shoot. Rather than provoke him, his wife remained calm. D backed away and fell down two flights of stairs.

On drugs the superoptimistic user may not operate as quickly as he needs to. One user observed about himself, "With drugs, I'm not in too much of a hurry."

Although drugs are necessary to minimize deterrent considerations, they do not always eliminate fear during the actual execution of a crime. A residue of fear may reemerge, and the user once again is afraid of getting caught. This fear makes him just that much more cautious. However, if the fears concurrent with the crime are too intense, they substantially diminish the excitement. To deal with a strong reemergence of fear, the user may use more drugs and thereby increase his excitement during and after the crime.

The user in a daily grind of crime establishes a cycle in which his appetite for excitement grows and he undertakes bigger crimes. If he is to execute these, he has to overcome even greater fears. This requires more drugs, and consequently there is mounting danger that he will be less careful.

> D had intended to remain a sneak thief, engaging in petty larceny, because he figured that if he were caught the penalty would be light. However, petty larceny lost its impact, and D's thievery expanded from shoplifting small items to stealing large sums of money wherever he could find them, such as from a temporarily untended cash register. As D became more daring, he used more drugs. He realized that as he was running greater risks, he was also losing his "finesse." One day he walked from one part of the city to another, conspicuously carrying a bag of stolen proceeds in his arms. He did so with a sense of total immunity from apprehension. Out of jail less than a month from a previous conviction, D was arrested. By the time this occurred, even other criminals did not want to associate with him because they regarded him as lacking in judgment.

A user like D is in constant danger of arrest not only for the crimes he commits but also for everything related to drug use—purchase, possession, usage, or sales. He associates with people who would betray him at any time to save themselves or to further their own objectives.

The drug user aims for "big scores," but rarely succeeds in achieving them. Consequently, he may be short of the money required for drugs and decides to "knock off little jobs." Most users obtain proceeds from crime in excess of what they need to continue drug use.

> D had been using amphetamines over a period of several days. An incident occurred in which a man pulled a knife on D's stepfather. Resolving to get even, D tried to follow the man, but lost him. He then went to a bar committed crimes from which he obtained more money and then used that money for drugs. The drugs permitted him to commit more daring crimes.

To an observer it would have appeared that D was stealing to support his habit. The fact is that he had plenty of money. What mattered to him was the criminal excitement that drugs facilitated. Of course, the drug user may be without money because he has lived lavishly. The money that he has is squandered on big cars, elaborate wardrobes, parties, gifts, and women. But he is not destitute simply because he has had to spend money for drugs.*

*Some drug-using criminals do not have the resources to live in an extravagant manner. This is because they are petty criminals who lack the "heart" to do things in a big way.

Some users assert that when the day comes that they give up drugs, they will also give up crime. However, this has not been the case. Even though some users do give up drugs later in life, their criminal output continues, although at a reduced level. This is because the desire for criminal excitement has been foremost all along.

THE DRUG USER AND VIOLENCE

Numerous statements in the professional literature contend that certain drugs, notably opiates, marijuana, and barbiturates, suppress violence. We have found that whether a user is violent has very little to do with his choice of a particular drug. What is important is the makeup of the user and not the drug. Thus, a person may commit a violent act while on virtually any drug.*

The drug-using criminal without drugs is more afraid of committing a violent act than the criminal who is a nonuser. Even though violence is recurrent in his thinking, he is tremendously frightened by the prospect of being injured. But drugs reduce fears and bring out what is present. Restraints are fewer in the forceful exercise of power and control. One user commented, "Without heroin, I would ignore a slap; under drugs I would not hesitate to commit murder for the same offense." On drugs the user is more likely to go on the offensive and resort to needless, and often reckless, acts of violence. Some routinely carry weapons, but without drugs they do not use them. Only when on drugs do they use a weapon to intimidate or assault a person.

D had been using amphetamines over a period of several days. An incident occurred in which a man pulled a knife on D's stepfather. Resolving to get even, D tried to follow the man, but lost him. He then went to a bar that employed a go-go dancer whom he knew. He selected a record for her to dance to, but she rejected his choice. He asked her whether she had trouble dancing to it. At this point, a man who claimed to be her husband approached him and asked defiantly, "Why don't you dance to it?" Undaunted D selected the same record on the jukebox and drew his gun, this time ordering his accoster to dance to it. A fight ensued, in which he beat the man on the head with the gun and left him badly injured. Loaded with amphetamines, D's mind was racing about what to do next. He had committed many felonies and suspected that it might not be long until the police apprehended him. So he drove to his mother's house and picked up an overnight bag and a sawed-off shotgun. He decided to commit an act that would really give people something to talk about. After buying and

---

*Fiddle (1967, p. 138) quoted a drug user's expression of astonishment at the fact that tuinol had an effect directly opposite to that which he had anticipated: "Goofballs [tuinol] is supposed to be like a sedative that's supposed to put you to sleep, but it doesn't. . . . It would make me like a wild man."

drinking some beer, D went to a hospital, shot out the windows, broke into the building, and held the police at bay before finally surrendering.*

As D talked with us later about this series of events, he stated that he was totally in control of his behavior. He said that drugs gave him the courage to do what he wanted – to draw his gun in the bar and to engage in the sensational series of events at the hospital.

Another criminal drug user related how his thinking expanded on LSD so that he seriously entertained the idea of killing his parents and later did so. In confinement he acquired more LSD, and homicidal thinking again occurred.

D had been in conflict with his parents most of his life. He opposed their expectations and restrictions, and regarded their lives as superficial and boring. His hatred for his parents was intense. D had used a variety of drugs, but preferred LSD because it gave him the highest high. On one occasion of LSD use, he thought seriously for the first time of how to go about killing his father and mother. A period ensued during which he restricted his drug use to marijuana. Thinking about the homicide continued and deterrents weakened. Finally, at a time when he was again on LSD, he obtained a shotgun and murdered his parents. He was eventually adjudged not guilty by reason of insanity. On the hospital ward, having obtained LSD, he thought again about killing. This time the fantasied targets were his two brothers and the ward doctor, all of whom he professed to hate. This thinking continued until after the drug wore off. D observed of this experience: "While under the influence of LSD I thought about knocking off my two brothers and a doctor. However, when the drug wore off, I changed my mind. My conscience told me that I couldn't get away with it. But while I was under the drug's influence, I relished the idea."†

The desire to kill his parents did not spring *de novo* from the drugs. Rather there had been a long history of discord. In his thinking D had eliminated his parents from his life many times but had not actually planned the details of a homicide. With LSD he seriously considered what he was too frightened to think about without the drug.

---

*D was brought to trial and found to be mentally ill. At that time, he never served a sentence for any of the crimes for which he was wanted, but spent a relatively brief period confined in a psychiatric institution.

†It is interesting to note that D's illicit drug use in the hospital was discovered when he turned up the volume of the rock music to which he was listening so high that it drew the attention of the ward staff. Staff members came to D's room and noted his dreamy, distant appearance. This is yet another example of what we referred to above – the user's insufficient precautions when under drugs.

Drug users who have committed homicide while on drugs have expressed their doubt that they would have done so in a drug-free state. The central point, as expressed by one drug user, is that "anything you have in mind before you use drugs, you will be able to do after." Whereas drug users have particular preferences in their selection of drugs, any drug can facilitate violent thinking and action. The personality and predisposition of the drug user are the critical elements.

THE AFTERMATH OF THE CRIME

After a drug user has committed a crime, there is likely to be a resurgence of fear. Was he seen? Was he followed? Did he leave any evidence? Who might inform? There may be a return of conscience and self-recriminations. The user may worry about how he has disappointed his family and betrayed people who trusted him. The bigger the crime, the greater the worry. These fears limit the excitement of the crime's aftermath.

The user is dismayed when he perceives himself as unsuccessful in the crime. He may have counted on stealing $10,000, but only obtained $50 because he arrived at a store after the day's receipts had been deposited in the bank. There is a letdown from superoptimism and excitement as he faces the reality of his lack of accomplishment. Temporarily his evaluation of himself is lowered. More drugs obliterate his failure, remove an impending sense of worthlessness, and eliminate fears related to conscience and the possibility of arrest.

If he has been successful in his enterprise, the user wants to prolong the excitement and savor the triumph. To celebrate his success, he uses more drugs, not only to combat any fears that reemerge but also to facilitate additional exciting enterprises. More drugs may be used for the celebration than before or during the crime. Large amounts of a drug produce nodding or the further enjoyment of criminal fantasy. The user may be satisfied to retreat into such fantasy. He may play the big shot, giving away the proceeds, spending them lavishly on others, and sometimes giving away drugs.* By conducting himself in this way, the user not only builds himself up but obligates others. He swaggers about, boasting of his accomplishments. With every telling, he exaggerates the risks of the crime, the obstacles he overcame, the magnitude of the proceeds, the dangers of the getaway. With enough drugs in him, the user may be indiscriminate about whom he boasts to, thereby revealing himself to an informer or being overheard by someone who later "snitches." For many the major part of the celebration, and the main reason for drug use, is the

---

*As we pointed out in Chapter 6 of Volume I, the criminal often steals what he does not need or value. It is the excitement of the act rather than the proceeds that is paramount — the physical overpowering or the conning of a victim rather than the amount of money or value of the property extracted.

prospect of exciting sexual activity (see next section). No matter what form the celebration takes, the criminal drug user remains eager for more conquests and excitement. Thus he may move rapidly from one crime to another, using more drugs in the process.

The drug user is more likely to be arrested when on drugs than when he is not using them. Still, as is the case with criminals generally, he gets away with far more than is ever known to the authorities. When he is apprehended, it is often due to recklessness. In retrospect he sees himself as having been stupid with respect to poor operating procedure.

> D had committed more than three dozen breaking and entries in a six-week period. The only time that he was arrested, he was on drugs.

> D was using massive amounts of drugs at the time he committed a theft. He spotted a police car. Instead of trying to escape, he walked straight toward the vehicle. Because of his suspicious behavior, D was questioned by the police, who then found pills on him and arrested him on a drug charge.

Some users are so emboldened on drugs that they resist arrest, thus incurring additional charges.

> D was arrested as a pickpocket. He then began to assault the police officer. Later, after he was booked, it was discovered that he was on drugs. Charges were pressed not only for picking pockets but also for assaulting an officer and possession of drugs.

When held accountable, the drug user functions in the same manner whether or not he is on drugs at the time.* He plays cat and mouse with the interrogator, sizing him up and feeding him whatever the drug user thinks will work to his advantage. If he is on drugs, he is more facile in his lying, but less credible.

DRUGS AS POTENTIATORS OF SEXUAL PERFORMANCE

The role of drugs in enhancing sexual thinking and activity is one of the most prominent aspects of our findings. Criminals did not decide to use drugs initially for reasons related to sexuality. It was only after using drugs that users discovered that their sexual performance was enhanced. Some criminals then continued drug use only because of its positive impact on their sexual lives.

---

*For the psychology of accountability, see Chapter 6 of Volume I.

The criminal drug user assesses his stature as a man by his sexual conquests. The professional literature has not adequately taken into account the central place of sex in the criminal's drug use. Discussion of sexuality is mainly in terms of whether drug use potentiates or suppresses sexual drive and extent of activity. For example, literature on opiates reflects the point of view that this class of drugs reduces sexual drive. Wortis (1959, p. 178) observed that "opiates calm the user, create a pleasant dreamy state, and depress sexual drive." Rada (1975) cites evidence that "hard drug use does not predispose to the commission of sexual crimes but may, in fact, diminish sexual behavior and experience." We have found that this is usually not the case. The literature contains little information about the user's thinking about himself and his fantasized or actual partners. The exploitative aspect of the user's sexual activity is mentioned even less in the literature, except for street narratives of prostitutes and their pimps.

The criminal user's approach to a sexual conquest is quite similar to his approach to robbing a bank. There is the scheming, the careful working out of an M.O. (a *Modus Operandi*), the conquest, and the celebration. (One user even referred to his women during his celebrations as his "psychological Rolls Royce.") In this section we describe in detail the role that drugs play in the user's sexual life.*

THOUGHT AND TALK

The user's thinking about a sex partner is similar to his other criminal thinking.† He conjures up a fantasy of a potential partner or creates a fantasy about someone whom he already knows. He realizes that with drugs he will find sexual thinking and activity more exciting. When the user thinks about sex, he automatically thinks about drugs and vice versa. The two become practically synonymous.

In the user's mind, anyone attractive to him is a potential partner, whether or not he knows the person. The user can, of course, engage in sexual thinking without drugs, but drugs permit him to prolong that thinking, savor it, and elaborate on it. A common fantasy is to be surrounded by a harem that grants his every whim. Drugs facilitate thinking not only about the impossible, but also thinking about the possible.

Seated at a restaurant, D spotted an attractive young woman. Later he made her the subject of a fantasy, but the fantasy had little impact. After smoking marijuana, D had a very elaborate fantasy about this same woman. He thought about meeting her and giving her a potent alcoholic

---

*For more detail on the criminal's sexual life, see Chapters 3 and 4 of Volume I.

†The concepts here apply equally to heterosexual and homosexual pairings.

drink. The fantasy continued with his taking her to a deserted area where she then became incapacitated and her judgment was impaired. He then fantasized about undressing and exhibiting himself to her, and engaging in a variety of sexual activities.

In contrast to the earlier unstimulating fantasy when he was not on drugs, the fantasy when he was on drugs was highly charged. On drugs, fantasy is more vivid and immediate. The user cuts off the awareness that it is only a fantasy and becomes involved in it, not permitting the intrusion of reality to lessen the impact. Even if he is confined with no immediate sexual prospect, he need not be lonely. Aided by drugs, he is, in his thinking, the center of attraction, with partners able and willing to serve him. With a real partner he may have a fifty-fifty chance of having his way, but in fantasy there is 100 percent certainty that whatever he wants will be granted. He imagines himself to be the greatest lover in the world. One fellow on drugs regarded himself as unique in his sexual prowess and highly sought after as a partner. His estimation of himself was "I can ball a girl like nobody ever balled her."

During the drug user's prolonged fantasy, fears surrounding actual sexual performance are cut off. There is less hesitation than usual about approaching a partner. In his thinking, anyone is his for the taking. He is irresistible, and his prospective partner is lucky to have him. He is not beset with doubts about his physical makeup, notably genital endowment. He no longer fears ridicule or criticism of performance. He does not fret about prematurity, impotence, or disease.

The drug user considers almost anyone a prospective partner and entertains ideas about various types of sexual contacts such as rape, homosexuality, or child molestation that without drugs were abhorrent. He may fantasize violating his own standards by having sex with a woman whom he previously has regarded as untouchable or with someone toward whom he has been very sentimental.

> "You see, I have always had this thing about my penis being smaller than other people's. However, when I took LSD, it seemed more like normal. In fact, it was bigger than normal. When I took LSD, the things I had hesitated to do, the things I was afraid to do became possible. Often I have wanted to experience the excitement of raping without being under the influence of drugs, but I was so conscious of the smallness of my penis that without drugs I just didn't have the nerve."

Once D used drugs, many fears vanished. Not only did he think about rape, but he actually committed scores of rapes, every one of them when he was on drugs, usually something other than LSD.

Just as he brags about crime while on drugs, so the user exaggerates in narratives of his sexual exploits. Rarely is there anything approaching a true recapitulation of what transpired. Instead, boasting and lying are all in the interest of a self-buildup. Talk about sex is more exciting when the user is on drugs. His themes are the acquisition of a partner, the conquest, his sexual prowess and versatility, his exploitation of the partner, and his attempts to use the partner as an accomplice in crime.

SEXUAL ACTIVITY

It is the sexual potentiation that makes drug use worthwhile for many criminals. For the drug-using criminal, sex without drugs has little impact. Some users are poor performers without drugs and are ashamed of impotence or premature ejaculation. Several mentioned masturbating before a sexual encounter, because they were fearful of being premature without drugs. Because manhood and sexuality are regarded as synonymous, it is not surprising to hear a user say, "Without drugs, I was half a man."

> Without drugs D suffered from premature ejaculation. About to meet a woman who he knew was eager for sex, he tried to obtain heroin, but without success. Instead, he consumed a large portion of a quart of whiskey. He was a total failure in bed, but he persuaded his partner to try again. With two or three thrusts, he had an orgasm. Crestfallen that the alcohol did not bring him up to snuff, he thought, "my prick betrayed me." The woman was resentful because she had heard that D was a remarkable performer. This reputation was based on his performance when he used heroin.

Some drug users, like D, are less than competent without drugs. Yet many who are regarded as competent by their partners see themselves as insufficient.

> D described sex with his girl friend when he had not taken drugs. There was foreplay for a half hour, and he had no trouble getting an erection. He produced an orgasm in her, and after being restimulated by her, he reentered. She experienced orgasm twice more, and he had an ejaculation. D said that the experience was "dead," and he thought that he had performed poorly. Yet his partner told him how good he had been and compared him favorably with her former husband.

D told us that the whole experience lacked "voltage," that during it his mind was a blank. On drugs, however, he had the power to go on and on. The drug user's standard of his own adequacy is the same in his sexual life as it is else-where. He must be unique in his performance in that he is the best — the best lover who holds an erection the longest and pleases his partner the most. The buildup is critical; the user wants to be a sexual King Kong and have his part-ner admire him. He aspires to provide her with an incomparable experience. Evaluating himself against such a standard causes most of his experiences without drugs to result in disappointment and anger. On drugs he is more likely to achieve the supremacy that he seeks.

The M.O. varies in sex as it does in crime. The objective is to dominate the partner, whether through flattery and conning or through coercion. A drug user described his thinking about rape when he used LSD:

> "I thought about rape a lot. When I would take off on LSD, I would see the telephone poles as giant penises. Women seemed to be naked all around me, and I would imagine how it would be to grab them and rape them. I was walking down the street and this woman was in front of me. I had undressed her, and she was naked. I approached her from the rear where her ass was bouncing up and down and was just about to grab the cheeks of her ass when she turned around and startled me. I ran away."

This thinking was later translated into action, again at a time when this man was on drugs. "Another time I was in the swimming pool, and I would look in the water, and everybody seemed naked. The girls excited me, so I waited in the parking lot, and when this particular girl came out, I raped her at knifepoint in the back of a car." The criminal under drugs becomes increas-ingly brash in the sexual acts that he undertakes. As in other crimes he takes chances when on drugs that otherwise he would not take.

> Throughout his two marriages, D's rape pattern persisted. He never committed a rape without drugs. The bigger the challenge, the greater the excitement. Drugs allowed him to approach a female with absolute cer-tainty that he would have her for sex. He regarded himself as irresistible and the woman as wanting him. Usually he used only liquor to reduce his fears. He was discreet as to where and how he operated. He would be by himself and make his approach through conning. However, on one occa-sion, D had used barbiturates, amphetamines, and alcohol in combina-tion, and he departed from his usual pattern. He threatened a stranger as she left a function that she was attending and made her drive him to her apartment, forced his way in, and demanded sex. She began screaming, and that led to his apprehension.

Violent sex is not the only M.O. facilitated by drugs. The con man becomes slicker; he thinks of elaborate ways to entice and seduce a prospective partner and then is bolder about it than he would be without drugs.

The total domination of his partner is the chief aim of both the heterosexual and the homosexual drug-using criminal. The desire for total conquest overshadows the importance of the physical experience. On drugs the user may be more successful in persuading his partner to do what she might otherwise reject. He may convince her to use drugs in the hope that she will be receptive to a greater variety of sexual activities. He does not particularly care about what kind of sex they have, but surmounting her objections to a specific form of sexual activity is a triumph. In addition, his own objections to particular sexual activities may be overcome when he is on drugs.

> D was a homosexual prostitute, but did not like to assume the "female position" (being the receiver of his partner's penis) in anal intercourse. However, when he used heroin, this was no problem for him. "Playing the woman" was expedient to becoming quite the "man," as he later extracted money and favors from his partner.

Whether or not he is on drugs, if the drug user does something that he is later ashamed of, he can always resort to using a drug to rid himself of conscience.

> D exhibited himself to a young woman. Afterward he was filled with recriminations, but then a half hour after the event he shot some heroin. Anxiety was eliminated, and he slept peacefully.

Thus, in sexual offenses as in other crimes, the user resorts to drugs to deal with consequences of his own irresponsibility, whether it be the fear of apprehension or a bothersome conscience.

The professional literature is filled with statements that heroin diminishes sexual interest. Users in our study claim the opposite. They maintain that when they are on heroin they hold erections from one to sixteen hours. While the latter figure is undoubtedly an exaggeration, most claim that erections last several hours, enabling them to acquire a reputation as inexhaustible lovers. The heightened erectility occurs mainly with heroin, but it has been reported with amphetamines, liquor, and marijuana. Some rub cocaine on the penis to experience a "freeze." This drug, known for its anesthetic properties, is used to desensitize the penis. Some users report applying cocaine to their partner's clitoris to prolong cunnilingus.

With longer periods of erectility on drugs, the user indulges in long and elaborate fantasies during bouts of sexual activity. This further enhances his control over orgasm and permits him to bring his partner to a pitch of extreme excitement. In speaking of a marathon sexual experience while he was on heroin, one user commented, "I felt like Hercules."

Although erection is prolonged, it is often at the expense of ejaculation, especially with heroin use. The amphetamine user has better control of ejaculation. The user chooses his drug according to what he wants. Some equate their sexual prowess solely with how long they maintain an erection, and so ejaculation is unimportant. It is the status in the eyes of the partner that matters. The drug user offers himself to his partner for self-aggrandizement. This may be to achieve recognition as a great lover or to exploit the partner later for money, material goods, or other favors. Actually the drug user is functioning as a prostitute, but does not regard himself in that way.

A drug-using criminal may charm a responsible woman into having a sexual relationship with him. This occurs when she is unaware of his criminal background or, if aware, believes that she can reform him. The following describes the performance of a man with a long-standing pattern of drug use, who was not using drugs during a period when he was trying to convince his girlfriend that he was responsible.

> D met his girlfriend when she was through with work for the day. They went to a poetry reading and then to her apartment. They played chess, but D observed that she was inattentive and not in the mood for this. So they lay down on the bed. There was body play and they removed their clothes. D maintained an erection for 15 minutes, but then suddenly felt tired. Without ejaculating, he withdrew and was disinclined to try again.

In speaking with us, D compared this occasion with experiences he had had with irresponsible women while he was on drugs, during which his erection lasted for hours, producing multiple orgasms in his partners and winning their praise and admiration for his staying power. Whether or not a drug user like D is on drugs, sex with his wife or with any other responsible woman is of little interest because it lacks the excitement of the forbidden. Even when he has sex available in a consenting relationship with a responsible person, he seeks other outlets.

On drugs the user is far less discriminating in the choice of a partner than he otherwise would be. When off drugs he is contemptuous of some of the partners whom he selects when on drugs. The drug user has no difficulty in finding females who are irresponsible and are attracted to him.* Some of these women have sexual problems. Those who are frigid especially value prolonged sexual activity. So do those who are homosexual and require a long period of stimulation, during which they engage in homosexual fantasy in order to reach orgasm.

*We have interviewed some of the women with whom criminals in our study associated.

The drug user sometimes endures discomfort and fatigue while engaging in sex for a long time without reaching orgasm. He may admit that he finds these sexual marathons boring. Pleasing his partner is not the drug user's central concern; that is merely a means to an end. By satisfying his partner, the user obtains reinforcement of the belief that he is number one. In addition, he is in a more advantageous position to extract favors later. He may have sex to obtain money for other things, including drugs, from partners who know that sex will be better for them if the drug user is on drugs. He may move in with a partner, expecting her to be his servant. Because his associates are generally irresponsible, he sometimes succeeds in enlisting a partner in the commission of crimes, including buying and selling drugs. If she is already a drug user, he makes drugs available and may introduce her to a new substance. She is using him, however, as well as being used by him. Not only is she having sex, but she may also demand and obtain money, clothes, and lavish presents. More important, she shares the excitement of his criminal life.* Each partner prostitutes himself or herself. Each obtains what is valued and gives away what is worthless. Of course, neither believes that he is prostituting himself, and each believes that he is in control.

The finding that certain drugs reduce sex drive and hamper performance does have a basis. As the user increases the amount of the drug he takes, he reaches a point where he is no longer interested in sex. The elimination of interest is a direct consequence of high doses of drugs. Such a state of affairs is not easily accepted by men who consider themselves sexual King Kongs. When they are on high doses, some regulate drug use so that sexual interest is not totally diminished.

> On drugs D could maintain an erection for several hours. This brought him the approval of women and boosted his image of himself as a man. But there came a time when he was using such high doses of heroin that his interest in sex waned and he ceased sexual activity. D then decided to time his sexual activity so that it occurred many hours after heroin use. He used heroin at 7 P.M. and had sex early the next morning. He eliminated the 11 P.M. injection because he knew that more drugs would obliterate his sexual drive. Taking these precautions resulted in competence in sexual performance.

In such situations the user estimates the point at which he has had an optimal dose.

Some users become so distraught over waning sexual interest or competence when they are on high doses of heroin that they go through withdrawal

---

*If the drug user's partner is truly a responsible person, she not only shuns crime and tries to reform him but eventually severs all ties with him.

"to get my sex back." Some do this on their own, and some seek treatment to withdraw from the drug. Others who regard sex as something of an ordeal are temporarily relieved. When they are on heavy doses of drugs, the entire problem of sexual adequacy is eliminated. The pursuit of power is then manifested in other enterprises, and the user does not regard himself as less than a man.

In some instances, when sexual performance is unsatisfactory, the drug user resorts to extreme measures to assert his manhood. It is then that barriers to violence fall.

> Having consumed six ounces of liquor within an hour, D found that he was able to obtain an erection, which he had had trouble doing earlier. But when he consumed as much as a pint, erectility and interest both declined, and his sexual competence was markedly reduced. Even though sexual interest was less, his desire to prove himself increased, and he committed crimes in which he assaulted, choked, and mutilated women, in several instances masturbating on their bodies or raping them.

Alcohol did not cause the violence. But with conscience and fears of apprehension removed, there were fewer barriers to D's demonstrating, in the face of his faltering sexual performance, that he was still a man.

At times it is convenient to blame drugs for his lack of interest in sex. If he wants to discontinue a relationship with a woman, he may do this. Or when he cannot perform competently because he is on high doses of drugs, he tells himself, "horse [heroin] is my sex." He still believes that he retains his great sexual capacity, but that it is temporarily knocked out by the drugs. In short, the user blames a lack of interest in sex on drugs but also attributes heightened interest in sex to drugs. Both are viable positions, depending on what he wants and how much of a drug he is using.

DRUGS AS FACILITATORS OF CRIMINAL EQUIVALENTS

A criminal equivalent is a criminal's self-serving and usually exploitative search for power that does not violate the law.* Although his objectives may appear socially acceptable, he is trying to control other people for his own self-aggrandizement. Criminal equivalents may be concurrent with crime, or

---

*Criminal equivalents are discussed in Chapter 7 of Volume I. We quote from part of that chapter here:

> A criminal who is not thrusting for power through crime may be doing it in other ways. . . . When we speak of a "criminal equivalent," we are referring to an action or series of actions in which a criminal seeks *power for its own sake*. Wherever the criminal is—at home, at school, at work, on the street—he seeks to promote himself, usually at the expense of others. (pp. 459, 460)

they may be expressed during a phase when the criminal is not arrestable. Hundreds of times a day criminal equivalents are expressed in the simplest of transactions, and they afford as much excitement at the time as would a violation of the law. Because on the surface the activity itself often appears responsible, a careful probing of the person's thinking is necessary to discern whether the behavior in question is truly of a criminal nature. For example, the criminal is adept at gaining a forum and attracting listeners. Obviously nothing is irresponsible about a person's making a speech in support of a legitimate cause. It is only when one knows the criminal's mental state at the time that it becomes clear that the high from being the expert and center of attention overrides in importance the message he is bearing or the significance of the cause for which he is working. Later he may misuse any recognition he obtains to exploit others. The excitement generated by criminal equivalents does not satisfy the criminal for long, so he eventually goes to the forbidden and commits crimes.

Drugs alter the user's view of himself. (We described aspects of this in our discussion of the high.) On drugs the user is in his "own little world," by which he means that he is a significant figure — unique, in charge, accountable to no one.* He expects to prevail and others to bow to his wishes.

The drug user may couch his inner experience in terms of euphoria by which he means increased confidence. One user said that on drugs "I feel better, like another kind of person." This "confidence" is the experience of being "ten feet tall" and able to thumb one's nose at the world.

> "LSD is a very powerful thing, and I'll probably take it again. On LSD you really believe what's going on . . . I remember walking on a street, and all of a sudden I was filled with joy and tremendous happiness. The only thing that I could say to someone was, well, I was twenty years old, I had long hair, and I was high on LSD."

The young man who said this was describing a state of mind in which he was a very special person. In this conversation he went on to reflect how absurd and foolish the rest of the world seemed to him.

On drugs the user's thinking is more pretentious than usual. He has vivid fantasies about being rich and famous — a business tycoon, a leading activist for social change, the foremost proponent of humanitarian ideals, a renowned philanthropist and, in general, being the top person in any enterprise. In his thinking, such objectives are not merely possibilities; they are

---

*Larner and Tefferteller (1964) quote a drug user who was discussing what his thinking was like under heroin: "Like you're your own boss . . . you ain't got no problems whatsoever, you think freely, you don't think about things you were thinking about before shooting up, like you're in your own world, nobody to bother you or nothing."

certainties if only he wills them. Education, skills, and experience do not matter. He believes not only that he is the best, but that he is entitled to the best.

> Shortly after leaving a party where he had been drinking, D smoked some marijuana. He then drove a woman and her daughter to their home in a part of the city that was considerably more fashionable than where he lived. D's thinking was that he *deserved* to live in such a place and should own a luxury car to fill its garage.

Drug-induced reality obscures daily reality. Thus a drug user thinks about owning a limousine, a recreational vehicle, and a yacht, even though he has no legitimate source of income. A responsible person may think about owning such objects, but he does not consider himself immediately entitled to them; he knows he must earn them. The drug user imagines himself as the owner, and the drug facilitates his "taking possession" through commission of a crime.

Under drugs the drug user is not self-critical. Every criminal believes that he is a decent human being, and drugs enhance this opinion. On drugs, his estimate of his capability and performance is greatly exaggerated. He is superoptimistic about everything he undertakes and is generally complacent about his own functioning. If he applies for a job, he is certain that he will be hired, even though such a conclusion is unwarranted by anything that has transpired. On drugs he believes that he has penetrating insights. One user, discussing this phenomenon, stated, "I can grasp a lot of things I don't think I would grasp without a lot of psychological work. I can solve a lot of my problems on pot."

When on drugs the user vastly overestimates the quality of his performance. His thinking is expansive, and he sees himself as doing a first-rate job. Yet a more objective evaluation nearly always reveals that he is doing a poor job.*

> Several musically talented users observed that on drugs they regarded their musical productions as superior. However, later when they were off drugs and listened to tapes of their performance, they were surprised to hear how poor it was and how their technique suffered.†

---

*In its second report, the National Commission on Marihuana and Drug Abuse (1973, p. 149) stated: "Drugs may also interfere with the user's perception of his own abilities. Some studies have noted that student amphetamine users tended to overestimate their capacity to make sound judgments and solve mathematical problems, and amphetamine-using soldiers tended to overestimate their performance in certain routine monotonous tasks."

†Walton (1938, p. 121) commented on the belief that marijuana use improves musical performance: "As judged by objectively critical means, the standards of performance are no doubt lowered."

While he was on drugs, D had written a short story which he regarded as a virtual masterpiece. Later, when he was not on drugs, D read what he had written and cringed. He termed it a "disaster" because it made no sense.

On drugs the user regards himself as incapable of error. He plows ahead with his "I don't give a damn" attitude. This inevitably results in carelessness and mistakes. By being above mundane cares, he habitually creates problems for himself.

D used a combination of different drugs. Although he was a meticulous worker at certain office duties, he mailed five letters in the wrong envelopes.

While under drugs D was painting a room. Normally he was an extremely careful painter and a perfectionist about the final job. However, on this job he underestimated the quantity of paint, missed painting the bottom of the doorpost, neglected to paint the electric switch plate, and left five blue smudges on the white ceiling.

When held accountable, the user does not shoulder the blame for his carelessness, but becomes angry and takes it out on someone else. The attitude of being above it all often has consequences far more serious than missent letters or an unsatisfactory paint job.

The user has extravagant and pretentious thinking about himself, and he believes that everyone else shares his perceptions. In his view, people stand in awe of his talents and accomplishments or at least of his potential to accomplish great things. Generally this belief is totally a self-deception in that responsible people really distrust or fear him. The user's misperceptions of others' reactions may come forcefully to his attention at his job. The criminal who uses drugs at work is likely to conform to requirements because he does not want to alienate others and lose the job. He may succeed at this for a while, but an attitude of not caring eventually manifests itself. He becomes domineering and irritable with co-workers. When he is taken to task, he is surprised and defensive because he has been unaware of how others have perceived him. Of course he then criticizes his critics and finds a variety of excuses for his performance.

On drugs the user chooses what he desires to experience excitement. In doing so, he skips over material that requires concentration, study, and reflection, thereby missing central themes. Sometimes there is a false sense of being well-informed. An extreme instance of this occurred in a drug user who read the comments on a dust jacket and then considered himself an expert on the contents of the entire book. The user may locate a passage that he regards

as profound, but when off drugs he is puzzled as to why he found it so meaningful. On drugs he is likely to ignore details, regarding them as unimportant.
He becomes intensely involved with books that he might not otherwise pick
up. One user who had contempt for science fiction decided when on drugs to
immerse himself in a science-fiction novel. He was fascinated by it and
identified with the powerful beings in the story who could do the impossible.

> When he was not using drugs, D was fond of reading poetry. He was ex-
> tremely intense in the way he went about this, poring over every line,
> striving in a perfectionistic manner to understand every symbol and
> grasp every allusion, as well as to fathom basic meanings. On drugs,
> however, he avoided reading poetry because it required too much
> concentration.

What we have said about the choice of reading material and the approach to
reading is also true of the user's television and film watching. If he is on
drugs, he is most likely to view only programs that promise excitement and
will stimulate fantasy. Watching television or a movie while on drugs, he is
excited by the wheeling and dealing or outright violent actions performed by
people in positions of power.

> Without drugs D found Western movies very dull. On drugs, he found
> himself identifying with the fast gunslinger. Whether the guy who was
> quick on the trigger was on the side of good or evil made no difference to
> him.

> When D read the newspapers, he customarily covered a variety of arti-
> cles. While on drugs he concentrated on the crime and corruption stories.
> He imagined himself to be on the side of either the cops or the robbers de-
> pending on which aspect of the story seemed most exciting.

Drug users claim that drugs enhance their appreciation of music. Although
the music is said to be psychedelic, it is not the music that expands the user's
thinking, but the drugs that he has used as he retreats into fantasy with the
music in the background. The greater enjoyment and appreciation is less of
the music than it is of the attendant fantasy.

Since the 1960s, a controversy has swirled around the issue of whether certain rock music promotes drug use. It was said, for example, that the Beatles'
song "Lucy in the Sky with Diamonds" is about an LSD-induced fantasy. It
does not promote anything in the responsible person except enjoyment of the
music and perhaps pleasant images if one stops to think about the lyrics. It
would not occur to many that the song has anything to do with drugs. The

drug user may enjoy the melody and the lyrics, but of overriding significance is the quality of his thinking as he is listening. While he is on drugs, he listens to music and expands his thinking into fantasies, some of which are later expressed in criminal equivalents and, ultimately, violation. For more than two decades the controversy has persisted as to whether listening to certain rock music *causes* drug use. Millions of youths listen to this music, but only a minority use drugs. It is unlikely that anyone becomes a drug user merely because he is a rock music devotee.

Drug users have claimed that on drugs they are more sociable. The user may indeed be more outgoing, but the quantity of talk is less important than the attitude displayed. He becomes less reluctant to assert himself, and he attempts to dominate a conversation. He cares less about what he says than to whom he says it. Associating with others who, like him, are irresponsible, he brags about his accomplishments, past and projected. Constantly, he indulges in verbal "oneupmanship." When we interviewed criminals while they were on drugs, we found that they were more evasive, less truthful, less receptive to us, and played more games than when they were off drugs. These qualities permeate their interactions with others.

The user's sociability often takes the form of holding forth as the expert. In one-to-one discourse or at a party, the user acts as though he is the authority on any topic that arises. A number of our drug users have recounted how on drugs they have been "supercharged" with energy and filled many hours discussing what they considered profound issues, viewing themselves as fonts of wisdom. Conversation about drugs is a favorite topic. Especially if he is on drugs, the user glamorizes drug use and offers long accounts of what he considers to be his own unique experiences. If he has not elected to retreat into fantasy, the drug user dominates a group, and if the group is composed entirely of drug users, competition among them for the spotlight is keen. Even the user's sense of humor contains elements of criminal equivalents in that laughter is invariably at the expense of another person who is made to look foolish.

DRUGS AS FACILITATORS OF RELIGIOUS EXPERIENCE

Nearly all our drug users were exposed to organized religion as children and have gone through periods in their lives when religious interest was again evoked. By "religious experience" we refer not only to attendance at services and belief in God but also to an attempt to live a life of purity. Some drug users have been monastic at times without invoking a supreme being. This monasticism is an attempt, no matter how brief, at self-reform in which the drug user concentrates on the spiritual, repents for sin, and disavows materialism. He does not use drugs during such a phase. Although most drug users have had such periods, they generally have been reluctant to discuss openly this dimension of their inner lives, regarding such expression as a sign of weakness.

For the criminal, religion is a set of concrete acts and thoughts compartmentalized from the rest of life.* Religious beliefs and practices, although they may be sincerely followed at the time, are not sustained, and thus monastic periods do not last.

It is characteristic of the criminal that he goes to extremes. In striving to be pure, he vows that his conduct will be beyond reproach. In trying to outshine all of humanity in virtue, he experiences a sense of power. He may approach others with missionary zeal, trying to convert them to his beliefs. In the process he promotes himself more than the message. Whether or not he makes his religious life public, such periods of monastic existence add to the drug user's belief that he is a good person and that he has absolved himself from wrongdoing. Eventually this phase comes to an end. Either the drug user concludes that he can never live up to the hypermoralistic standards he sets for himself and refuses to live in fear of failure, or else he becomes bored and turns to competing excitements.

Only on rare occasions have drug users in our study used drugs specifically to achieve a spiritual or religious state. When they do, restraints to religious expression are knocked out by drugs, just as deterrents to crime were previously eliminated. Some users report that on drugs they become humble and contrite. The most striking example of this is the religiosity that is so strongly expressed in a drug-induced psychosis discussed at the end of this chapter.

Drugs facilitate the user's approaching hell or heaven, depending on his mental state at the time.

> D decided to use LSD because he thought it would bring him closer to a state of goodness. He temporarily rejected his life of crime. He had the idea that if in his mortal state he went on a trip to heaven, he might find it easier to get into heaven later.

The desire for power during our users' religious experiences under drugs is prominent. They report not only that their world expands but also that they have a sense of being at the center of it. The experience is extraordinary and highly exciting. The user arrives at a powerful position in which he is at the hub of a limitless world. He believes he is at one with the universe and on a par with God.

He is excited by his belief that he is achieving insights into the nature of God, existence, and the universe that no one else has and that no one else can

---

*See Chapters 3, 4, and 7 of Volume I for discussion of the criminal's religiosity and monasticism.

possibly share. Some users attempt to communicate these insights to others with great passion.

While on drugs (but not in a monastic phase), the user may invoke God's blessing for an avowedly criminal act.* This allows him to remove the barrier of conscience and sometimes results in his committing extremely serious crimes. Without drugs he may have had fleeting thoughts about particular crimes; with drugs these ideas coalesce into the possible and immediate. Considering a crime within a religious framework further legitimizes it. Although he believes that he has God on his side, the user nevertheless maintains control over his own actions. He is the one who sought God's sanction. He knows that he was not directed by external forces. If he is later held accountable, he tells others that God instructed him and claims that his crime was "God's will." Some users fabricate hearing God's voice directing them to commit a crime. These are self-serving excuses. After a fashion, a user is being truthful if he says simply that he received God's approval because that is what he convinced himself of after he had already decided what he wanted to do. In a state of great spiritual fervor (facilitated by drugs), he convinced himself that God was on his side. This is quite different, however, from being at the mercy of forces outside himself, a defense he uses when held accountable.

DRUGS AS FACILITATORS OF DEPRESSION AND SUICIDE

Every criminal whom we have studied has had sporadic suicidal thinking, although actual suicide attempts are rare.† In comparing drug users and nonusers, we found a greater proclivity for such thinking and for suicidal efforts among the former. This appears to be largely because they have a much more difficult time cutting off fears about themselves and about life in general.

Suicidal thinking occurs when the criminal drug user's opinion of himself as a good person collapses. This may happen when he is not confined. Suicidal thinking and action occur most often, however, when the criminal faces prolonged confinement because he has failed in crime and his opinion of himself is at a low ebb.

When self-disgust is present, it is intensified by drugs. The criminal enters a state in which he believes that he amounts to nothing, that this is apparent to others, and that things will never get better.‡ Perceiving life as having nothing to offer, he can fathom little reason to continue to exist.

---

*In Chapter 4 of Volume I we describe the self-serving aspects of religious belief and observance. An example is praying to God for help in completing a bank robbery.

†See the section on suicide in Chapter 7 of Volume I.

‡The zero state is described in Chapter 4 of Volume I.

D had been released from prison to a halfway house. He was in the community only a few days before his resolution to change began to erode. He spoke of getting a job, but found many excuses not to. He spent time instead with other former prison inmates in the halfway house, talking about crime, sizing up the women, drinking, and using marijuana. It was not long before D broke parole and left the area. He knew that the FBI would pursue him, but he believed that he could lose himself in familiar haunts in his large native city. Shortly after leaving the halfway house, D phoned us. (He had participated in our program several years earlier but had dropped out.) He said that he was in poor physical condition with a tormenting rash and suffering from exhaustion. He had been using large amounts of amphetamines and marijuana and had been awake for days. In an attempt to sleep, he began using barbiturates. D declared that there was no hope. He maintained that life was empty and that he was going to kill himself. He commented that his entire life had been a waste and that many people, especially his mother, had suffered because of him. He stated that he knew that the FBI was pursuing him and that he would go to jail and there deteriorate further. This life offered nothing. Not long after his call to us, D was apprehended by the authorities.

When D had used drugs previously, it had usually been to expedite a particularly daring and serious crime. However, his state of mind since leaving prison had fluctuated between total despair about his future and the desire to commit a very big crime. After D left the Washington area, he soon became overwhelmed with fear — specifically fears about his physical well-being, fear of apprehension by the law, fears of conscience about the suffering he had caused his mother, and an all-encompassing despondency about the future. Drugs only exacerbated this view of life.

The state of mind before using drugs is obviously critical. If the user cares little for life without drugs, he cares even less with them. If he is depressed and uses drugs to remove the depression and if there is no desire for crime or sex, then he becomes even more depressed.

A drug-using criminal said to us, "I don't care about living. Nothing is important. It doesn't make any difference what I do or what happens. I feel trapped in a hopeless situation. I don't care if I drop dead." D's attempt to come to terms with this state of mind consisted of drinking a fifth of whiskey and injecting heroin. He hoped that his thinking would change so that he would be excited about crime. Instead he reported, "When I tried to think about crime, it was like being impotent. I got very depressed because I was totally incapable of committing any crime." D thought about death and even went to the library to see whether he could discover a painless means of committing suicide.

This was a prime example of a case where drugs did not produce a high. A longtime user resorted to drugs and got nothing from them because at the time there was no ongoing criminal thinking. This man did not kill himself but resolved his conflict by deciding to cooperate in our program for change. Eventually he wearied of that and returned to crime.

Any aspect of his physical or mental makeup that the user is currently unhappy about may be brought out and exaggerated with drugs. One man had always been self-conscious about varicosities of his scrotum. He was embarrassed whenever he was nude, whether it was in the presence of a male or a female. Depressed prior to using LSD, he experienced intense shame during a sexual experience while on the drug over what he considered a severe physical defect.

A collapse of the criminal's good opinion of himself is one component of depression and suicidal thinking. The other is anger at a world that does not accommodate him and recognize him in a manner commensurate with his inflated self-image. When he is on drugs, the injustices of the world are magnified and his indignation is even greater than when he is without drugs. Although confined in a psychiatric hospital, one drug user had illegitimately obtained tranquilizers and amphetamines that he was using in large amounts. At one point he wrote a description expressive of his mental state:

"The world keeps going around and around. Let me go I say, but I cannot go . . . I want to cry, but cannot. For some reason, the tears just will not come anymore . . . I want to die, but cannot die. Just like the fly around the light. It cannot die. Why should it die? He is locked up, but still he is free. Free to go around and around my head. Why can't he go bother some other person and not me . . . Oh God, I have to get away from this place on the ward. I can't see the trucks and see the night, the free night is the thing—the light and the air. All the people."

In another part of the writing, D expressed his view on the permanency of depression: "Depression is something that will never, never stop." Being confined was depressing enough, but both his despair and anger were intensified by drugs. In a burst of energy D spent the day at the typewriter, typing his recollections of the past. The full account is laced with self-pity and indignation at what others did to him. His writing expresses a wish to die, but it lacks a genuine resignation to death. At one point in his writing, D said: "I have to keep going. I do not know how, but there is so much to tell that I have to tell someone." Suicidal thinking that has been recurrent intensifies with drugs.

Even though the drug user thinks there is no way out, he lacks the "heart" to commit suicide. As much as he may not want to live, he is equally afraid to die. (As we indicated previously, the drug user is extremely fearful of injury or death.) Only rarely is a drug user so depressed that when he resorts to drugs, he becomes despondent enough to make a suicidal gesture or actually kill himself.

Rather than live in despair the drug user most frequently seeks excitement as his antidote. He angrily decides to regain control and strives to assert his power in this world that he has deemed so unacceptable. He cuts off fears and once again recharges himself by seeking criminal excitement. His pervasive anger is directed at whatever targets are convenient. The enormity of the crimes to be committed may be directly proportional to the intensity of his depression.

A NOTE ON FACILITATION OF PSYCHOSIS

We have had only limited experience with psychosis induced in criminals during drug use. Among the 255 participants in our study, less than 3 percent have experienced transient psychotic states, and all but one of these was a drug user. Generally psychosis among criminal drug users is rare, and there is little in the literature about it. Weil (1972, p. 56), although not referring specifically to criminals, reported that the percentage of drug users who become "negatively psychotic" on chemical highs is no larger than the percentage of students who become psychotic while attending college.

The literature reports that psychosis may emerge with a variety of drugs, notably amphetamines, cocaine, hallucinogens, and occasionally marijuana. In addition, psychosis may attend withdrawal from barbiturates. There is a consensus that drugs produce a psychosis mainly in those with a predisposition to psychosis. De Long (1972, p. 94) pointed out that it is not clear that even the hallucinogens cause psychotic effects, but that they "may serve only to precipitate them in someone who is about to have such a problem anyway."

Some drugs are more likely than others to bring out psychosis, notably amphetamines, LSD and PCP (phencyclidine). In discussing the effects of hallucinogens, it is important to distinguish the psychoticlike ("psychotomimetic") alterations in perception and sensation experienced by most users, who do not then become psychotic, from what are bona fide psychotic states in which a person loses contact with reality.*

The toxic psychosis is a special case that results when a person has had a very large dose of a drug.† It is a temporary state that disappears when a sub-

---

*We shall say more about this in the next chapter.

†Weil (1972, p. 50) describes a toxic psychosis as "a nonspecific reaction of the brain to an overdose of anything that affects it."

stance has been metabolized and excreted. In a toxic psychosis the user truly lacks control over his mental state and is confused and disorganized. In such a condition, users in our study were so incapacitated that they were unable, even to plan, much less execute, a crime.

Our experience has been that the content of the psychosis is anticrime.* In Chapter 7 of Volume I we characterized psychosis as a backlash of conscience. The drug user is more bothered by conscience than the nonuser, because, to repeat, the user has greater difficulty cutting off all deterrents. If a criminal is preoccupied with issues of conscience and is having trouble ridding himself of them and then uses drugs, conscience haunts him all the more.

> D was taken to the hospital after he had disturbed several people in their home at four in the morning. He had been using amphetamines, marijuana, and LSD for nine months. Having been at a "pot party," he reported that after eight or ten drags on the pipe, he began seeing flashing red lights and then noticed that his friends turned into devils who were pursuing him. He ran from them, fell on his knees, and prayed to God for help. He then ran up a street, believing that he was directed by "a light beam from God."

> He wound up on the front steps of a church. Looking across the street at the white door of a private home, he thought he was looking at the "pearly gates," and then he frantically pounded on the door to get in. The police were summoned, and D was taken to the hospital.

Another user mentioned that during an amphetamine-induced psychosis, he became very frightened of an atomic bomb attack on Washington, DC and believed that he would experience sudden death and go to hell.

Although the content of the psychotic state is often religious, psychosis differs from the transient monastic phases described. Monasticism involves a rational person's self-imposed restraint in order to live a pure life. In a psychosis the drug user is convinced that he is personally appointed by God. One drug user thought that he was God's personal emissary dispensed to punish sinners. Such beliefs indicate a loss of contact with reality. In such a condition, there is a sense of supreme power; the user believes that he has a special mission or has been selected by God for a particular purpose.

A remarkable facet of the drug user's psychosis is that even though he has partially lost contact with reality, he still maintains considerable control over his behavior. He can, as it were, step back and watch the psychosis in pro-

---

*Even in the confused state of the toxic psychosis, anticrime elements are present. In one such case, a user atoned for his sins, holding a Bible in one hand and his scrotum in the other.

gress, concealing it from others so that no one (not even his family) suspects its presence. If he does reveal the psychosis, he can use it to further his own objectives, later capitalizing on it to establish a record of mental illness to support an insanity defense. If he has ever been referred for psychiatric treatment during a psychotic episode, such a history verifies his "instability."

BIBLIOGRAPHY

De Long, J. V. (1973). The drugs and their effects. In Drug Abuse Survey Project, *Dealing with Drug Abuse: Report to the Ford Foundation,* pp. 62–123. New York: Praeger.

Fiddle, S. (1967). *Portraits from a Shooting Gallery.* New York: Harper and Row.

Larner, J., and Tefferteller, R. (1964). *The Addict in the Street.* New York: Grove Press.

McKee, M. R. (1975). Drug abuse knowledge and attitudes in "middle America." *American Journal of Public Health* 65:584–590.

National Commission on Marihuana and Drug Abuse. (1973). *Drug Use in America: Problems in Perspective,* Second Report of the National Commission on Marihuana and Drug Abuse. Washington, DC: Government Printing Office.

Rada, R. T. (1975). Alcoholism and forcible rape. *American Journal of Psychiatry* 132:444–446.

Walton, R. P. (1938). *Marijuana: America's New Drug Problem.* Philadelphia: J. B. Lippincott.

Weil, A. T. (1972). *The Natural Mind: A New Way of Looking at Drugs and the Higher Consciousness.* Boston: Houghton Mifflin.

Wortis, S. B. (1958). A physician views today's narcotics problem. In *Narcotic Drug Addiction Problems,* ed. R. B. Livingston, pp. 174–183. Washington, DC: Government Printing Office.

Chapter 6

The Choice of a Drug

THIS CHAPTER IS NOT an exhaustive account of drugs and their effects. Rather, it contains a series of observations based on our study of drug-using criminals. The purpose of presenting this material is to relate why the criminal chooses specific drugs to facilitate crimes. Material on drugs and sexual behavior has been included because sexual exploitation is so frequently an element of the user's criminality.

The criminals in our study have used a variety of drugs to achieve their desired mental state. The choice of a specific drug is largely a matter of individual preference. If one drug is not available, another may be substituted. But irrespective of which substances are used, all facilitate the thinking, talk, and action that the criminal desires.

Drugs do not manage the criminal. He regards drugs as he regards the rest of the world. Nothing manages him. He learns what to expect pharmacologically and endeavors to regulate his frequency of drug use and dosage accordingly.

All our drug users realized that they would fare better without drugs. Drug use entails risks of arrest, of being cheated in a transaction, and of being harmed physically. But there is yet another cost. As we pointed out earlier, when he is on drugs, the criminal is prone to take greater risks in crime and exercise poorer judgment. As one user commented, "on drugs it's bigger schemes but poorer execution."

The user is acquainted with the risks of drug use, but cuts off fears along these lines as he searches for the highest high. One user described this quest in the following manner; "I want something that will make life smooth and easy, that will give me the energy to accomplish what I want. Then I can be happy." By "happy" he means being "ten feet tall" and able to overcome impediments to his objectives.

The culmination of the search for the highest high is often polydrug use, in which the user is indiscriminate in what he uses. The drug users in our study rarely restricted themselves to one drug. All drugs have facilitating effects; if the user cannot obtain one drug, he uses another or several in combination. A given drug may be more readily available in one neighborhood than in another. The user searches for what he wants. When drugs are scarce, he takes what he can get. When he is confined, his access is even more limited, and again he uses what he can obtain. The user adapts to circumstances but is not a victim of them. Availability does not determine whether he uses drugs, but only which drugs he uses at a specific time.

The choice of a drug may depend on the user's assessment of the quality of what is available. It is difficult for a drug user to determine accurately the quality of the drug he is using. He knows how much alcohol he is consuming, but he does not know the extent to which a substance sold to him as heroin is adulterated with other substances. He endeavors to determine what constitutes an optimal dose (for him) and often relies on word of mouth about the quality of what is available.

OPIATES

Our heroin users reported that to knock out fear and facilitate excitement, heroin was their drug of choice. They asserted that their judgment in crime was less impaired when they were on heroin (unless the dose was extremely high) than when they used other drugs. The heroin user finds that he is sharp and alert and maintains good coordination. He is poised, in control, and prepared to undertake bigger crimes. No matter what kind of crime was contemplated, our users claimed that during the execution they were more efficient on heroin than they were on other drugs. One criminal who was drinking heavily switched to heroin because his recklessness on liquor resulted in belligerent encounters that brought him to the attention of the authorities. On heroin he was "smoother" and less assaultive. In the previous chapter we discussed the tremendous advantage of heroin to the user in his attempts at sexual conquest; indeed, some users rely on heroin mainly to enhance sexual performance.

One dilemma of the heroin user is that he rarely knows what he is buying. Street heroin is heavily adulterated and sometimes laced with toxic substances, such as arsenic, strychnine, and formaldehyde. If the user unknowingly obtains an unusually pure batch and injects it as he regularly would, he risks an overdose.* Although heroin can be snorted, injection is

---

*Not even the dealer knows how the drug that he is selling has been "cut," i.e., what the relative concentrations of the drug and adulterants are. Unusually pure heroin infrequently appears on the streets. Users who do not know the strength of what they have obtained may take an overdose if they inject the regular amount. This is especially likely to happen with inexperienced users. Four deaths were reported in Washington, DC, from such a batch of "killer stuff" (*Washington Star* 11/14/76). A death and numerous hospitalizations occurred in Detroit from the use of white Mediterranean heroin that was as much as ten times as strong as the more widely available and cheaper Mexican brown heroin (*Detroit News* 9/21/77).

usually the preferred method of administration, but injection itself has drawbacks: Some users have had to overcome a strong fear of the needle, there is jeopardy in having the drug "paraphernalia" on one's person, and there is a risk of infection (especially hepatitis) from unsterilized needles.

The main disadvantage of heroin is the physical dependence and daily grind to satisfy it. However, the heroin users in our study have reported that withdrawal is not the agonizing process that it is reputed to be. Indeed, some heroin users withdraw on their own when they want to give up the daily grind or when they are under pressure from their families. Some voluntarily reduce the size of their habit so as to gain greater impact from a smaller dose or to recover their sexual interest.

Others have said that the heroin user slows down and becomes less aggressive. This does happen when he drifts into a nod. But as we explained in Chapter 4, although he may be less physically active when in a nod, there is an increase in criminal thinking. Thus the nod is a precursor of more criminal activity. Our users have reported that when they used heroin in an attempt to sleep, they became agitated and restless, because their thinking was accelerated; if they finally fell asleep, their sleep was often disturbed by frightening dreams.

Heroin is the opiate of choice among users of opiates in our study. It provides the highest high. However, if heroin is unavailable, the user has recourse to other narcotics. Some, such as Darvon (dextropropoxyphene) and Demerol (meperidine), and Dilaudid (hydromorphone) are relatively inexpensive and are available through prescription. Such drugs produce a high when used alone or, as is more common, in combination with other drugs.

Methadone, another opiate, is dispensed in programs treating heroin dependence.* Users in our study have reported that in using methadone, they were simply substituting one mind-altering drug for another. They stated that a methadone high is not as intense as a heroin high, nor is there a rush. Methadone, according to most of our users, relieves the physical distress attending heroin withdrawal but does not greatly lessen the desire for heroin.

STIMULANTS

COCAINE

The drug-using criminal knows that cocaine increases the speed of his thinking and increases the physical energy available for instant action. Cocaine users in our study reported experiencing a "cocaine nod." One user observed that he fantasized "big scores" on heroin but was more inclined to pursue them on cocaine. Cocaine provides a sharper cutoff of fear than do most other drugs. A user described the cutoff in terms of a "calming effect."

*See the discussion in Chapter 7 of the literature on methadone treatment.

"Within my system I was much more calm. I was able to think better, and I did things more efficiently."

Another commented that on cocaine the consequence of the sharp cutoff of fear was a "state of unimaginable ecstasy associated with a feeling of supreme power." Such a cutoff removes restraints, so the criminal is prepared to engage in crime of virtually any sort and has fewer inhibitions to the use of violence. "When I take cocaine, I will do anything and give up everything for self-preservation. Cocaine is the drug that will make me commit any kind of crime." The criminal who said this was on cocaine when he committed a rape for which he was later arrested. The "no-holds-barred" aspect of both the thought and the action is contained in this statement:

"On cocaine all the larceny comes out. I could see a woman's pocketbook lying there. I have no need for money, but I would take its contents anyway. Under cocaine I wouldn't give a damn whether I ever saw her again or not. I might even kill her if she caught me or protested too much about it."

Cocaine is reputed to facilitate sexual activity. In contrasting heroin and cocaine, one user reported that heroin led to a great deal of thinking about sex, but cocaine energized him so that he would actually go out, find a woman, and enact his thoughts.

Another attraction of cocaine is its reputation as the drug of celebrities. One user commented, "It was rare, not easily available. Not everyone could afford it."* The cost of the drug made it "prestigious" and desirable for our users, but it was relatively unavailable to them (compared with other drugs), and before its increased availability in the mid-1970s, it was used infrequently.

The effects of cocaine are short lived, relative to those of heroin. As the effects wear off, there is an immediate letdown. However undesirable his mental state before cocaine, the user fears even more the state that will ensue as the drug wears off. Consequently if he has a supply available, he may use more and more to ward off the letdown. A few criminals reported isolated instances of hallucinations as they were coming off the drug. Another drawback to cocaine is that because the cutoff of fear is so sharp, the user's heightened superoptimism may lead him to be more reckless than he would be on opiates. In fact, some criminals distrust cocaine users, perceiving them as unpredictable because they are so inclined toward immediate action.

*Chaplin (1977) calls cocaine the "Rolls Royce of drugs" and observes on the part of its users "a strange, secret satisfaction to paying $100 for an infinitesimal amount of illegal powder."

AMPHETAMINES

Amphetamines are easily available and may be taken in pill form or for a more rapid effect injected intravenously. Injection produces a rush; pills do not. Amphetamines are much like cocaine in that the user finds that he has a great deal of energy instantly available.

The mental state on amphetamines is expansive — the user believes that he is totally in control of everything in his environment. There is an acceleration of exciting thinking. Schemes are conceived, one after another: "Methedrine increases the speed of my thoughts to such an extent that one thought enters before I can complete the one going out before." The quality of that thinking is such that almost any means to an end are considered acceptable. Humanitarian ideals, present at times without drugs, are eliminated with the use of drugs.* Acts of violence are more readily contemplated. One user had thought many times about hijacking an oceanliner; on amphetamines he began discussing methods, although he stopped short of actually committing the crime. He reported that he reacted much more violently in day-to-day situations on amphetamines than he did on marijuana or on no drugs at all. For example, when he was on amphetamines he angrily threatened his sister with a knife as she reached past him for the butter. He made the same threats to youngsters whom he saw making obscene gestures at him.

As is often the case with cocaine, the amphetamine user is inclined to be bold to the point of recklessness: "You get the feeling you can't do anything wrong when you can't even walk straight." A small obstacle may be perceived by the amphetamine user as an enormous personal affront and thus trigger a rapid and severe response. Some drug users who are aware of their proclivity to react this way will not use amphetamines in connection with commission of a crime, especially when a complex scheme is to be carried out with precision. They reserve amphetamine use for parties, where they act like big shots, making plays for women, engaging in exciting conversations, and holding forth as experts on any and all subjects that arise. For some, amphetamines are the drugs of choice for prolonged sexual activity. They find not only that they are able to maintain an erection for hours but also that there is less interference with ejaculation than when they use opiates.

A major drawback to amphetamine use is what happens on cessation of use of the drug. Especially if he is on a high dosage, the user anticipates "crashing" or a severe depression that is followed by general apathy and insomnia. To preempt this, the frequent and heavy user of amphetamines increases his dosage. In addition to the risk of overdosage, there is a possibility of psychotic reactions. In several of those users in our study who had histories of transient psychotic episodes, such episodes were triggered by amphetamine use.

*For a discussion of the criminal's sentimentality see Chapter 4 of Volume I.

DEPRESSANTS

Depressants, namely sedative-hypnotic and anti-anxiety drugs, are relatively easy to obtain, some being readily prescribed. Because some of the drugs in this class, such as barbiturates, are considered extremely dangerous, public officials have recommended removing them from the public market and limiting their use to hospital patients. Depressants were used only occasionally by criminals in our study, generally in combination with other substances.

Surprising as it might seem, our drug-using criminals used "downers," as these drugs are called, to seek a high. As with other drugs, the state of mind is expansive, and deterrents are cut off. Users describe the mental state produced as one of oblivion, in which they "don't give a damn." One user of Seconal (secobarbital) and chloral hydrate reported that when on these drugs, he would respond in a hair-trigger fashion to anyone who offended him. Normally quite fearful of physical injury, he would lash out verbally and then, with little provocation, physically. Users of Quaalude (methaqualone) reported a heightened sense of power and a feeling of more control over themselves than on other substances, such as alcohol.

Users find it hard to regulate the dosage of some depressant substances. They may experience a grogginess or fogginess of mind that is truly incapacitating for a criminal enterprise. Frequent use of some of these drugs, especially barbiturates, results in a physical dependence from which withdrawal is more difficult and poses more risk than withdrawal from most opiates. Unregulated withdrawal from barbiturates can have severe consequences, including convulsions and death. There is also a considerable risk of overdose, especially when sedative-hypnotics are indiscriminately combined with other drugs, particularly alcohol.

MARIJUANA

No drug-using criminals in our study relied heavily on marijuana to commit crimes. However, they all had had experience with the drug. With marijuana they could achieve a mild high without the paraphernalia of the opiates, without fears of physical dependence, and without the unpredictable consequences of "popping" pills. Criminal users claimed that marijuana was principally a drug for relaxation. By this they meant that it was a stimulant to thinking and talking about whatever they found exciting—usually crime or criminal equivalents. They found marijuana especially desirable in social situations. It was a good party drug. It enhanced their view of themselves and thus boosted their confidence so that they could be more outgoing. One user observed that on marijuana he was able to ignore features in himself that otherwise disturbed him. Other users reported that with heightened perception of their own importance and expertise, they were more disposed to dominate and control conversations. Sometimes the opposite was true. They enjoyed themselves more at a party when they retreated from socializing and engaged in fantasy. While on the drug in a criminal milieu, they engaged in freewheeling conversation about past and anticipated crimes and regaled others with their sexual exploits.

Some valued marijuana for sexual activity. When they used the drug, they were bolder in approaching prospective partners. If they could induce a partner to use marijuana, barriers to sexual experimentation fell. Throughout the sexual experience, the user's view of his virility and prowess was enhanced.

Some users reported that combining marijuana with alcohol resulted in lessening inhibitions to committing crimes. However, they asserted that in crime they were wary of using marijuana either alone or with alcohol. By itself, marijuana was not potent enough to knock out deterrents completely and give them the "heart" for a major crime; in combination with alcohol, it impaired judgment, so that a user was more likely to err in the course of committing a crime.

Except perhaps for alcohol, marijuana use entailed the least personal or social risk. Even while using the drug, they could function at school, work, and home without significant impairment in performance. Thus they were able to be high without others detecting it. Those who moved away from "hard" drug use (in their forties) continued to use marijuana later in life.

HALLUCINOGENS

Drug-using criminals readily discuss the changes in perception and sensation that they experience when they use the drugs known as hallucinogens.* In probing the thinking of our drug users, we have found that true hallucinations are not experienced. Rather, they have perceptual distortions.† The exception to this is the user's experiencing "nonpsychotic hallucinatory deterrents" (described in Chapter 5).

A hallucination is a "sense impression for which there is no appropriate external stimulus" (Kendler 1963, p. 689). Drug users in our group employ the word hallucination simply to refer to vivid fantasy that they can conjure up at

---

*Hallucinogens most commonly used by criminals in our study were lysergic acid diethylamide (LSD), psilocybin, and mescaline. Also used were a variety of others, including dimethyltryptamine (DMT), dimethoxyphenylisopropylamine (DOM or STP), and phencyclidine (PCP). For more background material on this class of drugs, the reader is referred to Chapter 2.

†De Long (1972, p. 92) made a similar observation: "The hallucinogens do not produce hallucinations in the classic sense. It is rare for a user to see things that are not there. Rather, perception is altered."

will. One man said to us, "I can hallucinate about you." He meant that he could fantasize about a specific object in his environment. In another example of calling a fantasy a hallucination, a criminal stated that he had the hallucination of himself as lord and master of the hospital where he was confined.

When a user engages in a transaction to purchase hallucinogenic drugs, he usually has little knowledge of what he is procuring. Not only are the potency and purity of the substance unknown, but its very identity may be concealed. The user may believe that he is buying one drug, but gets another, so total is the misrepresentation by the seller.

Among criminals who use drugs in search of the highest high, curiosity about hallucinogens is great. The knowledge that others have experienced adverse effects is rarely a deterrent, for they believe that these drugs offer new frontiers to explore. If they know that someone has had a "bad trip," this establishes a challenge for them to get high yet prove they are in control.

> "I was an explorer, and I wanted to see if I could control it. I was afraid, but I still believed I could master it. I wanted to experience the things I had heard about LSD. I wanted to see if they were true and if it would do for me the same things it did for others."

Hallucinogen users in our series were most familiar with LSD, although on occasion they used other drugs in this class.* They reported tremendous acceleration of thinking and a sense of expansiveness that reflects an elimination of internal and external deterrents:

> "I had the power of God."

> "I felt that I had it made. I thought that the world was my oyster. Nobody could touch me."

> "When I am under the effect of LSD, I can do anything I want. Reality doesn't exist. Time and space are not in control of me. I can do and be where I choose to be, nothing can contain me. I am in another world, a world of my own."

As is the case with other drugs, the "world of my own" is one in which the user is free to pursue any objective. One man stated, "Anything you have in mind before you take LSD, you will be able to do." In the preceding chapter, we referred to the facilitation of violence and homicide by a user on LSD.

---

*Some users temporarily stopped using LSD and switched to other hallucinogens in the wake of reports that LSD use results in chromosomal and brain damage.

However, it was sexual thought and action that were paramount in the experience of hallucinogen users in our study. One user reported a rush of sexual fantasy and an orgasm in the shower. Another reported that on hallucinogens he could engage more readily in homosexual prostitution.

Upon ingesting a hallucinogen, gastrointestinal distress may be experienced, sometimes resulting in severe nausea and vomiting. The "coming down" from the drug may be accompanied by discontent, restlessness, and quickly expressed anger. But most important in the list of adverse effects is the "bad trip." For the most part, our drug users avoided hallucinogens in the commission of crimes because they experienced greater difficulty in controlling their thinking and behavior than with other drugs. It was more difficult to cut off fear with this class of drugs than with any of the others. Only very infrequently did inner fears or self-destructive thinking emerge. When they did, it was a reflection of the immediacy of such a mental state prior to the use of the drug.

Our users experienced far more good trips than bad, but even after a bad trip, they knew that the odds of having a good trip remained great. They continued to perceive the hallucinogens as affording the best opportunity to experience the highest high. "When I took LSD, I would not want anything else. Nothing else would bring me to the point I was at, and everything else would bring me down. When I take LSD, everything else is a bummer."

The user of hallucinogens has a convenient excuse if he is held accountable for something he does while on the drug. Because this class of drugs is reputed to render people unpredictable and "crazy," he may obtain a sympathetic response to a claim that he was out of control and not responsible for his behavior.* If he is a known drug user, conceivably he could argue such a position in defense of a crime, whether or not he actually used the drug at the time of the offense at issue.

ALCOHOL

We are discussing here the use of alcohol by criminals who used other drugs as well. As alcohol is the most available drug, the criminals in our study came to it early. Among their forbidden activities were procuring alcohol illicitly, consuming it with companions, and selling it to others. Nearly all have continued alcohol consumption throughout their lives, the extent of use varying according to the individual and circumstances. The quantity of intake can be adjusted easily; the user generally knows the potency and quality of what he is getting.

*A defendant who murdered five women after using LSD claimed that the drug caused him to commit the homicides and resulted in his having no memory of the slayings (*Washington Post* 10/18/77).

As is true of all other drugs he uses, the criminal is certain that he is in control of his alcohol consumption. He knows of the possible adverse physical effects of chronic, heavy drinking. He knows how drinking can impair his judgment and coordination. He knows that if he is arrested for a crime, alcohol may complicate his situation, and he knows that its use may give him away as it is detectable through behavioral signs, odor, and blood tests. But he is confident that he can regulate his intake so that he will experience none of these unwanted effects.

Alcohol may facilitate planning a crime, but it is often a liability in executing it. Some drug users choose to avoid alcohol before a crime because it makes them too cocky and, as a result, careless. Heavy drinking results in a decrease in coordination and deftness, as well as impairment of judgment. Consequently the drinker may fail to take precautions that are necessary to the successful execution of a crime. He may fail to assess accurately the security arrangements, leave a telltale sign, or draw attention to himself unnecessarily — for example, by speeding as he leaves the site of the crime.

With alcohol the response to a perceived insult is quick. Sober, the criminal might avoid a physical confrontation because of intense fears of bodily injury. With alcohol he is hypersensitive, emboldened and more prone to fight. One man who had unmercifully stamped on another's face and body later reflected, "I wouldn't dare do that without alcohol." With alcohol he takes chances that he otherwise would not.

> D described an incident typical of his drinking behavior in military service. One night after a bout of drinking, D was returning from committing several crimes. As he strolled along, he walked into a signpost. A military policeman observing him became suspicious and halted D in order to interrogate him. D refused to cooperate and assaulted the MP. The outcome was D's being beaten badly and reported to the company command, where charges were placed against him for drunken and disorderly conduct. Thereafter he was watched more closely.

After getting into trouble enough times through such incidents, some drug users moderate their use of alcohol.

Criminals in our study have used alcohol more frequently and heavily for a celebration after a crime than before committing it. Some reported that alcohol facilitated sexual activities. Their view of themselves as irresistible was enhanced, and they were bolder in their approach to prospective partners.

> D was out on the town drinking and acting the "big shot." He danced with a girl on a stage where patrons of the bar were prohibited. He crumpled up money and threw it at the dancing girls. Then he took a $20 bill and stuffed it into the G-string of one of the dancers.

In searching out partners, they were more likely to use force to get what they wanted than if they had not been drinking.

> D attempted to gauge carefully the amount that he drank. Without alcohol he had little sexual drive and either had trouble attaining an erection or was unable to ejaculate. With alcohol he regarded himself as a superman. He would establish a liaison with a woman and then, if she resisted his sexual overtures, he would rape her.

The drug users in our group often combined alcohol with other drugs. One man said that the outcome of this practice was that "you operate with total abandon." Although the state of mind produced had its desirable aspects, functioning with "total abandon" had its drawbacks when precision in planning and executing a crime was essential.

POLYDRUG USE

Throughout this volume we have reiterated the point that the drug user continually searches for the highest high. This usually entails combining drugs rather than always using the same substance. Use of one drug reduces barriers to the use of others. Taking a drink increases thinking about using other substances. A commonplace example in the life of the heroin user is to have a drink and then begin thinking about obtaining heroin to enact a crime or sexual conquest. Thus, in the user's mind, drinking becomes synonymous with drugs and criminal action.

The general view is that if one obtains the desired effect from one drug, the effect can be enhanced by other drugs. In seeking the most intense and prolonged high, there is an erosion of caution, and so, the user may become indiscriminate about the drugs that he tries. Thus, there is the phenomenon of the party where pills are passed around, and users sample them without knowing the identity of the substances. If the user is scheming to commit a complex crime that requires precision, he is more discriminating and chooses his drug to facilitate the execution of that crime successfully. But if he is in a social situation or in the midst of celebrating a crime, there are fewer restraints. Not atypical was the practice of one man who combined methadone, marijuana, heroin, alcohol, and tranquilizers — all in the course of a single day.

One kind of drug may be followed by another to prolong and heighten the experience, especially in the case of sexual activity.

> D was picked up by his girlfriend, and they went to her apartment. There they snorted heroin and drank beer. This was followed by a long bout of sexual activity, in which D maintained an erection for one-and-a-half

hours. They went out to see if they could find marijuana. Being unsuccessful, they went to sleep at 5 A.M. At 7A.M., still under the influence of drugs, D went to work. After work he and his girlfriend went to a motel to continue the "party." They snorted heroin, then found a source for marijuana and had another orgy. The next day D was in no condition to go to work and phoned in sick.

The first time that D had sexual intercourse, he was on heroin. From that time on he found that heroin increased his ardor and his ability to maintain an erection. But on heavy doses of heroin he had flagging interest and erectility. To stimulate his sexual interest, he used cocaine while maintaining his heroin habit.

Each drug user has phases in which he prefers different substances or combinations of substances. Availability, of course, is one determinant. Heroin users experiment with a variety of combinations, but they must have heroin as one of the ingredients, if they are to avoid withdrawal symptoms. Cocaine is often a desired ingredient, because it is an energizer. It is used with heroin — heroin for fantasy and scheming, and cocaine for the energy to initiate action. Another frequent combination is barbiturates and amphetamines — the former for an "I don't give a damn" attitude, and the latter to counteract the effect of barbiturate-induced grogginess. The combinations are varied, depending on what the user wants to pursue at a particular time, what he has heard from other users, and what his own experience has been.

The above represents a series of observations about criminals who make conscious, deliberate choices to use specific drugs for specific purposes. On some occasions they are highly selective as they pursue particular objectives. At other times they are indiscriminate, using anything they can acquire to obtain the highest high. In any event, a wide variety of substances and combinations are used to achieve very similar effects.

BIBLIOGRAPHY

Chaplin, G. (1977). Cocaine in Washington. *Washington Post* (*Potomac Magazine*), June 5.

De Long, J. V. (1972). The drugs and their effects. In Drug Abuse Survey Project. *Dealing with Drug Abuse: A Report to the Ford Foundation,* pp. 62-97. New York: Praeger.

Detroit News (9/21/77). Deadly heroin traced to girl, 11.

Kendler, H. H. (1963). *Basic Psychology.* New York: Appleton-Century-Crofts.

Washington Post (10/18/77). Rissell gets 5th life term, claims LSD influence.

Washington Star (11/14/76). Police seeking source of heroin batch that killed 4.

Chapter 7

Treatment of the Drug User

IN THE FOLLOWING SECTIONS we shall survey approaches to drug abuse treatment and prevention. The first to be considered is the effort to utilize external deterrents, including confinement, probation, and civil commitment; second, sociologic programs that are directed toward the improvement of social conditions regarded as causing drug use; third, psychologic approaches, especially the widely used therapeutic community; fourth, medically oriented programs; and finally, other measures employed to deal with the drug use problem.

Our focus on the outcome of each approach ("Does the program work?") requires two considerations: the concept of change and the evaluation of change. Few practitioners speak of a "cure." Reichard (1947) noted that cure mandates total change:

> If we actually could "cure" a person addicted to alcohol who for years prior to addiction had been able to drink in moderation, we should expect him then to be able to return again to moderate drinking. Such results of treatment are so uncommon as to be virtually non-existent; therefore, it is better to use other terms, e.g., control, successful treatment, total and permanent abstinence, when referring to a successful solution of an addict's problem by total and permanent abstinence. (p. 722)

Louria (1971) pointed out the difficulty inherent in evaluation:

> The concept of evaluation is terribly important. The problem of addiction is an emotional one, and every program quite naturally develops an emotional proprietary interest in its own methods. Because this is true, no program can assess itself adequately. (p. 198)

The 1914 Harrison Narcotics Act was intended to control the dispensing of narcotics. According to this law, a person caught using unprescribed narcotics had broken the law and faced the possibility of confinement. Under the

233

Harrison Act, government-operated clinics provided narcotics under medical supervision. However, the clinics established for this purpose were closed before 1930, because of abuses (including black market sale of legally dispensed drugs) and poor management. Since the closing of the clinics, the alternatives in handling drug dependence have been confinement without treatment, confinement with treatment, and mandatory treatment without confinement.

Wallis (1926), Commissioner of Corrections for New York City, declared that "the medical profession has nothing to offer" as a cure for addiction. Opinions changed with the times. For example, thirty-five years earlier, Lett (1891), a physician, was imploring:

> I would enjoin you to pour out your full sympathy towards the unfortunate opium habituate. . . . He needs your help. He needs care. . . . Give credence to what he tells you. Extend a rescuing hand to the drowning man. Pour oil and wine on his smarting wounds. (p. 833)

After the closing of the government clinics, about the only recourse for medical treatment was civil commitment to government hospitals at Lexington, Kentucky and Fort Worth, Texas, whose programs began in the 1930s. In the early 1960s, the tide began to turn again to a medical approach to treatment. Glaser (1967) called this trend "the most distinctive development in crime and drug addiction treatment in the United States in recent years." Some segments of society regarded punishment as futile and as possibly damaging to the addict, who was viewed less as a criminal and more as a sick person. With the Robinson case in 1962* the Supreme Court moved toward defining addiction as an illness. In that decision the Court held that imposing criminal sanctions on a person for being an addict constituted cruel and unusual punishment. Addiction was to be considered an illness, but the Court ruled that states could compel an addict to undergo treatment and were to apply criminal sanctions only if he did not comply with the treatment program.

Thus, in the 1960s treatment facilities proliferated, and funds were made available for a variety of programs. Yolles (1973) observed that as a result of the Drug Abuse Prevention and Control Act of 1970, for the first time the nation could devise programs to treat and prevent drug abuse. Increasingly, the thrust of programs was away from punishment and toward "rehabilitation," although, as Ball (1972) and Schoolar et al. (1973) observed, the term *rehabilitation* is a misnomer in that most addicts have never established themselves as responsible citizens.

*California v. Robinson [370 U.S. 660 (1962)].

MOTIVATION FOR TREATMENT

Rarely will an opiate addict voluntarily consent to treatment. Treatment is usually accomplished as a result of some type of coercion. (Blachly 1966, p. 742)

The most potent factor in bringing addicts into treatment is the courts ordering them into programs (Ausubel 1958, p. 77). A team of psychologists in
a government-commissioned study concluded that legal coercion and treatment have to be integrated "into a single cooperative effort" (*APA Monitor*
8/72). The team suggested indeterminate civil commitment to "heroin
camps" for uncooperative addicts. Kolb (1962, p. 127) observed that some
drug users are propelled into treatment by pressure from families and
friends. Another source of external pressure is the unavailability of drugs, a
periodic problem. As Primm (*New York Times* 12/26/72) stated: "Whenever
you have good law enforcement you reduce availability on the street. When
that happens you either drive [addicts] into the program or you drive them to
other drugs of abuse."

Personal factors may also bring the drug addict into treatment. He may
want to reduce his habit to more manageable proportions so that he can obtain the desired effects with less frequent or smaller doses of the drug. Thus
he will seek detoxification with "no intention of remaining clean" (De Ropp
1957). Lindesmith (1968) described this vividly when he quoted a drug user
rubbing the veins of his arm and saying, "Boy, will I be able to hit that when I
get out."

Some drug addicts, however, have periods when they are exhausted, in despair, disillusioned, and "sick of the hassles" of drug addiction (St. Pierre
1971). As Brunner-Orne (1956) observed, the addict in such a period is similar to the alcoholic who is remorseful, subdued, and willing to do almost anything when he is emerging from a binge after having hit rock bottom. De
Ropp (1957) described the role of self-disgust: "Absolutely nothing [can be
done] until he has reached a fixed decision to help himself. Only when he has
grown utterly disgusted with his dependence, when he has sunk to the bottom
of the pit and come to loathe his self-inflicted degradation can he be helped to
help himself" (p. 134). The most common pattern for the drug user is to vacil-
late between abstinence and drug use. Cohen (1969, p. 123) observed that
"after a few bad trips, a psychotic break, or disillusion with the drug way of
life, the devotee will want out." An older person who is addicted to drugs may
have been through many such periods of disillusionment and decide that suicide is the only way out (Lindesmith 1968, p. 135).

In light of the factors of external coercion, transient states of despair, and
the desire to maximize benefits from the drug by reducing the size of one's
"habit," it is not surprising that most authorities are skeptical about the addict's receptivity to eliminating drug use. Gerard and Kornetsky (1954) ob-

served that addicts resent classification as psychiatric patients, although su-
perficially they conform to program requirements and "serve their time."
Skepticism was expressed about the sincerity of those who entered the former
Public Health Service Hospital at Lexington. De Ropp (1957) reported the
views of the New York Academy of Medicine: "To vary the monotony, the
addict goes to the federal hospital at Lexington to take 'the cure' at a cost to
taxpayers of about $4,000. He has in most instances no intention of re-
maining off opiates and in about 75 per cent of cases is back on the drug again
soon after release" (p. 158).

Tennant et al. (1973) made a study of the reasons for 702 drug users wanting medical help in two Los Angeles free clinics.

> Over 90 per cent were heroin or barbiturate addicts requesting ambula-
> tory detoxification. In reality, the majority of the addicts probably de-
> sired medication to reduce the size and cost of their habit or to suppress
> abstinence symptoms until they obtained enough money to purchase
> more illicit drugs. This is evidenced by the fact that over 85 per cent of
> these addicts did not return to the clinic after the initial visit. (p. 50)

In other words, outpatient medical help was exploited by addicts and, in the
long run, contributed to maintaining their drug use patterns.*

Moffett et al. (1975) observed the "striking dichotomy" in perception between the addict and the therapist. Describing addicts in a Philadelphia methadone program, Moffett et al. pointed out that from the addicts' point of
view, they were being treated for an illness that they did not have.

> These addicts sought treatment in the methadone program primarily in
> order to alleviate their drug problems—craving, physical illness, and
> weariness of the hectic life on the streets. They viewed themselves as pri-
> marily beset by this dependency upon drugs; they did not conceive of
> themselves as either physically or mentally ill, or suffering from psychiat-
> ric problems. . . . The primary interest of the patients was not in re-
> socialization, and they did not conceive of the program as having this as
> its primary objective. (p. 60)

Newman (1973) described the plight of the involuntary patient in therapy:
"By definition, the involuntary patient enters the enforced therapeutic relationship rejecting that which the clinician sees as the desirable objective. Cure
and rehabilitation therefore become synonymous with achieving that which

---

*Silsby and Tennat (1974, p. 170) observed that the greater success in detoxification of inpatient
addicts may be attributed to their not being as easily able to procure drugs as are outpatients in
detoxification programs.

the addict does not want" (p. 95). Goldberg (1975) described the difficulties in retaining psychologists in drug abuse treatment, one of the problems being that "clients have little motivation to change their drug use or life styles."

Because motivation is initially lacking in most drug users, many authorities believe that it has to be developed after treatment begins. St. Pierre (1971) has described the slow process by which this occurs. He and others believe that motivation emerges when a person is confronted by what he is doing, acquires intellectual and emotional awareness, and finally develops a conviction that drugs are harmful and that he must change his life. Some believe that no single form of treatment can overcome lack of motivation: "I doubt that a single treatment of choice will ever be established for narcotic addiction, for the addicts represent a heterogeneous population with varied readiness and motivation and capacity to engage in one form or another of treatment" (Maddux, 1974).

In short, most drug users are not self-motivated to seek help. Legal coercion, family pressures, and their own transient state of self-disgust (in that order) are the factors in bringing them to agents of change. The basic question is: "Given the attitude of the drug user, can anything of enduring value be accepted and implemented?"

EXTERNAL DETERRENCE

Whether severe penalties will deter people from drug use is controversial. For the purpose of deterrence, society has imposed penalties in the form of confinement, probation and parole, and civil commitment. Brill and Lieberman (1969) observed that the "punitive treatment modality" has been the most widely used "treatment" afforded addicts since the early 1920s. Reichard (1947), a former medical director of the Public Health Service Hospital at Lexington, stated that it is necessary to resort to external controls when "internal controls are inadequate or misdirected."

During the last thirty-five years, incarceration for drug-related offenses has been widely condemned. Over thirty years ago, Lindesmith (1940–1941) stated that imprisonment is "as cruel and pointless as similar treatment for persons infected with syphilis would be."

> The treatment of addicts in the United States today is on no higher plane than the persecution of witches of other ages, and like the latter it is to be hoped that it will soon become merely another dark chapter of history. (p. 208)

Incarceration has been criticized because its main result is the temporary removal of the individual from the drug supply, only to have him emerge later with his "basic problem" unresolved (Ploscowe, 1961).

A physician cannot treat addicts in prison without being struck by the futility of jailing them....Jail does not eliminate the reason for the crimes, namely addiction. Addicts are not deterred or cured by confinement. In fact, the prison system, as it is now constituted, returns the addicts to the community in worse condition than when they entered, because social deterioration is added to their medical problem. (Dole 1972, p. 369)

Civil commitment is the "nonpunitive incarceration of an addict for purposes of rehabilitation" (DeLong 1972, p. 183). The prime example of this has been commitment to the federal narcotics facilities at Lexington, Kentucky, and Fort Worth, Texas. The Lexington facility has been termed a 1930s "hybrid of prison and hospital" (Walsh 1973). It evolved from an institution with a "life on the farm" approach to rehabilitation in the 1930s to a therapeutic community in the 1960s. In 1974 it was transferred from the National Institute of Mental Health to the Bureau of Prisons to be used as a treatment center for federal prisoners with histories of drug use. Title I of the 1966 Narcotic Addict Rehabilitation Act (NARA) authorizes federal courts to commit addicts for treatment, rather than prosecute narcotic addicts charged with federal offenses. If an addict fails to respond positively to treatment, his commitment may be terminated and prosecution for the original criminal charge may be instituted. Title II provides for a sentencing procedure to commit for treatment some addicts who are convicted of crimes in federal court. Title III provides for civil commitment of addicts who were not charged with a federal crime. We shall describe later the treatment methods, such as the therapeutic community, that have been used at the Lexington and Fort Worth facilities.

The shortcomings of coercive and inflexible civil commitment procedures have been repeatedly described (Thorpe 1956; Schur 1965; Meyer 1972, pp. 54–60). DeLong (1972) has identified what he believes to be severe limitations of the procedure:

Many drug experts believe that programs of civil commitment offer little more than custodial care in a predominantly penal setting. Counseling and therapy, when employed, are imposed on the patients by the staff and are of questionable value. Apparently, most addicts are committed as an alternative to criminal prosecution or sentencing, and view commitment as such. Most do not appear to be motivated toward inner change, and those who do succeed might succeed equally as well in a voluntary commitment program. (p. 190)

Friedman, Horvat, and Levinson (1983) described the motivation of inmates of a NARA unit as "suspect." That is to say that some entered the program solely to obtain early release. "All this legal maneuvering results in a prisoner taking no responsibility for initiating a course of personal development. This is not a desirable way to begin a meaningful therapeutic process" (p. 109). The Bureau of Prison psychologists did note, however, that despite the suspect initial motivation "a prosocial reorientation might take place given the proper therapeutic environment."

Some have advocated the type of restraint provided by a parole or probation arrangement. This calls for supervision by a community agency (Reichard 1947, Brunner-Orne 1956). Peck and Klugman (1973) described a program operated by the Los Angeles Suicide Prevention Center and the Institute for the Study of Life-Threatening Behavior. Services were provided for federal parolees, beginning with a pre-release program. Also offered were a variety of services in the community, such as counseling, job placement, methadone maintenance, health care, residential treatment, and group therapy. Each parolee was required to report to a parole officer during a three-year period. Peck and Klugman stated that between 62 and 86 percent of the participants were functioning satisfactorily; 83 percent were not using drugs, 75 percent were not rearrested, and 58 percent were employed, attending school, or both.

In many areas of the United States, either residential or outpatient drug treatment programs are court-mandated. The Community Diversion Incentive Programs of the State of Virginia supervise nonviolent convicted felons who are permitted to reside in the community while their prison sentences are suspended.* Urine screenings, attendance at Alcoholics Anonymous (or Narcotics Anonymous), counseling, community service, and participation in other activities are required as part of an arrangement that is more intensive than probation. If the offender fails to comply with the program, he can be returned to court for imposition of the full sentence. If he completes the program and stays crime- and drug-free during an additional period of probation, he does not serve additional time in confinement.

Legal leverage is considered essential because addicts are viewed as not wanting to be cured or not knowing how to get proper help if they desire it (Brown 1961, p. 285; Rosenthal 1973). Thus legal control helps to maintain "motivation."† Arneson (1973), commenting on the success of Project Joy, a group therapy program for addicts, stated that "it wasn't until he was threat-

---

*For information on the Virginia Community Diversion Incentive Act, contact Virginia Department of Corrections, Richmond, Virginia.

†In Volume II we described our experiences in the process of changing criminals into responsible citizens. We found that the confidence and firm support of the court were essential conditions to a criminal's implementing our program.

ened with a prison sentence that he seemed to straighten out and start "achiever remission" and "building up his ego strength . . . making his defense more appropriate" (p. 33). Jaffe (1969) proposed a "supervisory-deterrent" model that is basically a probationary arrangement. As he saw it, the addict's choice is between "abstinence with freedom or drug use with the risk of penalties." Obviously, there is initial coercion, but, then, according to Jaffe, "the more demonstrable the beneficial effects to the drug user of these involuntary stages, the less appropriate is the term 'punitive' as a descriptor." Kurland et al. (1966) described a program in which court-referred narcotic addicts received inpatient psychiatry care. A daily urine analysis was to serve as a deterrent to drug use. This was not successful: thirty-one of forty-six patients were either returned to court or eloped from the hospital. A similar effort with a group of parolees treated as outpatients was more successful. Only six of twenty-nine patients were remanded to correctional institutions.

Brill and Lieberman (1969) proposed a system of "rational authority" with "graded sanctions or coercions which would help the addict internalize controls and be rehabilitated even, and often, in spite of himself." Such a program would derive its coercive powers through court authority. They have viewed the use of "rational authority" as a "humane, constructive manner" of rehabilitation. Brill and Lieberman developed a program with major objectives to alter criminal attitudes and behavior, as well as to promote change in use of leisure time, family responsibility, work, friendships, and interpersonal relationships. Rehabilitation workers, cooperating with probation officers, were assigned to work with the addict. Brill and Lieberman believed that it was "through the holding function of rational authority" that they could "engage an addict long enough to develop his *tolerance for abstinence*" (p. 19).

Those favoring and those opposing coercive treatment agree that there is no sustained internal force in the drug user (especially the addict) leaning to change. One finds an entire spectrum of reactions by workers in the field to punitive or compulsory ways of dealing with drug addiction. Brown (1961) has stated that coercive measures are necessary because the individual addict cannot be trusted, being a "liar and [a] thief and . . . weak-willed," and, most important of all, having no motivation to terminate his habit (p. 263). Yet others flatly oppose compulsory measures. Keilholz and Battegay (1963, p. 233) have asserted that to "subject addicts to compulsion . . . makes them refractory and they relapse almost immediately after they leave the hospital." Schur (1965, p. 150) has said that compulsory treatment may "promote and reinforce the addict's deviant self-image." Arguments have been made that punitive legislation simply is not effective in deterring drug use. The President's Advisory Commission on Narcotic and Drug Abuse (1963) said:

As the Commission pointed out in its introduction, it is difficult to believe that a narcotic addict who is physically and psychologically dependent on a drug will forego satisfaction of his craving for fear of a long prison sentence. . . . The weakness of the deterrence position is proved every day by the fact that the illicit traffic in narcotics and marijuana continues. (p. 40)

A Senate Committee (Ploscowe 1961, p. 16) stated that despite punitive legislation and efforts by the Bureau of Narcotics, the United States has "more narcotic addicts, both in numbers and population-wise, than any other country of the Western World." McMorris (1966) and Cohen (1969) have argued that a decree or law will not eliminate conduct of a private nature that reflects individual tastes and preferences and that to believe otherwise is to be as naive as expecting "that a chemical potion will magically change character" (Cohen 1969, p. 124). With respect to the use of drugs on the campus, Keniston (1969) stated that the harshness of penalties for possession and use of marijuana "has had no deterrent effect." However, Rouse and Ewing (1972) maintained that the legal risks of marijuana use are a more weighty deterrent than alleged physical or psychologic hazards.

When one tries to decide in practical terms what to do, one confronts the ever-frustrating problems of the drug user's lack of motivation for treatment. Sentiment in many quarters is against coercive treatment. However, when it is left to the user to commit himself voluntarily, he usually does so only if it helps to reduce the external pressures of the court or his family. When the pressure has disappeared, he is likely to reject whatever program he is in and return to the streets and drugs.

SOCIOLOGIC MEASURES

The environment rather than the mind or body of the individual is the primary target of sociologic attempts to change those who already are drug users, as well as to prevent drug use by others. The sociologic contention is that drug use (as well as other deviant behavior) will not decline "unless there are broader social changes" (McBride and McCoy, 1981, p. 299). This view asserts that better housing, reduction of unemployment, elimination of discrimination, and increased opportunities for education and job training all are conducive to a person's joining and remaining in the mainstream of society and avoiding drug use. Maurer and Vogel (1967, p. 195) called for a "long range attack on the social and economic conditions which break down the individual personality." Raymond (1975) stated that "measures should be taken to reduce addicts' group isolation by making it possible for them to attain the goals of the broader society. This suggestion presupposes improvements in educational opportunities and stronger laws governing equal employment rights and fair housing" (p. 18). As we pointed out in Chapter 2 of Volume II, numerous economic and social projects have been undertaken by federal, state, and local governments and by private organizations to combat crime. Similarly, efforts are also directed at lessening crime that is generally considered the result of drug use.

Few people oppose projects that will improve the quality of American life. However, such writers as Meyer (1972) have warned that these undertakings must not be viewed as the answer to the drug problem itself. "Programs to improve the quality of life among the poor must be considered in their own right and not as programs for the prevention of drug abuse" (p. 127). One specific objective is to reduce availability of drugs and thereby the "contagious" spread of drug use. Anslinger (1934) proposed isolating drug addicts from the community at large. Bejerot (1972) and Mushkin (1976) proposed that chronic addicts live in communities remote from the big cities. There they could be maintained on drugs under medical supervision. Coombs (1972) advised similar measures: "This is what we must now do to the addicts in our midst. They must be swept off the streets and placed in addiction villages in the deserts of the West. And the pushers of heroin must know that once they are caught they will spend the remainder of their lives in the dungeons that we call prisons."

An alternative to isolating drug users is removing the supply of drugs. Neumann (1973) and Dole (1973) concluded that from a public health standpoint, the most effective way to deal with the "heroin epidemic" is to curtail the supply.

> Reducing the availability of heroin is a key to prevention. Here (despite much adverse publicity) the enforcement agencies have been quite effective, as shown by the high price and poor quality of heroin on the black market today, compared with the more potent supply available fifteen years ago. The fallacy in the enforcement approach, however, is the assumption that the epidemic of heroin use could be stopped by enforcement alone. . . . Enforcement and treatment are complementary, and both essential, if the epidemic is to be controlled. (Dole 1973, pp. 206–207)

As Brown (1961, p. 244) pointed out, the government has tried to control drug traffic into the country through international treaties and domestic laws. Of the 1975 federal drug abuse funds, 40 percent was allocated to drug traffic prevention (National Clearinghouse 1974). Lundberg (1973) has warned the medical and pharmaceutical professions that unless they regulate more carefully the drugs they dispense, federal intervention will become necessary. Most writers in the field have recognized that, by itself, the suppression of supply is not sufficient to deal with the problem (King 1961, p. 122; Lindesmith 1968, p. 238; Wald and Hutt 1972).

COMMUNITY SERVICES

Community services have been provided both to assist known drug users living in the community or returning to it from confinement and to prevent drug use, primarily through education. Brill and Lieberman (1969) observed that a community-based treatment approach has been advocated because "the addict's problems developed within the social context of a specific community, and . . . rehabilitative efforts are therefore best directed to changing him within the same community setting" (p. 5). The federal government has seen the addict's plight in the same way.

> It is also recognized that the community in which an addict lives has a key role in introducing him to addiction, and that a discharged addict needs powerful motivation and support to rehabilitate himself in an unchanged community. . . . A new approach to the problem of narcotic addiction became Federal policy with the passage of the Narcotic Addict Rehabilitation Act of 1966. Under the provisions of this Act, known as NARA, narcotic addicts are civilly committed to a Federal program which provides them with treatment, followed by supervised aftercare in their own community for up to 3 years. (National Institute of Mental Health 1971)

Federal grants and matching fund programs facilitated the development of community services throughout the country that offer treatment, aftercare, and rehabilitation. *U.S. Medicine* (4/15/73) reported that from mid-1971 until early 1973 the number of these programs increased from 36 to over 400. Helms et al. (1975) observed that at one point federal funding of community-based drug rehabilitation programs had reached the point where capacity exceeded utilization. He suggested that facilities be extended to drug-using prison inmates.

A public health approach described by Meyer (1972) involved the coordination of resources at the federal, state, and local levels. Meyer regarded the establishment of the Special Action Office on Drug Abuse Prevention as a step toward implementing this approach. He differentiated between "community-based" and "community-controlled" programs, warning of the drawback of the latter. "Competing power groups within the community demand to control programs for goals that frequently run counter to the interests of addiction treatment. No facility should voluntarily accept community control and those that are hassled with it will have to find some way of mitigating its objectionable effects" (p. 147).

One community-based program that has reported some success is the California Youth Authority's Community Centered Drug Program. A study by Breed (1975) revealed that only 22.2 percent of those involved in the program failed on parole, compared with 41.3 percent of those not in the program. The major problem with community programs of any sort, as pointed out by Brill and Lieberman (1969, p. 6), is that addicts do not continue the therapeutic relationship after the crisis that initially brought them to the agency has been resolved.

In a community educational effort for families with drug-using teenagers reported by Gottschalk et al. (1973), two psychiatrists conducted meetings at an evening clinic in Laguna Beach, California. Their purposes were "to provide sound medical opinion about drugs"and to try to "reduce the generation gap." This was an informal, low-budget operation established primarily for education, not for indepth treatment. One difficulty reported was that many youngsters thought that they had no problem and argued that they were attending the meetings only because they were forced to by parents, school, or the court; 82 percent of the parents felt strongly favorable toward the services provided at the clinic, but little more than half the youths found it useful or expressed interest in continuing.

Because the drug user generally does not seek help voluntarily, some drug counseling problems take the initiative and contact the users. Such a community program was that undertaken by the Youth Direction Council at Levittown, New York: "We have taken our program into the heart of one of the most difficult areas in the community" (Edmundson 1974). Establishing its headquarters at a shopping mall where youths congregated, the Council offered the services of social workers, social work aides, a school psychologist, group leaders, and volunteers.

Some communities maintain "transitional centers" that offer reentry programs entailing short-term residence for drug-dependent people. Residence in such homes is sometimes offered as an alternative to prison. The purpose of the halfway house is to attempt to rehabilitate the drug user in the community, giving him access to community resources rather than isolating him in confinement. Some communities operate a "hotline," a telephone service to provide information to drug users and families about drugs and referrals for emergency treatment. Another type of local program is the "rap house." Such a facility, which may be established in a storefront, is oriented toward youth, relying on adult counsel and peer pressure to change attitudes through discussions or "rap sessions." The sessions offer alternatives to drug use and referral to other agencies for special problems.

Chinlund (1975, p. 133) suggested that "power-seeking" drug users participate in community organizations such as scouting, the 4-H Club, and Camp Fire Girls. He stated that these activities provide "ways in which young people can feel important and realize they have made important achievements."

Nearly all treatment and aftercare programs require that drug users work. No one claims that a job itself cures drug use, but most authorities believe that employment is an integral part of rehabilitation in that it prepares the drug user "to resume an active role in society" (Karras and Cohen 1974, p. 1; Inskeep 1981, p. 293). Lamb and Mackota (1973, p. 157) pointed out that "a feeling of inadequacy in the world of work is frequently a major contributing factor to turning to drugs." They believed that work serves an essential purpose in a person's return to society:

> Work is an entree back into society. The drug addict becomes part of a social group valued by society rather than an isolated individual in an anti-social group. . . . He has a reason to get up in the morning and some feeling of being a part of the large group of other workers who go to work every day . . . The addict, forced into close contact with co-workers, must learn to handle himself in these relationships. His acquiring the ability to cope with the personal interchanges that go on may decide whether or not he can survive off drugs. (p. 158)

Drug abusers are even being offered help at their job sites. Both prevention and treatment programs are sponsored by employers and trade unions.* Kolben (1982) described the availability of such services as a trend for the 1980s. She reported that troubled employees are served by either an in-house staff or are referred to private consultants or public agencies. An employee's retaining his job may depend on his getting help: "When a supervisor concludes that an individual's work performance is no longer acceptable, the worker will be told that he has the option to such help through the counseling service or face the threat of dismissal" (p. 187).

---

*The growth of Employee Assistance Programs in corporations has been sizeable in the 1980s. An article on "corporate caring" in a national airline magazine (Thompson, 1986) pointed out the following facts:

Lost productivity due to drug abuse costs the United States $8.3 billion annually; the cost of alcohol abuse is $30.1 billion a year. The drug abuse problem on the job is so great that at least 30 percent of Fortune 500 companies are using pre-employment screenings to detect users.

The author of the article points out that there has been a recent change in employer attitudes toward drug abuse among employees. Instead of ignoring the problem or simply firing the offending workers, many companies are trying to get them help:

"Today's growing company interest in EAPs is helping substance abusers receive help that, on their own, many never would have sought.

COMMUNITY EFFORTS AT PREVENTION

In considering preventive measures, society has turned to the schools, suggesting that they focus their efforts on combating drug use by making the curriculum more relevant to youth, ensuring successful experiences, and taking many of the same steps that reformers have advocated to combat delinquency.* Schools have been urged to conduct specific programs in drug education. As early as the 1920s it was proposed that education about the dangers of narcotics be provided in schools. Thomas (1926) urged that the public school "put over this program and call to its aid every moral force available." Clark (1970, p. 89) suggested that "courses in the dangers of drugs should be integrated into school curricula with supporting evidence as solid as geometry." School courses and seminars have been established to present information about drugs. Johnson (1968) described the goal of such a program in a junior high school: "to help each student establish a set of values, to look at himself in HIS world, to look at his peers who are such an important part of life, to determine just what HE was going to do when faced with decisions about the use of these dangerous drugs" (p. 84–85). Wattenberg (1973, p. 387) asserted that drug education programs are a "stock solution." He observed that two faulty premises underlie such efforts: that youngsters are ignorant about the effects of drugs, and that fear will prevent them from experimenting. He argued that teachers do not credit their students with being as knowledgeable as in reality they are. Psychologic studies have shown that scare tactics do not work. Wattenberg held that drug education is not a panacea, but offers an opportunity for young people "to weigh evidence and make decisions."

McMorris (1966) pleaded that unless the mass media join "in an all out campaign" for education, "the American dream will evaporate into a nightmare of generally self-imposed narcotic insanity from which there will be no return." In 1971 the Federal Communications Commission issued a directive in which it served notice to local radio stations that if they played songs with lyrics "tending to promote or glorify the use of illegal drugs," they could lose their licenses (*Yale Alumni Magazine* 12/73). For years the media have presented public service messages describing the dangers of drug use and publicizing resources for drug information.

Griffenhagen (1973) described a "philatelic war on drug abuse" in which the post offices of countries throughout the world have produced postage stamps with a drug-abuse prevention theme. The United States issued such a commemorative stamp in 1971. Griffenhagen stated that the entire history of drug abuse education and prevention could be traced through postage stamps.

*See Chapter 2 of Volume II.

The federal government has combated drug use through massive educational programs, especially through the Department of Health and Human Services. That agency has produced radio and television spot announcements, posters, pamphlets, brochures, and films. Believing that particular segments of the population should be targeted, materials have been designed for specific age and ethnic groups. The Department of Justice also has published an abundance of material. Pointing out that most states have laws requiring drug education, the Department of Justice has suggested resources that include informed speakers, group discussions, and peer group pressure. It has provided specific information as to inclusion of drug materials in science or health curricula and has suggested activities as alternatives to participation in the "drug scene." The Drug Enforcement Administration of the Department of Justice has issued dozens of posters, many with full color photographs of football players and slogans such as "You have the ball, make the right decision," "Rise above the wrong crowd," and "You can see through a drug play." The National Coordinating Council on Drug Education (undated) has published *Super Me, Super Yo,* a bilingual book (English and Spanish) designed to help children to develop a positive self-image. The Council believed that this publication, issued more than a decade ago, represented a "dramatic breakthrough from the traditional approach to drug education."

> Rather than focusing on drugs, we are attempting to prevent the problems which often lead people to abuse drugs — unhappiness with themselves, their families, and their lives. We believe that drug abuse prevention can best be achieved by zeroing in on these potential problems before they arise. (Cocoran, undated)

The book pays no attention to drugs and is therefore different from other drug use prevention materials.

In some quarters considerable skepticism has been expressed as to the effectiveness of educational programs in the prevention of drug use. Brown (1961) claimed that information campaigns may be having an effect opposite from what was intended. The National Coordinating Council on Drug Education suggested that 85 percent of the hundreds of information films may be doing more harm than good, leading to the perpetuation of myths about drugs and thus furthering the "credibility gap" that already existed (*APA Monitor* 2/73). A University of Michigan study (Sackler 1973) found that the students who took part in a drug education program "sharply *increased* their experimentation with drugs of abuse." Greden et al. (1974), reporting on drug use at a military base, stated that "the attitude changes from 1970 to 1972 were puzzling. Marijuana was generally viewed more favorably, and there was little perceptible change in opinions about hallucinogens and heroin. This was true despite an intensive educational campaign to make drugs less appealing" (p. 80). Others evaluating drug information programs have found that they have not reduced drug use or prevented experimentation with drugs (Ross 1973; Weaver and Tennant 1973; Einstein 1983).

The National Commission on Marihuana and Drug Abuse (1973) concluded that no drug education program in the United States or anywhere else had been sufficiently successful to warrant its recommendation. The Commission therefore suggested a moratorium on all drug education programs in the schools and the repeal of legislative requirements for such courses in school curricula.* Later, the tide turned strongly toward school-based education programs. By the 1980s, many public school systems had made drug education a part of the required health curriculum even during the elementary grades.

During the last twenty years, drug education has been community-based. Bender (1963) recommended family life and educational and recreational programs for "bored, neglected kids" to avert drugs and crime. Meyer (1972, p. 14) believed that programs in community service "can usually tap a wellspring of idealism while discouraging drug usage" in young people. He cited as an example the 1968 presidential campaign in which youthful supporters of Senator Eugene McCarthy were encouraged to stay off drugs in order to "keep clean for Gene" and thus be more effective campaigners.

McKee (1975) questioned the need for drug education. He compared the attitudes toward drugs of users and nonusers and found a sharp difference between the two:

> There is definitely a genuine line of attitudinal demarcation present, in that one group does not use any form of illegal drug and reflects this in their response in a variety of ways, and the other, smaller group does use drugs and thinks (and therefore acts) quite differently. (p. 590)

McKee concluded that more factual drug education is not the solution and implied that the nonusers do not need such education at all and the users do not profit by it.

In summary, the trend in sociologic approaches to drug use is to curb and prevent drug use in ways identical with those used in curbing and preventing non-drug-related crime. The emphasis is on environmental change, with community programs and services in the forefront. Critics of sociologic mea-

---

*An example of such legislation is cited by Ross (1973, p. 70): Education and training, relating to "dangerous drug usage" has become mandatory in the schools in New York State since May, 1969, when amendment to the mental hygiene law made it compulsory."

sures do not oppose those measures *per se,* but are skeptical of the extent of their impact on individual drug users.

PSYCHIATRIC-PSYCHOLOGIC APPROACHES

INDIVIDUAL PSYCHOTHERAPY

Individual psychotherapy for drug users has been practiced, but in recent times this has largely given way to newer forms of therapy.* Maddux (1974) pointed out that considerable "personal strength" was required for an addict to succeed in outpatient psychotherapy and that most needed the external control of commitment. Occasionally those who enter treatment do so voluntarily, but usually it is required. Chein et al. (1964) have decried compulsory psychotherapy.

> The latest development in the approach that takes as its central goal the suppression of the evil is that of compulsory therapy. The idea is to sentence addicts to indefinite terms of psychotherapy in prisons-turned-hospitals. . . . Little thought is given to the question of whether psychotherapy is something that can be administered by force. Or to the question of whether even the willing addict patient can benefit from continuous psychotherapy uninterrupted by bouts with the responsibilities and temptations of freedom. (p. 332)

Although many writers on the subject share the reservations of Chein et al., they continue to regard psychologic treatment as important.

> Psychologic treatment directed toward the patient's personality needs is necessary if any permanent success is to be expected. . . . Individual treatment of the addict is a challenging problem. . . . Experience indicated that psychiatric treatment should be directed toward young patients with relatively well developed ego strengths who express, or are capable of expressing, overt anxiety and whose strivings and goals show good contact with reality and awareness of social and cultural demands. (Fraser and Grider 1967, p. 72)

Currently, individual therapy is recommended for users of various classes of drugs, but there is less enthusiasm about its use for those who are physically dependent. Meyer (1972), a spokesman for this position, advocated psy-

*Individual treatment has never been widely used with addicts. It had its greatest use before other forms of treatment came into existence in the 1960s.

chotherapy as the "treatment of choice" for drug users, but noted its ineffectiveness with addicts:

> Traditional psychoanalytic and other forms of individual psychotherapy and counseling which have attempted to break the cycle of addiction have generally failed. (p. 62)

> The treatment of an individual heroin addict by an individual private physician or psychiatrist should be avoided. (p. 79)

Doubt exists as to the effectiveness of any type of psychotherapy for both drug users and addicts. In a footnote to his text, Ausubel (1958, p. 82) stated that even though the cause of addiction may be primarily psychologic, psychotherapy may not be the best avenue of treatment. Ausubel claimed that even the more widely used group psychotherapy becomes for the addict an exercise in "group rationalization."

In this section we shall cover a spectrum of individual treatment, from formal psychoanalysis five times a week with an analyst to informal crisis counseling by "ex-addicts." The psychoanalytic efforts described here occurred primarily in circumstances in which the drug user participated voluntarily. The other individual approaches have been used for both compulsory and voluntary patients. In the 1920s and in the 1930s, psychoanalysis was the procedure of choice for a variety of psychiatric disorders. It was used to treat drug dependence at a time when few other methods were available. "It is true the psycho-analyst is justified in asserting that the only radical approach to drug habits is through psycho-analytic treatment" (Glover 1932, p. 298).

Proponents of psychoanalysis regard drug use as symptomatic of an underlying personality defect. Successful treatment entails identification and resolution of that defect. Jones (1920) stated that repressed homosexuality plays "a highly important, and perhaps the essential part" in addiction to both drugs and alcohol. Benedek (1936) believed that the analysis of depression "would constitute the essential task of the analysis of the addict," and she described a case in which addiction was regarded as a defense against depression. From her paper it is unclear whether either depression or addiction was cured.

Psychoanalytic treatment calls for, "initially, a tolerant and permissive atmosphere" (Savitt 1954). Simmel (1929) described how in sanitorium treatment the drug-dependent patient is provided with "transitory substitute-gratifications in order to help him to renounce his symptom." In the hospital the patient is encouraged to be like a little child and lie in bed, with a special nurse assigned to him, ministering to his every need; thus, the patient's unconscious "receives the uttermost fulfillment of his deepest longing, in spite of the torments which he suffers consciously" in giving up the drug. This situation is then analyzed and, "as treatment progresses, the infantile phase spontaneously disappears." In 1955 Glover observed that the analyst should expect to be drawn from his "analytical seclusion" if he takes an addict into treatment. He warned that addicts sometimes have to be extricated from "awkward social situations." This "protective support" might well provide secondary gains and complicate the transference. However, Glover saw no option but to provide this protection and work through the consequences.

The search for hard data to evaluate the results of psychoanalytic treatment reveals nothing substantial, merely sporadic case reports. During the last two decades orthodox psychoanalysis has been used only rarely to treat drug use, but modifications of psychoanalytic techniques have been applied. Wieder and Kaplan (1969) reported several cases in which they used psychoanalysis or psychoanalytically oriented psychotherapy. They claimed success in treating a seventeen-year-old marijuana user and a fourteen-year-old alcoholic. In several other cases, young adults continued to use drugs after treatment. Goldberg and Goldberg (1973) described an "existential-analytic" group procedure emphasizing "here and now" confrontation. In their residential treatment program, "insight therapy" followed attitudinal and behavioral change. These authors observed that causal explanations were obstacles to change. They asserted that reconstructive work is useful only after behavioral change has occurred. Goldburgh (1968) described his intensive work with a young man with whom a "gentle, skilled and knowledgeable" psychoanalyst had made no headway in months in five-times-a-week treatment. Goldburgh used hypnosis followed by increasingly more conventional analytically oriented therapy. The treatment, lasting six years, was so intensive that the therapist took his patient with him on vacations. Finally, he claimed success, but there is no report of prolonged follow-up. Levine and Ludwig (1966) used "hypnodelic treatment" with narcotic addicts that involved the controlled administration of LSD and hypnosis, combined with analytic interpretation. Patients were reported to have worked closely with the therapist during hypnotic induction. After the three-hour session, patients continued thinking and working on their problems. A factor in the procedure was the development of the "ability to produce a mental state in which thoughts and feelings assume an exaggerated sense of meaning, importance and significance." The effectiveness of the treatment on the addicts' abandonment of drug use, both in the hospital and later, is not clear.

In common with psychoanalysis, Janov's (1970) "Primal Therapy" emphasizes the uncovering of childhood experiences that resulted in a person's denial of needs and repression of feelings.* This treatment entails the "dis-

*Although Primal Therapy differs in many respects from psychoanalysis as currently practiced, Janov stated that "in some respects, Primal Therapy has returned full cycle to early Freud" (p. 206).

mantling of the causes of tension, defense systems and neurosis" (p. 20). During therapy the addict learns to feel "primal pain," which is the consequence of believing, "I am not loved and I have no hope of love when I am really myself" (p. 25). "When Primal Pain is gone, it will no longer be necessary to berate or plead with an addict to stop his behavior" (p. 363). Janov recommended that the addict be confined for ten to fifteen weeks during Primal Therapy. He has maintained that Primal Therapy of addicts is "quick and to the point" (p. 363), and has asserted that addicts, whose main defense is heroin, are more treatable than many neurotics with elaborate networks of defenses.

Most professionals in the drug abuse field have found that psychoanalytic procedures have failed.* Savitt (1954) pointed out that because of their inability to delay gratification, addicts are generally considered poor prospects for analytic treatment. He said that the "major technical problem" facing the analyst is keeping the patient in treatment long enough for the latter "to gain effective insight into the meaning of his condition." Critics of psychoanalysis have contended that this mode of treatment is not effective with addicts or other drug users. Carlson (1974) observed: "The assumption that I run into in the psychoanalytical community in terms of treating addiction problems is that 'if you understand yourself, you will get well,' and that is translated 'cognitive insight produces cure,' and that ain't so!" Kramer (1971, p. 668) also observed that traditional psychiatric techniques with a psychoanalytic frame of reference "have not been useful in the management of opiate dependence" because they overlook social determinants, such as drug availability and peer pressure. In addition, he said, drug dependence can be so strong that it "assumes a life of its own" that is not affected by "solving the underlying conflict."

Asserting that conventional individual psychotherapeutic methods "oriented to educated, middle class patients" have generally failed with the heroin addict, A. M. Freeman (1963, p. 204) advocated "social therapy" that would help the addict reenter the community. Messinger and Zitrin (1965) maintained that it was wasteful to expend energy and money and "fatuous" to expect psychiatry "to achieve any substantial result with the drug-addicted psychopathic criminal."

The literature contains little concerning the application of rational therapy to the individual drug user. In his discussion of "integrity therapy," Drakeford (1967) implied that his approach could be implemented with individual sociopaths, including addicts. In a talk, Ellis (1976) claimed that "rational-emotive therapy" could be successful with drug addicts if their belief systems

---

*In Chapter 2 of Volume II we presented reports of the failure of psychoanalytic procedures in changing the criminal.

were attacked and their attitudes toward themselves and the outside world were changed.

Fort (1972, p. 243) stated that ideally in an outpatient setting, users of drugs other than heroin should be offered individual psychotherapy, whether it be "Freudian, Bernian, eclectic, etc." Meyer (1972) suggested that through psychotherapy, adolescent hallucinogen users could be helped to resolve adolescent adjustment reactions. At the Langley Porter Youth Drug Unit in San Francisco, Salasnek and Amini (1971) reported that the combination of individual psychotherapy and the social therapies "fit together hand in glove" in treating adolescent narcotic addicts: "It is through the use of individual psychotherapy that these people are helped in a more protected setting to get a glimpse of their defensive systems and to begin to repair some of their ego deficits" (p. 142). It is not clear from most program descriptions what issues are explored in individual psychotherapy and by what techniques.

Multimodality drug treatment programs usually include a form of individual counseling. The counseling may be psychologic, social, vocational, educational, or religious. Individual counseling is often combined with pharmacotherapy as in methadone programs. It is also an adjunct to detoxification programs. Counseling sometimes is performed both by paraprofessionals and "ex-addicts." The patient may meet with his counselor as often as once a day while he is an inpatient (e.g., Raynes and Patch 1973, description of the Boston City Hospital Drug Detoxification Unit) or less frequently. At New York's Beth Israel methadone treatment unit, "patient assistants" have the function of talking with an addict about his problems (Nyswander 1967). Beth Israel has also used counselors (not "ex-addicts") who offer "pragmatic" counseling (Glasscote et al. 1972, p. 77).

Counseling is the core of many aftercare programs. Describing the NARA (Narcotic Addict Rehabilitation Act) units in federal prisons, Farkas et al. (1970) reported that the counselor coordinates everything for the patient's aftercare. He "handles personal, marital, family, educational, vocational and emotional crises as they arise." The same is true of counselors of NARA parolees in the Los Angeles area. Peck and Klugman (1973) stated that half the "rehabilitation specialists" treating this group are ex-addicts and half are ex-felons. There is no single theoretical approach. Rather, "any reasonable pragmatic approach that has some promise of working is given a try."

In short, a survey of the literature indicates that many drug treatment programs offer what is called "individual therapy" or "counseling." There is considerable variability in the frequency of treatment, the scope of treatment, and the therapist's administration of treatment. The literature contains very little descriptive material on content, process, or follow-up of individual psychologic treatment efforts.

GROUP PSYCHOTHERAPY

The origin of group psychotherapy is in dispute. Dreikurs (1969) regarded Alfred Adler and his co-workers in the 1920s as the "pioneers of group therapy" when they opened counseling centers to work with groups of parents and children.* The traditional group therapeutic efforts were psychoanalytic in orientation, with variations introduced by Horney, Sullivan, Slavson, and others. The major emergence of group therapy was in the 1950s, when it was perceived to be "a viable solution to the shortage of trained personnel, . . . the lack of adequate community resources for psychiatric patients, and the high cost of individual treatment" (Kaplan and Sadock, 1971, p. vii). In the mid-1960s, group therapy was regarded as "the treatment of choice for a widening range of patients with highly diverse problems" (Kaplan and Sadock). Anthony (1971, p. 28) has observed that "a cascade of experimental approaches has inundated the group arena." These include Gestalt therapy, self-confrontation groups, marathon therapy, transactional analysis, family therapy, behavior modification, and many more.

Delinquents and criminals have participated in institutional therapeutic groups as a requirement, but only occasionally voluntarily.† They have not been treated in most outpatient clinics and practices. The same is true of physically dependent drug users.‡ According to Craig (1982, p. 139), group therapy is now a part of nearly all drug abuse programs. He asserted: "Group therapy can have dramatic and exciting effects on a drug addict. If the addict can form a therapeutic alliance, it can be the modality that makes the ultimate difference in the patient's eventual rehabilitation." Kaplan and Sadock (1971) pointed out that no article has discussed group treatment of younger drug users because very little group therapeutic work had been done. Before the 1970s many practitioners believed that drug users (especially "addicts"), old or young, were unsuitable candidates for group psychotherapy and so were unwilling to treat them. Johnson (1963, p. 99) pointed out that addicts do not tolerate anxiety and when made anxious resort to drugs. Yalom (1970, p. 158) listed addicts among the groups of poor candidates for outpatient intensive group psychotherapy. However, no other mode of treatment was any more successful. Lowinson and Zwerling (1971, p. 602) observed that because individual therapy had failed with drug addicts, group therapy began to be widely used, especially in hospitals.

---

*Anthony (1971) pointed out that it was Freud who first outlined a group psychology. However, Freud himself did not practice group therapy.

†See Chapter 2 of Volume II.

‡Here we shall use the word addict because this is the term employed in the literature.

In the 1950s a professional literature started to emerge describing attempts to treat drug addicts in groups. McClain (1951) reported holding group discussions with addicts at the Lexington facility. There the therapist did not attempt to change the addict's basic character but, with a permissive attitude, tried to "increase 'external' superego forces." McClain asserted that he was successful in helping addicts to understand their drug problem better, but he did not indicate that they ceased using drugs after they left the institution. Abrams et al. (1958) described informal group discussions with addicts at the Cook County Jail. In a "permissive, yet cooperative atmosphere," addicts were encouraged to express themselves and relate to others. Again no results were included, other than successful "ventilation of feelings." Haskell (1958) reported some success in helping groups of Riker's Island Penitentiary inmates to learn new occupational, community, and family roles.

In addition to role playing and discussion groups, more traditional group therapy was conducted with drug addicts in the 1950s. Techniques were not strictly psychoanalytic, but therapists conceived of group process and content in analytic terms. Thorpe and Smith (1953) described phases in the group therapy of addicts.

> The group [changes] from a conglomerate of chaotic individuals griping about how badly they are being treated to individuals who have arrived at a consensus that *they* are the source of their own problems. They then progress to a group of persons who are tentatively being tested, and accepted by each other and by the therapist, and finally to a stage where they begin to confide in one another. (p. 75)

In this group experience, addicts learned to acknowledge parts of themselves that they considered "bad," and consequently they were believed not to need drugs to deal with denial-caused anxiety. The practitioners did not share the then-current pessimism about successful psychiatric treatment of drug addicts. In fact, three years later Thorpe (1956) declared that "the most useful tool for the beginning exploration of an addict's problems is a group" (p. 70). He then described several different types of group organization and stressed the importance of the therapist's exploring his own countertransference feelings. Thorpe warned that "unless these are explored and dealt with, the group invariably disintegrates" (p. 70).

Sabath (1964) attempted to treat addicts on a voluntary basis, emphasizing the sharing of experiences rather than focusing on and interpreting patients' psychodynamics. His evaluation of group process was conceptually psychoanalytic. Sabath believed that group treatment was advantageous because transferences could be played out. When a negative transference developed toward a drug addict or staff member, the addict could still develop a positive transference to others in the group. Another benefit of group treatment was a decrease in pressure from authority figures, accompanied by an increase in pressure from peers. Peer pressure has been regarded by many workers as the most important aspect of the treatment. Sabath emphasized the development of personal relationships with other group members rather than disclosure and emotional ventilation. He noted that "addicts' telling their story [was a] repetitive exaggeration and invention of their past glories." Some addicts believed that they would be cured merely by relating their most painful memories and thoughts to the group therapist. Sabath claimed that his work led to the discovery that his approach was successful in maintaining "some continuous relationships with hard-core addicts on a voluntary outpatient basis for longer periods than had been possible with other techniques in the past." He did not discuss the extent of the participants' drug use or of his own follow-up.

D. X. Freedman (1974) observed that group processes evolve in the therapy of the addict in much the same way that they evolve in drug cults. He stated that "for the larger proportion of addicted persons, the sharing of therapeutic experience, reinforced by frequent contact with peers, seems important." Freedman observed that in the group setting the reformed addict is compelled to relinquish his "false autonomy."

Psychoanalytic concepts have been incorporated into many different forms of group treatment. Gradually, however, psychoanalysis has given way to the rational therapies as they have emerged into prominence. Berne (1966) claimed that transactional analysis was applicable to the treatment of drug addicts. He said that the "primary game" of the addict is similar to that of the alcoholic (inviting persecution and seeking rescue) and that "secondary games" are played with a variety of people—policemen, doctors, judges, and prison personnel. However, Berne did not report having treated addicts personally.

Farkas et al. (1970) described a program for treating addicts at the Federal Correctional Institutional at Milan, where Glasser's reality therapy served as the basis of treatment. Quartets of addicts formed groups to participate with other quartets in the large inmate community. In addition, small therapy groups, called "T-groups," were the "basic interacting units" that met twice a week for one-and-a-half hours. Each T-group was composed of a staff person, a "linker," and a pair of patients from a quartet. Reinstein (1973) described an outpatient rational therapy group in which the emphasis was on managing immediate problems effectively rather than "attempting to unravel unconscious psychodynamics" (p. 840). Carlson (1974) described transactional analysis (T.A.) in outpatient group treatment of drug and alcohol users in the "velvet ghetto," a middle- and upper middle-class population. In T.A. "growth groups," T.A. principles were taught, life "scripts" were analyzed, and there was a "rational-behavioral script revision." Patients signed contracts to make behavioral changes, and those contracts were reviewed weekly in the group meeting.

In the 1970s when the United States was alarmed over an apparent "epidemic" of drug use, the mental health profession was subjected to more and more pressure to provide treatment. Community and institutional programs elected group therapy as the primary mode of treatment.* Different types of therapy groups proliferated, all designed for drug users: "rap" groups, group therapy groups, psychodrama groups, meditation groups, creative writing groups, social skills groups, recreation groups, and assertiveness training groups. In 1977, King declared that "group therapy is the most usual choice of treatment in programs for adolescent drug abusers generally" (p. 23). Zucker and Waksman (1973) said that for the young male drug addict population that "is typically refractory to individual psychotherapy," group treatment seems to be "particularly applicable," especially if it is part of a total rehabilitation program.

In most institutions some form of "milieu therapy" is used, in which the "group" is the entire patient or inmate community. Ramirez (1967) advocated "total milieu therapy" as the means to modify negative attitudes and to reinforce positive attitudes.† This entailed peer group discussions and "confrontations" with professionals and ex-addicts. Within the milieu, therapy subgroups of ten patients each met three times a week. The guiding idea behind milieu therapy is that change is best promoted twenty-four hours a day by what happens in the entire living unit, rather than in isolated therapeutic contacts in smaller groups or between individual patients and their therapists.

> We attempt to make the social milieu stable, firm, consistent, orderly and giving. By giving, I do not mean indulging; I mean responding with attentive interest and concern for the patient's feelings and behavior. Every employee having contact with patients is therefore conceived of as having a therapeutic role. (Maddux 1965, p. 170)

The entire residential milieu assists the patient to learn that "anxiety does not mean catastrophe" and that anxiety can be mastered without drugs (Maddux). Gold and Coghlan (1973) described a residential treatment milieu for

---

*In institutions long accustomed to treating drug-dependent individuals, the shift to group therapy came before the 1970s. Samuels (1966), describing the situation at the Lexington facility stated; "Until about 10 years ago, doctors emphasized individual psychotherapy, given one hour a week. But even an hour a week was too big a load for the staff and the emphasis has shifted to group therapy with eight or 10 patients" (p. 36).

†Ramirez's milieu therapy evolved into what he called a "therapeutic community."

adolescent drug users at the Holy Cross Campus of the Pius XII School at Rhinecliff, N.Y. The primary concept was that a person would change because of the "total environmental press" of the milieu:

> "Cure" is obtained by extinguishing the unacceptable behavior patterns and learning new acceptable ones that are reinforced by peer pressure and a total environmental press toward associating good feelings with this new learned behavior. Learning new behaviors leads to changes about oneself. (p. 2)

By its very structure, psychodrama is a form of group treatment. Deeths (1970) described a technique wherein the addict ventilates his feelings. In a presumed "rebirth," he gets in touch with long-buried feelings that emerge when past traumas are reconstructed and reenacted. Boylin (1971) reported how psychodrama helped a female addict to express her feelings about entering a male treatment community. This resulted in the patient's outpouring of rage and profanity, with the therapist yelling to facilitate more self-expression.

In much group work with drug users, and especially in the therapeutic community, the techniques of encounter are used (e.g., Perkins 1972). Hollander (1973) described treating a group of ten adolescents, some of whom were drug users. Warm-up exercises were practiced first, such as pounding on a sofa to release inhibited aggressive feelings. The sessions were then devoted to assessing and improving interpersonal relationships through encounter techniques.* Hollander reported that all members of the group benefited. The non-users were able to see the users as individuals, rather than as junkies. Five of the six users abstained from drugs for nearly a year after termination of the group.

Frakas et al. (1970) described marathon groups used at Terminal Island. In sessions of eight to twelve hours, over one or two days, group pressure was said to "lower the defenses of the participants [addicts] and accelerate the therapeutic experience." Kilmann (1974) applied marathon techniques to female narcotic addicts. He reported that compared with control subjects who did not participate in the marathon, the addicts "became more interested in their obligations, made greater efforts to be more successful," and were highly positive about the experience. Hampden-Turner (1976) described marathon groups lasting forty-five or more hours at the Delancey Street Foundation, a San Francisco self-help residential and therapeutic community for drug-using as well as non-using criminals. In sessions called "Dissipa-

---

*Hollander referred specifically to the techniques described by William Schutz in *Joy* (New York: Grove Press, 1967).

tions," the participants' "deepest experiences and fears are explored as exhaustion wears down their defenses" (p. 19), thereby "dissipating" their self-hatred and guilt. Page (1982) and Page and Miehl (1982) reported that marathon group therapy was effective in helping drug users in a residential treatment setting explore problems and receive feedback from others.

Panio (1975) offered a preliminary report on "saturation group therapy" (SGT). Small groups of adolescent polydrug users spent weekends together, during which there were fifteen hours of structured group therapy per weekend. Although he did not present details, Panio claimed a "positive treatment effect."

In the late 1960s and into the 1970s, the encounter movement gathered momentum. Inevitably there were psychic casualties, and only after the initial enthusiasm had worn off did dispassionate evaluation of encounter techniques begin. In a book addressed principally to parents, Lieberman et al. (1973) indicated that he and his associates did not believe that the encounter experience promoted change in drug-using adolescents. The authors were critical of the "indiscriminate prescription and use of this method for experience, kicks or therapy — too often without any screening of the participants." They cautioned that the emphasis on "feelings" could be counterproductive in adolescents who needed instead "to learn to discriminate between freedom and license."

Many practitioners regard drug use as a symptom of a disturbed family system and contend that the entire family must be treated (e.g., Cleveland 1981). Hirsch (1961) contended that what is "basic in psychiatry" is that children are affected by their parents' unconscious conflicts; consequently parents must be treated as well as the child. In fact, Kaufman (1985, p. 112) declared, "Therapy can only begin when all family members are present." The task in family therapy is to uncover the function that drug use serves in a family and to "expose conscious or unconscious support of the addict by some family members" (Bartlett 1975, p. 272). Wolper and Scheiner (1981, p. 349) described the family therapist's aim as to "examine the way the family is organized around the symptom (drug use) rather than focus only on the symptomatic member." Stanton (1982, p. 145) found that the "function of the system" was to keep the family together: "The family system served to maintain the addiction." Wellisch and Hays (1973, p. 222) noted that parents in treatment focus on the "comfortable subject" of their offspring's drug use to avoid being confronted with their own problems. As Alexander and Dibb (1975) said, "the addiction seemed to serve as an agreed-upon safe locus for most of the criticism that did occur. Parents and addicts often asserted that the addiction was the only family problem they could think of" (p. 504). Hirsch claimed that the parents in a group that he treated were "indirect pushers," in that they covered for their children, paid their debts, and gave them money. The "tremendous guilt" experienced by mothers and fathers blocked them from examining their own involvement in their children's problems. Hirsch's article did not reveal the results of the treatment of drug users with whom he worked in family groups. Wellisch and Hays reported mixed results, such as moderation, but not discontinuance, of drug use. In an article about the treatment of drug-using adolescents and their families at the Detroit Medical Center, Kempler and Mackenna (1975) described the key objective as "restructuring the family as a means of reducing or removing symptoms and improving family functioning." Alexander and Dibb (1975, p. 510) said that a family therapist has two courses: to "pry the addict away from the family" and to alter family process to promote growth of the addict, rather than dependence. Each alternative has its problems. They concluded:

> In our opinion, the addict-family syndrome presents a vital challenge to family therapists to develop methods that are powerful and subtle enough to change families in which resistance is high, the connection between family process and the presenting problem is easily denied, and the need for intervention is great. (p. 511)

The "systems" approach has become increasingly popular. Einstein (1983, p. v) described this development as follows: "The literary 'fact' that no man is an island unto himself becomes translated, treatmentwise, into no man should be the sole and isolated focus of treatment because he represents and is represented by a variety of systems." Einstein followed this by asserting, "Unfortunately, the dynamics of this ongoing revolution in treatment philosophy have not seemed to touch or effect the treatment of the drug user." He suggests a "refocus" of attention upon treating the drug user because "at times, it seems that current opinions and data have an existence unrelated to the increase or decrease in drug use." There seems to have been no group treatment technique devised especially for drug users. Rather, the forms of treatment that have been used for other psychiatric populations have been adapted to drug users.* In the therapeutic community, new techniques have been introduced and old ones combined. It is to this widely used group treatment method that we now turn.

---

*We have not described recreational therapy, music therapy, occupational therapy, and other forms of therapy that are used with groups of drug users. These are standard modes of treatment that are offered to a variety of inpatient groups at institutions that are psychiatrically oriented. They have various therapeutic rationales. For example, Wittenberg (1974) described art therapy with adolescent drug users. She said that the therapeutic experience can provide an "escape valve for the emotions," improve interpersonal relations, contribute to the development of inner discipline, and, overall, help to "strengthen the ego."

THE THERAPEUTIC COMMUNITY

In the preface to Maxwell Jones's *The Therapeutic Community* (1953), Goodwin Watson stated that Jones's work was based on the belief that "a healthy group life would make healthy individuals." Watson observed that the therapeutic community "permits a psychiatrist to serve about twenty times as many persons as he could carry through psychoanalysis." At his Belmont Hospital unit Jones described the treatment of "some of the most anti-social elements in society." He stated that the entire time that a patient spends in a hospital should be considered "treatment," not only the relatively few hours that he might spend with an individual therapist. Resocialization was to occur through group education, and problem solving through group discussion. The program of the Belmont unit included regular meetings of the entire patient community, psychodrama, recreation, workshop training, and social activities. In the therapeutic community (T.C.), barriers to communication that were in part a product of the hospital hierarchy were broken down in order to foster greater openness between patients and staff. Jones was describing a cooperative group in which a democratic process was maintained by patients sharing in the decision making.

Because traditional methods of treatment have been ineffective with drug users, the therapeutic community has been embraced and has achieved popularity.* However, the T.C. approach used today in drug treatment programs is markedly different from that which Jones originally described in 1953.† The idea of living and working in a community has been retained, but many others ideas and procedures have been altered. Instead of being a democratic organization, each T.C. has a rigid heirarchy, and "ex-addicts" usually hold the primary roles in the power structure. The form of group therapy is that of "encounter," "confrontation," or "attack," in which the drug addict is regarded initially as an infant in an autocratic family structure. Kaufman (1973, p. 4) has described the T.C. as "a family which both loves its members and sets limits for them." He has typified T.C. leaders as "beloved but authoritarian parental figures" (Kaufman 1985, p. 91). In describing Daytop, one of the best known T.C.s, Shelly and Bassin (1965) observed that the addict is "regarded as a 3-year-old who must be told what to do with the expectation that if he disobeys he will be punished promptly. The whole design of

*We have included the therapeutic community in the literature review of Volume II, Chapter 2. In Chapter 11 of that volume we presented a detailed account of how criminals functioned in the therapeutic community at Saint Elizabeths Hospital, Washington, D.C.

†Smart (1976, p. 145) commented that "a reading of the program descriptions and attendance at actual sessions is likely to raise doubts...about how much shared decision making, multiple leadership, and therapeutic culture actually exists."

the program is to help him grow from a child of 3 to an adult" (p. 190). Some T.C.s reject professionals and anything that smacks of professionalism, although Meyer (1972) observed that even if there is an antiprofessional stance, a great deal of professional jargon is used:

> For good measure, pseudo-psychoanalytic jargon is sometimes thrown in where it is felt that individuals must progress through oral, anal, and genital phases of rehabilitation to the point where they can be responsible for their actions. It is not entirely clear to what degree these latter principles are of value in understanding the nature of the therapeutic process. (p. 65)

The grandfather, or archetype, of all therapeutic communities treating drug addicts is Synanon.* Charles Dederich, a layman and ex-alcoholic, is its founder. Synanon was established in 1958 as a one-room storefront operation in Ocean Park, California. At its height, it had close to 8,000 members and had $8 million worth of holdings in real estate in eight cities. The Synanon program served as the prototype for many other organizations that set up programs to help drug users become completely abstinent.

To be admitted to Synanon the addict had to prove that he wanted help. In his initial contact, roadblocks were deliberately set in his path. He might be required to wait for an appointment, then told to return on another day, and possibly asked to pay an entrance fee.† On entry into the residential community, the addict passed through withdrawal without the support of medication. After "kicking the habit," he was considered "an employee of the organization" (Yablonsky and Dederich 1965, p. 206). Synanon aimed to help the addict to grow from an "emotional infant" to a mature, responsible adult. In the initial period the addict's behavior was totally controlled by others. He began at the bottom of a structure that Yablonsky (1965) termed an "autocratic pyramid." The symposium-seminar, or "synanon," was the mode of group therapy used. It was a forum in which, according to a Synanon member, addicts could "dump their emotional garbage and learn about themselves, a kind of pressure cooker for working out what's bugging you" (Yablonsky 1973, p. 749). In these meetings the confrontations were often ruthless, with nothing barred except violence. A "standard therapeutic tool" of "attack

---

*The word 'synanon' originated with a newly arrived addict in the early days of the organization. In his attempt to say two 'foreign' words — 'symposium' and 'seminar' — in the same breath, he blurted out 'synanon': 'I want to get into another one of those — symp . . . Sem — *synanons*' " (Yablonsky 1965, p. ix).

†Glaser (1971) said that an admission fee of $1,000 places Synanon beyond the range of the street addict.

therapy" was called the "haircut," in which the addict's wrongdoing was "caricatured, exaggerated, and severely ridiculed" (Yablonsky and Dederich 1965, p. 215).* In addition to Synanon meetings three times a week, there were lectures, seminars, theatrical groups, and other programs. The most severe punishment was exclusion from the community, or "30 days on the street." As the addict progressed, he rose in the hierarchy of Synanon and eventually could become a therapist or executive. Dederich, quoted by Yablonsky (1973, p. 783), maintained that Synanon did a thorough job of reformation. "In Synanon, we don't violate the law or use social lubricants [alcohol] and we are opposed to this type of behavior. We are more square than our square friends. Perhaps we have to have a more rigid moral fiber than is believed to be necessary in the larger society." The success of Synanon was measured in terms of total "clean man days" (days without drug use) earned for the entire organization.

Rosenthal (1973, p. 85) observed that Synanon viewed remaining within the Synanon community as preferable to leaving it. Glaser (1971, p. 618) pointed out that, for the addict, Synanon became "a way of life in itself, rather than a means to the end of re-entering the general society." Partly because Synanon was an entity unto itself, it was observed that the organization was strongly antiprofessional. Glaser stated that professionals were viewed with suspicion, and Dederich himself was quoted as having declared, "We do not want or need interference from professionals" (Yablonsky 1965, p. 386).

A second well-known program was that of Daytop Village ("Daytop" standing for "Drug Addicts Treated On Probation"). David Deitch, a heroin addict for fourteen years and a graduate of Synanon, was Daytop's main architect and first executive director. Daytop offered a voluntary, residential abstinence program. Unlike Synanon it had professionals on its staff; a physician served as "psychiatric superintendent." Casriel and Deitch (1966) described Daytop as having a "highly organized, paternalistic, tribe-like family structure." Daytop had three house rules: no drugs or alcohol, no violence, and no shirking of responsibility (Shelly and Bassin 1965). When he entered, the addict went through withdrawal; he was then "taught to grow up" (Casriel and Deitch). No excuses for his behavior were permitted. Encounter group therapy sessions differed from more traditional group therapy in that there was no formal leader, no search for causes, and a focus on current, rather than past, behavior. In these encounters, the addict was embarrassed, ridiculed, scolded, and laughed at for behavior that was not approved of. The "haircut" was administered here, too. "Every member is expected to react spontaneously on a visceral level employing, if he feels the need of it, the crudest terminology and vehement verbal expression" (Shelly and Bassin

---

*In some programs, the addict *literally* is given a haircut: his head is shaved.

1965, p. 192). In addition to the regularly scheduled encounters, group marathons lasting more than thirty hours were held. Other features of the program were seminars and a job-status system. Casriel and Deitch (1966) stated that 84 percent of the addicts who remained for a month would stay for the duration and "get well." The addicts were said to remain in the program voluntarily because they develop an "anaclitic identification" and "positive transference" to the group and to the facility.* When the addict has participated from eighteen to twenty-four months, according to Casriel and Deitch (1966), "a new personality has emerged, one starkly different from that of the 'dope fiend' who entered." As an "ex-addict," he was prepared to reenter life outside Daytop, or he could remain to assume administrative or teaching responsibilities.

Synanon and Daytop were models for many later efforts at helping people give up drugs. Heavy confrontation by peers in residential therapeutic communities has remained for nearly two decades as the most widely practiced group treatment modality. (See Rosenthal and Biase 1969; Farkas et al. 1970; Glaser 1971; DeLeon et al. 1972; Perkins 1972; Rosenthal 1973; Treffert and Sach 1973.) In some of these communities, rewards for acceptable behavior consist of advancement in the organization's hierarchy. The staff of some programs is composed largely of former residents.

T.C.s differ in length of residence required, initiation procedures, frequency of group meetings, and provision of ancillary services.† However, the primary objective of all the T.C.s is to achieve a drug-free state and rehabilitation through resocialization. This is to be accomplished by rewarding socially acceptable behavior and penalizing unacceptable behavior. Glasscote et al. (1972, p. 37) described the factors in a T.C. addict's progress from "applicant to graduate" as "motivation, isolation, deprivation, denunciation, confrontation, participation, elevation, and graduation."

Controversy has arisen as to the usefulness of mixing addicts and other patients. Barr et al. (1973) described an "abstinence, interdisciplinary community" at the Eaglesville (Pennsylvania) Hospital and Rehabilitation Center. They found that treating drug addicts and alcoholics together was beneficial:

> The presence of each group helps to counteract certain typical characteristics of the other group that interfere with the ability to profit from treat-

---

*Even in this treatment format, psychoanalytic terminology is used in describing psychologic process.

†Many different programs have been used within the T.C. Goldfield and Lauer (1971) described the use of creative writing as an adjunct to treatment of young addicts at Langley Porter. Lebow (1973) mentioned the use of T'ai Chi Ch'uan, a Chinese martial art involving ritualized exercise in slow motion. This, along with "biodynamic self-regulation" and "autogenics," was part of a T.C. at the Federal Correctional Institution at Lompoc, California.

ment, in particular, the impulsivity of the drug addicts and the passivity of the alcohol addicts. The mix of addictions brings into the hospital persons of varied social and cultural backgrounds. . .who, along with the heterogeneous staff, provide a microcosm of the larger outside community.

Pokorny and Wiggins (1972) described a T.C. composed of addicts and "straights." The addicts asserted their "superiority" over the others and assumed control, becoming virtual policemen as well as counselors of others. The drug-free addicts repeatedly put down those who were not drug-free. Rosenfeld (see Glasscote et al. 1972, p. 188) has stated that mixing patient groups "leads to endless disruptive, impulsive acting out and regressive behavior."

Opinion is divided over the effectiveness of the therapeutic community itself. Boorstein (1967) has stated that the T.C. is the "only approach" that "can possibly deal with the numbers involved and the ego defects present." Rosenthal (1973a), speaking of the T.C., proclaimed, "Today, there is a cure." He maintained that the T.C. returns addicts to "drug-free and fully functional lives." Evaluations of the T.C. appear to range from unqualified endorsement to a total dismissal of its usefulness. But Brill and Lieberman (1969) observed that there is often a lack of carry-over of a new behavior into the community once the addict is discharged. Levy (1973a) was critical of the ex-addict staffs for ignoring the expertise of professionals. Goldberg (1975) observed that ex-addicts and "confrontational models" tend to shut some professionals out. Turnover in personnel on ex-addict staffs is commonly high; consequently, administration of therapeutic communities is poor. Specific techniques of the T.C. have been criticized. Walder (1965) said that from the standpoint of learning theory, the humiliation, ridicule, and sarcasm of "attack therapy" constitute punishment, and punishment is an ineffective means of eliminating socially undesirable behavior. He stated that in Synanon the positive aspect of "attack therapy" is that the members appear to be concerned about the addict's behavior. "Whatever the value of punishment in Synanon, it is accepted only by virtue of the stronger rewards administered, since without these rewards attack would elicit negative motivations and cause the member to "split" (p. 304). Zarcone (1982) criticized other aspects of the Synanon approach: "There is not enough modeling of an alternative perceptual style, and the Synanon game often violates what should be an axiom: too much anger can make learning impossible" (p. 86).

Coulson et al. (1974), advocates of the T.C., voiced their objection to the confrontation method, especially for adolescent amphetamine users: "We feel confrontation is very reminiscent of the (amphetamine user's) life style, i.e., a high level of tension and suspicion and no moderation in approaching either people or drugs" (p. 10). Glasscote et al. (1972) questioned whether persuading the addict of his worthlessness is conducive to repairing defective egos and raising self-esteem. *Time* (12/11/72) cited an American Psychiatric Association report that said that no T.C. had managed to graduate more than a tiny fraction of those who had entered.

Smart (1976) cited problems in evaluating therapeutic communities and halfway houses that treat addicts. One difficulty is that recovery rates are inflated because they are based on the number of graduates, not on the number of original entrants. For example, Coghlan and Zimmerman (1972) stated that Daytop based its success rate on the number of participants who graduated and stayed drug-free, rather than on the total number of addicts who entered the program initially. These investigators presented the following statistics about Daytop treatment for the period January 1969 to January 1970:

694 entered   175 dropouts returned to the program
535 dropped out   38 graduates, four of whom returned to drugs
23 expelled

If one uses the 694 entrants as a base, the success rate ("graduation" rate) is 5.5 precent. However, if one uses the thirty-eight graduates as a base, the success rate (staying off drugs) is 89 percent (Coghlan and Zimmerman).

In addition, it has been noted (Smart, 1976) that it is impossible to determine which characteristics of a program are associated with high recovery rates. Another problem is that some programs have large numbers of polydrug users who are not opiate addicts. From recovery statistics it is not feasible to tell how this group responds.

The concept of the therapeutic community was oversold, according to Iverson and Wenger (1978, p. 90): "Their selling techniques were excellent but their product, although good, could not possibly reach the public's expectations. Few, if any, of the therapeutic communities can produce valid statistics which indicate such a high degree of success." All that Iverson and Wenger could conclude from their survey of research is that T.C.'s "have a positive influence on many of their residents" (p. 91). Karras (1979, p. 266) flatly stated that the T.C. has "not been demonstrated to be effective for the drug user, the mental health patient or alcoholic."

Gould (1972) maintained that the T.C. fails to change the user's values and life-style. He contended that most addicts change from manipulating in the drug world to manipulating in the straight world. He observed that other drugs are used, even though heroin use may decrease or be eliminated. Not impressed by T.C. results, Gould recommended that "ninety percent of the money should go to prevention."

MEDICALLY ORIENTED APPROACHES

Many descriptions of drug dependence emphasize that it is a problem requiring medical management. The drug user is considered physically dependent (addicted)* if he experiences physical withdrawal symptoms upon discontinuation or reduction in the use of the drug. Hoffman (1983, p. 82) noted that heroin withdrawal symptoms include perspiration, yawning, nausea, vomiting, diarrhea, pupil dilation, "goose-flesh," tremors, chills, rise in blood pressure, increase in heart rate, and pain from muscle spasms.

The drug-dependent person is usually regarded as "sick," and illness is treated by medical intervention, not punishment. Kolb (1962), Lindesmith (1968), Jaffe (1969), and others have advocated an alteration of laws so that people who are addicted can be treated medically and, if necessary, provided with adequate doses of medication for self-administration. "First of all, it must be recognized that the addict is, above all, a sick person, a patient in need of specialized medical and psychiatric services" (Freedman 1963, p. 202).

DETOXIFICATION

Detoxification entails withdrawing the drug from the addict until he is drug-free, and limiting treatment to his physical symptoms. Most references in the literature are to detoxification from opiates. Withdrawal may be abrupt ("cold turkey"); it may be fairly rapid, taking place over a period of two weeks or less; or it may be prolonged. There has not been agreement as to the desired course to follow. Kolb and Himmelsbach (1938) stated that until the 1890s withdrawal was managed as a slow process, over a period of a month or more. Lanphear (1890) called for a gradual withdrawal from morphine, which was the prevalent addicting drug during the late nineteenth century. Abrupt withdrawal has been regarded as inhumane and dangerous (Lett 1891; Vogel 1952), although abrupt withdrawal was recommended by Kolb and Himmelsbach for addicts with "weak habits" and Fraser and Grider (1953) advocated "abrupt and total withdrawal" for cocaine and marijuana "addiction."

Some observers have minimized the suffering of the person who is withdrawing stating that it is like living through a case of the flu. "Many psychopaths who have made up their minds to go through with the treatment, come what may, do not complain at all" (Kolb and Himmelsbach 1938, p. 760).

---

*Elsewhere in this volume we do not use the terms *addict* or *addiction*. They are used in this chapter to represent as faithfully as possible the thinking of others.

Brill (1963) pointed out that many addicts "kick the habit in the streets" and achieve withdrawal voluntarily, without medical assistance. "The average addict is prone to histrionics which he uses to manipulate the environment to get more drugs and to express his intolerance of frustration and even moderate discomfort but, in the long run, withdrawal pains are the most easily treated problem" (p. 154). Berger (1964, p. 62) asserted that "cold turkey" is probably not as horrible as most physicians believe.* Alexander and Dibb (1975) commented that "the pain of physical withdrawal is not the chief obstacle to overcoming addiction. The inability to create a satisfying alternative life style following withdrawal can be crucial" (p. 506).

In the late nineteenth century there were many peddlers of opium antidotes. Mattison (1886) claimed that some of their "nostrums are nothing but disguised solutions of morphia" and observed that "the vast volume of failures is a sealed book of blasted hopes of vain endeavors." In 1892 Crothers recommended that "a long preliminary course of baths, mineral waters and tonics" precede withdrawal from opium.

Between 1900 and 1930 the belladonna group of drugs was used to treat opium addiction. Because of a belief that physical addiction was caused by intestinal intoxication, a purgative compound with strychnine was used to cleanse the system of toxic matter. Kolb and Himmelsbach (1938), historians of the period, stated that the treatment regimen during this time was useless and even harmful. They described many other early remedies for drug addiction, including peptization, water-balance, lipoid, endocrine, and immunity treatments. They advocated three ten-minute warm baths a day, intravenous glucose for those who do not eat well, bromides to reduce restlessness, and sedatives to promote sleep.

Insulin, adrenalin (epinephrine), subcutaneous oxygen, and endocrine substances were mentioned in the notes of the Royal Society of Medicine (1931) as useful in withdrawing addicts from opiates. Summarizing early efforts at treatment, Kolb and Himmelsbach (1938) stated: "No adequate theory of the ultimate nature of opiate addiction has been presented and treatments based on theories have been failures" (p. 793). Twenty-four years later Kolb (1962) reflected that "more useless, harmful, and even lethal treatments have been invented for the withdrawal of opiates than for the treatment of any other disease of modern medicine" (p. 129).

Traditionally, withdrawal has taken place in hospitals, where the drug user is an inpatient. Crothers (1892) had warned that some addicts "shall live in institutions for years." Vogel (1952) stated that one of four general principles in narcotic addiction treatment is that the addict be treated in a closed institu-

---

*The chief narcotics officer for Japan's Ministry of Health and Welfare advocated that addicts "sweat out" withdrawal. He commended "the experience of pain and suffering" as "the best medicine" (*Washington Star* 11/28/73).

tion. (The other principles were that there be an element of compulsory treatment, that the hospital be a psychiatrically oriented institution treating only addicts, and that from four to six months of treatment be provided.) However, it has been observed that addicts frequently come to a hospital for a respite, not a cure: "The voluntary patients are utilizing the hospital merely to reduce "the size of their habits" and thereby ease their financial burdens" (Rice 1965, p. 464). Meyer (1972, p. 24) observed that after detoxification, the addict can get a "high" more easily. That is, he requires a lower dose to achieve the same effect. Through detoxification he reduces the cost of his "habit."

Since 1940 addicts have been administered a variety of agents to relieve their symptoms during withdrawal. Avery and Campbell (1941) advocated shock therapy with Metrazol (pentylenetetrazol) accompanied by the inhalation of carbon dioxide and oxygen to aid in withdrawal from morphine. Gallinek (1952) regarded electro-convulsive therapy as an aid in managing the addict's withdrawal and recommended two or three treatments per day for as long as a week. Before 1948 Thigpen et al. (1953) were using electro-convulsive treatments to eliminate adverse effects of withdrawal. They claimed that patients were discharged from the hospital "physiologically free of their habituation." Boswell (1951) advocated the administration of cortisone to counteract withdrawal of opium derivatives. Laverne (1973) advocated carbon dioxide therapy for detoxification and management of addicts. Wen pioneered the use of acupuncture for detoxification. He reported (see *China Medical Reporter* 12/73) that thirty opium and ten heroin addicts were cured of withdrawal symptoms and lost the urge to use the drug to which they were addicted. There is a growing literature on the use of acupuncture in drug treatment (e.g., Kao and Lu 1947; Shaowanasai and Visuthimak 1974).

Various methods have been advocated to treat other aspects of withdrawal. Berger (1964) recommended that barbiturates be prescribed for sleep problems — 200 to 300 mg of phenobarbital or 200 mg of pentobarbital. He also advocated the use of tranquilizers, such as 100 mg of Librium (chlordiazepoxide) daily or 400 to 1,000 mg of Thorazine (chlorpromazine). A. L. Goodman (1968) said that Lomotil (diphenoxylate), an antidiarrheal agent, allayed severe symptoms of withdrawal. Glatt (1972, p. 253) pointed out that Lomotil has the advantage of not being suitable for injection and therefore is less likely to be abused. He said that an effective combination was Lomotil with chlormethiazole, a sedative-hypnotic used for withdrawal from alcohol.

The most frequently used agent for detoxification is methadone. During the Second World War, German chemists synthesized methadone while carrying out a research program on analgesics.* Isbell and Vogel (1949) stated

*The drug was named "Dolophine" after Adolf Hitler.

that, in small doses (5-10 mg), methadone could help in withdrawal by serving as a substitute for morphine; the methadone dosage could be reduced in seven to ten days. Isbell and Vogel called this proceudre "the most satisfactory method of withdrawal we have used" (p. 912).

Vogel (1952) reported that methadone had been used for detoxification at the federal facility at Lexington since 1948.* Fraser and Grider (1953) recommended that 5 to 40 mg of methadone be administered three times a day (the dosage depending on the severity of the abstinence symptoms). After two days the dosage was to be cut to 50 percent. It was then to be progressively reduced every other day, to 30 percent, 10 percent, and 5 percent of the amount that initially prevented the appearance of abstinence symptoms. Rice (1965) endorsed this method of detoxification as "comfortable for the patient, problem-free for the nursing staff, and easy to administer" (p. 459). Dole (1972b) reported successfully detoxifying more than 22,000 addicts in New York City jails with decreasing doses of methadone administered orally during a period of one to two weeks. Canada (1972) reported a similar program with 270 patients treated in the Seattle area.

Although it was formerly believed that detoxification must take place in an inpatient setting, the recent trend has been toward outpatient detoxification. Meyer (1972) pointed out that the success rate of the Public Health Service hospitals with their inpatient services had been only 5 percent. With the increasing use of heroin, not enough beds were available to accommodate everyone. It was discovered that detoxification could be accomplished in an outpatient setting at less cost and with at least as good a success rate as that of the Public Health Service hospitals. At the outpatient clinic the addict is given methadone in liquid form once a day and detoxification is completed within three to twenty-one days.†

Chambers (1973a) observed that in ambulatory detoxification there is a "social-interactional and motivational process" rather than a purely "medical process." That is, the addict, still in the community, can learn new patterns while being treated. Furthermore, outpatient treatment is less expensive than inpatient care. Chambers claimed that when the addict is treated as an outpatient, he must assume the largest share of responsibility. He observed that some addicts exploit ambulatory detoxification either by obtaining methadone to maintain them until they obtain heroin or else by reducing the degree of their heroin habit. In a two-year trial of ambulatory detoxification in Philadelphia, just 25 percent of the addicts who had entered were discharged

---

*The technique for detoxification in hospitals today was developed at Lexington (Brecher 1972, p. 137).

†Methadone can be administered orally, either as a liquid or as a pill. The advantage to the former is that it cannot be hoarded, as pills can (Rice 1965).

as detoxified. In another study, Chambers (1973b) observed that 68.6 percent terminated the program against medical advice. Chambers et al. (1973) reported extensive drug use during ambulatory detoxification. In the "initiation" stage (40 mg of methadone), addicts were using heroin 64.1 percent of the time; in the middle state (30 mg), they were using heroin 39.4 percent of the time; and in the later stages (20 mg), they were using heroin 34.3 percent of the time. Drugs other than heroin were used. Chambers et al. said that the most disturbing finding was that more than 25 percent of the urine specimens showed no trace of methadone — this indicated that the addicts were selling the methadone and then purchasing other drugs. Moffett et al. (1973) found that approximately a year after terminating outpatient detoxification, 9.5 percent of the participants were drug-free (versus 11.8 percent who left the program "against medical advice," or AMA), 38.1 percent had been arrested (versus 52.9 percent of the AMA group), and 38.1 percent were employed (versus 38.2 percent of the AMA group).

It should be noted that warnings about methadone's addictive potential were voiced long before the drug became popular:

> Methadon [sic] is a dangerous addicting drug. . . . The drug in sufficient dosage produces a type of euphoria which is even more pleasant to some morphine addicts than is the euphoria produced by morphine. . . . Morphine addicts like methadon because it produces a long sustained type of euphoria and because it will suppress signs of physical dependence when substituted for morphine. These qualities make methadon a particularly dangerous drug. (Isbell and Vogel 1949, p. 913)

Darvon-N (propoxyphene napsylate) is said to "suppress abstinence symptoms and eliminate the addict's craving for heroin in a manner similar to methadone" (Tennant et al. 1977, p. 23). Darvon-N has been used for detoxification and short-term maintenance of both heroin- and methadone-dependent people (Tennant et al. 1974). Peyton (*Drug Survival News,* 1976) stated that Darvon-N is "one of the most effective drugs we've found yet" for heroin detoxification and claimed that the drug has low potential for physical addiction and successfully blocks most symptoms of opiate withdrawal.

It has long been recognized that abrupt withdrawal from barbiturates carries potentially lethal consequences. Smith and Wesson (1971, p. 56) described withdrawal symptoms as including "muscular weakness, systolic postural hypotension, nausea, insomnia, major motor seizures, hyperpyrexia, and, in some cases, death." Fraser and Grider (1953) recommended that 0.2 to 0.5 gm of pentobarbital be administered either orally or by injection for immediate symptom relief and then tapered off in dosage. Among others advocating pentobarbital for gradual withdrawal were Blachly (1964), and

Rice and Cohen (1965), and Giannini et al. (1982). Smith and Wesson (1971) recommended substituting phenobarbital, a longer-acting barbiturate. They contended that the more constant blood level of the drug allowed for safer use of smaller daily doses of barbiturates during withdrawal. To treat users who were dependent on both heroin and barbiturates, they suggested withdrawing first barbiturates then heroin, while maintaining the addict with methadone, and, finally withdrawing the methadone. Isbell (1951) pointed out that withdrawal from barbiturates is only a first step in treatment. He advocated that four to six months of "rehabilitative therapy" follow the two- to three-week period of withdrawal.

It has been observed that grouping large numbers of addicts together for detoxification or for any other form of treatment presents difficulties. Schur (1965) pointed out that a patient may "experience a strengthening and reinforcement of his identification" with the drug world in such a place, "rather than being weaned away." Nyswander (1956, p. 116) contended that in any treatment center where large numbers of addicts are assembled, failure is virtually inevitable; she proposed that they be treated in general or psychiatric hospitals. Freedman (1963) noted the failure of specialized institutions, such as the one at Lexington, and advocated community-based medical and rehabilitative services. Vaillent (1966) stated that the most important determinant of abstinence is not so much where the treatment occurs but the "presence or absence of constructive but enforced compulsory supervision."

No one asserts that detoxification is a cure. In 1941 when Avery and Campbell were using shock therapy to relieve withdrawal symptoms during detoxification, they admitted that no personality change occurred: "very little was accomplished as far as a cure of the addiction [was concerned]" (p. 335). Similarly, Thigpen et al. (1953) said that helping the patient through detoxification was only a "first step toward real recovery" (p. 456). Vaillent (1966) reported that 96 percent of all addicts who sought hospitalization at Lexington relapsed within a year. Many clinicians were noting that detoxification was not promoting lasting abstinence, much less personality change.

DeLong (1972, p. 183), obviously believing that addicts commit crimes to support habits, said that detoxification offers a "short-term way of protecting society against crime rather than a long-term treatment for addiction." Silsby and Tennant (1974, p. 169) stated that "short-term, ambulatory detoxification is not usually associated with long-term abstinence." Finally, Cushman and Dole (173) warned: "It is important that rehabilitation and detoxification should not be confused with the concept of 'cure' in a pharmacological sense. Like the abstinent ex-alcoholic, the abstinent ex-addict can live a normal life without becoming normal in pharmacological response to the agent that caused his addiction" (p. 752). Most addiction programs offer other services once detoxification has been completed. These have been described earlier in this chapter.

MAINTENANCE

Drug maintenance usually refers to the legal and controlled administration of methadone, heroin, or other opiates. This method was tried in the United States about 1920, when narcotic distribution clinics were established. There, users could obtain a free daily dose of heroin, morphine, or cocaine. However, in clinic cities where drugs were dispensed freely, there was a marked increase in criminality, especially thievery, and black-marketeering (Brown 1961, pp. 172-174). The medical profession played a leading role in closing these clinics (Terry and Pellens 1928; Ploscowe 1961). However, Markham (1972) stated that by 1922 the Treasury Department, "in an inquisitorial campaign," had forced the clinics to close. Ploscowe (1961) believed that if clinics were to be established once again, the medical profession would have to do more than "merely serve as dispensaries for drugs"; it would be necessary to provide social work and psychiatric services "to deal with the personality problems of the addict."

Citing the current failure of law enforcement efforts to curb drug use, some people still believe that legal maintenance is the lesser of two evils (e.g., Kramer 1972). In medical and legal circles, this view has given impetus to methadone maintenance programs.

Methadone Maintenance

As mentioned earlier, methadone, a synthetic opiate, has been used for detoxification since the late 1940s. The guiding concept supporting methadone maintenance is that addiction is a metabolic, rather than psychologic illness. Dole and Nyswander argued that the "underlying cause" of addiction is a "persistent neurochemical disturbance" and that psychologic factors play only a secondary role in the process (Dole 1972). In the early 1960s methadone treatment programs proliferated to maintain the narcotic user. Methadone was acclaimed as an aid in controlling drug use, but not as a cure. The objectives of maintenance are to stabilize the addict so that he does not have to resort to crime to support his "habit" and to permit him to become receptive to concomitant forms of treatment that will help him change his life-style (Narcotics Treatment Administration, undated).

> Originally, methadone was not seen as "junkie insulin," but as something of a "medical lollypop" which could be used to lure addicts into contact with a treatment program. In their initial concepts of what a methadone program should be, Dole and Nyswander saw the drug as playing only a small part in a multifaceted rehabilitation program. . . . It allowed [the addict] to enter a program comfortably before committing himself to it. (Moffett 1975, p. 15)

In maintaining addicts, Dole and Nyswander began with a low dosage of methadone and then increased it until tolerance was reached. The addicts would then be maintained on that dosage for an indefinite period. Dole et al. (1968) outlined the three phases of treatment:

1. Six weeks on open medical ward; dosage brought to point where methadone blocks heroin effect
2. Discharge to outpatient clinic for daily treatment; eventually patient does not have to report daily, but can take out dosages
3. Stability of rehabilitation must be proved by normal life in community for one year; medically, treatment remains the same.

The objective in the first phase is to increase the dosage to a point where "drug hunger" or "craving" for narcotics is eliminated and the euphoriant effect of heroin is blocked.

When properly stabilized, the patient is firmly buffeted in the zone of normal function. He is protected against both abstinence and euphoria. If he takes heroin, he does not get 'high," as he otherwise would, nor is such an experiment followed by the "sick" feeling that in the past had forced him to seek relief with repeated injections of heroin. (Dole et al. 1966, p. 305)

Before methadone, as Dole and Nyswander (1965) pointed out, no substitute agent was available that would last very long, so an addict required several injections a day. A properly administered dose of methadone lasts between twenty-four and thirty-six hours, in contrast with four or five hours for heroin. Although the precise mechanism of methadone's action is unclear, as Perkins (1972) noted, this does not militate against the drug's use. Bowden and Maddux (1972) listed advantages of methadone maintenance over abstinence:

1. Patient remains in treatment program
2. Methadone ensures stabilization of addiction
3. No withdrawal symptoms
4. Blocking of the "rush" or euphoria
5. Keeps patients away from heroin community
6. Allows for different emotional setting, e.g., support by staff of a clinic
7. Reinforcers of heroin diminished, e.g., reduction of guilt and need for self-punishment.

In many quarters methadone maintenance was hailed as finally offering hope for the drug addict and society (Warshofsky 1970). Joseph and Dole (1970) claimed:

> We have available today in methadone maintenance an evaluated medical-counseling treatment which is capable of salvaging previously intractable, hardcore heroin addicts. Although other methods have had a degree of success, no other treatment for heroin addiction has had a documented success comparable to that of the methadone program. The voluntary retention of patients, the decrease in criminal activity, and the increase in productive behavior are unprecedented in the treatment of opiate addiction. (p. 48)

Meyer (1972, p. 47) asserted that "methadone maintenance treatment is the single most important breakthrough in the treatment of the heroin addict." Positive reports about methadone's success brought about a change in policy by the Food and Drug Administration, which lifted restrictions on methadone, making it available in approved clinics (*Psychiatric News* 5/3/72). In 1965 Beth Israel Hospital of New York City (where Dole and Nyswander had pioneered methadone therapy) was granted $1,380,000 by New York State to expand methadone work, then in the pilot stage. By 1970 funding had increased, and Beth Israel Hospital had $6 million to spend in that work.* New York State had allocated $15 million to methadone programs throughout the state (Trussell and Gollance 1970). Stimmel (1975, p. 292) pointed out that methadone maintenance had been the first treatment to "develop objective criteria to allow for independent evaluation." Success could be measured in terms of retention and arrest rates, and social productivity, as defined by employment, school attendance, or full-time homemaking. These have in fact been the criteria most commonly used in evaluating the effectiveness of methadone maintenance programs.

Paulus and Halliday (1967, p. 658) observed that only maintenance medication "seems to keep the hard-core addicts from continuing the in-and-out-of-jail pattern until death." However, proponents of methadone maintenance have never claimed that it was to be the sole modality for treating drug addicts. It was thought of as "a holding action rather than a lifelong proposition" (Krepick and Long 1973), inasmuch as the administration of the drug would keep the addict coming to a program so that he could be treated in other ways. The addict who comes to the clinic regularly for methadone can be persuaded or required to participate in counseling, vocational training,

*Goodman (1971) stated that, "since 1966, the Mecca of 'Methadone maintenance' has been the Bernstein Institute of the Beth Israel Hospital."

education, or other programs. Graff and Ball (1976) noted that methadone clinics are largely organized within two models, the metabolic and the psychotherapeutic. They called for a new "social psychiatric" model that would "provide comprehensive therapy not only for the manifest disease system, but for its underlying social causes" by bringing family, school, church, and other community organizations into the treatment program.

At one time, methadone maintenance, like detoxification programs, required a period of hospitalization, but the programs were later administered totally in outpatient settings. Kromberg and Proctor (1970) reported how this change occurred and what its consequences were. The staff at the Connecticut Mental Health Center found that addicts were difficult to manage in an inpatient setting because they frightened others, did not respond to conventional treatment, and failed to follow hospital rules. The staff decided to keep the addicts for day treatment but send them home at night. The focus shifted from inpatient to outpatient treatment, from individual to group therapy, and from staff control to "patient peer" control. Kromberg and Proctor stated that seventy-five of ninety-two patients in their study became "productive community citizens" under that regimen. They explained the success of methadone maintenance in the following manner:

> Unlike the heroin addict whose whole life revolves around the fear of withdrawal and the procurement of his next "fix" the methadone-maintained addict has more physical and psychic energy available for vocational and social rehabilitation. He can focus on supplanting artificial euphoria with real satisfactions from job success and improved family and interpersonal experiences. (p. 2577)

In other words, methadone, its proponents assert, permits an addict to become stabilized and thus have energy available for other rehabilitative programs.

In 1969 Gearing submitted an evaluative report of methadone maintenance treatment in New York to the New York Narcotic Addiction Control Commission. The program initiated by Dole and Nyswander was then in its sixth year; there had been 1,554 admissions, and 1,269 patients were being treated. The evaluation committee concluded: "The Methadone Maintenance Treatment Program continues to be an effective form of treatment for a substantial number of selected heroin addicts. None of the patients who have remained in the program have become readdicted to heroin, and the majority have become productive members of society as measured by schooling and employment records, in contrast to their previous records. They also demonstrate less anti-social behavior as demonstrated by records of arrest" (p. 7).

Favorable rates of retention of addicts in methadone programs have been cited in a number of studies — e.g., Nyswander (1967), 90 percent; Joseph and Dole (1970), 82 percent; and Trussell and Gollance (1970), 80 percent. The largest centralized data collection was that for New York City. From January 1964 to March 1973, data were collected on 43,853 patients (Kreek 1975). The retention rates were 86 percent during the first year, 67 percent for those in the program for three to four years, and 64 percent for those in treatment for five years or more. More than half the patients were employed. Their arrest rate fell dramatically to one-sixth of what it was before the patients entered the program. Dole et al. (1968) reported a 94-percent success rate in ending criminal activity of former heroin addicts. Cleveland (1974) strongly endorsed methadone maintenance in his report on the progress of 300 inner-city addicts who had participated in a program in which little but methadone maintenance was offered as a rehabilitative measure. Citing a retention rate of 76.6 percent after one year, reduction in arrests, and a decrease in heroin use, Cleveland stated that costly rehabilitation programs might not be needed, because methadone alone could do the job. Lahmeyer (1982, p. 50) concluded with respect to retention in treatment, "Methadone maintenance has proved superior to therapeutic communities and ambulatory drug-free clinics."

The primary criticism of methadone maintenance has been that it substitutes one addicting drug for another. Long before methadone maintenance programs were widespread, Isbell et al. (1948) reported that former morphine addicts became addicted to it. Twenty-four years later, Rosenthal (*Time* 12/11/72) warned: "Methadone is increasing the addiction rate among young people. I predict that in five years there will be millions of people on methadone and no reduction in crime. Methadone will turn out to be a tremendous national embarrassment." As methadone itself became a drug of choice, it began to be abused.* Diversion of the legitimate supply of methadone from programs was occurring, and the drug was finding its way into the streets (Dobbs 1971; *New York Times* 12/26/72; *U.S. Medicine* 5/15/75).† Stephens and Weppner (1973) found that 27 percent of patients on methadone maintenance were using the drug illegally, 19 percent using it regularly enough to become addicted. Some addicts preferred methadone to other

---

*Methadone abuse became increasingly widespread in Great Britain (Hawks 1971). James (1971) stated: "No longer is the London narcotic addict invariably a heroin addict. Many are now intravenous self-affixing methadone addicts ('methadone junkies') and a number of them have never used heroin to any great extent at all" (p. 127).

†Jaffe et al. (1971) reported that noninjectable methadone "disks" could be converted into an injectable form with a little ingenuity and then abused.

drugs because it was stronger, more dependable, of higher quality, and productive of a "good high." Greene et al. (1975) presented a picture of the severity of methadone abuse in Washington, D.C. Deaths from methadone overdose rose to a peak of fifty-one in Washington during 1972. Blum (1984, p. 19) cited 200 methadone-related deaths in 1977, half of these in New York City. In the fourth quarter of that year, 57 percent of patients included in a Narcotics Treatment Administration study were found to have used methadone illegally at some time in their drug use careers. Greene et al. pointed out that in their eagerness to use methadone to meet a national crisis, people in the field had disregarded warnings about the abuse potential of the drug. The decline in the illicit use of methadone since 1972 has been attributed (Greene et al.) to education about the hazards of methadone, better control over physician distribution,* improved security of supplies, and modification of methadone take-home privileges.

Methadone advocates have contended that reliance on methadone is "not too different from dependence of psychotic patients on major tranquilizers, of diabetics on insulin, and of epileptics on dilantin" (Brill and Chambers 1971, p. 51). However, the idea of helping a person give up one drug only to become dependent on another, aside from the potential for abuse of that second drug, raises moral-ethical issues. McCabe (1971, p. 126) stated that one could expect that methadone maintenance would "inevitably engender controversy, simply because the procedure collides with traditional American values [that hold that] it is 'bad' to foster drug dependency in any individual." Others have contended that the substitution of one drug for another, although not immoral, is an illusory solution to the problem. Dobbs (1971) has termed the practice "hypocritical." Lennard et al. (1972) stated that methadone may contribute to the wider American drug problem, rather than solve it: "One need only consider that the methadone 'solution' must surely reinforce the popular illusion that a drug can be a fast, cheap, and magical answer to complex human and social problems" (p. 881).

Another criticism is that the claims of success are unreliable because retention statistics are misleading. Brill (1973) stated that in the compilation of these figures, "not everyone counts." Perkins (1972) said that the success figures reflect experience only with participants who remained in a program *after* the "failures" either had been excluded or had voluntarily dropped out. "The limitations of any treatment approach cannot be understood if the size and composition of the group that fails remains unknown; this group needs to be identified"(p. 462). Although they pointed out the advantages of meth-

---

*Some physicians marketed methadone illegally (e.g., see *Washington Star* 11/14/72). Greene observed that conviction and imprisonment of a physician for doing just that provided a deterrent to others who were tempted to engage in such a practice.

adone maintenance, Maddux and Bowden (1972) critically examined the success claims of such programs. They cited the problem of the "shrinking sample": "As time passes, the sample shrinks to consist increasingly of subjects who refrain from behavior that prompts separation from the programs. The remaining sample becomes composed of 'successful' subjects partly because the unsuccessful subjects were separated" (p. 441). In evaluations of success, results are not what they seem to be when based on a shrinking sample. With respect to the criterion of frequency of criminal behavior, Maddux and Bowden pointed out that the number of arrests and convictions is an insufficient indicator, because it only "represents interactions between alleged offenders and the law enforcement system." Another drawback of arrest figures is that instead of being "status frequencies at a point in time," they are cumulative. For example, a decline from 92 percent arrested before treatment to 21 percent during maintenance implies a great change. But the 92 percent represented the total of those who had ever been arrested in all the years before they participated in the program, whereas the 21 percent was for a period of only fifteen months. Reviewing other reports of success with methadone, Maddux and Bowden concluded that "the reports of success with methadone maintenance appear both ambiguous and exaggerated."

It has been observed that methadone does not sufficiently "block" the effects of heroin, and so many methadone patients continue to use illegal opiates (Stitzer et al. 1984, 85–86). Lennard et al. (1972) observed that a large-enough dose of heroin will override the methadone blockade. But Havassy and Tschann (1984) reported that even after significant dosage increases of methadone, clients continued to abuse other opiates. Of a random sample of 100 clinic patients on methadone, a majority, Dobbs (1971) reported, were still using heroin. He was puzzled by the finding that patients who had been in treatment the longest showed evidence of more heroin use than those admitted more recently. Chambers (1972) cited results of a study of 173 addicts participating in an outpatient methadone maintenance program at the Philadelphia General Hospital: 15 percent were taking methadone purchased from other patients or obtained illegally through physicians' prescriptions, and 84.2 percent were also using heroin.

Chambers and Moffett (1973) stated that among 174 NARA Philadelphia addicts being maintained on methadone, 18.4 percent were found to be "cheating" with cocaine. The choice of cocaine was attributable to its ready availability and the ability of addict-patients to afford cocaine's high price after they had reduced their heroin habits by substituting free methadone.

Addicts have been reported to be using other classes of drugs. In fact Glasser (1983, p. 103) pointed out, "The polydrug abusing individual who is also addicted to heroin may represent the majority of maintenance clients." Methadone does not establish a "cross-tolerance" for nonopiates (Lennard et al. 1972), so the methadone patient has been "introduced to a 'cafeteria' of other drugs" (Kenny and Wright, 1975).

> Shortly after entering methadone treatment, he learned that he could "boost" his methadone by injecting amphetamines and achieve new levels of euphoria. He then learned that if he was "too high" he could "come down" with barbiturates. Perhaps he also started using alcohol to relieve withdrawal during methadone detoxification and is now becoming an alcoholic. (p. 277)

In the Philadelphia study cited by Chambers and Moffett (1973), 60.8 percent of the methadone patients were using amphetamines, 32.2 percent, barbiturates, and 18.5 percent, cocaine. Many other investigators have found considerable use of these substances by methadone maintenance patients (e.g., see *U.S. Medicine* 7/15/73; Kissin and Sang 1973). Greene et al. (1974) found that questionnaire data revealed that 42 percent of Narcotics Treatment Administration patients (in both detoxification and methadone maintenance) were using phenmetrazine, a "close relative" of amphetamines; 86 percent of these stated that they used the drug to "prolong the effects of heroin and/or methadone." Some have reported considerable collateral drinking, which Bigelow et al. (1973) called the "most frequent cause of failure in methadone treatment," occurring in 10 to 20 percent of methadone patients. Liebson et al. (1973) indicated that methadone treatment itself appears to precipitate alcoholism in many people. In a favorable review of a New York methadone program, Kreek (1975) noted that after three or more years of methadone treatment, 12 percent of the patients interviewed drank more than 12 oz of whiskey per day; 65 percent of these patients had abused alcohol before methadone treatment and continued to do so throughout the course of treatment.

Methadone programs do try to detect the illicit use of drugs by requiring that addicts submit to urine tests. "All the essential information about illicit drug use in a methadone maintenance program can be obtained by random urine testing at an average frequency as low as once in five days" (Goldstein and Brown 1970, p. 315). Felton (1973) has pointed out how "test-wise" addicts try to subvert the urine testing program:

1. Buying or "borrowing" clean specimens and submitting them
2. Releasing urine from a concealed plastic bladder in contact with the body, thus producing a warm, clean specimen
3. Holding off drug use for a few days, so that it will not show up
4. Stalling, claiming an inability to void
5. Presenting a pale urine specimen after a heavy intake of beer to dilute the specimen and diminish the chance of a positive finding. (p. 1020)

These ruses have been noted by others (e.g., Vista Hill Psychiatric Foundation 1972). Taylor (*U.S. Medicine,* 7/15/73) reported an unexpected finding in an analysis of urine samples. In a methadone program 17.4 percent of all specimens analyzed contained no methadone, which suggested that methadone was being diverted from the program. Goldstein and Brown (1970) recommended that a member of the program staff monitor the patient's urination directly to ensure that the sample being submitted is the patient's own. They advised that urine be tested every day or at random so that the addict does not try to beat the system by refraining from drug use on known scheduled days. Wang (1982, p. 237) noted that increasingly reliable methods have been developed for analyzing urine for drugs.

Some segments of society have opposed methadone on racial grounds. Brill (1973) pointed out that black militants and some Puerto Ricans believe that methadone maintenance is a form of genocide. Spokesmen for these groups have contended that white society is trying to enslave minority populations by perpetuating drug dependence. Goldmacher, a psychiatrist, claimed (*Washington Post* 5/14/72) that "methadone is legal dope. It is the planned, deliberate addiction of hundreds of thousands of drug abusers." Senay (1971) has observed that some people believe that methadone is being used as a "substitute for facing the basic problems of racisim and poverty."

Dole and Nyswander's ten-year perspective on methadone maintenance treatment (1976) acknowledged that their original projections had been "overly optimistic." They had not anticipated the resistance to the substitution of one drug for another. But they believed that politics, rivalries, antagonism, misinformation, and arbitrary bureaucratic decisions about regulation constituted impediments just as great. Observing the decline in available treatment facilities, Dole and Nyswander stated that "there are now more addicts on the street using methadone illicitly on an occasional or regular basis than there are patients in these facilities." They pointed out that methadone never was regarded as a panacea, but only as a first step in treatment. A follow-up of 204 people who left methadone treatment in 1974 revealed that only 22 reported no legal problems and denied the use of opiates, the use of other major drugs, or alcoholism. Dole and Nyswander concluded:

> In analyzing the ten-year experience, an optimist might point out that the failures of methadone maintenance treatment during the past five years have been due more to administrative than pharmacological problems. . . . The success of the pilot-study programs in the period from 1965 to 1970 should not be forgotten. These results have been well documented and independently evaluated. It is mainly the programs rather than the addicts that have changed, and, theoretically, at least, the administrative mistakes could be reversed. (p. 2119)

Dole and Nyswander continued to advocate methadone maintenance and social rehabilitation for the "previously intractable heroin addict."

Opinion has remained divided about the effectiveness of methadone maintenance. Many, like Meyer (1972), have affirmed that it is "probably the most universally applicable treatment for heroin addiction while also being the least expensive" (p. 48). And there are the criticisms just enumerated — the substitution of one drug for another, the illicit use of methadone, methadone's failure to "block" the effects of heroin, the failure of methadone maintenance to have an impact on the addict's use of other classes of drugs, and so forth. In 1972 Rosenthal predicted that in five years methadone maintenance would become a "national embarrassment." At a Congressional Hearing four years later, methadone maintenance was denounced (*Washington Post* 6/30/76). However, in 1982, Kalinowsky et al. stated, "Methadone is now by far the most widely used method against heroin addiction" (p. 316). And in 1983, Hoffman observed:

> Currently this approach appears to be gaining acceptance progressively (though not without criticism) as the method with the highest potential of all known therapeutic modalities for alleviation of drug-related crime and for restoration of the confirmed narcotic addict to an economically productive life." (p. 278)

Heroin Maintenance

Methadone maintenance programs in the United States have been compared with the "British system," a medical distributive approach in which people physically dependent on heroin are maintained on controlled amounts of the drug. In Great Britain, to be a drug addict is not illegal. Physical dependence is regarded totally as a medical problem, and addicts are treated as patients, not as criminals (Schur 1961). The medical profession's distribution of drugs is unchallenged by outside authority; the police have the function of protecting medical control, not controlling drug distribution itself (King 1961). The government monitors records kept by those who dispense drugs. Schur observed that because addicts have legal access to drugs, they do not resort to theft to support their "habits." King (1961) stated that Home Office enforcement officials have encountered no illicit trafficking in opiates.

Eldridge (1972, p. 111) described three circumstances under which British physicians may prescribe heroin to addicts: when a cure is being sought through gradual withdrawal, when withdrawal symptoms are so severe that an addict must continue to receive small amounts of the drug, and when an addict has demonstrated that he can lead a normal life only if maintained on heroin.

Initially the narcotics problem in Great Britain was regarded as relatively minor. Eldridge (1972, p. 112) stated that "the most extensive examination of the British system finds that the system is the result of a small narcotics problem." Schur (1961) claimed that there were between 300 and 500 addicts in Britain at the beginning of the 1960s — actually fewer than in 1935. At the end of the 1960s, however, Cohen (1969) reported abuses of the British system, noting a continuing trend toward addiction-related crime. "Unfortunately, the buildup of tolerance and the resale of heroin by the registered addict to his friends or for profit have caused sufficient abuse of this benign and humane effort that heroin addicts are increasing by 50 percent yearly in England" (p. 72). James (1971) observed that between 1960 and 1967 heroin was prescribed in amounts far in excess of those required for maintenance. In 1967 he noted that on the average, every prescription allotted an amount of heroin sufficient to sustain two addicts. Markham (1972) stated that addiction spread in Great Britain at an epidemic rate in the 1960s and attributed this to liberal dispensing of prescriptions. May (1972) said that the spiraling of addiction in Great Britain was somewhat curtailed when the government began to limit the prescribing of heroin to staff physicians in government-operated clinics. Mitcheson (1970) spoke of the "new-style addict" in Britain. This prototype was a male, in his late teens or early twenties, and indiscriminate in his drug use.* Mitcheson pointed out that after 1968 when heroin distribution was more carefully controlled, other drugs were still easily available. After the Dangerous Drugs Act of 1967, treatment centers were supervised by consultant psychiatrists. Lieberman and Blaine (1970) pointed out that prescriptions for heroin and cocaine were written only by physicians with a license to prescribe "restricted" drugs. As of 1970, however, the restrictions applied neither to morphine nor to Demerol (meperidine). Lieberman and Blaine presented statistics demonstrating the extent to which addiction had "mushroomed" in the 1960s. According to them, there were 132 heroin addicts in Britain in 1961 and 2,240 in 1968. Heroin addicts under twenty years of age numbered 2 in 1961 and 709 in 1968. Cocaine users increased from 84 in 1961 to 564 in 1968.† Stimson and Ogborne (1974) surveyed a representative sample of addicts who received heroin in London clinics. Eighty-four percent of the heroin addicts admitted that in the month before the interview, they had used drugs other than those prescribed at the clinic, and 37 percent said that they occasionally sold, exchanged, or loaned some of the drugs that had been prescribed for them. Edwards (1979, p. 7) concluded,

*Stimson and Ogborne (1974) reported that the mean age for heroin use was nineteen in their sample of heroin addicts attending clinics in London.

†All but a few cocaine users were also using heroin. Addicts using both drugs were included in each statistical tally.

"The belief that prescribing would prevent a black market has proved illusory."

In 1972 Edward Lewis, chief medical officer of the U.S. Bureau of Narcotics and Dangerous Drugs (*U.S. Medicine* 9/1/72), observed that the British system was moving away from heroin maintenance to methadone maintenance—the "American system."

Following the passage of the Harrison Narcotic Act in 1914, there appeared in the United States a number of clinics that treated narcotic addiction by providing addicts with maintenance doses of morphine (Henry 1974). Many of these facilities were essentially unregulated, and narcotic drugs were easily diverted to the black market. These clinics were declared illegal in 1923 and closed down.

Advocacy of heroin maintenance in the United States has been limited. A committee of the American Bar Association was reported as favoring experimentation with heroin maintenance (*Washington Post* 2/12/72). Stachnik (1972) cited advantages to a system that would provide addicts who refuse other forms of treatment an opportunity to be maintained legally on heroin:

1. The crime rate would be reduced for that percentage of crimes which are committed to support a habit
2. The intravenous use of heroin at clinics would be with clean equipment, thus guarding against disease
3. Fatal accidental doses would be precluded because the quality of the drug would be uniform
4. Contact would occur between a benign "establishment" and the heroin subculture. (pp. 641–642)

According to Stachnik, heroin maintenance would not be an end in itself. He hoped that addicts could be persuaded, perhaps by ex-addicts, to enter some other form of treatment. Waldorf et al. (1974) commented that in view of the fact that one opiate (methadone) has been dispensed legally, consideration should be given to dispensing others.

Since we have made one opiate available for maintenance, we might consider others as well. The time is past when everyone reacted hysterically to the idea of giving opiates to addicts; we have been doing just that on a large scale for nearly six years. Rather than limit maintenance to one drug, we think it is time to bring in the other opiates and try them in new ways. (p. 45)

Markham (1972) described the proposal of the Vera Institute of Justice in New York for heroin maintenance programs. Hard-core addicts would be attracted by the provision of short-term heroin maintenance; after twelve months they would be "eased into methadone maintenance, or onto a narcotic antagonist." The heroin would be administered seven days a week, four or five times daily to prevent diversion into the black market. The proposal was controversial and to our knowledge was not implemented.

Heroin maintenance has been opposed in the United States on medical, legal, psychologic, and moral grounds. Dole (1972) presented the following objection:

> The weak point in the scheme is the assumption that addicts can be satisfied with heroin. Proponents of the heroin clinics appear to believe that 250,000 addicts could be kept happy with a daily ration of this drug, and thereafter would desist from crime. No one familiar with the pharmacology of heroin could make such an assumption. Heroin addicts cannot be maintained with a stable dosage because the drug produces an increasing tolerance and physiological dependence in the user. (p. 1493)

As far as we know, no heroin maintenance programs have been instituted in the United States since the closing of the government maintenance clinics in the 1920s. However, Zimmerman (1977) reported that methadone maintenance pioneers Drs. Vincent Dole and Marie Nyswander conducted a maintenance experiment using morphine in 1964. The experiment was regarded as a failure because subjects' dosages could not be stabilized. The results of this experiment were never reported in the scientific literature.

Narcotic Antagonists

During the last twenty-five years, much research has been conducted to find narcotic antagonists — "nonaddictive" drugs that would block the euphoric effects produced by narcotics. With such narcotic antagonists, the physically dependent drug user would not experience the desired effects; this would result in the elimination of both conditioned physical dependence and drug-seeking behavior (Freedman et al. 1968). Administered before an opiate, the antagonist, it is claimed, blocks opiate-induced effects; given after, it antagonizes or reverses the effect. Glasscote et al. (1972) described the operation of narcotic antagonists:

> Narcotic antagonists do not cause nausea but rather interfere with any pleasurable effect from narcotics, evidently by actually occupying the particular receptor sites in the body at which heroin effects are realized. . . . Two such antagonists, cyclazocine and Naloxone, have been used experimentally with somewhat promising results, but they have

drawbacks. The former frequently produces unpleasant side effects, the latter is expensive and has an active life of only a few hours. (p. 28)

In 1954 Strober reported a case in which nalorphine (*N*-allylnomorphine, NAM, Nalline), a nonaddicting morphine derivative, reversed the effects of acute heroin intoxication.* Isbell and his associates at the federal facility at Lexington conducted the first experiments with Nalline to determine the extent of addiction for each patient so that appropriate treatment could be prescribed. Fraser et al. (1956) found that administration of 3, 6, or 10 mg of Nalline simultaneously with 30 mg of morphine reduced or blocked the euphoric effects of morphine. The same is true when 10 mg of Nalline is given 1¾ hours after 30 mg of morphine. The disadvantage to Nalline is that its effects are brief in duration.

Nalline became widely known for its effectiveness in identifying those addicts who had returned to opiate use. The drug can precipitate noticeable signs of withdrawal in a person who uses opiates within forty-eight to seventy-two hours after subcutaneous injection of 2–3 mg of the drug (Bailey 1968). The main criterion for diagnosis of opiate use is an increase in the diameter of the pupils after injection of Nalline. The "Nalline test" has been used by law enforcement agencies. It was widely used in California beginning in 1956. "This test . . . is an innocuous, time-saving and safe test which can be administered by any physician with little practice in an office or clinic. The procedure is simple and takes but a few minutes" (Brown 1961, p. 294). Bailey (1968) stated that three positive tests were regarded as grounds for filing a petition of violation and returning a parolee to court. Brown (1961, p. 317) maintained that use of this Nalline test by parole officers acts as a deterrent to drug use. He quoted a drug user as saying, "This Nalline, man! I knew it would catch me, and I wasn't going back to San Quentin this time." Because the addict is not on drugs, Brown contended, he can hold a job and need not resort to crime to maintain his habit. "The addict who of necessity (Nalline) has cut down his habit, has in many cases been able to support himself and his family; he has been able to keep a job, stay out of jail and out of trouble on a more or less permanent basis so long as he knows he has to live with Nalline. This is his crutch and society's control" (p. 317).

William R. Martin, a pharmacologist at the Addiction Research Center at Lexington, originally proposed that narcotic-blocking drugs be used for treatment of the heroin addict. He described studies in which his team had

---

*Today Nalorphine is on the shelves of pharmacies and hospital emergency rooms throughout the country. It is an effective antidote to a heroin overdose, bringing a victim out of a coma or stupor within minutes (Brecher 1972, p. 102). Nalorphine is also used for overdoses of other narcotics, including methadone.

administered cyclazocine to volunteer prisoner-patients at the Lexington facility. Martin et al. (1965) stated that the drug did produce "a type of euphoria, tolerance, and physical dependence," but that its effects were qualitatively different from morphine. They noted that the potential for abuse of cyclazocine was low. In 1966 Martin et al. reported that the drug antagonized toxic and euphoric effects of very large doses of heroin and morphine. Four milligrams per day not only provided protection against the euphoria produced by large doses of narcotics but also prevented physical dependence. When the addict was gradually withdrawn from the cyclazocine over a two-week period, abstinence symptoms were very mild (e.g., light-headedness) and did not lead to renewed drug-seeking behavior. Martin et al. recommended the use of cyclazocine for the "ambulatory management of abstinent narcotic addicts" who are "highly motivated."

After an intensive study of the effects of cyclazocine, Martin and Gorodetzky (1967) stated that "the use of cyclazocine is really an extension of the drug-free environment approach to treatment; it provides, paradoxically, in essence a pharmacologically enforced and maintained state of abstinence" (p. 92). Martin and Gorodetzky asserted that with the use of narcotic antagonists, other treatment approaches would be more effective because they would not be undermined by physical dependence and drug-seeking behavior. A further advantage of cyclazocine is its prolonged action. Freedman et al. (1968) said that a maintenance dose of this drug blocks heroin challenges for longer than twenty-four hours. They also recommended it for terminating the addict's use of narcotics, thus rendering him more amenable to rehabilitation efforts. They reported that addicts treated with cyclazocine became less interested in criminality and more interested in vocational activities. A drawback was that the addict's use of marijuana, amphetamines, and barbiturates was not affected by the antagonist.

Resnick et al. (1970) reported that fourteen patients treated with cyclazocine for up to two and one-half years became less dependent on opiates. Nevertheless, there were intermittent periods of heroin use, during which the addicts took less cyclazocine. Chappel et al. (1971) viewed the major role of cyclazocine as helping former addicts to maintain abstinence during the difficult months after withdrawal. They surmised that the dropout rate early in cyclazocine treatment was high because patients had not achieved full blockage doses and thus were using narcotics to experience the "high" from them.

Another narcotic antagonist is Naloxone. Fink et al. (1968) reported that Naloxone, even at the lowest dose tested (0.7 mg), abolished the effects of heroin within one-half to two minutes. When Naloxone is administered before heroin, it blocks the effect of heroin. Fink et al. estimated that 1 mg of intravenous Naloxone could block the effects of 40 mg of heroin. The main drawback of Naloxone is that its effects do not last as long as those of heroin.* Kurland et al. (1974) studied the effects of Naloxone on 119 parolee-addicts who volunteered to participate in a controlled setting. Their urine specimens were examined daily at an outpatient clinic to determine the extent of narcotic use. The naloxone dose ranged from 200 to 800 mg, depending on the outcome of the urine analyses. A control group received a placebo. There was little difference between the number in each group that remained in the program, but the Naloxone group used considerably fewer narcotic drugs. Kurland et al. did not envisage Naloxone as a panacea, but regarded its principal value to be in its deterrent action.

> As with other antagonists, there is no pharmacological reason to expect that Naloxone will insure complete abstinence since it does not reduce the urge to take narcotics. Its specific usefulness lies in its deterrent action once narcotic drugs are again taken. (p. 669)

"Narcotic antagonists" other than methadone have been developed and only within the last decade used widely in the treatment of addiction. Naltrexone, an analogue of Naloxone, is one of these. It is said to "block opiates from reaching their sites of action in the brain" (Crowley 1983, p. 105) while having no narcotic effect of its own.

Gorodetzky et al. (1975) found that naltrexone is twice as potent as naloxone and seventeen times as powerful as Nalline in precipitating abstinence in morphine-dependent users. These investigators claimed: "Because of its antagonistic potency, oral effectiveness, duration of action and lack of agonistic effects, it should offer significant advantages over Naloxone and probably cyclazocine in the treatment of heroin dependence" (p. 753). Schecter and Grossman (1975) observed that naltrexone does not produce physical dependence, its abuse potential is minimal, and no euphoric effects were noted.

The National Institute on Drug Abuse (NIDA) (see Willette and Barnett 1981) published an entire volume on the use of this substance which is administered in either liquid or capsule form. It is described by NIDA as a "potent narcotic antagonist" that is free of side effects and whose effectiveness can last for three days from one oral dose. Patients who are physically dependent on an opiate substance must first be detoxified before they are placed on naltrexone. Like methadone, naltrexone is primarily a maintenance drug. "As a maintenance drug, naltrexone offers protection against impulsive drug use which can easily lead to the resumption of chronic heroin dependence"

---

*Fink (1971) stated that the "ideal antagonist" would make it possible for mass inoculation of the antagonist with a "bio-degradable plastic implant" to be administered to "susceptible populations." It is conceivable that casings can be implanted in the body that would slowly release the antagonist into the bloodstream. This "depot" form of administration is being researched (Maugh 1972).

(Renault 1981, p. 19). Renault went on to point out that this substance is hardly a "cure." The motivational issue of the patient is again crucial. "From a practical point of view, only a minority of patients will use naltrexone as a maintenance drug. Most patients tend to drop out of treatment prematurely" (pp. 19–20).

Rawson and Tennant (1983) followed up 58 heroin addicts treated with naltrexone. Five years after treatment, 90 percent had become re-addicted for various periods. Rawson and Tennant concluded that instead of viewing naltrexone as a cure, it should be seen as a means "to eliminate their opiate problem for as long as they are in treatment" (p. 295). Ostensibly, these patients at least had the "learning experience" of being abstinent from illegal opiates for a time.

Dole (1972) has criticized the use of narcotic antagonists on the grounds that blocking the euphoric effect does not prevent relapse. He contended that a metabolic "underlying drive" is not mitigated by a narcotic antagonist; the drive might be increased if "traces of physical dependence persist."

The narcotic antagonists have been regarded, not as competitors, but as alternatives to methadone (Freedman et al. 1968; Chappel et al. 1971). Kissin and Sang (1973) pointed out that antagonists might be more palatable to some minority group members who oppose methadone. Brecher (1972) has stated that the antagonists are inferior to methadone.

> First, they do not assuage the postaddiction syndrome — the anxiety, depression, and craving that recur for months and perhaps years after the last shot of heroin. . . . The other major difference is that since antagonists are not addicting, a patient can stop taking them at will. Most patients do stop taking them — and then promptly return to black-market methadone. (pp. 159–160)

The current literature reveals that treatment efforts with narcotic antagonists are not widespread. At best these drugs are useful adjuncts to treatment only when the physically dependent drug user is highly motivated to change. Most users lack this motivation.* As is often the case with other reports of treatment outcome, observations of the success of narcotic antagonists are mainly short term.

Other Examples of Pharmacotherapy

There is a growing literature on attempts to treat abusers of other substances with medication. Gawin and Kleber (1984) reported successful treatment of certain cocaine abusers using a combination of psychotherapy and

---

*Markham (1972, p. 31) observed that compelling addicts to take antagonist drugs "would present logistical and civil liberties dilemmas of major proportions."

either an antidepressant (desipramine) or lithium carbonate. They attributed this success partially to "an actual pharmacologic effect" that reduced craving for the substance.

Cranson and Flemenbaum (1978) noted that there is "a large body of evidence" indicating that lithium has a place in the treatment of amphetamine abuse. They also reported treatment cases in which lithium had an effect adverse to cocaine.

PSYCHOSURGERY

Reports of the use of psychosurgery specifically to cure drug dependence are few. It has long been known that some patients become physically dependent on the narcotics used to manage intractable pain in serious illnesses such as cancer. When such patients were psychosurgically treated, they no longer required opiates, because the surgery relieved the pain. Smolik (1950) observed this in patients who had undergone prefrontal lobotomy.

Wikler et al. (1952) noted that bilateral frontal lobotomy resulted in the reduction of "purposive" features of the opiate-abstinence syndrome. That is, the person no longer craved drugs as he did before the surgery. Knight (1969) said that stereotactic surgery is very efficient and results in minimal destruction of tissue.

> Stereotactic surgery now provides the means of producing accurate lesions of small size at selected points in the nervous system where concentrations of nerve cells or fibre pathways subserving a particular form of activity permit some small area of destruction to produce widespread physiological effects. (p. 583)

Knight found that psychosurgery was successful in curing barbiturate addiction in patients who experienced severe anxiety or depression. He also reported success with nonpsychopathic heroin addicts. These patients had what he called a "better personality," meaning that drugs were used not so much for excitement but to escape anxiety or depression. Knight reported that stereotactic surgery modified the intensity of withdrawal symptoms, thus making it easier to terminate the patient's drug use. In some cases, craving was eliminated, rendering the patient more amenable to rehabilitation. A six-month follow-up after such surgery revealed the elimination of drug use. Göktepe et al. (1975) reviewed the cases of 208 psychiatric patients two-and-one-half to four-and-one-half years after a stereotactic subcaudate tractotomy had been performed. Nine of these patients had been drug dependent; of these, five were available for follow-up. Although they reported that the operation did not worsen the psychiatric condition in any case, there was no evaluation of the effect of surgery on drug use.

Most of the reports cite no beneficial effects of psychosurgery on drug addicts. Freeman and Watts (1950), who pioneered psychosurgery in the United States, concluded that it was of no value to drug addicts. "Chronic alcoholism and drug addiction, when they are manifestations of an underlying psychopathic state or even of a very disorganizing psychoneurotic process, are contraindications. Even though the emotional tension may be relieved the compulsion may remain and result in complete irresponibility" (p. 518). Freeman (see Ackerly 1954) said that he would not operate on drug users who seek "gratification of certain unfilled wants." In 1972 Freeman stated that "lobotomies failed almost completely with drug addicts. The few examples of successful lobotomies in alcoholics and drug addicts could be attributed to the high level of anxiety that underlay their addiction." Heath (see Ackerly 1954) reported failure with psychosurgery on one drug addict. A. Miller (1954) reported a similar failure with a psychopathic person dependent on drugs. Ausubel (1958, p. 82) said that, although lobotomy "may render the need for morphine superfluous," the operation was not conducive to "motivational maturity or social productivity." In fact, he declared that it "intensifies a pre-existing personality defect." Maurer and Vogel (1967), reviewing results of psychosurgery, stated that

> in the light of present information . . . it may be concluded that bilateral frontal lobotomy does tend to reduce markedly the craving for opiate drugs in addicted patients; however, in patients whose addiction is related to serious personality defects, a relapse to addiction may be expected. It should be noted that frontal lobotomy *per se* does not prevent the abstinence syndrome in narcotic addicts. (p. 218)

Maurer and Vogel pointed out that "personality defects consequent to lobotomy" may be worse than problems associated with the addiction.

In the 1970s and 1980s recommendations for psychosurgery to cure drug dependence have been nonexistent. Psychosurgery has been discontinued with criminals and drug users, both because of a lack of convincing beneficial results and also because of ethical and moral objections.*

MEGAVITAMIN THERAPY

There is a growing literature on "orthomolecular psychiatry," a biochemical approach to mental illness. In the 1950s Hoffer and Osmond pioneered research on the value of megavitamin therapy in treating schizophrenia. After following patients for five to ten years, they concluded:

*See Chapter 2 of Volume II for a discussion of the controversy over psychosurgical treatment of criminals.

Our findings showed clearly enough that there is a strong probability that large doses of niacin, especially if given early in the disease, change the outcome for the better. . . . We had evidence that we could improve the long term outcome of schizophrenia by very simple means. (Osmond 1967, pp. 128, 129)

According to the Do It Now Foundation (1972), a national organization involved in drug abuse education, the administration of large doses of vitamins to schizophrenics has resulted in a recovery rate of approximately 85 percent. Do It Now speculated that "many persons who were prone to schizophrenia . . . are now having it brought out through drug experimentation."* Ryback (1972) said that drug users are often helped as members of Schizophrenics Anonymous (S.A.), a self-help organization founded by Hoffer. A chapter for teenagers, founded in Boston, had a number of drug users among its members. Ryback observed that the majority of drug users attending S.A. meetings are in the "psychotic category." Vitamin therapy is part of the S.A. program, in which participants take niacin (nicotinic acid) in conjunction with vitamins B6, C, and E.

Even if drug users are not schizophrenic, the mental phenomena they experience as a consequence of drug effects, especially after using hallucinogens, resemble symptoms of schizophrenia. " 'Drug Wipeout' as it exists today among at least several million present or former drug users, is a condition which appears to be identical in nature to borderline or full-scale schizophrenia" (Do It Now Foundation 1972). Megavitamin therapy has been administered to those who have had "bad trips" on psychedelic drugs. According to a report on vitamin therapy (Bill 1968), large amounts of niacin were distributed in the Haight-Ashbury district of San Francisco to those suffering from LSD psychosis. Hawkins (1973) said that the LSD rescue service operating in many cities has administered megavitamin therapy to counteract adverse effects of psychedelic drug reactions.†

The Do It Now Foundation has claimed that large doses of niacin and vitamin C "help lessen the intensity of a 'comedown' off of heavy doses of amphetamine, either oral or intravenous." Niacin is also suggested to counter manifestations of amphetamine psychosis. In addition, Do It Now advocated megavitamin therapy for barbiturate and opiate addicts. Niacin was

---

*For a detailed first person account of a schizophrenic illness that followed shortly after ingestion of mescaline, the reader is referred to Vonnegut (1975). Vonnegut "cracked in very hip surroundings" and was later treated by megavitamin therapy for schizophrenia.

†Hawkins (1973) cited Bronsteen's observation (in *The Hippy's Handbook*) that modern psychiatry is out of touch with young people, and that in the case of bad LSD "trips," the psychiatric establishment should be avoided and niacin embraced.

proposed as a "guarantee against convulsions and as postwithdrawal therapy" for heroin users. The Foundation claimed that the advantages of niacin over methadone are that it costs less, requires fewer visits to a doctor, and "paves the way for complete drug and chemical independence," instead of serving as a substitute drug.

Vitamins have long been used to treat alcoholics during the postwithdrawal period. Hawkins (1973) said that many members of Alcoholics Anonymous were unable to remain sober until they were placed on sugar-free diets fortified with vitamins. In 1972 between 20,000 and 25,000 alcoholics were taking large doses of vitamins. R. F. Smith (1974) reported the result of a five-year trial of niacin given alcoholics in Michigan. He found that in "severe advanced alcoholism" with a toxic organic brain syndrome, niacin therapy is most valuable. He claimed that 30 percent of the total alcoholic population can benefit from such treatment.

There is little in the professional literature concerning the application of megavitamin therapy to drug users. The only statistics we have located provide an estimate of results: "Response to megavitamins seems to be proportionate to the 85% statistic reported in treatment of normal schizophrenia, though in the last four years, we have kept no careful records of successes or failures, and have been unable, due to staff limitations, to initiate any sort of foolproof follow-up" (Do It Now, 1972). On this thin evidence, no conclusion can be drawn on the value of this treatment.

OTHER APPROACHES

SELF-HELP

Alcoholics Anonymous (AA), founded in Ohio in 1935, had 100 members by 1939 and 350,000 by 1965 (Bellwood 1973). In 1985, national membership is estimated to be over one million.* Although A.A. is not an organized religion, it has been referred to as an "evangelical movement" (Chafetz and Demone 1962). God is referred to directly or by implication in eleven of the twelve "steps" necessary to achieve sobriety.† If an A.A. member cannot place his faith in a power greater than himself, he is advised to have faith in his fellow A.A. members. Initially A.A. restricted its membership to the "pure alcoholic," avoiding those with criminal records and other socially de-

---

*A telephone check with A.A.'s World Headquarters Office in New York in 1985 produced an estimate of national membership of over one million.

†In step four, each member is to take a "searching and fearless moral inventory" of himself. In Volume II, Chapter 9, we described the "moral inventory" that the criminals in our program take as a necessary step in the deterrence of criminal thinking and action.

viant patterns. However, this position was regarded as intolerant, and in recent years the only requirement for membership has been problem drinking. Today Alcoholics Anonymous groups operate in prisons and institutions. A.A. has expanded its services to include wives of alcoholics (Al-Anon) and teenage children of alcoholics (Alateen). Blum (1984, p. 284) stated what is a widely shared evaluation: "A.A. has probably been the most successful approach to the rehabilitation of the alcoholic."

Other groups have patterned themselves after Alcoholics Anonymous, including Narcotics Anonymous (N.A.). N.A. was founded in 1949 by Daniel Carlson, who was dependent on drugs for twenty-five years. In 1985 it had chapters in every state in the United States and in 30 foreign countries. Thirteen "steps" are recommended for the addicts to become drug-free. Patrick (1965) said that the spirit of the first twelve is summarized by the thirteenth: "God Help Me! Without God I am lost. To find myself I must submit to Him as the source of my hope and my strength." With respect to N.A.'s effectiveness, Brown (1961) said: "Narcotics Anonymous groups have been organized in several major cities and while their effectiveness is not documented, many of them are valuable as an adjunct to self-rehabilitation" (p. 272). The organization itself is quoted as taking this position: "We know that through Our Way of Life some addicts can stop using drugs, and if it's only one in twenty or even thirty that's more than enough to keep us together and trying" (Patrick 1965, p. 157).

Reports of systematic follow-up are not available. But it is important to note that many, if not most, treatment programs that target abstinence require their patients to attend A.A. or N.A. meetings. Describing his approach to family therapy, Kaufman (1985, p. 168) stated:

> Another critical aspect of my approach . . . is requiring a commitment to a system for achieving abstinence, which involves A.A., N.A, . . . etc.

RELIGION

> Over at least a century of experience in organizing rescue for the drug dependent, only those efforts using religion have been successful. (Jones 1971)

In 1926 Cantala stated that adherence to religious principles is "undoubtedly one of the strongest barriers checking the development of drug addiction." Increasingly there have been reports of drug users who turned to religion to replace drugs. Cohen (1969) has maintained that people will stop using drugs if they have an alternative that equally fulfills their needs. "The fact is that young people *will* cease using drugs if they are provided with some better nonchemical technique. The hidden ally here is the ultimate failure of drugs to fulfill the real needs of the users" (p. 2095). Cohen observed that some young people stopped using drugs when they discovered that spiritual leaders regarded drugs as deleterious to spiritual development.

Other groups propose spiritual conversion to counteract drug use. "The fact of religious conversion, while self-authenticating and needing no justification, can be cultivated and is an event to be desired in the religious care of the youthful addict" (Hageman 1965, p. 195). According to this writer, addicts find a "high" in the "ecstatic experience of conversion and post-conversion spiritual seizure."* Hageman described specific elements in the process of conversion, including crusades for social justice, capitalizing on the addict's artistic sensibility and redirecting his aesthetic interests to the liturgy, and inculcating in him a sense of community. It is claimed that religious conversion transforms the addict from "an other-worldly masochist into a truly human person at home in the world" (Hageman, p. 198). In this attempt to convert the addict, drug use is regarded not as a sickness but as a sin. The Pentecostal movement places the responsibility on the individual: "Each addict is a sinner and he himself bears the burden of guilt, not his parents, however sinful they may be, nor the environment, however vicious" (Langrod et al. 1972, p. 175).

Teen Challenge is the best known of the Pentecostal groups that work with drug users. It was founded in 1960 by David Wilkerson, a minister of the Assembly of God. His brother, Don, joined him in trying to persuade addicts to come to Christ. "I explained to them that the only way they can be cured is through a new kind of will power—their will power and God's power. . . . The key to our success is not man-made—the cornerstone of our program was Christ" (Wilkerson 1969, pp. 46–47). Teen Challenge provides residential treatment.† Wilkerson acknowledged that some addicts walk in from the streets just for comfort and convenience. Whatever the addict's motivation, the program staff tries to involve him in "faith therapy," the main therapeutic tool. The critical experience is conversion: "As is the tradition with religious experiences, conversion is seen as an event rather than a process. It is characterized by a sudden, presumably unexpected emotional experience following which a new attitude toward life prevails" (Glasscote et al. 1972, p. 163). Langrod et al. (1972) observed that the program is very strict in its rules, requiring the drug user to make and stand by his commitment to God. Brill and Lieberman (1969), impressed "by the apparent power of conversion and

---

*The "high" from religious conversion has also been described in a first-person account by Bennett (1972). He described his experience selling religious books: "I'd walk out of that house, and it was better than any heroin high I ever had or all of them put together. That's worth it, right there—helping people, sharing, selling Bible books, and praying" (p. 185).

†Teen Challenge was still functioning in 1986.

missionary activities" in changing the lives of addicts, cautioned: "It is obvious, however, that not all addicts can respond to such missionary zeal or can maintain the deep religious conviction required of them, although a recent evaluation of their results is encouraging" (p. 6). Langrod et al. stated that this religiously oriented program has the same problem as most other residential drug programs in that a substantial majority of those who enter drop out. Glasscote et al. (1972) said that 600 to 700 addicts were in Teen Challenge (T.C.) in its first six years. Without a systematic follow-up, it was estimated that 22 percent of these completed all phases and left drug-free. According to T.C.'s own records, 70 percent of those who graduated from the one year program remained drug-free at least five years (McKee et al. 1971).

There have been accounts of other programs that rely on spiritual conversion. Some clergymen go into the community, bringing religion to the drug user. A book about Father Daniel Egan (Harris 1969), known as "the junkie priest," describes such a mission.* In the early 1970s Reverend Danny Morrow talked with drug users in the Virginia Beach, Virginia, community, telling them "how they could find freedom from drugs through a personal relationship with the Saviour" (Broken Needles, undated). Leech (1970) described the church's contacts with drug users in the Soho area of London: "A good deal of time is spent visiting and hanging around, particularly during the night hours, bringing the care and love and sensitivity of Christ" (p. 38). Wilson (1973) described a ministry among London drug addicts in which he brought those who were willing to a "spiritual therapeutic centre" at a farm 80 miles from London. "The only way an addict can keep off drugs is to change his direction by a spiritual rebirth. . . . Many of the young men in our care have had a deep spiritual experience since their conversion. Some have had a Pentecostal experience and spoken in tongues. Some are working and living in a world free of drugs" (pp. 120–121). Wilson claimed that of 150 residents, 60 percent completed a six-to-twelve-month course of rehabilitation, and 55 to 60 percent of these have remained off drugs and "have taken up responsible places in society."

Drug Addicts Recovery Enterprise (DARE) in Albuquerque, New Mexico, is an innovative, religiously oriented program, the focus of therapy being the love of Jesus Christ. Psychotherapy, vocational training, and "redirection of life-style" are combined with "faith therapy" and total abstinence from drugs. This residential program requires rigorous adherence to strict rules regarding personal appearance and habits, contacts with the outside, associations within the center, and general deportment. A minimum of nine months in residence is usually required. Graduates of the program have an opportu-

---

*In 1973, Father Egan was listed as being with New Hope Manor, a residential drug-abstinence program in Garrison, New York (New York State, 1974, p. 204).

nity to participate in a three-month outreach program that provides jobs and schooling for those reentering the community. DARE claims an 83-percent cure rate, although it mentions no system for follow-up.

The "Jesus movement" among white, middle-class youth is a more recent phenomenon that has attracted a number of drug users. The *Washington Post* (12/12/71) reported that youngsters became caught up in the excitement of the movement and therefore did not need the excitement of drugs. News items and human interest stories have appeared about former drug users who found peace through a religious conversion. We have not located any professional literature that evaluates the results of such conversions to determine whether they are lasting. Skeptics have suggested that this kind of conversion may be merely another temporary "high."

Protestant, Jewish, and Catholic agencies across the nation offer prevention programs, referral services, and treatment programs without necessarily invoking religion as such. A perusal of listings of drug programs in most states shows that many programs are operated by religion-oriented agencies. The clergy has always offered guidance to its congregants. However, the field of pastoral counseling is becoming increasingly sophisticated, paying considerable attention to the training of clergymen in the techniques of helping with specific problems, including alcoholism and drug use.*

In short, religious institutions are actively trying to combat drug use, some through programs that do not invoke religion at all, and others that base their approach totally on religious conversion. Striking claims have been made, particularly in the case of the latter, but a systematic evaluation of results is lacking.

ALTERING STATES OF CONSCIOUSNESS: OFFERING ALTERNATIVES TO DRUGS

Weil (1972a) has taken a positive view of the steps that people devise to "satisfy their needs for altered states of consciousness by means that do not require external tools" such as drugs. Cox (1971–1972) stated that the task is to provide drug users with worthwhile alternatives. "Experts agree that most people could stop drug use if a sufficiently desirable and simple alternative were offered to make them want to stop."

Many methods have been suggested for altering states of consciousness. Brecher (1972, p. 509) listed sensitivity training, encounter therapy, Zen Bud-

---

*Kennedy (1968) defined the aims and purposes of a National Clergy Conference on Alcoholism as education of the Catholic clergy through annual Pastoral Institutes on alcohol problems, prevention of alcoholism through dissemination of information and through educational programs, especially in the seminaries, and recovery of alcoholics through the Sacraments of the Church and the programs of A.A.

dhism, yoga, Transcendental Meditation, massage, hypnosis, and self-hypnosis as nonchemical ways of "turning on" or "getting high." Hyde (1968) referred to the "nonchemical turn-on" that one may experience through yoga under the leadership of Maharishi Mahesh Yogi, an Indian guru.* "His here-and-now pleasure seeking, or instant ecstasy, has somewhat the same appeal as the promise of some drugs, but there is little or no danger of insanity, as may be the case with some hallucinogens" (p. 129). Hyde declared that "turning on" without drugs helps students "in solving their identity crises." One drug center, according to Brecher (1972), was considering introducing parachute jumping, an activity that has been called "clean fun for a new high" (*Washington Star* 6/20/72). Greaves (1974) has stated that everyone needs to have "euphoric experiences" in life. The problem is that the drug user does not know how to experience pleasure through normal channels. Among activities that Greaves recommended were body-sensory awareness programs and meditation.

Bauman (1974) found hypnosis to be a viable alternative to consciousness alteration through drugs. He outlined a technique whereby hypnosis was induced by reliving a "good trip" or happy drug experience. Through practice the patient would then use self-hypnosis to develop this simulated drug experience into a more intense and rewarding high than had originally been achieved with drugs.

Wallace and Benson (1972) described yoga as follows: "The state called yoga (meaning 'union') has a generally agreed definition: a 'higher' consciousness achieved through a fully rested and relaxed body and a fully awake and relaxed mind." Different paths are charted to approach this state of mind, including engaging in strenuous physical exercise, control of such bodily functions as respiratory rates, and inward focus on one's own mental processes. Transcendental Medication (TM) is the most widely practiced form of meditation.† In 1973 (see Sykes) it was estimated that some 160,000 Americans meditate—a tremendous growth from 221 in 1965.‡ In 1975, 205 World Plan Centers were offering TM courses (Bloomfield et al. 1975), and instruction in TM was provided in more than 300 American universities (Cox 1971–1972).

*It was Maharishi Mahesh Yogi who founded the International Meditation Society, in which Transcendental Meditation is taught.

†It is not our purpose here to describe the actual process of Transcendental Meditation. Many articles, books, and courses are available.

‡Newspaper columnist Colman McCarthy (1976) described the extent to which Americans were flocking to TM: "The inner life boom, for a start, is said to involve 600,000 Americans who are spending $20 million annually for commercially run transcendental meditation courses, with 30,000 newcomers a month."

Weil (1972b) said that many drug users give up drugs for TM, but "one does not see any meditators give up meditation for drugs." Encouraged by this observation, some people believe that TM could be an effective substitute for drugs. Marcus (1974) stated that "TM may satisfy the needs of drug abusers to alter consciousness as well as satisfying the needs of those drug abusers, whether or not addicted, seeking relief from tension or stress" (p. 129). *Time* (10/23/72) noted that the Army had permitted experiments with TM to help drug addicts.*

There have been testimonials as to the effectiveness of the varous forms of meditation in helping people cease drug use (see Rubottom 1972; *Washington Post* 5/3/73; *San Jose News* 8/4/73), but only a few studies have appeared in the professional literature. Marcus (1974) reported that the first study of the effects of TM on drug use was conducted in 1969 at a Squaw Valley residential TM course. Of 143 "regular" drug users, 83 percent ceased using all drugs after their practice of TM, 15.5 percent reported a decrease in the use of one or more drugs, and 1.5 percent increased their use of drugs. Of the same group, 49 percent said that their drug use patterns changed because, after TM, life had become more fulfilling; 24 percent said that the drug experience had become less pleasurable; and 8 percent reported no further desire for drugs.

Benson (1969) stated that nineteen drug users between twenty-one and thirty-eight years of age stated that they ceased using drugs because "drug-induced feelings became extremely distasteful as compared to those experienced during the practice of transcendental meditation." Benson and Wallace (1972) cited similar positive results in a sample of 1,862 subjects. "Individuals who regularly practiced Transcendental Meditation (1) decreased or stopped abusing drugs, (2) decreased or stopped engaging in drug-selling activity, and (3) changed their attitudes in the direction of discouraging others from abusing drugs" (p. 374).

According to Benson and Wallace, TM is offered "as a program for personal development." Reduction or cessation of drug use is "merely a side effect of the practice." Benson (1975) pointed out several weaknesses in the study. First, it included only people who were actively engaged in meditation and who were planning to continue it; thus it was difficult to determine how many started TM and then dropped it and resumed drug use. Furthermore, the subjects had a vested interest in the study because they were in training to teach TM. Another limitation was that the information about drug-use practices was retrospective and thus subject to exaggeration or distortion.

Schwartz (1973), reporting on his study with Goleman, stated that a reduction in the use of marijuana and psychedelics occurred in subjects who medi-

---

*According to Driskill (1974), TM is practiced at fifteen military posts, some of which incorporate it into drug abuse programs.

tated regularly. Shafii et al. (1974) stated that the practice of meditation seems to contribute significantly to reducing the use of marijuana and hashish. In their study almost half the users who practiced meditation one to three months decreased or stopped their use of marijuana. The longer a person practiced TM, the greater the probability that he would discontinue marijuana use. The average frequency of marijuana use for the mediator group before TM was 7.3 times a month; after TM, this dropped to 2.8 times a month.

Ramirez (1975) studied drug-using inmates who practiced TM at the Milan Federal Correctional Institution. Inmates who practiced TM regularly were evaluated on the basis of psychologic test results as having improved in "emotional stability and maturity." However, TM did not produce a significant change in behavior, as measured by staff ratings and records of infractions. The author did not mention whether drug use was affected by practicing TM.

Marcus (1975) strongly endorsed TM: "Presently, at least for those dependent on drugs, TM may be used in conjunction with therapeutic communities, but TM may be effective even when it is the sole means of treatment. . . . It is not necessary to view TM as an alternative to drugs. The termination or reduction of drug use is said to occur naturally as life becomes more fulfilling" (p. 178). Marcus commended TM for its simplicity and applicability to any group of people, its low cost, the lack of stigma associated with it, and the fact that TM itself abjures drug use.

Bloomfield et al. (1975), in support of TM, pointed out that TM "improves self-regard, decreases anxiety and improves self-reliance" (p. 106). "Despite all the specific effects for which people take drugs, the purpose of drug abuse is the restoration of physiological equilibrium and a feeling of well-being. Because TM restores equilibrium by reducing stress and maximizes the enjoyment of life, it may well offer a plausible solution for all forms of drug abuse" (p. 107). Bloomfield et al. stated that government officials in Illinois, Michigan, New Hampshire, New York, and five foreign countries were looking into the use of TM to combat drug use. The Illinois House of Representatives passed a resolution in May 1972, noting that TM "shows promise of being the most positive and effective drug prevention program being presented in the world today," and advised that TM be incorporated in drug abuse programs sponsored by the state mental health department. Monahan (1974), appearing before the Subcommittee on Alcoholism and Narcotics of the U.S. Senate Committee on Labor and Public Welfare, asked that the federal government support TM "as an additional weapon in the therapeutic arsenal to be used in the national struggle against drug abuse."

Marcus (1974) saw great potential in TM for prevention of drug use. He said that TM can be taught to children as young as seven years of age – before the age of susceptibility to drug use. Marcus regarded TM as producing an expansion of consciousness and a "natural high" without drugs. And TM provides "healthful group pressure" to meditate, rather than use drugs. Although there has been much fervor about TM, little exists in the way of careful study of its impact on drug use.

BEHAVIOR MODIFICATION

Behavior modification is a psychologic procedure that focuses on changing undesired behavior, rather than on resolving conflicts that presumably underlie the behavior. Cheek et al. (1973), in recommending behavior modification as an approach to addiction, wrote: "Because of the nonverbal orientation of the lower class to which many addicts belong, behavior modification probably appeals in terms of its practical, direct, behavioral approach, emphasizing immediate problem situations and how to handle them, rather than analysis in terms of past experiences" (p. 994).

Much of the rationale for the application of behavioral techniques is based on Wikler's two-factor theory that accounts for the drug addict's relapse after withdrawal from drugs (National Institute of Mental Health 1968). The first factor is classical Pavlovian conditioning. A conditioned response is established through repeated temporal association between sporadic, accidental abstinence periods and contact with specific aspects of the environment (e.g., a bar or street corner). Even when there is no physiologic basis for withdrawal symptoms, the addict's presence in a situation where he had used drugs in the past triggers symptoms that mimic physiologic withdrawal. The second factor in relapse is operant conditioning. When the consequences of an act are rewarding, the act is repeated. Thus, the act of acquiring drugs is repeatedly reinforced by relief from withdrawal symptoms. Wikler (1965) believed that successful treatment requires the extinction of both opiate-seeking behavior and the conditioned abstinence phenomena.

Behavior modification has been used to treat a wide variety of disorders not related to drug use.* Although much has been done with alcoholics,† relatively little has been attempted with other drug users. Here we shall summarize some efforts to treat drug users with behavioral techniques that were found valuable with other groups of patients. For a more comprehensive account of behavior modification applied to drug users, the reader is referred to Callner's review (1975).

Most accounts of behavior therapy with drug users report aversive condi-

---

*For a discussion of behavior modification applied to the criminal, see Chapter 2 of Volume II.

†Wisocki (undated) has compiled a bibliography of studies in which learning principles were applied to alcoholism in the period 1942-1968. More recent studies are cited by Baekland et al. (1975) in their review of treatment methods of chronic alcoholism.

tioning as the treatment of choice. Meyer (1972, p. 75) described aversive therapy as "an effort to apply 'punishment' as a means of reducing the frequency of unwanted behavior." Three methods of presenting aversive stimuli are used: administration of drugs that produce unpleasant effects, application of electric shocks, and "covert sensitization." The last, also termed "verbal aversion," entails the drug user's imagining unpleasant situations that he has experienced.

Wolpe (1965) described the treatment of a physician for dependence on Demerol. The patient carried with him an apparatus with which he could shock himself whenever he experienced the onset of craving for the drug. Using the device for twelve weeks, the patient experienced only minor craving. Then the apparatus broke down, he discontinued therapy, and his drug use recurred.

Lesser (1967) described combining aversive conditioning with relaxation and self-assertion training to treat a morphine-dependent user. The viewing of pictures of the various steps in self-administration of narcotics was combined with administration of electric shock (as the aversive stimulus). Lesser reported that the patient stopped using "hard drugs," although he occasionally smoked marijuana. O'Brien et al. (1972) reported combining aversive conditioning with relaxation therapy and desensitization (described below) in the successful treatment of two heroin users. O'Brien and Raynes (1972) reported the use of electroshock, verbal aversive imagery, relaxation procedures, and systematic desensitization in treating three patients who had been dependent on heroin for at least ten years. Follow-up showed a cessation of heroin use in two of the three; the third was using the drug less than he had before treatment. Blachly (1971) described a plastic syringe constructed so that when the addict pressed the plunger, a shock was administered. In an extension of this procedure to group treatment, electrodes were connected to all group members; if one pressed the plunger, everyone received a shock.

Raymond (1964) treated a narcotic addict by aversive conditioning with apomorphine, an emetic. The apomorphine was injected, and then the narcotic. Within a few minutes after the latter procedure, the patient became nauseated. Lieberman (1968) reported one apomorphine success and one failure. He stated that the unpleasant effects of the aversive stimulus were nausea, vomiting, cold sweats, and dizziness. Lieberman acknowledged that aversive conditioning is not a cure in itself, but maintained that it has potential value when combined with other treatments.

Two British investigators, Thomson and Rathod (1968), reported using the drug Scoline (suxamethonium chloride). As the addict prepared to inject a narcotic, an anesthetist injected 30 mg of Scoline. A paralysis of breathing set in, at which time the addict was forcefully told about the dangers of drugs. After the development of mild cyanosis (turning blue because of lack of oxygen), oxygen was administered. Thomson and Rathod stated that nine of the ten patients treated remained off all drugs for an average of thirty-three weeks.

To participate voluntarily in aversive conditioning a drug user must be highly motivated. We have encountered no studies of forced treatment of drug addicts. Meyer (1972) stated that "aversion therapy has not been attempted widely in [the United States], and there are no data which support the general efficacy of aversion therapy in any of the drug abuse syndromes" (p. 75).

"Covert sensitization" (verbal aversion) has the advantage of not requiring any "external agent" (Anant 1968). It is a purely verbal procedure, relying on communication of images. Kolvin (1967) described the case of a fifteen-year-old gasoline sniffer. He was to pair thoughts of gasoline sniffing with frightening thoughts of falling. Kolvin reported that the patient was cured after twenty half-hour sessions. Thirteen months after the treatment ended, he still was not sniffing gasoline.

Steinfeld (1970) treated institutionalized narcotic addicts, both individually and in groups, with relaxation and covert sensitization. The aversive imagery included scenes of vomiting and of attacks by rats as the addict imagined himself ready to use narcotics.

Wisocki (1973) reported directing outpatient treatment of a heroin user at three levels: "reinforcing thoughts and behaviors antagonistic to the use of heroin, eliminating positive thoughts and urges for heroin, and creating an aversion for all aspects of heroin usage." A typical "covert sensitization" or aversive conditioning session had the patient think about obtaining drugs and then imagine that he was attacked by wasps. As the patient pictured the drug pusher, he was to imagine hordes of wasps swarming all over him. Then as he thought that perhaps it was not worth going to the city for drugs, he was to imagine the wasps leaving and his being happy that he had resisted the urge. An eighteen-month follow-up showed that he had not used heroin. He had also gained an improved self-concept and "new pro-social attitudes and behaviors."

According to Brady (1972), "systematic desensitization" is the most widely used behavior therapy in treating psychologic disorders. It entails training in progressive relaxation, construction of anxiety hierarchies, and a combination of both these steps during the actual desensitization. The objective of systematic desensitization is to make the patient increasingly comfortable through suggestion and reassurance in anxiety-arousing situations (Anant 1968). Kraft (1968) stated that the drug user takes refuge in drugs because he has difficulty in making contact with other people. Correction of this problem, in his opinion, would eliminate the need for drugs. Kraft (1969) reported the successful treatment of two amphetamine (Dexamyl) addicts through systematic desensitization and relaxation induced by hypnosis. The patients were taught to be at ease first in social situations at the hospital and later in the drug area of London. Increasingly they were granted more time away from the hospital, with longer intervals between therapy sessions. When they could function on their own without drugs for two weeks, formal treatment was terminated, and they were eligible to attend a weekly meeting of the Post Behavior Therapy Club with the therapist present. Both patients in Kraft's study were drug-free after a nine-month follow-up.

Another form of behavior modification is "contingent reinforcement," in which the desired "prosocial behavior" is specified and reinforced according to a prearranged program. Contingency reinforcement may be carried out through contractual agreements between patient and therapist ("contingency contracting") or in a token economy. Boudin (1972) described a contact between himself and a female graduate student who was a heavy user of amphetamines. The therapist had to be available at all times for this treatment procedure. In fact, at one point in the therapy, the patient resided in the therapist's home. The patient was to keep the therapist informed of her whereabouts, checking in three times a day. She had to cease using drugs. The patient opened a joint bank account in her name and her therapist's, into which she deposited her money. If she wavered in her determination and used drugs, she had to write a check to the Ku Klux Klan for fifty dollars. (The patient was black.) Boudin reported that two years later she had not used amphetamines.

Glicksman et al. (1971) described a "token-economy" milieu for inpatient rehabilitation of narcotic users. Civilly committed, youthful addicts who had been unresponsive to traditional psychotherapeutic methods were placed on a ward of the Bayview Rehabilitation Center in New York, which used contingent reinforcement. The resident could "eventually buy his discharge from the institution" by earning enough credits for desirable behavior. Credits could be amassed in proportion to the amount and quality of participation in various programs, as well as the quality of behavior on the ward. The authors reported that these patients were discharged from the center after an average stay of four months, compared with seven and one-half months for residents on other wards not in this program. The token-economy group boasted about their "high paycheck totals," whereas residents of other units regarded compliance as "phony" or "hypocritical." Glicksman et al. reported that the experimental group not only got out faster but also became increasingly involved in an "honest dialogue" with staff.

Ross and Jones (1973) reported that contingency contracting appears promising in modifying specific kinds of behavior, such as the addict's learning to relax without drugs. One drawback that these investigators met in their contingency-contracting trials was the addict's attitude that "whatever behavior I can get away with is OK if it is not in any of my contracts."

Callner and Ross (1973) described behavioral training in assertiveness for drug addicts. Their premise was that if drug users learned to respond to situations with "appropriate assertive behavior," it was more likely that they would be integrated into society. The patients engaged in structured role playing, modeling, rehearsal, and videotaping procedures and were then asked to practice the new behavior with one another in different settings. Pretreatment and posttreatment assessment showed that the experimental group was more assertive than the control group, which was not given the assertiveness training. The effect of this treatment on drug use was not reported.

The application of behavior modification to the drug user is still relatively recent. Individual case studies suggest that the patients who participated were highly motivated for treatment. Wolpe's addicted physician (1965) had had three years of psychoanalytic treatment, but his addiction was affecting his work, marriage, and social life. Nevertheless, behavioral techniques failed with him. Lieberman's success (1968) was with a person who "eagerly accepted the conditioning therapy." Wisocki's youthful heroin addict (1973) was described as "highly motivated" and willing to pay for treatment. Callner (1975) said that only 57 percent of the studies that he surveyed reported follow-up data, and 87 percent of these relied on self-reports of drug use. "In general . . . the reluctance to follow patients after treatment and the lack of reliable follow-up measures strongly points to another obvious area for future refinement."

THE CURRENT SITUATION

Faced with the crisis of increasing drug use and a need to take some kind of action, society has expanded its programs and services to deal with the drug user. Much of this expansion occurred in the "Great Society" programs of the 1960s. In response to political pressures, drug programs proliferated in an atmosphere of crisis and professional rivalry. The explosion of new programs continued into the 1970s.*

The National Commission on Marihuana and Drug Abuse (1973) declared that the United States was spending over $1 billion a year without knowing whether the money was reducing drug use or only perpetuating government activity.

The cry, "do something," forced the Federal government to spend the money without an opportunity to evaluate the programs in advance or to assess their likely impact on larger social welfare policies. . . . "Drug

---

*A survey of directories of federal, state, and local programs shows hundreds of offerings in drug abuse treatment and prevention. The New York Drug Abuse Control Commission, for example, had a 262-page directory that listed only the local programs for fiscal 1974.

abuse" spending in the last decade can be summarized thus: an ill-defined problem emotionally expressed, led to ill-defined programs, lavishly funded. (pp. 281, 283)

The Commission stated that "a drug abuse industrial complex" had been created. In 1974 Thomas Bryant, the president of the Drug Abuse Council, maintained that knowledge was not keeping pace with the programs developed. "It is a sad commentary that despite the growing investment in drug programs, a huge information gap exists in this critical area. We don't know a great deal about mind-altering drugs. . . . Current prevention and education programs have suffered from a lack of adequate evaluation as to their effectiveness" (*U.S. Medicine* 2/1/74). Field, of London's Metropolitan Hospital, asserted in a letter to *Lancet* (1968) that psychiatry had failed to make an impact on drug dependence:

> The alleged treatment of drug addiction by psychiatrists is merely another example of the lack of humility on the part of psychiatrists and their refusal to face what must be a painful fact to them — namely that there are conditions which are not amenable to their "treatment." There is not the slightest evidence that any form of treatment administered by psychiatrists is statistically significantly better in curing drug addicts compared with what can be expected without such treatment.

Some have concluded that drug dependence is an incurable disease: "We have certainly not been successful in 'curing' any kind of addiction. . . . Rehabilitation efforts are a failure. . . . The British system's rationale is that drug dependence is an incurable disease" (Barbara and Morrison 1975, p. 33).

Because of the urgency of coping with drug use, there has been little critical examination of the results of the programs that have been used. Callner (1975), in reviewing behavioral treatment approaches to drug use, criticized the total lack of follow-up in approximately half the studies that he surveyed and added that "considering the long-term nature of drug abuse problems, followup assessment is perhaps the most critical appraisal of treatment effectiveness" (p. 153). The diversity of approaches to the treatment of drug users closely parallels the variety of points of view about the causation of drug use. As indicated above, sociologic, psychologic, and medically oriented approaches have all been applied to drug treatment with varying degrees of claimed success. Still the fact remains that drug use remains high on the list of unsolved national problems.

Agreement as to the most effective methods of treating drug users is as rare as agreement as to the causes of drug use and the effects of drugs on human behavior. Following the passage of the Harrison Narcotics Act in 1914, private physicians, who had regarded physical dependence on drugs as a disease, were prevented from maintaining their patients on morphine, and the federal government assumed the role of providing treatment for drug users. Poorly administered government-established clinics lasted until 1925, and then for the next ten years, drug treatment was virtually nonexistent. The federal institutions at Lexington, Kentucky, and Fort Worth, Texas, were the only major drug treatment facilities in the country until the increase in drug use in the 1960s made imperative the establishment of new facilities and a search for more effective methods of treatment (National Clearinghouse 1975).

Some people believe that the drug problem is predominantly a consequence of society's intervention. Ashley (1975, p. 187) contended that prohibitions against cocaine and other illicit drugs should be abolished. Reinert (1974) raised the question of whether society is "morally justified in depriving an individual whose life is without purpose, hope and direction . . . of the chief pleasure of which he is capable." Szasz (1971), arguing that drug abuse and addiction are moral rather than medical problems, stated: "The Constitution and the Bill of Rights are silent on the subject of drugs, implying that the adult citizen has or ought to have the right to medicate his own body as he sees fit" (p. 546).

We believe that the issue of drug use is far more than a person's right to what he considers pleasure. In this book, we have emphasized that criminals use drugs, to a considerable extent, to facilitate the commision of both more numerous crimes and more serious crimes than they commit when they are not on drugs. Accordingly, we have endeavored to bring our understanding of the criminal to the task of developing a program to help him change. It is the process of change which forms the substance of the next chapter.

BIBLIOGRAPHY

TREATMENT OF THE DRUG USER

Ball, J.C. (1972). On the treatment of drug dependence. *American Journal of Psychiatry* 128:873-874.

DeLong, J. V. (1972). Treatment and rehabilitation. In Drug Abuse Survey Project, *Dealing with Drug Abuse,* pp. 173-254. New York: Praeger.

Glaser, D. (1967). Problems in the evaluation of treatment and rehabilitation programs. In *Rehabilitating the Narcotic Addict,* Vocational Rehabilitation Administration. Washington, D.C.: Government Printing Office.

Lett, S. (1891). Treatment of the opium neurosis. *Journal of the American Medical Association* 17:828-833.

Louria, D. B. (1971). *Overcoming Drugs.* New York: McGraw-Hill.

Reichard, J. D. (1947). Addiction: some theoretical considerations as to its nature, cause, prevention and treatment. *American Journal of Psychiatry* 103:721-730.

Schoolar, J. C., Winbum, G. M., and Hays, J. R. (1973). Rehabilitation of drug abusers – a continuing enigma. *Rehabilitation Literature* 34: 327-330.

Wallis, F. A. (1926). The criminology of drug addiction. In *Narcotic Education,* ed. H. S. Middlemiss, pp. 21-28. Washington, D.C.: H. S. Middlemiss.

Yolles, S. F. (1973). General perspective on drug abuse. In *Yearbook of Drug Abuse,* eds. L. Brill and E. Harms, pp. 239-264. New York: Behavioral Publications.

MOTIVATION FOR TREATMENT

APA Monitor (8/72). Government study lauds "treatment" camps for addicts.

Ausubel, D. P. (1958). *Drug Addiction.* New York: Random House.

Blachly, P. H. (1966). Management of the opiate abstinence syndrome. *American Journal of Psychiatry* 122:742-744.

Brunner-Orne, M. (1956). The utilization of group psychotherapy in enforced treatment programs for alcoholics and addicts. *International Journal of Group Psychotherapy* 6:272-279.

Cohen, S. (1969). *The Drug Dilemma.* New York: McGraw-Hill.

De Ropp, R. S. (1957). *Drugs and the Mind.* New York: St. Martin's Press.

Friedman, S. B., Horvat, C. L., and Levinson R. B. (1982). The narcotic addict rehabilitation act: its impact on federal prisons. *Contemporary Drug Problems* II: 101-111.

Gerard, D. L., and Kornetsky, C. (1954). A social and psychiatric study of adolescent opiate addicts. *Psychiatric Quarterly* 28:113-125.

Goldberg, F. J. (1975). Why so few psychologists in drug abuse? Paper presented at the 83rd Annual Convention of the American Psychological Association, Chicago.

Inskeep, R. (1981). Vocational rehabilitation/employment development for drug dependent women. In National Institute on Drug Abuse., *Treatment Services for Drug Dependent Women.* Rockville: National Institute on Drug Abuse, 293-243.

Kolb, L. (1962). *Drug Addiction.* Springfield, IL: Charles C Thomas.

Lindesmith, A. R. (1968). *Addiction and Opiates.* Chicago: Aldine.

Maddux, J. F. (1974). Current approaches to the treatment of narcotic addiction. In *Psychotherapy and Drug Addiction, I: Diagnosis and Treatment,* pp. 106-122. New York: MSS Information Corporation.

Moffett, A. D., Adler, F., Glaser, F. R., and Horvitz, D. (1975). *Medical Lollypop, Junkie Insulin, or What?* Philadelphia: Dorrance.

Newman, R. G. (1973). We'll make them an offer they can't refuse. In *Proceedings of the 5th National Conference on Methadone Treatment,* pp. 94–100. Vol. 1. New York: National Association for the Prevention of Addiction to Narcotics.

New York Times (12/26/72). Youths rejecting heroin, but turn to other drugs.

Silsby, H., and Tennant, F. S., Jr. (1974). Short-term, ambulatory detoxification of opiate addicts using methadone. *International Journal of the Addictions* 9:167–170 (Reprinted by courtesy of Marcel Dekker, Inc.).

St. Pierre, C. A. (1971). Motivating the drug addict in treatment. *Social Work* 16:80–88.

Tennant, F. S., Glasser, M., McMillan, C., and Shannon, J. (1973). Changing face of the contemporary drug scene. *Medical Digest* 19:49–52.

EXTERNAL DETERRENCE

Arenson, G. A. (1973). In reply . . . drug rehabilitation. *Psychiatric Opinion* 10:33.

Brill, L, and Lieberman, L. (1969). *Authority and Addiction.* Boston: Little, Brown.

Brown, T. T. (1961). *The Enigma of Drug Addiction.* Springfield, IL: Charles C Thomas.

Brunner-Orne, M. (1956). The utilization of group psychotherapy in enforced treatment programs for alcoholics and addicts. *International Journal of Group Psychotherapy* 6:272–279.

Cohen, S. (1969). *The Drug Dilemma.* New York: McGraw-Hill.

DeLong, J. V. (1972). Treatment and rehabilitation. In Drug Abuse Survey Project, *Dealing with Drug Abuse,* pp. 173–254. New York: Praeger.

Dole, V. P. (1972). Comments on "heroin maintenance." *Journal of the American Medical Association* 220:1493.

Jaffe, J. H. (1969). A review of the approaches to the problem of compulsive narcotics use. In *Drugs and Youth: Proceedings of the Rutgers Symposium on Drug Abuse,* eds. J. R. Wittenborn et al., pp. 77–91. Springfield, IL: Charles C Thomas.

Keniston, K. (1969). Search and rebellion among the disadvantaged. In *Drug Dependence: A Guide for Physicians.* American Medical Association, Council on Mental Health. Chicago: American Medical Association.

Kielholz, P., and Battegay, R. (1963). The treatment of drug addicts in Switzerland. *Comprehensive Psychiatry* 4:225–235.

Kurland, A. A., Wurmser, L., Kerman, F., and Kokoski, R. (1966). Urine detection tests in the management of the narcotic addict. *American Journal of Psychiatry* 122:737–741.

Lindesmith, A. R. (1940–1941). "Dope fiend" mythology. *Journal of the American Institute of Criminal Law and Criminology* 31:199–208.

——— (1973). Patent medicine for the drug problem. *American Journal of Orthopsychiatry* 43:512–514.

McMorris, S. C. (1966). What price euphoria: the case against marijuana. *Medio-Legal Journal* 34:74–79.

Meyer, R. E. (1972). *Guide to Drug Rehabilitation.* Boston: Beacon Press.

Peck, M. L., and Klugman, D. J. (1973). Rehabilitation of drug dependent offenders: an alternative approach. *Federal Probation* 37:18–23.

Ploscowe, M. (1961). Some basic problems in drug addiction and suggestions for research. In *Drug Addiction: Crime or Disease?,* pp. 15–120. American Bar Association and American Medical Association, Joint Committee on Narcotic Drugs. Bloomington, IN: Indiana University Press.

Reichard, J. D. (1947). Addiction: some theoretical considerations as to its nature, cause, prevention and treatment. *American Journal of Psychiatry* 103:721–730.

Rosenthal, M. S. (1973). A hard line must be drawn. *American Journal of Orthopsychiatry* 43:526–528.

Rouse, B. A., and Ewing, J. A. (1971). Marijuana use by graduate and professional students. Paper presented at the 5th World Congress of Psychiatry, Mexico City, November–December.

Schur, E. M. (1965). *Crimes Without Victims.* Englewood Cliffs, N.J.: Prentice-Hall.

Thorpe, J. J. (1956). Addicts. In *The Fields of Group Psychotherapy,* ed. S. R. Slovson, pp. 59–75. New York: International Universities Press.

Walsh, J. (1973). Lexington Narcotics Hospital: a special sort of alma mater. *Science* 182:1004–1008.

SOCIOLOGIC MEASURES

Anslinger, H. J. (1934). The narcotic problem. In *Attorney General's Conference on Crime.* Washington, D.C.: Government Printing Office.

APA Monitor (2/73). Study finds most drug-abuse films do more harm than good.

Bejerot, N. (1972). *Addiction: An Artificially Induced Drive.* Springfield, IL: Charles C Thomas.

Bender, L. (1963). Drug addiction in adolescence. *Comprehensive Psychiatry* 4:181–194.

Breed, A. F. (1975). California's Youth Authority reports successful program for chronic drug abusers. *American Journal of Correction* 37:8–9.

Brill, L., and Lieberman, L. (1969). *Authority and Addiction*. Boston: Little, Brown.

Brown, T. T. (1961). *The Enigma of Drug Addiction*. Springfield, IL: Charles C Thomas.

Chinlund, S. (1975). Juvenile offenders and the drug problem. In *Fundamentals of Juvenile Criminal Behavior and Drug Abuse,* eds. R. E. Hardy and J. G. Cull, pp. 125-138. Springfield, IL: Charles C Thomas.

Clark, R. (1970). *Crime in America*. New York: Simon and Schuster.

Coombs, O. (1972). It's blacks who must stop crime. *Washington Post,* December 3.

Corcoran, J. F. (Undated). Letter accompanying *Super Me/Super Yo*. Washington, D.C.: National Coordinating Council on Drug Education.

Dole, V. P. (1973). Heroin addiction — an epidemic disease. Reprinted from The Harvey Lectures, Series 67. New York: Academic Press.

Edmondson, J. A. (1974). Personal communication by executive director of Youth Direction Council of Levittown-Island Press, Inc., Levittown, N.Y., May 31.

Einstein, S. (1983). Drug education: a primer. *International Journal of the Addictions* 18:1157-1169.

Gottschalk, L. A., Morrison, G. C., Drury, R. B., and Barnes, A. C. (1973). The Laguna Beach experiment as a community approach to family counseling for drug abuse problems in youth. In *Children and Their Parents in Brief Therapy,* eds. H. E. Barten and S. S. Barten, pp. 214-226. New York: Behavioral Publications.

Greden, J. F., Morgan, D. W., and Frenkel, S. I. (1974). The changing drug scene: 1970-1972. *American Journal of Psychiatry* 131:77-81.

Griffenhagen, G. B. (1973). Philatelic war on drug abuse. *Drug Forum* 3:1-36.

Helms, D. J., Scura, W. C., and Fisher, C. C. (1975). The treatment of the addict in correctional institutions. In *Medical Aspects of Drug Abuse,* ed. R. W. Richter, pp. 360-366. Hagerstown, MD: Harper and Row.

Johnson, B. B. (1968). A junior high school seminar in dangerous drugs and narcotics. *Journal of School Health* 38:84-87.

Karras, A., and Cohen, M. (1974). The genesis and evaluation of two rehabilitation programs for drug abusers. In Proceedings of the Institute of Clincial Toxicology Conference: Clinical Perspectives of Non Narcotic Drug Abuse, Houston, TX.

King, R. (1961). An appraisal of international British and selected European narcotic drug laws, regulations and policies. In *Drug Addiction: Crime or Disease?,* pp. 121-155. American Bar Association and American Medical Association, Joint Committee on Drugs. Bloomington, IN: Indiana University Press.

Kolben, N. S. (1982). Employer- and Union-sponsored employee counseling programs: trends for the 1980s. *Contemporary Drug Problems* II:181–202.

Lamb, H. R., and Mackota, C. (1973). Using work therapeutically. In *Drug Dependence and Rehabilitation Approaches,* eds. R. E. Hardy and J. G. Cull, pp. 157–169. Springfield, IL: Charles C Thomas.

Lindesmith, A. R. (1968). *Addiction and Opiates.* Chicago: Aldine.

Lundberg, G. D. (1973). Barbiturates: a great American problem. *Journal of the American Medical Association* 224:1531.

Maurer, D. W., and Vogel, V. H. (1967). *Narcotics and Narcotic Addiction,* 3rd ed. Springfield, IL: Charles C Thomas.

McBride, D., and McCoy, C. (1981). Crime and drug-using behavior. *Criminology* 19:281–302.

McKee, M. R. (1975). Drug abuse knowledge and attitudes in "middle America." *American Journal of Public Health* 65:584–590.

McMorris, S. C. (1966). What price euphoria: the case against marijuana. *Medio-Legal Journal* 34:74–79.

Meyer, R. E. (1972). *Guide to Drug Rehabilitation.* Boston: Beacon Press.

Mushkin, S. (1976). Politics and economics of government response to drug abuse. *Annals of the American Academy of Political and Social Science* 417:27–40.

National Clearinghouse for Drug Abuse Information. (1974). Drug abuse prevention report. Report Series 2, No. 1. Washington, D.C.: Government Printing Office.

National Commission on Marihuana and Drug Abuse. (1973). *Drug Use in America: The Problem in Perspective.* Second Report of the National Commission on Marihuana and Drug Abuse. Washington, D.C.: Government Printing Office.

National Coordinating Council on Drug Education. (Undated) *Super Me/ Super Yo.* Washington, D.C.: National Coordinating Council on Drug Education.

National Institute of Mental Health. (1971). Comprehensive community programs for narcotic addicts and drug abusers. Public Health Service, Publication No. 2149. Washington, D.C.: Government Printing Office.

Raymond, F. B. (1975). A sociological view of narcotics addiction. *Crime and Delinquency* 21: 11–18.

Ross, F. T. (1973). The group process in the drug programs of the independent schools. In *Drug Abuse and Drug Addiction.* ed. M. Rosenbaum, pp. 69–74. New York: Gordon and Breach Science Publishers.

Sackler, A. M. (1973). On drugs and good intentions. *Hospital Tribune,* June.

Thomas, M. G. (1926). Teaching of narcotics in the schools. In *Narcotic Education,* ed. H. S. Middlemiss, pp. 203–208. Washington, D.C.: H. S. Middlemiss.

Thompson, D.C. (1986). Corporate caring. *Pace* 13: Piedmont Airlines, January, pp. 39–42.

U.S. Medicine (7/15/73). Methadone use seen possible MD "folly."

Wald, P. M., and Hutt, P. B. (1972). The Drug Abuse Survey Project: summary of findings, conclusions, and recommendations. In *Dealing with Drug Abuse,* pp. 3–61. Drug Abuse Survey Project. New York: Praeger.

Wattenberg, W. W. (1973). *The Adolescent Years.* New York: Harcourt, Brace & Jovanovich.

Weaver, S. C., and Tennant, F. S. (1973). Effectiveness of drug education programs for secondary school student. *American Journal of Psychiatry* 130:812–814.

Yale Alumni Magazine (12/73). WYBC loses censorship appeal.

PSYCHIATRIC-PSYCHOLOGIC APPROACHES

Abrams, A., Roth, D., and Boshes, B. (1958). Group therapy with narcotic addicts, method and evaluation. *Group Psychotherapy* 11:244–256.

Alexander, B. K., and Dibb, G. S. (1975). Opiate addicts and their parents. *Family Process* 14:499–514.

Anthony, E. J. (1971). The history of group psychotherapy. In *Comprehensive Group Psychotherapy,* eds. H. I. Kaplan and B. J. Sadock, pp. 4–31. Baltimore: Williams and Wilkins.

Ausubel, D. P. (1958). *Drug Addiction.* New York: Random House.

Barr, H. L., Rosen, A., Antes, D. E., and Ottenberg, D. J. (1973). Two year follow-up study of 724 drug and alcohol addicts treated together in an abstinence therapeutic community. Paper presented at the 81st Annual Convention of the American Psychological Association, Montreal.

Bartlett, D. (1975). The use of multiple family therapy groups with adolescent drug addicts. In *The Adolescent in Group and Family Therapy,* ed. M. Sugar, pp. 262–282. New York: Brunner/Mazel.

Benedek, T. (1936). Dominant ideas and their relation to morbid craving. *International Journal of Psychoanalysis* 17:40–56.

Berne, E. (1966). *Principles of Group Treatment.* New York: Oxford University Press.

Boorstein, S. (1967). A psychoanalytical overview of the offender: implications for therapy. *Psychoanalytic Forum* 2:245–269.

Boylin, E. R. (1971). Using psychodrama to introduce a new drug addict to members of a concept house: a case study. *Group Psychotherapy and Psychodrama* 24:31–32.

Brecher, E. M. and the editors of *Consumer Reports* (1972). *Licit and Illicit Drugs.* Boston: Little, Brown.

Brill, L., and Lieberman, L. (1969). *Authority and Addiction.* Boston: Little, Brown.

Carlson, W. P. (1974). Out-patient treatment of drug-alcohol abuse in the velvet ghetto. Paper presented at the 82nd Annual Convention of the American Psychological Association, New Orleans.

Casriel, D., and Deitch, D. (1966). New success in permanent cure of narcotics addicts. *Physician's Panorama,* October.

Chein, I., Gerard, D. L., Lee, R. S., and Rosenfeld, E. (1964). *The Road to H: Narcotics, Delinquency and Social Policy.* New York: Basic Books.

Cleveland, M. (1981). Family and adolescent drug abuse: structural analysis of children's roles. *Family Process* 20: 295–304.

Coghlan, A. J., and Zimmerman, R. S. (1972). Self-help (Daytop) and methadone maintenance: are they both failing? *Drug Forum* 1:215–225.

Coulson, G., Went, H., and Kozlinski, E. (1974). Comments on "414": A therapeutic community for the treatment of adolescent amphetamine abusers. *Corrective and Social Psychiatry and Journal of Behavior Technology Methods and Therapy* 20:10–12.

Craig, R. J. (1982). Group therapy with drug addicts. In *Drug Dependent Patients,* eds. R. J. Craig and S. L. Baker, pp. 127–140. Springfield, IL: Charles C Thomas.

Deeths, A. (1970). Psychodrama, crisis intervention with delinquent male drug users. *Group Psychotherapy and Psychodrama* 23:41–43.

De Leon, G., Holland, S., and Rosenthal, M. S. (1972). Phoenix House: criminal activity of dropouts. *Journal of the American Medical Association* 222:686–689.

Drakeford, J. W. (1967). *Integrity Therapy.* Nashville, TN: Broadman Press.

Dreikurs, R. (1969). Early experiments with group psychotherapy. In *Group Therapy Today,* ed. H. M. Ruitenbeek, pp. 18–28. New York: Atherton Press.

Ellis, A. (1976). Workshop presented at the United States District Court sponsored by the Office of the Probation Officer. Washington, D.C., April 8.

Einstein, S. (1983). Treating the drug user: built-in conceptual problems. *International Journal of the Addictions.* 18:iii–vii.

Farkas, G. M., Petersen, D. M., and Barr, N. I. (1970). New developments in the Federal Bureau of Prisons Addict Treatment Program. *Federal Probation,* December, pp. 52–59.

Fort, J. (1972). The treatment of sedative, stimulant, marijuana, and LSD abuse. In *Major Modalities in the Treatment of Drug Abuse,* eds. L. Brill and L. Lieberman, pp. 237–256. New York: Behavioral Publications.

Fraser, H. F., and Grider, J. A. (1967). Treatment. In *Narcotics and Hallucinogens: A Handbook.* Rev. ed. Ed. J. B. Williams, pp. 67–74. Beverly Hills, CA: Glencoe Press.

Freedman, A. M. (1963). Treatment of drug addiction in a community general hospital. *Comprehensive Psychiatry* 4:199–207.

Freedman, D. X. (1974). Implications for research. In *Psychotherapy and Drug Addiction, I: Diagnosis and Treatment,* pp. 253–263. New York: MSS Information Corporation.

Glaser, F. B. (1971). Gaudenzia, Incorporated: historical and theoretical background of self-help addiction treatment program. *International Journal of the Addictions* 6:615–626. (Reprinted by courtesy of Marcel Dekker, Inc.)

Glasscote, R. M., Sussex, J. N., Jaffe, J. H., Ball, J., and Brill, L. (1972). *The Treatment of Drug Abuse.* Washington, D.C.: American Psychiatric Association.

Glasser, W. (1965). *Reality Therapy.* New York: Harper and Row.

Glover, E. (1932). On the aetiology of drug-addiction. *International Journal of Psycho-Analysis* 13:298–328.

——— (1955). *The Technique of Psycho-analysis.* New York: International Universities Press.

Gold, S. R., and Coghlan, A. J. (1973). Effect of residential treatment on adolescent drug abusers: a preliminary report. Paper presented at the 81st Annual Convention of the American Psychological Association, Montreal.

Goldberg, C., and Goldberg, M. (1973). *The Human Circle.* Chicago: Nelson-Hall.

Goldberg, F. J. (1975). Why so few psychologists in drug abuse? Paper presented at the 83rd Annual Convention of the American Psychological Association, Chicago.

Goldburgh, S. J. (1968). An eclectic approach with hypnosis in the therapy of a drug addict. *Psychotherapy: Theory, Research and Practice* 5:189–192.

Goldfield, M. D., and Lauer, R. (1971). The use of creative writing in groups of young adult drug abusers. *New Physician,* July, pp. 449–457.

Gould, R. E. (1972). An evaluation of the therapeutic community's contribution to the management of drug addiction. Paper presented at the 125th Annual Meeting of the American Psychiatric Association, Dallas.

Hampden-Turner, C. (1976). *Sane Asylum.* San Francisco: San Francisco Book Co.

Haskell, M. (1958). The drug addict, role playing and group psychotherapy, the need for a new approach. *Group Psychotherapy* 11:197–202.

Hirsch, R. (1961). Group therapy with parents of adolescent drug addicts. *Psychiatric Quarterly* 35:702–710.

Hollander, M. (1973). Programs for drug abuse prevention and treatment in a suburban community. In *Drug Abuse and Drug Addiction,* pp. 47–61. New York: Gordon and Breach Science Publishers.

Iverson, D. C., and Wenger, S. S. (1978). Therapeutic communities: treatment practices in view of drug dependency theory. *Drug Forum* 7:81–103.

Janov, A. (1970). *The Primal Scream.* New York: G. P. Putnam's Sons.

Johnson, J. A. (1963). *Group Therapy: A Practical Approach.* New York: McGraw-Hill.

Jones, E. (1920). *Treatment of the Neuroses.* London: Baillere, Tindall, and Cox.

Jones, M. (1953). *The Therapeutic Community.* New York: Basic Books.

Kaplan, H. I., and Sadock, B. J., eds. (1971). *Comprehensive Group Psychotherapy.* Baltimore: Williams and Wilkins.

Karras, A. (1979). Rehabilitating the drug abuser: a variation on a theme. *Drug Forum* 7: 265–272.

Kaufman, E. (1973). Group therapy techniques used by the ex-addict therapist. In *Drug Abuse and Drug Addiction,* ed. M. Rosenbaum, pp. 3–19. New York: Gordon and Breach Science Publishers.

Kaufman, E. (1985). *Substance Abuse and Family Therapy.* Orlando: Grune & Stratton.

Kempler, H. L., and Mac Kenna, P. (1975). Clinical observations and brief family therapy of drug abusing adolescents and their families. Paper presented at the 52nd Annual Convention of the American Orthopsychiatric Association, Washington, D.C.

Kilmann, P. R. (1974). Marathon group therapy with female narcotic addicts. Paper presented at the 82nd Annual Convention of the American Psychological Association, New Orleans.

King, C. S. (1977). Coping with drugs through changing the environment. *Los Angeles Herald-Examiner,* 5/8/77.

Kramer, J. C. (1971). Prepared Statement before the Select Committee on Crime. 92nd U.S. Congress. House. *Hearings Before the Select Committee on Crime,* Part 2. Washington, D.C.: Government Printing Office, pp. 662–670.

Lebow, K. E. (1973). The drug abuse treatment center at the Federal Correctional Institution at Lompoc. Paper presented at the 81st Annual Convention of the American Psychological Association, Montreal.

Levine, J., and Ludwig, A. M. (1966). The hypnodelic treatment technique. *International Journal of Clinical and Experimental Hypnosis* 14:207–215.

Lieberman, F., Caroff, P. and Gottesfeld, M. (1973). *Before Addiction: How to Help Youth.* New York: Behavioral Publications.

Lowinson, J., and Zwerling, I. (1971). Group therapy with narcotic addicts. In *Comprehensive Group Psychotherapy,* eds. H. I. Kaplan and B. J. Sadock, pp. 602–622. Baltimore: Williams and Wilkins.

McClain, J. (1951). An experiment in group psychothearpy with the narcotic addict. *American Journal of Psychotherapy* 5:24–31.

Maddox, J. F. (1965). Hospital management of the narcotic addict. In *Narcotics*, eds. D. M. Wilner and G. G. Kassebaum, pp. 159–176. New York: McGraw-Hill.

——— (1974). Current approaches to the treatment of narcotic addiction. In *Psychotherapy and Drug Addiction, I: Diagnosis and Treatment*, pp. 106–122. New York: MSS Information Corporation.

Messenger, E., and Zitrin, A. (1965). A statistical study of criminal drug addicts: psychosis, psychoneurosis, mental deficiency, and personality types. *Crime and Delinquency* 11:283–292.

Meyer, R. E. (1972). *Guide to Drug Rehabilitation*. Boston: Beacon Press.

National Clearinghouse for Drug Abuse Information. (1972). National directory of drug abuse treatment programs. Prepared by the Institute of Behavioral Research, Texas Christian University, Fort Worth, TX. Washington, D.C.: Government Printing Office.

Nyswander, M. (1967). The methadone treatment of heroin addiction. *Hospital Practice* 2:27–33.

Page, R. C. (1982). Marathon group therapy with users of illicit drugs: dimensions of social learning. *International Journal of the Addictions* 17:1107–1115.

Page, R. C., and Miehl, H. (1982). Marathon groups: facilitating the personal growth of male illicit drug users. *International Journal of the Addictions* 17:393–397.

Panio, A. M. (1975). Saturation group therapy with poly drug users. In *Developments in the Field of Drug Abuse*, eds. E. Senay et al., p. 572. Cambridge, MA: Schenkman.

Peck, M., and Klugman, D.J. (1973). Rehabilitation of drug dependent offenders: an alternative approach. *Federal Probation* 37:18–23.

Perkins, I. H. (1972). A unique approach to hospital treatment of narcotic addicts. *Adolescence* 7:29–50.

Pokorny, A., and Wiggins, G. (1972). Straights and addicts mix: rationale, results. Paper presented at the 125th Annual Meeting of the American Psychiatric Association, Dallas.

Reinstein, M. J. (1973). The role of drug counselors in a hospital drug-cure program. *Hospital and Community Psychiatry* 24:839–841.

Rosenthal, M. S. (1973a). A hard line must be drawn. *American Journal of Orthopsychiatry* 43:526–528.

——— (1973b). New York City: Phoenix House: a therapeutic community program for the treatment of drug abusers and drug addicts. In *Yearbook of Drug Abuse*, eds. L. Brill and E. Harms, pp. 83–102. New York: Behavioral Publications.

Rosenthal, M. S., and Biase, D. V. (1969). Phoenix House: therapeutic communities for drug addicts. *Hospital and Community Psychiatry*, January, pp. 26–30.

Sabath, G. (1964). The treatment of hard-core voluntary drug addict patients. *International Journal of Group Psychotherapy* 14:307–317.

Salasnek, S., and Amini, F. (1971). The heroin addict in a therapeutic community: a cultural "rip-off." *Journal of Psychedelic Drugs* 4:138–144.

Samuels, G. (1966). A visit to Narco. *New York Times Magazine,* April 10, pp. 32–42.

Savitt, R. A. (1954). Extramural psychoanalytic treatment of a case of narcotic addiction. *Journal of the American Psychoanalytic Association* 2:494–502.

Shelly, J. A., and Bassin, A. (1965). Daytop Lodge — a new treatment approach for drug addicts. *Corrective Psychiatry and Journal of Social Therapy* 11:186–195.

Simmel, E. (1929). Psycho-analytic treatment in a sanitorium. *International Journal of Psycho-analysis* 10:70–89.

Smart, R. G. (1976). Outcome studies of therapeutic community and half-way house treatment for addicts. *International Journal of the Addictions* 11:143–159. (Reprinted by courtesy of Marcel Dekker, Inc.).

Stanton, M. D. (1982). Family therapy of drug dependent veterans. In *Drug Dependent Patients,* eds. R. J. Craig and S. L. Baker, pp. 141–152. Springfield, IL: Charles C Thomas.

Thorpe, J. J. (1956). Addicts. In *The Fields of Group Psychotherapy,* ed. S. R. Slavson, pp. 59–75. New York: International Universities Press.

Thorpe, J. J., and Smith, B. (1953). Phases in group development in the treatment of drug addicts. *International Journal of Group Psychotherapy* 3:66–78.

Time (2/11/72). A glimmer of light.

Treffert, D. A., and Sack, M. (1973). A drug unit for life-style change: the Tellurian Community. *Hospital and Community Psychiatry* 24:326–340.

Walder, E. (1965). Synanon and the learning process: a critique of attack therapy. *Corrective Psychiatry and Journal of Social Therapy* 11:299–304.

Wieder, H., and Kaplan, E. H. (1969). Drug use in adolescents. *Psychoanalytic Study of the Child* 24:399–431.

Wellisch, D., and Hays, J. R. (1973). Development of family therapy as a new treatment modality in a drug abuse program for adolescents. In *Current Issues in Adolescent Psychiatry,* ed. J. C. Schoolar, pp. 221–232. New York: Brunner/Mazel.

Wittenberg, D. (1974). Art therapy for adolescent drug abusers. *American Journal of Art Therapy* 13:141–149.

Wolper, B., and Scheiner, Z. (1981). Family therapy approaches and drug dependent women. In National Institute on Drug Abuse. *Treatment Services For Dependent Women,* pp. 343–408. Rockville: National Institute on Drug Abuse.

Yablonsky, L. (1965). *The Tunnel Back: Synanon.* New York: MacMillan.

———— (1973). Synanon. In *Direct Psychotherapy,* ed. R. R. M. Jurjevich, pp. 747–794. Coral Gables, Florida: University of Miami Press.

Yablonsky, L., and Dederich, C. (1965). Synanon: an analysis of some dimensions of the social structure of an antiaddiction society. In *Narcotics,* eds. D. M. Wilner, and G. G. Kassebaum, pp. 193–216. New York: McGraw-Hill.

Yalom, I. D. (1970). *The Theory and Practice of Group Psychotherapy.* New York: Basic Books.

Zarcone, V. (1982). Residential treatment for drug dependence. In *Drug Dependent Patients,* eds. R. Craig and S. L. Baker, pp. 67–91. Springfield, IL: Charles C Thomas.

Zucker, A. H., and Waksman, S. (1973). Results of group therapy with young drug addicts. *International Journal of Social Psychiatry* 18: 267–269.

MEDICALLY ORIENTED APPROACHES

Ackerly, S. S. (1954). Evaluation of psychosurgery in psychopathic personality. *Proceedings of the 3rd Research Conference on Psychosurgery.* Department of Health, Education, and Welfare. Washington, D.C.: Government Printing Office.

Alexander, B. K., and Dibb, G. S. (1975). Opiate addicts and their parents. *Family Process* 14:499–514.

Ausubel, D. P. (1958). *Drug Addiction.* New York: Random House.

Avery, L. W., and Campbell, L. K. (1941). Shock therapy as an aid to withdrawal of morphine in addiction. *Disease of the Nervous System* 2:333–335.

Bailey, W. C. (1968). Nalline control of addict-probationers. *International Journal of the Addictions* 3:131–137. (Reprinted by courtesy of Marcel Dekker, Inc.)

Berger, H. (1964). Treatment of narcotic addicts in private practice. *Archives of Internal Medicine* 114:59–66.

Bigelow, G., Liebson, I., and Lawrence, C. (1973). Prevention of alcohol abuse by reinforcement of incompatible behavior. Paper presented to the Annual Meeting of the Association for Advancement of Behavior Therapy, Miami.

Bill, W. (1968). *The Vitamin B-3 Therapy: A Second Communication to A.A.'s Physicians.* Phoenix, AZ: Do It Now Foundation.

Blachly, P. H. (1964). Procedure for withdrawal of barbiturates. *American Journal of Psychiatry* 120:894–895.

Blum, K. (1984). *Handbook of Abusable Drugs.* New York: Gardner Press, Inc.

Boswell, W. H. (1951). Narcotic addiction: management of withdrawal symptoms with Cortisone. *U.S. Armed Forces Medical Journal* 2: 1347–1351.

Bourne, P. G. (1973). Methadone diversion. In *Proceedings of the 5th National Conference on Methadone Treatment,* Vol. 2, pp. 839–841. New York: National Association for the Prevention of Addiction to Narcotics.

Bourne, P. G., and Slade, J. D. (1973). Why is methadone maintenance successful? In *Proceedings of the 5th National Conference on Methadone Treatment,* Vol. 2, pp. 1086–1092. New York: National Association for the Prevention of Addiction to Narcotics.

Bowden, C. L., and Maddux, J. F. (1972). Methadone maintenance: myth and reality. *American Journal of Psychiatry* 129:435–440.

Brecher, E. M. and the editors of *Consumer Reports.* (1972). *Licit and Illicit Drugs.* Boston: Little, Brown.

Brill, H. (1963). Misapprehensions about drug addiction: some origins and repercussions. *Comprehensive Psychiatry* 4:150–159.

Brill, L. (1973). Opposition to methadone maintenance therapy: a study of recent sources of criticism. In *Methadone: Experiences and Issues,* eds. C. Chambers and L. Brill, pp. 315–324. New York: Behavioral Publications.

Brill, L., and Chambers, C. D. (1971). A multimodality approach to methadone treatment of narcotic addicts. *Social Work* 16:39–51.

Bronsteen, R. (1967). *The Hippy's Handbook.* New York: Canyon Books.

Brown, T. T. (1961). *The Enigma of Drug Addiction.* Springfield, IL: Charles C Thomas.

Canada, A. T. (1972). Methadone in a 30-day detoxification program for narcotic addicts: a critical review. *International Journal of the Addictions* 7:613–617 (Reprinted by courtesy of Marcel Dekker, Inc.).

Caruso, F. S., Gordon, M., and Pachter, I.J. (1973). Methadone and naloxone in combination (Naldone) for the treatment of heroin addicts. In *Proceedings of the 5th National Conference on Methadone Treatment,* Vol. 2, pp. 1336–1341. New York: National Association for the Prevention of Addiction to Narcotics.

Chambers, C. D. (1972). The incidence of cocaine use among methadone maintenance patients. *International Journal of the Addictions* 7:427–441 (Reprinted by courtesy of Marcel Dekker, Inc.).

––––––– (1973a). A description of inpatient and ambulatory techniques. In *Methadone: Experiences and Issues,* eds. C. D. Chambers and L. Brill, pp. 185–194. New York: Behavioral Publications.

––––––– (1973b). Characteristics of attrition during ambulatory detoxification. In *Methadone: Experiences and Issues,* eds. C. D. Chambers and L. Brill, pp. 195–202. New York: Behavioral Publications.

Chambers, C. D., and Brill, L., eds. (1973). *Methadone: Experiences and Issues.* New York: Behavioral Publications.

Chambers, C. D., and Moffett, A. D. (1973). Drug abuse in Philadelphia. In *Yearbook of Drug Abuse,* eds. L. Brill and E. Harms, pp. 129–156. New York: Behavioral Publications.

Chambers, C. D., Taylor, W. J. R., and Walter, P. V. (1973). Drug abuse during ambulatory detoxification. In *Methadone: Experiences and Issues,* eds. C. D. Chambers and L. Brill, pp. 203–213. New York: Behavioral Publications.

Chappel, J., Jaffe, J. H., and Senay, E. C. (1971). Cyclazocine in a multimodality treatment program: comparative results. *International Journal of the Addictions* 6:509–523 (Reprinted by courtesy of Marcel Dekker, Inc.).

Chicago Sun-Times (3/29/76). Acupuncture aid in heroin addiction.

China Medical Reporter (12/73). Acupuncture used for treating drug addicts.

Cleveland, W. H. (1974). Outcomes of methadone treatment of 300 innercity addicts. *Public Health Reports* 89:563–568.

Cohen, S. (1969). *The Drug Dilemma.* New York: McGraw-Hill.

Cronson, A. J., and Flemenbaum, A. (1978). Antagonism of cocaine highs by lithium. *American Journal of Psychiatry* 135:856–857.

Crothers, T. D. (1892). Some new studies of the opium disease. *Journal of the American Medical Association* 18:227–230.

Crowley, T. J. (1983). A biobehavioral approach to the origins and treatment of substance abuse. In *The Addictions,* eds., H. B. Milkman and H. J. Shaffer, pp. 106–107. Lexington, MA: Lexington Books.

Cushman, P., and Dole, V. P. (1973). Detoxification of rehabilitated methadone-maintenance patients. *Journal of the American Medical Association* 226:747–752.

DeLong, J. V. (1972). The drugs and their effects. In Drug Abuse Survey Project. *Dealing With Drug Abuse,* pp. 62–122. New York: Praeger.

Dobbs, W. (1971). Methadone treatment of heroin addicts. *Journal of the American Medical Association* 218:5136–5141.

Do It Now Foundation. (1972). *Megavitamin Therapy and the Drug Wipeout Syndrome.* Phoenix, AZ: Do It Now Foundation.

Dole, V. P. (1972a). Comments on "heroin maintenance." *Journal of the American Medical Association* 220:1493.

——— (1972b). Narcotic addiction, physical dependence and relapse. *New England Journal of Medicine* 286:988–992.

——— (1976). Methadone maintenance treatment: a ten-year perspective. *Journal of the American Medical Association* 235:2117–2119.

Dole, V. P. and Nyswander, M. (1965). A medical treatment for diacetylmorphine (heroin) addiction. *Journal of the American Medical Association* 193:646–650.

Dole, V. P., Nyswander, M. E., and Kreek, M. J. (1966). Narcotic blockade, *Archives of Internal Medicine*. October, pp. 304-309.

Dole, V. P., Nyswander, M. E., and Warner, A. (1968). Successful treatment of 750 criminal addicts. *Journal of the American Medical Association* 206:2708-2711.

Drug Survival News (1/2/76). How useful is Darvon-N?

Edwards, G. (1979). British policies on opiate addiction. *British Journal of Psychiatry* 134:1-13.

Eldridge, W. B. (1972). *Narcotics and the Law*. New York: American Bar Association.

Felton, J. S. (1973). Preemployment drug screening: pros and cons. *Journal of the American Medical Association* 226:1020.

Fink, M. (1971). A rational therapy of opiate dependence: narcotic antagonists. *Journal of Psychedelic Drugs* 4:157-161.

Fink, M., Zaks, A., Sharoff, R., Mora, A., Bruner, A., Levit, S., and Freedman, A. M. (1968). Naloxone in heroin dependence. *Clinical Pharmacology and Therapeutics* 9:568-577.

Fraser, H. F., and Grider, J. A. (1953). Treatment of drug addiction. *American Journal of Medicine* 14:571-577.

Fraser, H. F., van Horn, G. D., Isbell, H. (1956). Studies on n-allynormorphine in man: antagonism to morphine and heroin and effects mixtures of n-allynormorphine and morphine. *American Journal of the Medical Sciences* 231:1-8.

Freedman, A. M. (1963). Treatment of drug addiction in a community general hospital. *Comprehensive Psychiatry* 4:199-207.

Freedman, A. M., Fink, M., Sharoff, R., and Zaks, A. (1968). Clinical studies of cyclazocine in the treatment of narcotic addiction. *American Journal of Psychiatry* 124:1499-1504.

Freedman, W. (1972). Lobotomy in limbo? *American Journal of Psychiatry* 128:3115.

Freedman, W., and Watts, J. W. (1950). *Psychosurgery*. Springfield, IL: Charles C Thomas.

Gallinek, A. (1952). Controversial indications for electric convulsive therapy. *American Journal of Psychiatry* 109:361-365.

Gawin, F. H., and Kleber, H. D. (1984). Cocaine abuse treatment. *Archives of General Psychiatry* 41:903-909.

Gearing, F. R. (1969). Evaluation of methadone maintenance treatment program. Report submitted to the State of New York Narcotic Addiction Control Commission, June 23.

Giannini, A. J., Slaby, A. E., and Giannini, M. (1982). *Handbook of Overdose and Detoxification Emergencies*. New Hyde Park, NY: Medical Examination Publishing Co., Inc.

Glasscote, R. M., Sussex, J. N., Jaffee, J. H., Ball, J., and Brill, L. (1972).

The Treatment of Drug Abuse. Washington, D.C.: American Psychiatric Association.

Glatt, M. M. (1972). The treatment of the withdrawal stage in narcotic addicts by diphenoxylate and chlormethiazole. *International Journal of the Addictions* 7:593-596 (Reprinted by courtesy of Marcel Dekker, Inc.).

Glosser, D. S. (1983). The use of a token economy to reduce illicit drug use among methadone maintenance clients. *Addictive Behaviors* 8:93-104.

Göktepe, E. O., Young, L. B., and Bridges, P. K. (1975). A further review of the results of stereotaxic subcaudate tractotomy. *British Journal of Psychiatry* 126:270-280.

Gold, R., and Chatham, L. R. (1974). Characteristics of NARA patients in after care during June, 1971. DHEW Publication No. (NIH) 74-659. Washington, D.C.: Government Printing Office.

Goldstein, A., and Brown, B. W. (1970). Urine testing schedules in methadone maintenance treatment of heroin addiction. *Journal of the American Medical Association* 214:311-315.

Goodman, A. L. (1968). Use of diphenoxylate hydrochloride in the withdrawal period of narcotic addiction. *Southern Medical Journal* 61: 313-316.

Goodman, W. (1971). The choice for thousands: heroin or methadone? *The New York Times Magazine*, June 13, pp. 14ff.

Gorodetzky, C. W., Martin, W. R., Jasinski, D. R., Mansky, P. A., and Cone, E. J. (1975). Human pharmacology of naltrexone. In *Developments in the Field of Drug Abuse,* ed. E. Senay et al., pp. 749-753. Cambridge, MA: Schenkman.

Green, M. H., Turner, N., and DuPont, R. L. (1974). Amphetamines in the District of Columbia, III: Stimulant abuse in narcotics addicts in treatment, with an emphasis on phenmetrazine. *International Journal of the Addictions* 9:653-662 (Reprinted by courtesy of Marcel Dekker, Inc.).

Greene, M. H., Brown, B. S., and DuPont, R. L. (1975). Controlling the abuse of illicit methadone in Washington, D.C. *Archives of General Psychiatry* 32:221-226.

Graff, H., and Ball, J. C. (1976). The methadone clinic: function and philosophy. *International Journal of Social Psychiatry* 22:140-146.

Havassy, B. E., and Tschann, J. M. (1984). Chronic heroin use during methadone treatment: a test of the efficacy of high maintenance doses. *Addictive Behaviors* 9:57-65.

Hawkins, D. (1973). Orthomolecular psychiatry: treatment of schizophrenia. In *Orthomolecular Psychiatry: Treatment of Schizophrenia,* eds. D. Hawkins and L. Pauling, pp. 631-637. San Francisco: W. H. Freedman.

Hawks, D. V. (1971). The dimensions of drug dependence in the United Kingdom. *International Journal of the Addictions* 6:135-170 (Reprinted by courtesy of Marcel Dekker, Inc.).

Henry, G. M. (1974). Treatment and rehabilitation of narcotic addiction. In *Research Advances in Alcohol and Drug Problems,* Vol. 1, eds. R. J. Gibbins et al., pp. 267–301. New York: John Wiley and Sons.

Hoffman, F. G. (1983). *A Handbook on Drug and Alcohol Abuse.* New York: Oxford University Press.

Isbell, H. (1951). Treatment of barbiturate addiction. *Postgraduate Medicine* 9:256–258.

Isbell, H., and Vogel, V. H. (1949). The addiction liability of methadon (Amidon Dolophine, 10820) and its use in the treatment of the morphine abstinence syndrome. *American Journal of Psychiatry* 105:909–914.

Isbell, H., Wikler, A., Eisenman, A. J., Daingerfield, M., and Frank, K. (1948). Liability of addiction to 6-dimethylamino-4, -4 diphenyl-3 heptanone (methadone, "Amidone" or "10820") in man: experimental addiction to methadone. *Archives of Internal Medicine* 82:362–390.

Jaffe, J. H. (1969). A review of the approaches to the problem of compulsive narcotics use. In *Drugs and Youth: Proceedings of the Rutgers Symposium on Drug Abuse,* eds. J. L. Wittenborn et al., pp. 77–91. Springfield, IL: Charles C Thomas.

Jaffe, J. H., Fritz, K., and Kaistha, K. K. (1971). Methadone disks: injectable-noninjectable tablets. *Archives of General Psychiatry* 25: 525–526.

James, I. P. (1971). The changing pattern of narcotic addiction in Britain—1959 to 1969. *International Journal of the Addictions* 6:119–134. (Reprinted by courtesy of Marcel Dekker, Inc.).

Joseph, H., and Dole, V. P. (1970). Methadone patients on probation and parole. *Federal Probation* 34:42–48.

Kalinowsky, L. B., Hippius, H., and Klein, H. E. (1982). *Biological Treatments in Psychiatry.* New York: Grune and Stratton.

Kao, A. H., and Lu, L. (1974). Acupuncture procedure for treating drug addiction. *American Journal of Acupuncture* 2:201–207.

Kenney, J. P., and Wright, D. F. (1975). A requiem for the heroin loyalty myth. In *Developments in the Field of Drug Abuse,* eds. E. Senay et al., pp. 275–277. Cambridge, MA: Schenkman.

King, R. (1961). An appraisal of international British and selected European narcotic drug laws, regulations and policies. In *Drug Addiction: Crime or Disease?,* pp. 121–155. American Bar Association and American Medical Association, Joint Committee on Drugs. Bloomington, IN: Indiana University Press.

Kissin, B., and Sang, E. (1973). Treatment of heroin addiction. *New York State Journal of Medicine* 73:1059–1065.

Knight, G. (1969). Chronic depression and drug addiction treated by stereotactic surgery. *Nursing Times* 65:583–586.

Kolb, L. (1962). *Drug Addiction.* Springfield, IL: Charles C Thomas.

Kolb, L., and Himmelsbach, C. K. (1938). Clinical studies of drug addiction, III: a critical review of the withdrawal treatments with method of evaluation abstinence syndromes. *American Journal of Psychiatry* 94:759-799.

Kramer, J. C. (1972). Controlling narcotics in America. *Drug Forum* 1:153-167.

Kreek, M. J. (1975). Methadone maintenance treatment for chronic opiate addiction. In *Medical Aspects of Drug Abuse*, ed. R. W. Richter, pp. 167-185. Hagerstown, MD: Harper and Row.

Krepick, D. S., and Long, B. L. (1973). Heroin addiction: a treatable disease. *Nursing Clinics of North America* 8:41-52.

Kromberg, C. J., and Proctor, J. B. (1970). Evolution of a day program. *American Journal of Nursing* 70:2575-2577.

Kurland, A. A., Hanlon, T. E., and McCabe, O. L. (1974). Naloxone and the narcotic abuser: a controlled study of partial blockade. *International Journal of the Addictions* 9:663-772 (Reprinted by courtesy of Marcel Dekker, Inc.).

Lahmeyer, H. (1982). Methadone maintenance. In *Drug Dependent Patients*, eds. R. J. Craig and S. L. Baker, pp. 37-66. Springfield, IL: Charles C Thomas.

Lanphear, E. (1890). Treatment of morphine habit. *Journal of the American Medical Association* 14:648-650.

Laverne, A. A. (1973). Carbon dioxide therapy (CDT) of addictions. *Behavioral Neuropsychiatry* 4:13-28.

Lennard, H. L., Epstein, L. J., and Rosenthal, M. S. (1972). The methadone illusion. *Science* 176:881-884.

Lett, S. (1891). Treatment of the opium neurosis. *Journal of the American*

Lieberman, C. M., and Blaine, J. D. (1970). The British system of drug control. *Drug Dependence*, March, pp. 12-16.

Liebson, I., Bigelow, G., and Flamer, R. (1973). Alcoholism among methadone patients: a specific treatment method. *American Journal of Psychiatry* 130:483-485.

Lindesmith, A. R. (1968). *Addiction and Opiates*. Chicago: Aldine.

McCabe, O. L. (1971). Methadone maintenance: boon or bane? In *The Drug Abuse Controversy*, eds. C. Brown and E. Savage, pp. 115-132. Baltimore: National Educational Consultants.

Maddux, J. F., and Bowden, C. L. (1972). Critique of success with methadone maintenance. *American Journal of Psychiatry* 129:440-446.

Markham, J. M. (1972). What's all this talk of heroin maintenance? *The New York Times Magazine*, July 2, pp. 6ff.

Martin, W. R., and Gorodetzky, C. W. (1967). Cyclazocine, an adjunct in the treatment of narcotic addiction. *International Journal of the Addictions* 2:85-93 (Reprinted by courtesy of Marcel Dekker, Inc.).

Martin, W. R., Gorodetzky, C. W., and McClane, T. K. (1966). An experimental study in the treatment of narcotic addicts with cyclazocine. *Clinical Pharmacology and Therapeutics* 7:455–465.

Martin, W. R., Fraser, H. F., Gorodetzky, C. W., and Rosenberg, D. E. (1965). Studies of the dependence-producing potential of the narcotic antagonist 2-cyclopropylmethyl-2'-hydroxy-5, 9-dimethyl-6, 7-benzomorphan (cyclazocine, WIN-20, 740, ARC II-C-3). *Journal of Pharmacology and Experimental Therapeutics* 150:426–436.

Mattison, J. B. (1886). Opium antidotes and their vendors. *Journal of the American Medical Association* 7:568–570.

Maugh, T. H. (1972). Narcotic antagonists: the search accelerates. *Science* 177:249–250.

Maurer, D. W., and Vogel, V. H. (1967). *Narcotics and Narcotic Addiction,* 3rd ed. Springfield, IL: Charles C Thomas.

May, E. (1972). Narcotics addiction and control in Great Britain. In *Dealing with Drug Abuse,* Drug Abuse Survey Project. pp. 345–394. New York: Praeger.

Meyer, R. E. (1972). *Guide to Drug Rehabilitation.* Boston: Beacon Press.

Miller, A. (1954). *Lobotomy: A Clinical Study.* Toronto: University of Toronto.

Miller, R. (1974). Towards a sociology of methadone maintenance. In *Sociological Aspects of Drug Dependence,* ed. C. Winick, pp. 169–198. Cleveland: CRC Press.

Mitcheson, M. (1970). Polydrug abuse. In *ABC of Drug Addiction,* pp. 89–93. Bristol, England: John Wright and Sons.

Moffett, A. D., Adler, F., Glaser, F. R., and Horvitz, D. (1975). *Medical Lollypop, Junkie Insulin, or What?* Philadelphia: Dorrance.

Moffett, A. D., Soloway, I., and Glick, M. X. (1973). Post-treatment behavior following ambulatory detoxification. In *Methadone: Experiences and Issues,* eds. C. D. Chambers and L. Brill, pp. 212–227. New York: Behavioral Publications.

Narcotics Treatment Administration. Undated. Facts about Methadone. Washington, D.C.: Narcotics Treatment Administration.

New York Times (12/26/72). Youths rejecting heroin, but turn to other drugs.

Nyswander, M. (1956). *The Drug Addict as a Patient.* New York: Grune and Stratton.

——— (1967). The methadone treatment of heroin addiction. *Hospital Practice* 2:27–33.

Osmond, H. (1967). Background to niacin treatment. *Journal of Schizophrenia* 3:125–132.

Paulus, I., and Halliday, R. (1967). Rehabilitation and the narcotic addict: results of a comparative methadone withdrawal program. *Canadian Medical Association Journal* 96:655–659.

Perkins, M. E. (1972). Methadone maintenance: expanding the concept of service. *American Journal of Psychiatry* 129:461–462.

Ploscowe, M. (1961). Some basic problems in drug addiction and suggestions for research. In *Drug Addiction, Crime or Disease?*, pp. 15–120. American Bar Association and American Medical Association, Joint Committee on Narcotic Drugs. Bloomington, IN: Indiana University Press.

Psychiatric News (5/3/72). FDA lifts methadone restriction in reversal of former decision.

Rawson, R. A., and Tennant, F. S. (1983). Five-year follow-up of opiate addicts with naltrexone and behavior therapy. In *Problems of Drug Dependence, 1983.* ed. L. S. Harris, pp.189–295. Rockville: National Institute on Drug Abuse.

Renault, P. F. (1981). Treatment of heroin-dependent persons with antagonists: current status. In *Narcotic Antagonists: Naltrexone Pharmacochemistry and Sustained-Release Preparations,* eds. R. E. Willett and R. Barnett, pp. 11–22. Rockville: National Institute of Drug Abuse.

Resnick, R., Fink, M., and Freedman, A. M. (1970). A cyclazocine typology in opiate dependence. *American Journal of Psychiatry* 126:1256–1260.

Rice, J., and Cohen, L. (1965). Narcotic drug addiction: one year's experiences at Pilgrim State Hospital. *Psychiatric Quarterly* 39:457–465.

Royal Society of Medicine. Section of Psychiatry. (1931). Prevention and treatment of drug addiction. *Lancet* 220:587–588.

Ryback, R. S. (1972). Schizophrenics anonymous and the drug abuser. In *Drug Abuse: Current Concepts and Research,* ed. W. Keup, pp. 387–391. Springfield, IL: Charles C Thomas.

Schecter, A., and Grossman, D. (1975). Experiences with naltrexone: a suggested role in drug abuse treatment programs. In *Developments in the Field of Drug Abuse,* eds. E. Senay et al., pp. 754–766. Cambridge, MA: Schenkman.

Schur, E. M. (1961). British narcotics policies. *Journal of Criminal Law, Criminology and Police Science* 51:619–629.

——— (1965). *Crimes Without Victims.* Englewood Cliffs, NJ: Prentice Hall.

Senay, E. C. (1971). Methadone: some myths and hypotheses. *Journal of Psychedelic Drugs* 4:182–185.

Shaowanasai, A., and Visuthimak, A. (1975). Acupuncture in the treatment of heroin addiction. *International Criminal Police Review* 292:256–258.

Silsby, H., and Tennant, F. S., Jr. (1974). Short-term, ambulatory detoxification of opiate addicts using methadone. *International Journal of the Addictions* 9:167–170 (Reprinted by courtesy of Marcel Dekker, Inc.).

Smith, D. E., and Wesson, D. R. (1971). Phenobarbital technique for treatment of barbiturate dependence. *Archives of General Psychiatry* 24: 56–60.

Smith, R. F. (1974). A five-year field trial of massive nicotinic acid therapy of alcoholics in Michigan. *Orthomolecular Psychiatry* 3:327–331.

Smolik, E. A. (1950). Lobotomy in the management of intractable pain and narcotic addiction. *Diseases of the Nervous System* 11:327–331.

Stachnik, T. J. (1972). The case against criminal penalties for illicit drug use. *American Psychologist* 27:637–642.

Stephens, R. C., and Weppner, R. S. (1973). Legal and illegal use of methadone: one year later. *American Journal of Psychiatry* 130:1391–1394.

Stimmel, B. (1975). *Heroin Dependency.* New York: Stratton Intercontinental Medical Book Corporation.

Stimson, G. V., and Ogborne, A. C. (1974). A survey of a representative sample of addicts prescribed heroin at London clinics. *Bulletin on Narcotics* 22:13–22.

Stitzer, M. L., Bigelow, G. E., Liebson, I. A., and McCaul, M. E. (1984). Contingency management of supplemental drug use during methadone maintenance treatment. In *Behavioral Intervention Techniques in Drug Abuse Treatment,*. eds. J. Grabowski, M. L. Stitzer, and J. E. Henningfield, pp. 84–103. Rockville National Institute on Drug Abuse.

Strober, M. (1954). Treatment of acute heroin intoxication with nalorphine. (Nalline) hydrochloride. *Journal of the American Medical Association* 54:327–332.

Tennant, F. S., Russell, B. A., McMarns, A., and Cassas, M. K. (1974). Propoxyphene napsylate treatment of heroin and methadone dependence: one year's experience. *Journal of Psychedelic Drugs* 6:201–211.

Tennant, F. S., Russell, B. A., Tate, J., and Bleich, R. (1977). Comparative evaluation of propoxyphene napsylate (Darvon-N) and placebo in heroin intoxication. *International Journal of the Addictions* 12:565–574. (Reprinted by courtesy of Marcel Dekker, Inc.).

Terry, C. E., and Pellens, M. (1928). *The Opium Problem.* New York: Bureau of Social Hygiene.

Thigpen, F. B., Thigpen, C. H., and Cleckley, H. M. (1953). Use of electric-convulsive therapy in morphine, meperidine, and related alkaloid addictions. *Archives of Neurology and Psychiatry* 70:452–458.

Time (12/11/72). A glimmer of light.

Trussell, R. E., and Gollance, H. (1970). Methadone maintenance treatment is successful for heroin addicts. *Hospital Management* 110:56–62.

U.S. Medicine (9/1/72). Maintenance with heroin a "mistake."

——— (7/15/73). Methadone use seen possible MD "folly."

——— (5/15/75). Methadone abuse increases.

Vaillent, G. E. (1966). A twelve-year followup of New York narcotic addicts: 1. The relation of treatment to outcome. *American Journal of Psychiatry* 122:727–737.

Vista Hill Psychiatric Foundation. (1972). Urine testing for abusable drugs.

Drug Abuse and Alcoholism Newsletter. 1.

Vogel, V. H. (1952). The treatment of narcotic addiction. *Postgraduate Medicine* 12:201–206.

Vonnegut, M. (1975). *The Eden Express.* New York: Praeger.

Waldorf, D., Orlick, M., and Reinarman, C. (1974). *Morphine Maintenance: The Shreveport Clinic, 1919–1923.* Washington, D.C.: Drug Abuse Council.

Wang, R. (1982). Issues and problems in the toxicologic analysis of drugs of abuse. In *Drug Dependent Patients,* eds. R. J. Craig and S. L. Baker , pp. 235–261. Springfield, IL: Charles C Thomas.

Warshofsky, F. (1970). Methadone: a drug to lick a drug. *Family Health* 2:22–27.

Washington Post (3/4/69). Addicts hail "methadone miracle."

―――― (2/12/72). Heroin-maintenance backed by ABA unit.

―――― (5/14/72). U.S. methadone role scored.

―――― (6/30/76). Methadone flayed at heroin hearing.

Washington Star/News (11/14/72). Dr.―――― gets 14 to 45 years.

―――― (11/28/73). Japan's drug cure: pain and suffering.

Wikler, A., Pescor, M. J., Kalbaugh, E. P., and Angelucci, R. J. (1952). Effects of frontal lobotomy on the morphine-abstinence syndrome in man. *Archives of Neurology and Psychiatry* 67:510–521.

Willette, R. E., and Barnett, G. (1981). *Narcotic Antagonists: Naltrexone Pharmacochemistry and Sustained-Release Preparations.* Rockville: National Institute on Drug Abuse.

Williams, J. B. (1974). *Narcotics and Drug Dependence.* Beverly Hills, CA: Glencoe Press.

Zaks, A., and Fink, M. (1971). Naloxone treatment of opiate dependence. *Journal of the American Medical Association* 215:2108–2110.

Zimmerman, D. (1977). Narcotic maintenance has been tried in U.S. *U.S. Journal of Drug and Alcohol Dependence* 1:p. 1ff.

OTHER APPROACHES

Bauman, F. (1974). Hypnosis and the adolescent drug abuser. In *Psychotherapy and Drug Addiction I: Diagnosis and Treatment,* pp. 172–176. New York: MSS Information Corp.

Baekland, F., Lundwall, L., and Kissin, B. (1975). Methods for the treatment of chronic alcoholism: a critical appraisal. In *Research Advances in Alcohol and Drug Problems,* Vol. 2, eds. R. J. Gibbins et al., pp. 246–327. New York: John Wiley and Sons.

Bellwood, L. R. (1973). Alcoholics anonymous. In *Direct Psychotherapy,* ed. R. R. M. Jurjevich, pp. 795–817. Coral Gables, FL: University of Miami Press.

Bennett, B. (1972). *The Cross and the Needle*. Mountain View, CA: Pacific Press.

Benson, H. (1969). Yoga for drug abuse. *New England Journal of Medicine* 281:1133.

——— (1975). *The Relaxation Response*. New York: William Morrow.

Benson, H., and Wallace, R. K. (1972). Decreased drug abuse with transcendental meditation—a study of 1,862 subjects. In *Drug Abuse— Proceedings of the International Conference*, ed. C. J. D. Zarafonetis, pp. 369-376. Philadelphia: Lea and Febiger.

Bloomfield, H. H., Cain, M. P., Jaffe, D. T. (1975). *TM: Discovering Inner Energy and Overcoming Stress*. New York: Delacorte Press.

Blum, K. (1984). *Handbook of Abusable Drugs*. New York: Gardner Press.

Brecher, E. M., and the editors of *Consumer Reports*. (1972). *Licit and Illicit Drugs*. Boston: Little, Brown.

Brill, L., and Lieberman, L. (1969). *Authority and Addiction*. Boston: Little, Brown.

Broken Needles, Inc. (Undated). Fact sheet. Crewe, VA: 24-hour Printing Co.

Brown, T. T. (1961). *The Enigma of Drug Addiction*. Springfield, IL: Charles C Thomas.

Cantala, J. (1926). Opium, heroin, morphine: their kingdoms. In *Narcotic Education*, ed. H. S. Middlemiss, pp. 232-268. Washington, D.C.: H. S. Middlemiss.

Chafetz, M. E., and Demone, H. W., Jr. (1962). *Alcoholism and Society*. New York: Oxford University Press.

Cohen, A. Y. (1969). Inside what's happening: sociological, psychological, and spiritual perspectives on the contemporary drug scene. *American Journal of Public Health* 59:2092-2095.

Cox, S. B. (1971-1972). Transcendental meditation and the criminal justice system. *Kentucky Law Journal* 60 (reprint).

D.A.R.E. (Undated). *Facts*. Albuquerque, New Mexico: Drug Addicts Recovery Enterprise.

Driskill, R. (1974). Transcendental meditation: a look at what it can do for the soldier. *Fort Campbell Courier*, February 15, p. 11A.

Glasscote, R. M., Sussex, J. N., Jaffee, J. H., Ball, J., and Brill, L. (1972). *The Treatment of Drug Abuse*. Washington, D.C.: American Psychiatric Association.

Greaves, G. (1974). Toward an existential theory of drug abuse. *Journal of Nervous and Mental Diseases* 159:263-274.

Hageman, L. (1965). Adolescent addiction and religion. In *Drug Addiction in Youth*, ed. E. Harms, pp. 192-198. Oxford: Pergamon Press.

Harris, J. D. (1969). *The Junkie Priest*. New York: Pocket Books.

Hyde, M. (1968). Turning on without drugs. In *Mind Drugs,* ed. M. Hyde, pp. 127-134. New York: McGraw-Hill.

Illinois, State of. (1972). House Resolution No. 677, 77th General Assembly. House of Representatives. Adopted May 24.

Kaufman, E. (1985). *Substance Abuse and Family Therapy.* Orlando; Grune & Stratton.

Kennedy, R. J. H. (1968). Introduction. In *Alcoholism: A Sourcebook for the Priest,* National Clergy Conference on Alcoholism, pp. vii-ix. Indianapolis, Indiana: National Clergy Conference on Alcoholism.

Langrod, J., Joseph, H., and Colgan, K. (1972). The role of religion in the treatment of opiate addiction. In *Major Modalities in the Treatment of Drug Abuse,* eds. L. Brill and L. Lieberman, pp. 167-190. New York: Behavioral Publications.

Leech, K. (1970). The drug scene and the Christian community. In *ABC of Drug Addiction,* pp. 37-40. Bristol, England: John Wright and Sons.

McCarthy, G. (1976). Inner life for sale. *Washington Post,* April 4.

McKee, M. R., Lehigh, J., and Miller, R. (1971). Prognosis for heroin addicts in three rehabilitative programs. *Journal of Drug Education* 4:359-372.

Marcus, J. B. (1974). Transcendental meditation: a new method of reducing drug abuse. *Drug Forum* 3:113-136.

——— (1975). Transcendental meditation: consciousness expansion as a rehabilitative technique. *Journal of Psychedelic Drugs* 7:169-179.

Monahan, R. J. (1974). Transcendental meditation and drug abuse. *Congressional Record* 120 (no. 67), May 14.

Patrick, S. (1965). Our way of life: a short history of Narcotics Anonymous, Inc. In *Drug Addiction in Youth,* ed. E. Harms, pp. 192-198. Oxford, England: Pergamon Press.

Ramirez, J. (1975). The transcendental meditation program as a possible treatment modality for drug offenders: evaluation of a pilot project at Milan Federal Correctional Institution. Los Angeles: Institute for Social Rehabilitation, unpublished.

Rubottom, A. (1972). Transcendental meditation. *Yale Alumni Magazine,* February, pp. 27-29.

San Jose News (8/4/73). Meditation replaces drugs.

Schwartz, G. E. (1973). Pros and cons of meditation: current findings on physiology and anxiety, self-control, drug abuse and creativity. Paper presented at the 81st Annual Convention of the American Psychological Association, Montreal.

Shafii, M., Lavely, R., and Jaffee, R. (1974). Meditation and marijuana. *American Journal of Psychiatry* 131:60-63.

Sykes, D. E. (1973). Transcendental meditation — as applied to criminal justice reform, drug rehabilitation and society in general. *University of Maryland Law Forum* 3:37–50.

Time (10/23/72). TM: the drugless high.

Wallace, R. K., and Benson, H. (1972). The physiology of meditation. In *Altered States of Awareness (Reading from the Scientific American)*, pp. 125–131. San Francisco: W. H. Freedman.

Washington Post (5/3/73). "Path of bliss" leads girl from drugs.

Washington Star (6/20/72). Getting high — naturally.

Weil, A. T. (1972a). Man's innate need: getting high. *Intellectual Digest* 11:69–71.

———— (1972b). Altered states of consciousness. In *Dealing with Drug Abuse,* Drug Abuse Survey Project, pp. 345–394. New York: Praeger.

Wilkerson, D. (1969). *The Gutter and the Ghetto.* Waco, TX: Word Books.

Wilson, F. (1973). *Counselling the Drug Abuser.* London: Lakeland.

BEHAVIOR MODIFICATION

Anant, S. S. (1968). Treatment of alcoholics and drug addicts by verbal aversion techniques. *International Journal of the Addictions* 3:381–388 (Reprinted by courtesy of Marcel Dekker, Inc.).

Blachly, P. H. (1971). An electric needle for aversive conditioning of the ritual. *International Journal of the Addictions* 6:327–328 (Reprinted by courtesy of Marcel Dekker, Inc.).

Boudin, H. M. (1972). Contingency contracting as a therapeutic tool in the deceleration of amphetamine use. *Behavior Therapy* 3:604–608.

Brady, J. P. (1972). Systematic desensitization. In *Behavior Modification: Principles and Clinical Applications,* ed. W. S. Agras, pp. 127–150. Boston: Little, Brown.

Callner, D. A. (1975). Behavioral treatment approaches to drug abuse: a critical review of the research. *Psychological Bulletin* 82:143–164.

Callner, D. A., and Ross, S. M. (1973). The assessment and training of assertive skills with drug addicts: a preliminary study. Paper presented at the 81st Annual Convention of the American Psychological Association, Montreal.

Cheek, F. E., Tomarchio, T., Standen, J., and Albahary, R. S. (1973). Methadone plus — a behavior modification training program in self-control for addicts on methadone maintenance. *International Journal of the Addictions* 8:969–996 (Reprinted by courtesy of Marcel Dekker, Inc.).

Davidson, S., Robinson, J., and Stegbauer, V. (1973). Behavioral contracting workshop. In *Proceedings of the 5th National Conference on Methadone Treatment,* vol. 2, pp. 1203–1206. New York: National Association for the Prevention of Addiction to Narcotics.

Glicksman, M., Ottomanelli, G., and Cutler, R. (1971). The earn-your-way credit system: use of a token economy in narcotic rehabilitation. *International Journal of the Addictions* 6:252-531 (Reprinted by courtesy of Marcel Dekker, Inc.).

Kolvin, I. (1967). Aversive imagery treatment in adolescents. *Behavior Research and Therapy* 5:245-248.

Kraft, T. (1968). Successful treatment of a case of drinamyl addiction. *British Journal of Psychiatry* 114:1363-1364.

——— (1969). Treatment of Drinamyl addiction. *International Journal of the Addictions* 4:59-64. (Reprinted by courtesy of Marcel Dekker, Inc.).

Lesser, E. (1967). Behavior therapy with a narcotics user: a case report. *Behaviour Research and Therapy* 5:251-252.

Lieberman, R. (1968). Aversive conditioning of drug addicts: a pilot study. *Behaviour Research and Therapy* 6:229-231.

Meyer, R. E. (1972). *Guide to Drug Rehabilitation.* Boston: Beacon Press.

National Institute of Mental Health. (1968). The role of learning in the relapse of narcotic addicts. *Mental Health Reports* 2:1-10.

O'Brien, J. S., and Raynes, A. E. (1972). Treatment of heroin addiction with behavioral therapy. In *Drug Abuse: Current Concepts and Research,* ed. W. Keup, pp. 434-440. Springfield, IL: Charles C Thomas.

O'Brien, J. S., Raynes, A. E., and Patch, V. D. (1972). Treatment of heroin addiction with aversion therapy, relaxation training and systematic desensitization. *Behaviour Research and Therapy* 10:77-80.

Raymond, R. J. (1964). The treatment of addiction by aversion conditioning with apomorphine. *Behaviour Research and Therapy* 1:287-291.

Ross, S. M., and Jones, C. G. (1973). Contingency contracting with drug abusers. Paper presented at the 81st Annual Convention of the American Psychological Association, Montreal.

Steinfeld, G. J. (1970). The use of covert sensitization with institutionalized narcotic addicts. *International Journal of the Addictions* 5:225-232 (Reprinted by courtesy of Marcel Dekker, Inc.).

Thomson, I. G., and Rathod, N. H. (1968). Aversion therapy for heroin dependence. *Lancet* 2:382-384.

Wikler, A. (1965). Conditioning factors in opiate addiction and relapse. In *Narcotics,* eds. D. M. Wilner and G. G. Kassebaum. New York: McGraw-Hill.

Wisocki, P. A. (Undated). The application of learning theory principles to the problem of alcoholism — a bibliography of references — 1942-1968. Amherst, Massachusetts: University of Massachusetts, (u.p.).

——— (1973). The successful treatment of heroin addiction by covert conditioning techniques. *Journal of Behavior Therapy and Experimental Psychiatry* 4:55-61.

Wolpe, J. (1965). Conditioned inhibition of craving in drug addiction: a pilot experiment. *Behaviour Research and Therapy* 2:285-288.

THE CURRENT SITUATION

Ashley, R. (1975). *Cocaine: Its History, Uses and Effects.* New York: St. Martin's Press.

Barbara, J., and Morrison, J. (1975). If addiction is incurable, why do we try to cure it? *Crime and Delinquency* 21:28-33.

Callner, D. A. (1975). Behavioral treatment approaches to drug abuse: a critical review of the research. *Psychological Bulletin* 82:143-164.

Field, L. H. (1968). Letter. *Lancet* 2:1350.

National Clearinghouse for Drug Abuse Information (1975). Treatment of drug abuse: an overview. Report Series 34, No. 1. Washington, D.C.: Government Printing Office.

National Commission on Marihuana and Drug Abuse (1973). *Drug Use in America: Problem in Perspective.* Second Report of the National Commission on Marihuana and Drug Abuse. Washington, D.C.: Government Printing Office.

New York State Drug Abuse Control Commission (1974). *Comprehensive Index to the Drug Abuse Control Commission's Local Abstinence Drug Abuse Treatment and Preventive Education Programs.* Albany, New York: New York State Drug Abuse Control Commission.

Reinert, R. E. (1974). Drugs and the discontents of civilization. *Bulletin of the Menninger Clinic* 38:49-56.

Szasz, T. S. (1971). The ethics of addiction. *American Journal of Psychiatry* 128:541-546.

U.S. Medicine (2/1/74). Addicts' funding declines.

Chapter 8

The Drug-Using Criminal
in a Program for Change

OUR FORMAT FOR HELPING criminals become responsible human beings is presented in detail in Volume II, *The Criminal Personality: The Change Process*. In this chapter we offer an overview of our format for change. The bulk of the chapter is devoted to particularly troublesome problems that arise in working with drug-using criminals. The reader is referred to Volume II for the details of our techniques and for the concepts that we inculcate in criminals as they learn to become responsible citizens. As we have stated throughout the present volume, the criminal who is a drug user and the criminal who is not a drug user are similar in their mental makeup. Therefore the same format has been used in helping both to change. The groups that met daily to undertake the process of change were composed of drug users and nonusers.

In this volume we have not directly addressed the contention that alcohol and drug abuse are diseases. This widely held view is a fundamental tenet of many treatment programs, including Alcoholics Anonymous (A.A.) and Narcotics Anonymous (N.A.)* Smith et al. (1983, pp. 157–158) stated, "The disease concept is currently regarded by the mainstream of addiction specialists as the best model for understanding and treating a broad spectrum of chronic substance abuse patterns."

That physiological processes occur in the body as a consequence of alcohol and illegal drug use is indisputable. It is also the case that withdrawal from certain substances requires medical supervision. But it is equally true that the criminal *chooses* to use alcohol and drugs and that such choices are part of a pattern of seeking excitement through doing the forbidden.

In a program for change, it is essential that the criminal's substance abuse be addressed within the context of making a choice. He does not contract an illness from the use of alcohol and illegal drugs in the way one might catch the flu or develop a condition like diabetes. Being afflicted by a contagious or he-

---

*N.A. (1983, p. 3) states, "After coming to N.A., we realized we were sick people who suffered from a disease like Alcoholism, Diabetes, or Tuberculosis."

reditary disease is not a consequence of choice. The criminal, however, makes the choice to use alcohol or illegal drugs.

Throughout all three volumes, we have emphasized the importance of choice as the cornerstone of our program for helping criminals become responsible citizens. If one conceives of the criminal's alcohol and drug use as an illness, it is essential that such a view not dilute or eliminate the critical focus upon choice. If a criminal is regarded simply as afflicted by a disease, then the already difficult process of change through the exercise of choice, effort, and endurance is further impeded.*

To date, there is no medication that alone ensures a criminal's living an alcohol- or drug-free life. For him to change the way he thinks and behaves, the exercise of choice is critical. The criminal must become fed up with himself, choose to abstain from alcohol and drugs, and learn to deal with life's problems and frustrations.

The task of changing the criminal is much greater than was believed when this work began. It entails far more than changing his environment or providing him with insights into his past. One does not "rehabilitate" a criminal. Rehabilitation implies that one brings the criminal back to an earlier desirable state. We have to teach the criminal an entirely different way of thinking; he requires "habilitation," not rehabilitation. The task is to restructure totally his thinking about himself and the world. In that endeavor we function more as educators than as therapists. The process is rational, with a focus on thinking rather than feelings. (The criminal can justify anything with his feelings.) There is no going into why his criminality began because such an exegesis is counterproductive: it only provides the criminal with reasons not to change and with a means to justify further criminal thought and action.

Our approach to a criminal begins when his life situation is critical. He has been arrested and either wants to avoid confinement or wants to get out of confinement. In short, he has failed as a criminal. At our initial interview, we do not ask him about himself. Rather, during a three-hour period, even though we have never met him before, we tell him the truth about himself as society sees him. It is as though we were holding up a mirror that shows his past—how he has functioned in life and what has resulted. We talk about the stages of self-disgust he has experienced even when he was active in crime and about how short-lived they have been. In our early meetings we capitalize on his discouragement with his lot in life and his fears about the future. We point out that he has three options—continued crime and its possible consequences (i.e., injury to self and others, death, confinement), change, or suicide.

___

*Gossop et al. (1982) reported that British inpatient addicts who perceived their addiction as a form of "sickness" were least likely to remain in treatment.

We are aware that he is examining us more closely than we are examining him. So we let him know in a straightforward manner what our view of him is. He learns that we are not fascinated by his crimes and that we are not going to court his favor. We do not ask him about particular crimes, and we do not use his language. Our tactics are not those of "encounter" or "confrontation," as they are often practiced. We are intense and firm, but not angry. We never use ridicule, sarcasm, or profanity. Our purpose is to establish some facts about the criminal and to point out his options. The criminal has made many choices in his life; now he is free to make new ones. We do not expect an immediate commitment to a way of life that he has eschewed. However, because he is fed up with himself and his current way of life, he may be willing to listen to us and consider what we have to offer. From the beginning we promise him only blood, sweat, and tears. He will have to work very hard; in turn, we shall work hard to help him change. If he chooses to change, he has to endure the consequences of that choice. Endurance is the expression of "will." The price that he has to pay is to be deprived of the oxygen of his life — criminal excitement.

What occurs in the daily group meetings is the heart of the change process. After we have extensively interviewed the criminal individually, he enters a small group, the members of which are criminals at different points in the process of change. Coming in, he sees that there is an established format. He becomes aware that there are others like him who are actually changing. And those who are advanced in the change process see themselves all over again in the new, unchanged criminal. The objective of the program is to change the thinking of a lifetime because it is the thought of today that results in the crime of tomorrow. To elicit that thinking, we train the criminal in phenomenologic reporting — that is, reporting his thinking without addition, subtraction, reservation, or interpretation.* It is as though we were viewing a videotape of all his thinking for a twenty-four-hour period.

Criminals are often perceptive about others and enjoy pointing out faults, but they have to be taught to apply their observations to themselves. The emphasis in these groups is on each member's self-criticism and on the application to his own life of what others report. The climate is very much like that of a classroom, except that the teaching is not didactic. The agent of change selects themes from criminals' reports for each day's meeting. Initially every time an unchanged criminal opens his mouth, he reveals an error in thinking. We pay close attention to what might appear to an observer to be an insignificant detail. That detail will demonstrate an error that has widespread ramifications for the criminal and others. Corrective concepts are then introduced that apply not only to the concrete incident reported but also to similar events

*Phenomenologic reporting is discussed at length in Chapter 5 of Volume II.

that have occurred and will occur in the future. We are teaching concrete thinkers to be conceptual about responsible functioning. For example, a criminal might think about taking some supplies home from where he works. We treat the thought as seriously as though he were thinking about committing an armed robbery because it reveals an attitude. A basically responsible person may take home some supplies, but his irresponsibility stops there. For the criminal, appropriating what is not his is a way of life. There are many ways in which to approach such thinking because a number of thinking errors are involved: the pursuit of control for its own sake, an unrealistic sense of ownership, the failure to put himself in the place of others, a lack of interdependence, a lack of a concept of injury to others, and so forth.* Even though others in the group may not have thought of taking supplies from work, every one of them has stolen in some way. We are teaching fundamental concepts that appear self-evident to the responsible person but are as "foreign as the dark side of the moon" to the criminal. As we move from the concrete to the conceptual, we extend the discussion to a view of life. How does the criminal view himself? How does he view the world? How does he expect others to see him? What does he want out of life? Eventually it is one's evaluation of oneself and of the world that must be changed. This occurs through a long, repetitive process of giving meticulous attention to what appear to be the most minor details.

The criminal can feed us what he thinks we want to hear, just as he has fed others. Because of the techniques we use and our knowledge of how he operates, we provide him with fewer chances to lead us astray than other change agents might offer. Nevertheless, sometimes he does con us. Anyone going into this work has to avoid developing the two extreme attitudes of gullibility and unbridled cynicism. It is the criminal's life. Time will tell whether he is sincere and truthful; his implementation of correctives is critical, not his intentions. In order to have some outside information about the criminal, we make it a condition of his participation in this program that we have access to someone who knows him well, such as a wife, girl friend, or employer.

Self-disgust grows as the criminal implements his new knowledge and contrasts his new way of life with the old. To facilitate this, we require him to take a moral inventory, much as Alcoholics Anonymous requires "a searching moral inventory." Formerly the deterrents were the fear of getting caught and some fragments of conscience, both of which were cut off when it suited the criminal. Increasingly deterrence becomes part of life. Temptations are not savored but are rapidly deterred, and former stimuli for criminal thinking no longer serve as stimuli. As he makes some modest achievements, he has increasing impetus to deter criminal thinking.

---

*See Chapters 7 and 8 of Volume II.

Fear and guilt are indispensable to responsible functioning. In the past, the criminal has been intolerant of fear, viewing it as weak. In the process of change he comes to value fear as an impetus for constructive activities. This program has as its cornerstone a set of values that has survived for centuries. They are part of the fabric of civilization. Although we do not preach or invoke any particular religious doctrine, we teach the criminal a way of life that is commensurate with these values and antithetical to injuring others.

The course is arduous. It often begins with a honeymoon period in which the criminal is determined to change faster and do it better than anyone else. Eventually the excitement of this new enterprise wanes, and he becomes bored and angry at the restraints imposed — no drugs, sex only with his wife, a fully programmed day, total accountability for money, etc. As the honeymoon comes to an end, he tries to alter the program to suit his needs and to convert the agent of change to his point of view. Failing at this, some drop out and go their own ways. Others stay in, complaining and full of self-pity. Legal leverage is often critical at this stage. If a criminal does not cooperate with the program, we report this to his probation or parole officer. Privileged communication is maintained; it is only his noncooperation that is revealed. Of course, if we know that he plans to harm someone, confidentiality may be breached. As change occurs, legal leverage becomes less important; eventually, the criminal comes to seek help even after all legal holds have expired. He perceives the task of change as far from completed and desires guidance in decision making, a process with which he is still relatively lacking in experience.

Several other processes are going on concurrently. We continue to hold a mirror up to the criminal to increase his self-disgust; we remind him constantly that it is his life and that he has the three choices: crime, change, or suicide; and we teach him new thinking patterns.

As he lives responsibly, there are rewards — internal, interpersonal, and material. Instead of self-esteem based on inflated pretensions and unrealistic expectations, he begins to have self-respect based on solid, responsible achievements. He starts to earn the respect of co-workers, receives a promotion by an appreciative employer, the trust and love of a woman, and the affection of others, including his children, who before were afraid of him and distrusted him. He experiences a sense of cleanliness. No longer does he have to look over his shoulder for the policeman. Although he is a "slave" to this program, it allows him to experience a new freedom.

The drug-using criminal must engage in the same process as the nonuser. The same thinking patterns must be changed. However, the drug-using criminal presents specific additional obstacles, the most obvious being his drug use. *Giving up drugs is only a beginning; the major task is to change the thinking and action patterns that have been present for years.*

PITFALLS DURING EARLY CONTACTS
WITH THE DRUG-USING CRIMINAL

ASKING WHY THE CRIMINAL USES DRUGS

The unchanged drug-using criminal deploys numerous tactics to mislead an interviewer or change agent.* If the issue under discussion is drugs, a user justifies his drug use in a variety of ways. Asking him why he uses drugs only offers him a clear field to present his self-serving statements and, in addition, control the interview. The user's accountability explanations are totally misleading inasmuch as they rarely have anything to do with his thinking at the time that he actually decided to use drugs.† To dispute the whys of drug use with him only invites a contest, which he relishes because in most transactions with people he seeks a triumph.

Asking "why" not only provides the drug user with an arena for justifying drug use *per se* but also affords him an opportunity to blame drugs for problems that develop afterward. He proclaims that he used drugs because he was unhappy and life was difficult. Then he asserts that the drugs were responsible for further misery. By blaming drugs or conditions that he claims led to drug use, he strives to absolve himself of blame. His asking for help often reflects a desire that others bail him out of a difficulty that he has created for himself but then he blames it on his drug use, as though drugs constituted a problem external to him.

The user quickly senses how his interrogators regard him, and he feeds them what he thinks they want to hear. Sometimes others make excuses for him.

> D's mother died, and D was granted permission to leave the hospital to attend the funeral. En route D stopped to visit in the city and purchase drugs from friends. Consequently he never attended the funeral. When he returned to the ward, his drug intoxication was obvious. However, he hardly had a chance to make excuses before the doctor bailed him out. The doctor stated that he understood why D had used drugs. It was clear to him that an addict, so overcome by grief at his mother's death, had tried to cope with that grief by using drugs. The doctor did not know that the user was not saddened by his mother's death. Mother and son had hardly spoken to each other for years. Rather, D had used the funeral as a pretext for an occasion to leave the hospital and seek excitement.

In Chapter 1 we described how we not only accepted the drug-user's excuses

---

*For a complete description of the criminal's tactics, see Chapter 8 of Volume I.

†For a detailed description of the criminal's thinking in accountability situations, see Chapter 6 of Volume I.

as to why he used drugs, but unwittingly provided him with more. Our observation is that this is a common occurrence, especially in psychiatric settings.

The user responds to questions of "why" with a part of the truth and leads the examiner to think it is the whole truth. If the examiner is focusing on "hard drugs," the user will make "addiction" his central problem. He conceals the fact that he has long used other drugs on which he is not physically dependent.* The dialogue then centers on his physical dependence, whereas other antecedent drug-using and criminal patterns remain unrevealed or are overlooked.

We do not probe the sociologic and psychologic origins of drug use. Instead we control the interview and attempt to establish facts about the effects of drugs on the criminal's thinking. This reduces the user's faulting others, his justifying further drug use because of "addiction," and his blaming the drug use on feelings of fear, anger, depression, and boredom. (Some summon the courage to face us and tell the truth.) Using our methods, we still encounter obstacles, especially initially, although fewer than we used to with more conventional techniques.

In short, it is essential for the interviewer not to make a difficult situation worse by asking *why* the drug user acted as he did. To do so is to invite obfuscation and diversion. It also results in the user's regarding the interviewer as someone who can be easily led and controlled. Telling, rather than asking, the drug user who he is is conducive to eliciting information, derailing unproductive tactics, and establishing rapport based on the drug user's respect for the interviewer. Drug users interviewed by another doctor about meetings with Dr. Yochelson made the following comments about Yochelson's approach:

Subject A: "He did not beat around the bush. I did not dig him as a person, but enjoyed talking with him. He did not bullshit around."

Subject B: "He knew when I was lying and how. He was a heavy person. He talked to me like I was a normal man, direct, straight to the point. He showed me no pity."

Subject C: "The doctor cut me down, which made me mad at first, but I got over it because I knew what he said was true."

Subject D: "He was very forward, and I like his approach. He told me what I was going to do, and I had to agree with him."

*He may conceal the use of hard drugs and admit the use of other substances, but minimize the latter because they are "nonaddictive" and he terms them "socially acceptable."

VIEWING DRUG USE AS THE PROBLEM

A formidable obstacle to an agent of change or to any other interviewer is the drug-using criminal's perception that his drug use constitutes the source of his difficulties. He then focuses on drugs to the exclusion of other considerations. In doing so, he takes the position that he is a victim of his own drug use, over which he has little control. However, this is not the case. Some drug users have stopped using drugs on their own initiative. This has occurred when they were faced with unavailability of drugs, family pressures, or fear for their own health and safety.

The fear of physical deterioration and death is perhaps the most critical factor in the longtime user's decision to stop using drugs. He has witnessed people who have suffered ill health or who have taken overdoses. Some older drug users also stop using drugs because they no longer experience much of a high—"It gets to be a bummer." Even though a user in his forties stops using hard drugs, he is likely to continue with others, such as marijuana and alcohol. From time to time he may "chip" or use drugs of other types.

Various other factors may be contributing to the criminal's desire to stop drug use. He may be under pressure from a wife, girlfriend, or parents who threaten to have nothing to do with him unless he ceases drug use. Drug users have envied criminal nonusers who have had the "heart" to commit major crimes without drugs. Some decide that they will give up drugs because they want to be more effective in crime. They are weary of the daily grind and want to get "the monkey off my back." They believe that procuring and using drugs entail undesirable risks. Furthermore they think that their judgment will be better without drugs and that this will reduce the risk of apprehension. Some criminals on high doses lose their sexual interest (see Chapter 5), so they stop using drugs to "get my sex back." Several of our drug users voluntarily committed themselves to narcotic treatment programs for this purpose. Some criminals are disgusted with more than drug use itself. They perceive drugs as one element of a life that is generally rotten. One man reported that he hit rock bottom when he stole from his daughter's piggy bank. He called himself "a pretty poor excuse for a human being." Reviling himself as malicious and sadistic, he commented, "I had never sunk this low." Such disgust with one's whole way of life is short-lived. It is an attitude that is more pervasive among criminals who do not use drugs than those who do, because the latter try to convince others and even themselves that drugs constitute "the problem."

A major obstacle confronted us when the drug user sincerely wanted to stop using drugs but formulated this as the entire problem. He viewed himself as a basically good person—who happened to have a drug problem. He asserted that his irresponsibility was drug related, and that if he could only stop using drugs, he would be responsible. In focusing on drugs and not on his criminality (which preceded drug use), he was similar to the rapist who asserted that sex alone was his problem whereas, in fact, it was his pursuit of conquests and many other criminal patterns that were the critical features.

The scope of the change process affects every aspect of life of the criminal who uses drugs, as well as of one who does not. If a user adheres to a position that his drug use is all that requires changing, his personality will remain unaltered, and criminal patterns will continue whether or not he uses drugs.

In our initial interview we spend little time on drugs. Instead we identify other patterns of irresponsibility that have been almost lifelong. Every time the person tries to make drug use the focal point, we demonstrate that he was criminal long before drugs came into the picture. In further interviews we make it clear to him that if we help him only to stop using drugs (which he is capable of doing on his own), we shall have as a product a criminal who does not use drugs, rather than a criminal who does use drugs. He will still be a criminal.

TRYING TO DETERMINE WHETHER THE CRIMINAL IS ON DRUGS

An ongoing concern of the agent of change is whether the criminal with whom he is working is still using drugs. When this becomes a preoccupation, the agent of change starts to function like a detective, and this impairs the relationship. Actually there is no way to know for certain whether a criminal is on drugs at a particular time unless he is on such a high dose that there are observable signs, such as slurred speech, grogginess, awkwardness in gait, and so forth. These signs are rare. A criminal may be high on drugs during an interview, yet appear alert and attentive. The stance that the agent of change must take toward this issue is the same one that he assumes with respect to whether the person is committing other violations. We never know for sure whether a criminal is reporting accurately. However, if one is helping criminals change, he can be neither gullible nor cynical in his attitude. The criminal perceives the gullible person as a "mark," someone whom he can easily control. He perceives the cynic as not believing anything he says, and thus as not worth bothering with. Both gullibility and cynicism preclude a dialogue. It is essential for a change agent to remind himself, as well as the criminal, that it is the criminal's life that is at stake, not the change agent's self-esteem. Time will reveal the criminal's sincerity and truthfulness. We have had drug users take militant stands against using drugs only to fall away from that position later. To demonstrate his intentions to abstain, one user turned in marijuana reefers and surrendered marijuana seeds that he intended to plant. Soon after, he returned to drugs. At the time of his opposition to drug use, we had no certain way of determining whether he was expressing a sincere desire to change or was conning us. Whatever his intentions initially, the aftermath was the same. Had we challenged his sincerity at the time, we would have had little basis for a useful conversation.

In no way do we tolerate or condone drug use. Rather, we are stating that it is futile for a change agent to become consumed by the issue of whether, at any given point, the criminal is still using drugs. If we find out from others (e.g., institution staff members or the criminal's family) that he is using drugs, we let him know it. Our position, which we repeat often, is that he is wasting his time and ours by using drugs, especially as he professes that he wants to change.

THE CLOSED CHANNEL WHEN THE CRIMINAL IS ON DRUGS

The three components of the wide-open channel of communication are disclosure, receptivity, and self-criticism. We know from the start that we are dealing with a person who has been untruthful throughout his life. The only incentive he now has to be truthful in a program for change is that he has reached rock bottom. He is in a period of disgust with himself, and he knows what his options are. He realizes that to be-untruthful now is like going to a doctor with a serious condition, but not allowing the doctor to examine him. We can help him only if he allows us to examine his thinking through phenomenologic reporting.

Even though he has decided he wants to change, it is usually with reservation. Therefore it is quite some time before he totally opens the channel to permit an examination of his thinking. But whatever thinking he does report allows us considerable opportunity to identify errors and begin the long task of setting forth correctives for him to implement.

If the criminal is on drugs, the obstacles to full disclosure in a wide-open channel are increased. On drugs he is generally a much poorer reporter than when he is off drugs. He is not reflective and makes little effort to monitor and note his thinking. Thus, reporting is superficial. As one man put it, "I have done no thinking about myself." This was truthful. With drugs he was "ten feet tall" and had his mind on things that he found a lot more exciting than our program. Our requirement that the drug user disclose all his thinking is sometimes responded to with the accusation that we are invading his privacy. On drugs he is even more secretive and evasive than usual. There is more verbal fencing, and more cat-and-mouse tactics are employed as he faces the agent of change and other group members. As we pointed out in Chapter 5, lying is so frequent that the user loses track of what he said, whether it was yesterday or fifteen minutes ago. Lies also become more brazen with drug use.

Receptivity is minimal. Although physically present at a group meeting, the user is in another world. Although he may spend three hours in a session, he emerges remembering remarkably little, usually only that with which he agrees.

The drug user is basically closed minded and derisive of other's attempts to be constructive. He is impervious to criticism, or he tries to overcome whoever is the source of the criticism. Instead of evaluating the merit of what is said, the drug user responds to it as a put-down and tries to vanquish the critic. When he perceives himself as under attack, he becomes argumentative. He may quibble endlessly with semantics, minimize the importance of what is said or denounce it as irrelevant, become verbally abusive, and otherwise assume a rejecting stance.

When he is on drugs, self-criticism is practically nonexistent. His view of himself and of his place in the world is superoptimistic. Even though by his own volition he is participating in a program for change, he actually sees very little about himself that needs changing. He may agree that what was said during a meeting was sound and then shrug it off as not applying to him.

Off drugs he may maintain that he is fed up with himself and wants to change. On drugs, he is certain that he is already well advanced in change. To him it's all very simple. When he is pressed to scrutinize his own behavior, excuses flow. He harps on others' faults and wrongdoings, but sees none in himself. On drugs there is no incentive to engage in a moral inventory because such an exercise would negate his view of himself. He believes that he can function independently and does not need anyone's help. If he uses drugs over a substantial period, he is likely to begin staying away from meetings. When he reappears, it is with an arsenal of excuses for his absences. Although certain that he no longer has need of such a group and program, he may not drop out altogether but continue to participate in a token manner to keep others off his back.

Clearly, no transaction with a criminal can be productive while he is on drugs. We do not exclude him from a meeting, but we recognize and point out to him and other group members the futility of his participation when his mind is altered. In fact, perhaps the most constructive thing that happens is that other group members see a full-blown case of how drug use affects the wide-open channel. For the man on drugs, all we can do is reiterate that he makes his own choices in life—we can only help him if he desires to help himself.

SELF-PITY AND THE REFUSAL TO ENDURE

All criminals are cowards, having numerous fears and being easily threatened, but the drug-using criminal is the most cowardly. His fears are so intense that he requires drugs in order to proceed with a major crime. After committing a crime, he uses more drugs to eliminate the fear that he will be caught or that he was unsuccessful. He is short on endurance both in his crim- inal life and in his resolution to change. During the change process he com- plains constantly of how he is suffering. What he regards as suffering are the stresses and uncertainties of living that the responsible person endures as or- dinary parts of life. The latter learns to take these in stride and, indeed, may perceive them as challenges; the drug user refuses to endure mental or phys- ical stress. He demands a tension-free existence as a nonnegotiable condition of life.

The task of developing endurance is more onerous to the drug user than to the criminal nonuser. The criminal who does not use drugs is more resolute both in crime and in change. In contrast with the more indecisive, frag- mented drug user, the nonuser is more steadfast in making up his mind and in enduring the lack of excitement.

Once the drug user handles a difficult situation well, he believes that he is thereafter entitled to a problem-free life. He converts his failure to endure what he regards as a boring existence into an excuse or justification by asser- tions such as, "You know, all junkies are weak."

Like other criminals the drug user refuses to take life as it is. Something not going his way threatens his inflated view of himself. If others do not function as he expects, he reacts as though he personally has been put down. A self- limitation constitutes a put-down. An unfavorable attitude expressed toward him is a put-down. The drug user maintains a stubborn, uncompromising view of life in which it is better to die than to endure a lack of excitement and put his shoulder to the wheel. Confronted with any task that he seeks to avoid, he thinks about drugs. When he views the future as an endless series of problems, he thinks about drugs. When bored, he thinks about drugs. When tense and experiencing psychosomatic symptoms, he thinks about drugs. As the drug user discovers that change requires much more tenacity than he thought, he feels sorry for himself. Anger is a major component of self-pity. In a state of self-pity the criminal drug user desires drugs. As he thinks about drugs, he contemplates other violations that drugs would facilitate.

D reported an increasing amount of sexual thinking and more frequent erections as he stared at women. Aware of this, he resolved to remain at home all weekend. He was determined to end his pattern of sexual exploi- tation. As he forced himself to stay in, D became increasingly tense and developed a persistent headache. He experienced enormous self-pity with outbursts of tears as he reflected on the emptiness of his life. He saw him- self as a tragic figure with nothing worthwhile in the present and nothing to look forward to in the future. He deplored his own laziness in not pro- gramming his time for the weekend. As he wearied of being home, he be- gan thinking about drugs and the sex that drugs would facilitate. Instead of deterring that thinking, he savored it. Finally he called a girl who he knew was available for sex. En route to her house, he stopped to buy cocaine. Meeting the girl's mother at the front door, he lied in saying that he was a longstanding friend. The girl had the "works" for cocaine. After injecting the drug, the two went out for a beer. They returned to the house for sex, going through elaborate precautions to avoid being discovered by the girl's mother. D went home in the early hours of the morning and began to regret what he had done.

As we talked with D on Monday, he began to conceptualize how absurd was his view of suffering — somewhat like the view of the criminal who complains that he has only a $200 suit, not a $400 suit. He realized that the drugs had removed his fears about irresponsibility and illegal drug transactions, making life again exciting. Our response was as follows:

> What can we do for him? First, he has an opportunity to reveal what happened, to express his regret, and then to express his intentions. We can clarify certain issues. Is association with a woman like this worth the sacrifice of a job and a future? Everytime he does this, there can be trouble. What could have prevented another boyfriend from coming and presenting further difficulties? What could have prevented the mother from discovering him? Whenever a person sneaks, lies, and cheats, he is open to trouble.

Self-pity does not always result in violation. However, accompanying self-pity is an inertia with respect to responsible initiatives. The following episode (a dictation by Dr. Yochelson) reflects the state of mind that often gives way to violation (even though no violation occurred on this particular occasion).

> When D did not call, I assumed it was a bad day. I did not foreclose the possibility of drugs or other violations. As it turned out, over the weekend there was tiredness and a desire to be alone. The application of energy to do what had to be done was absent. Instead of pounding the pavement to look for a job, he was thinking about the past when he was fancy-free. The prevalent state was self-pity. D alternated between self-pity because of the dullness of his present life and self-disgust with his past. The idea of suicide occurred passively to him, taking the form "I wish I were dead." He thought fleetingly of rotting on a park bench indefinitely until he died. When D returned to his one little room, he regarded it as a jail cell and thought that perhaps jail offered a better option. In all this rumination, there was no desire to get busy and do something about himself. All the thinking about self-discipline and all the talk that had been generated in our office was for naught.

D's description of his weekend indicated a massive failure at putting the tenets of our program into practice. It was a state in which a drug user was deterred from crime but balked at doing anything constructive. His inertia resulted only in more self-pity and an assertion that he was incapable of change.

After a brief period of showing some initiatives, D returned to the same state of mind. Neither the high voltage of crime nor the dusty road of responsible living was acceptable.

> D was complaining about his contrived "flunky job." Yet he had no suggestions as to how to improve his income. He averred that our program confined him to low earnings. Our response was that at this time a flunky job is all that is realistically available to this criminal, who has few skills and is on probation. We have no objections to his doubling or tripling his income if he obtains a job honestly and meets the time requirements of this program. Generally D was whining and complaining about what he perceived to be the injustices of the world, including those inflicted on him by us. D asserted that he was in his early forties and would soon be ready for a rocking chair and retirement. He was overwhelmingly pessimistic about a future in which he would begin at the bottom in order to achieve modest successes. D said of responsible living, "I don't have what it takes to do that." This was the precise state of mind that had always plagued him whenever he had considered functioning responsibly. Age itself had nothing to do with it. As we held this discussion, we asked D for a solution to his situation. What were his ideas? He responded, "Now I'd like to kill myself, but I don't have the energy to do it."

D's statement about wanting to kill himself but lacking the energy is characteristic of the drug-using criminal. It illustrates his refusal to endure and his self-pity. At this point we were exerting more energy in working with D than he was.

The drug user goes through periods, sometimes extended, in which he does little for himself and whines about the injustices of life. He sees the agent of change as the source of his misery and constantly complains about the severity of the program's requirements. He is threatened with a zero state — being a nothing in a world that offers nothing.* No criminal, whether a drug user or nonuser, tolerates such a position very long. This is an especially dangerous state of mind in the drug user because he endures distress far less than his nonusing counterpart, who does not quit the program as readily when things are not going his way. The fearful drug user has many more ups and downs, and in a state of self-pity his fuse is extremely short.

*The zero state is discussed in Chapter 4 of Volume I.

On the day before Christmas, D waited on tables at his job. Lunch went well, and he earned twenty dollars. In the evening, despite a mix-up in reservations and D's not working in the busiest room, he earned sixty dollars. In terms of income, D's eighty-dollar day was satisfactory. However, D was angry because he believed that employees and supervisors had lied to him about the room assignments and were exploiting him. D said nothing, but went home to bed. On Christmas Day, he and his wife were planning to have dinner with friends. When D awoke on Christmas, he complained that he was tired and refused to go out. His wife was upset: she wanted to go, and their friends were expecting them. As they yelled at each other, D's wife threatened to call us for guidance, whereupon D grabbed a pair of scissors, snipped the telephone wires, and returned to bed. He awoke remorseful, thinking about all the injury he had inflicted on his wife. The rest of the day he treated her more kindly.

Reporting these events to us, D said that he did not like Christmas. As he reviewed his life at this holiday time, he experienced a sense of tremendous futility. In fact, as D spoke of this in our office, tears welled in his eyes. When D reported his conduct, we regarded his functioning as that of an unchanged criminal, even though he had not been arrestable and had abstained from drugs. Old patterns were still much in evidence. He was loaded with self-pity and anger. Guided by his feelings instead of reason, he had been violent in cutting the phone wires. Worse still, it was yet another in a long series of injuries to his wife. What we encountered typifies what the agent of change has to be prepared to meet with all drug-using criminals. Patience, firmness, and persistence are most important as one continues to face the drug user with who he is, what his lack of endurance has produced in the past, and what it will surely lead to in the future.

PSYCHOSOMATIC SYMPTOMS IN THE DRUG-USING CRIMINAL*

As he participates in the program, the criminal experiences a variety of psychosomatic symptoms as a result of the competition between the desire to do what is exciting and the desire to live within the restraints of responsibility. Psychosomatic symptoms are a direct reflection of restraints from criminality, whether imposed by the outside world or by the criminal himself. The drug users in our study have experienced them more frequently and more intensely than the criminals who do not use drugs.

In this chapter we are discussing symptoms that arise long after the user has been detoxified. However, the symptoms resemble those experienced during

---

*For a general discussion of psychosomatic symptoms and craving, see Chapter 4 of this volume.

withdrawal from drugs. The physical reaction includes chills, headaches, gastrointestinal disturbances, weakness, aches, perspiration, and diarrhea. In his mind a minor distress becomes a major disability, and he does not tolerate it well. If the user is confined, he often appears at sick call.

Psychosomatic symptoms are most frequent and intense early in the change process. It is then that the drug user wants to be responsible, but he knows so little about what this entails that there is not a strong commitment. A prominent theme in the early days of the program is "I can't," a position fortified by psychosomatic symptoms. When a criminal says that he cannot do something, this rarely refers to a real incapacity.* "I can't" means "I won't," in this case referring to living in a world that he considers boring and to a life that he views as empty. An espousal of "I can't" signifies that he refuses to live without the crime and sexual conquests for which drugs have been necessary. As he remains off drugs, the psychosomatic symptoms develop. His craving is far more for the excitement that drugs facilitate than for the drugs' physical effects. He cites the symptoms as evidence that he cannot change.

The severity of psychosomatic symptoms is in proportion to the degree of boredom, self-pity, and anger that the user experiences.

> Long after he had stopped using drugs, D was complaining about a severe headache that lasted throughout an entire weekend. He launched into a tirade, the theme of which was, "What the hell is this life?" He asserted that he was tired of being kicked around by others. He proclaimed that he would not take a back seat to anyone. Maintaining that people are phony, he said he did not care about society. He refused to be "on the bottom" and degraded. But then D said more quietly that he did not want to be defiant. He followed this by saying that his girlfriend was "like a French whore" and that he deserved a high-class woman. Then he again contradicted himself, exclaiming that she was a wonderful woman.

Headaches had been a frequent problem for D, who had renounced crime but still had not resigned himself to living what he considered a mundane life. The basic issue D raised here was that of excitement versus nothingness. The combination of psychosomatic symptoms and the dissatisfactions with life result in the drug user's dwelling on the former. His suffering then becomes an excuse for drugs.

Psychosomatic symptoms of the criminal are relieved quickly by excitement. Even the prospect of obtaining drugs removes the symptoms. As

*See Chapter 5 of Volume I for a development of the "I can't" theme.

change agents we take the position that he must endure the symptoms.* Instead of alleviating his distress, we establish the necessity of adopting a long-range view. He must suffer now in the interest of a remaining lifetime that could be radically different from the past. When he experiences these symptoms, the drug user learns to ask himself, "In what way am I thinking irresponsibly?" The objective is for him to determine the source of his discomfort and let that prompt him to examine his thinking and act more responsibly.

When the criminal is concentrating and productive, he is less likely to be bored. Fully programming his time is one means of dealing with the distress that attends boredom. Thoughts about drugs and concentration on psychosomatic symptoms are more frequent when he is idle than when he is occupied. When he pushes himself in responsible endeavors and attacks problems with zest, thinking about drugs decreases, and so does his physical discomfort. Each time psychosomatic symptoms and the attendant thinking about drugs and crime arise, the user must ask himself what the alternative is to enduring that which he considers boring.

> D had a headache and began thinking about drugs and women other than his wife. He took two aspirin tablets and then plunged into a deskful of work. On no one day during the last seventeen months had he processed as many orders as he did that particular day. The headache quickly vanished and did not return.

Diverting one's thinking through work is not a final solution. As the user becomes more fed up with his former way of life and as he habituates corrective patterns, he builds new values. These are antithetical to criminal excitement. He would then rather endure a hundred severe headaches and stomach upsets than risk what he has worked so hard to build. The worst thing possible, as he sees it, is a return to his old way of life.

FAILURE TO TAKE RESPONSIBLE INITIATIVES

The failure to take responsible initiatives is partially a reflection of inertia that accompanies self-pity. The drug user is ordinarily supercharged with energy, but during periods of dissatisfaction with the program for change, he applies little energy to responsible activity. In an interview he may express

---

*Dr. Yochelson did not administer psychotropic medication to drug-using criminals in the course of change. To do so would have run counter to the program's requirement that the drug user develop self-discipline and tolerate distress. Psychotropic drugs are ineffective in the unchanged criminal because their use does not relieve tension so that he can live responsibly and productively. The only relief from tension that he seeks is the "high" of criminal excitement.

this discontent by appearing listless, emotionless, apathetic, and generally fatigued. He ignores obligations, defers implementing correctives, and devotes little thought to what happens in daily meetings. One drug user wryly observed, "My sport is lethargy."

The drug user wants a life that offers more than a "treadmill to oblivion." This inertia can be transformed into action merely by removing restraints and allowing him to go his own way. The drug user does it himself when he cuts off deterrents. Then, with a rapid infusion of energy, he avidly socializes with other criminals, pursues sex, finds targets for exploitation, and is resourceful in planning and executing crimes.

Because his priorities are elsewhere, he defers and often defaults on the mundane chores that people face daily. Bills are ignored, laundry is left undone, the car is not taken through safety inspection, appointments are not kept, tax forms are not filed. The list is endless. Some drug users become apathetic about personal hygiene and tidiness and live in filth, with dishes piled up in the sink, appliances broken, trash strewn about their living quarters, light bulbs broken or burned out, and an empty refrigerator. Because of their deferment and default, they create more problems for themselves: creditors hound them, landlords threaten them with eviction, and others seek them out to redress grievances for broken promises and unfulfilled obligations.

When held accountable, the drug user contends that he has done nothing wrong and offers a variety of excuses. After visiting two places to look for a job, he gives up. He says that there are no jobs, that he has no chance with a criminal record, or that he is not qualified (meaning that no job is available that suits his tastes or fulfills his expectations). If asked why he has not visited a relative, he maintains that he does not have carfare, that he lacks the time, or that his family is too busy to see him.

Initiatives depend on the drug user's feelings and on whether he is interested. He claims that he is tired when confronted by any task that he does not want to do. Yet as a criminal, with or without drugs, he went for days at a time with a few hours of sleep and did not complain of fatigue. If an activity holds the promise of excitement and a buildup, he is rarely too tired. His attitude is, "If I like it, O.K. If not, to heck with it." He expects others to guarantee that change is worthwhile. Early in his contact with the agent of change, he was informed that the only guarantee possible was that he would have even more problems (though of a different sort) as a responsible person than he had as a criminal. But the drug user wants an assurance of success, still defining success in terms of being "number one." Otherwise why should he undertake initiatives to do what he perceives as unrewarding? He leaves the burden of proof to others.

Once he takes a responsible initiative, whether or not he sees it through to a conclusion, he expects others to regard him as heroic. If he recognizes the obligatory and begins to fulfill it, he thinks that he has accomplished all that is necessary for change. When he is confronted by a day without obvious pressures or tasks, there is little inclination to create a task. The lack of zest for change is far more obvious and prolonged in the drug user than in the criminal nonuser.

Throughout such periods of inertia, the agent of change continues to hold a mirror up to the drug user, presenting the facts as they are and demonstrating to him that his failure to take responsible initiatives will continue to result in an ever-widening circle of injury to others.

THE DEVELOPMENT OF A NEUROTIC REACTION

The drug user, more fearful in crime than the criminal nonuser, is also more fearful in change. He is like an infant in that he is functioning in a world new to him. Not wanting to make mistakes, he develops a virtual paralysis of initiative. There is a great deal of self-condemnation and a fear of the future. He is afraid that he will never change, never learn to do things right. His greatest concern is with how he impresses other people. He dreads making a fool of himself, and so there is exaggerated tension about his performance. He may be reluctant to enter a vocational or educational program for fear that he will not measure up to the standards. Once he enrolls, he doubts his ability to keep up with the class and master new skills. At a job he may refuse to assume new responsibilities for fear that he is inadequate. When he makes an error, he worries about it for days, regarding the slightest mistake as a calamity. Even a helpful suggestion by another person is interpreted as indicating that he has a severe deficiency.

> D arrived at work early to set up his busboy station perfectly. The hostess observed one small cover missing from a tray. In D's thinking he had been reduced to a hopeless incompetent.

The self-doubts occur on all fronts. He is no longer sure who he is and fears that other people will see the worst in him. This is especially true with regard to his sexuality.

> D knew that there were many priorities in change other than finding a woman. He realized that he was not ready for a responsible relationship with a woman. Yet everywhere he went — work, church, the laundromat — there were women who made it evident that they were available. D did not respond to flirtation, sexual suggestiveness, or physical brushes against him by waitresses and others at his job. He was polite, friendly,

and businesslike, as appropriate. Yet each day he came to us terrified that
others would perceive him as a homosexual. It was totally foreign to him
not to stake out sexual conquests. He also had the idea that some would
see him as unfriendly or snobbish. There was such fear about how
women would react to him that he often dreaded going to work.

The advantage of this neurotic state is that it ensures meticulous reporting
and a severe self-critical attitude. Doubt of one's self stimulates numerous examinations of conscience. The danger of this state lies in the drug user's extreme sensitivity. With the mounting tension, there is always the possibility
that he will react in his old way—interpret even the smallest constructive criticism as a global devaluation of himself, then react with anger, and either terminate his constructive efforts or lash out at others.

The agent of change does not reassure the drug user who has developed
neurotic anxiety. Our position has been that such a state is preferable to the
user's former pattern of not "giving a damn." Again we remind him of the
three options: he can use drugs and engage in crime, and then his most important problem will be getting hurt or arrested; suicide is another possibility; or
he can live with his tensions for a while, achieve something responsible, and
gain perspective. The drug user has known nothing about responsible living.
Now he is learning about how others live. The corrective for neurotic self-
doubt and perfectionism is to engage in a more realistic assessment of himself
and the world with objectives geared to reality.

DRUGS: THE INSTANT ANTIDOTE TO BOREDOM AND SELF-PITY

Excitement and drugs are synonymous in the criminal's thinking. Whenever he is dissatisfied, he thinks about drugs. This may occur when the user is
confronted by a specific task that he does not want to do, when he sees a person or place that reminds him of drugs, or when he despairs of the future.
Early in change the desire for drugs is likely to win in the competition between boredom and excitement.

Because drugs are so easily available and offer such a quick alternative, the
drug user is harder to work with than the nonuser, who lacks such recourse.
Even with no money the user finds it easy to get drugs. He has friends with
whom he has plenty of available credit.

Once he has decided to obtain drugs, the deterrent function of the agent of
change is cut off. Later the user provides a variety of excuses as to why he did
not contact the agent of change before using drugs. One user told Dr.
Yochelson that his reason for not calling was that he did not want to jeopard-
ize Yochelson's health by causing him worry. Justifications are numerous,
but the fact is that the user decides what he wants and cuts off the program to

accomplish it. By using drugs, he generally creates more problems for himself. Then he may use more drugs to find a way out.

The recourse to drugs is so rapid and seems so automatic that it appears that the user is at the mercy of an irresistible impulse or compulsion. But because a course of thought and action is habitual, it is not necessarily beyond the person's control. The criminal makes conscious choices and pursues what he wants. The process of making choices is indicated in the following excerpt from our notes that depicts a user's struggle with his desire for excitement.

This morning D described his behavior yesterday right after he left here. He was very much aware of an intense desire for sexual excitement, this along the usual lines of his view of himself as having great sexual powers.* These thoughts accelerated after he had seen Paula (a totally irresponsible woman) in a compromising position with a hospital patient. The vividness of this experience activated a great many memories of former exciting sexual conquests. As the day wore on, he became increasingly aware that he wanted high-powered sex. However, he was equally aware that this was not good for him. He indicated that his self-esteem was at issue. There was still a lingering need to be a number one sexual figure.

He described how, at 12:30, he thought he would take a bus ride to attenuate or remove these sexual ideas. He left the hospital and got off not far from his house, whereupon his first thought was to buy vodka. He thought of the effects that even a small amount of vodka had on him. He knew it would affect his thinking and judgment. He thought about this especially with respect to a late afternoon doctor's appointment and the evening with Diana (a responsible woman). He walked to the entrance of the liquor store, then turned away. Then he thought of obtaining cough syrup with codeine. He entered a drug store and the clerk asked what she could do for him. He paused as if paralyzed, and he realized that this was no good for him. He asked for dental floss and left. He then walked in the direction of another drug store, with a mounting desire for codeine. The same experience occurred, and he ended up by buying facial tissues. He went to a third drug store and had a similar experience. At this time, because the itch for excitement was still present, he decided to go home and masturbate to rid himself of tension. The masturbation fantasy only increased his desire for excitement. He thought once more about buying vodka, but rejected it. Finally he decided that he ought to return to the hospital. He kept his doctor's appointment and talked quite candidly

*This man had an extensive history of voyeurism and exhibitionism, in addition to many other types of crime.

about his state of tension and desire for drugs and excitement. In relating the events of the day to us, D made it clear that he could easily have presented himself as a victim of an overpowering urge of feelings that he could not control. The easiest thing in the world would have been for him to purchase liquor or drugs, and it would not have been difficult to find a woman for sex.

Here was a case of a series of choices being made that required an exercise of will. All that D would have needed was a drink of liquor, and the door would have been opened to other substances, exciting sex, and, in time, illegal acts.

ALCOHOL: OPENING THE DOOR TO CRIMINALITY

In helping hard-core criminals to change, we impose restraints and requirements that are severe. It took us years to realize that any irresponsible pattern of thought or action constitutes a danger because today's criminal idea is the forerunner of tomorrow's criminal act.

From the outset of the criminal's participation in this program, drug use other than that medically prescribed is ruled out. We receive little argument from the criminal about the wisdom of abstinence from opiates, amphetamines, barbiturates, and hallucinogens. Also, little opposition is expressed by him toward abstinence from marijuana. However, it is a different story with respect to alcohol. In requiring total abstinence from alcohol, we take the same position as Alcoholics Anonymous. This applies to all criminals, whether or not they are truly alcoholics. We have found that limiting people who have gone the whole route in crime to a modest amount of alcohol does not work. They must be dealt with as though they are alcoholics. In our objective of changing the thinking patterns of a lifetime, we require more than A.A. We insist not only on abstinence from drink but also on the eradication of even the thought of drinking.*

The drug-using criminal asserts that alcohol is permissible because it is legal and he can control his intake. He contends that nothing is wrong with a couple of beers at night or a glass of sherry to relax or, for that matter, a "social drink" at a party. The drug user attempts to defend his position by stating that "nothing happens" when he has a beer, meaning that he does not become intoxicated or commit a crime.

The appearance of the theme of "what's wrong with a beer?" indicates that the honeymoon phase is over. It signifies that the drug user is chafing at the restraints on his life. Another point at which the drug user is likely to make an exception for himself and use alcohol is when he acquires new freedom and

---

*See Chapter 6 for discussion of alcohol use by the unchanged drug-using criminal.

opportunity. Then he grows complacent and believes that he no longer needs the guidance of others. The lessening of restraints in the wake of complacency inevitably results in his traveling the paths he traveled when he was active in crime.

Alcohol use retards change. If the drug user is confined, the consumption of alcohol is a violation in that it is not permitted in an institution. We focus less on the "violation" aspect and more on what drinking reveals about the user's attitude toward change. Effort and endurance are required to transform one's life. The "calisthenics of change" are rigorous, calling for the development of self-discipline.* Abstinence is a part of that self-discipline. Furthermore, the criminal needs all the deterrents that are possible. Alcohol, like the other substances he has used, lessens deterrence. Even if the criminal has temporarily forsworn other drugs, we know that alcohol will remove fears, so that he will increase his drinking, eventually use other drugs, and finally land in the gutter. The best of intentions begin to corrode even before he takes the first sip.

Drinking may begin with a beer, then extends to sherry and wine, and before long includes hard liquor. The consequences his family will have to endure are his increased irritability, angry attempts to control others, chores left undone, and expenditure of scarce funds for liquor. With respect to work, there is tardiness and absenteeism, inefficiency, poor interpersonal relations, a deterioration in the quality of his work, and failure to meet deadlines.

D's wife phoned us one morning, angry and disgusted. Talking rapidly in a high-pitched voice, she threatened to leave and break up the family. She said that she had not objected to D's having a little beer or wine. In fact, she admitted that she occasionally had a beer. Now, however, she was furious at her husband's drinking heavily three nights a week at a neighbor's. She had become especially upset the previous night, when she saw a woman whom she knew to be a tramp going into the neighbor's house. D was usually home by 11 P.M., but this time he returned at four in the morning. His wife reluctantly let him in. That morning D decided that he was not going to work. When his wife asked him for an explanation, he retorted that she was not entitled to one. This attitude angered her even more.

In a session with us, D said that there had been no involvement with other women. He claimed that he had done nothing wrong. We pointed out that his life was at stake. He had cut off all deterrents. In the past D had inflicted injury on his family and others. Now old patterns were in evi-

*See Chapter 10 of Volume II.

dence, and he was failing to see the situation from his wife's point of view. Anger toward her, a refusal to go to work, and a lack of self-criticism augured poorly for change. It was D's choice. Was he going to risk his future over a drink?

Even when there is no obvious injury to others, the criminal's loss of perspective is dangerous.

> D was tense when a friend arrived with her three rambunctious children to visit his family. D tried to seclude himself and watch a basketball game on television, but he could not relax because of the commotion of the playing youngsters. In disgust he left the house and bought wine and beer. A few drinks calmed him down. However, his mood changed, and he began to view life pessimistically. He saw himself as a failure in family life, at work, and in all other endeavors. Although he was not considering ways to end his life, he thought that death would be welcome because so little was to be gained in continuing this dull, unrewarding life.

Throughout this chapter we have referred to the danger of such an attitude. A sure means of achieving relief is to engage once more in the exciting activities that had made life worthwhile in the past. Instead of our trying to relieve D of his fears of failure, we stressed the desirability of fears. If one is fearful of the right things for the right reasons, fear will lead to constructive initiatives and achievement.*

It is extremely difficult to convince a drug-using criminal that drinking is unwise at a time when he insists on indulging in it. Much more effective than our teaching or warning him is his seeing the salutary effects of abstinence after he has abstained. He has an enhanced sense of physical well-being. He finds that he is spending less money. Family life is more harmonious. He is calmer, participates more in activities, and is angry less often. He sleeps better and is more eager to attack problems each day. The criminal who gives up drinking is amazed that his thinking becomes clearer and that his performance everywhere improves. Perhaps most important is that abstinence from alcohol (and all other drugs) leads him to think less about drugs and crime than before. In time he radically changes his perspective about alcohol. Rather than seeing it as a tension reliever, he is finally convinced that it is a tension producer that will only compound his problems and result in failure of his efforts to change.

We insist that the drug-using criminal, no matter how advanced in change, abstain from alcohol. Our experience has shown that there is always risk associated with drinking. One of our drug users whom we have followed for eight years is functioning well, except that he drinks a beer most evenings. He

---

*See our development of fear as a corrective in Chapter 7 of Volume II.

has limited himself to this and reports that there has been no facilitation of criminal thinking or adverse effect on his performance at work. But there is evidence that when he drinks at home, he is more prone toward anger reactions. The way we continue to pose the issue to him and others is: "Is it worth even a remote chance of endangering all that you have worked for so hard and so long? Is it worth opening the door even the slightest crack?"

ONCE A DRUG-USING CRIMINAL, ALWAYS A DRUG-USING CRIMINAL

Throughout our work with all criminals, both users of drugs and nonusers, we have taken the position that the process of change is never concluded. This view is similar to that of A.A., which maintains, "once an alcoholic, always an alcoholic." Just as the alcoholic has the potential for backsliding, so does the drug-using criminal. Both must retain a self-critical stance toward their functioning in life—the criminal in a much broader sense.

We do not speak of criminals as changed, but rather as in a continuing process of change. There is always more to learn and always a better way of handling problems. They monitor their own thinking and seek assistance in that enterprise.* It is essential that the drug user continue to approach change with zest, attacking each problem responsibly as it arises. When such an attitude is absent, it indicates complacency and bodes future trouble. A complacent attitude renders the criminal vulnerable to the intrusion of old patterns of thinking. Such thinking may appear initially in a dream.

D had a dream in which he was in a room with men who were using drugs and with naked women. One of the men handed him some heroin, which he snorted. At this point D awoke. He did not find the dream exciting and did not savor any of the images that he recalled. Instead he was genuinely baffled as to why he had such a dream. For months he had abstained from drugs and had not even been thinking about using them.

We approached the dream from the standpoint of D's relatively recent self-satisfied attitude. We pointed out that he had rested on his laurels at home and had done nothing to improve relationships. At work he was functioning to others' satisfaction, but had taken no new initiatives. This dream was to be reacted to as a stimulus to be more self-critical and thereby avoid complacency.

Our experience has been that even if challenges are not presented to the drug user by others, he must create his own challenges. If he is working at a store where business is slow, he must take it upon himself to develop a project, such as mastering the inventory and learning more about the business. If

*See our description of our extensive follow-up in Chapter 10 of Volume II.

home life is harmonious, he must find ways to improve it. He can initiate projects with his children or find ways to be more helpful to his wife. One user decided that he ought to show more interest in his children's schoolwork. After helping his son locate places on a map in the encyclopedia, he commented, "No drugs ever made me feel this high."

The drug user has been accustomed to finding shortcuts, ignoring others' requirements, and generally seeking a problemless existence. Now the attitude must be the diametric opposite as he strives to be meticulous and thorough and to assume the attitude that there is always room for improvement in any endeavor or relationship. Greater effort and imagination can always be exerted. When difficulties arise, he must persevere in the face of them.

> D strained again a hamstring muscle that he had strained the preceding week. Then he pulled another muscle and developed a corn on his foot. In the past he has used any physical problem as an excuse for not going to work or for loafing while at work. This time he remained on his feet with these disabilities, working as a busboy fourteen hours a day.

This kind of effort and endurance becomes automatic in the change process. Regardless of how he feels, the drug user sticks with the job and looks for ways to improve.

It is critical in change that the drug-using criminal continue his examinations of conscience or moral inventory. Numerous events every day can serve as stimuli for a review of the past. The drug user makes opportunities for these self-examinations, no matter how busy he is. These occur on a bus ride to work, while he is waiting in line in the cafeteria, before he retires at night, as he performs a tedious chore, and at any other time that he can find. A regular practice of making such inventories indicates that he is still keenly aware of his past and considers himself still vulnerable. In addition, the moral inventory reinforces new initiatives and contributes to greater zest in attacking problems. The more vivid his past, the more vigor with which the drug user approaches change. The moral inventory gives added meaning to what a drug user said was one of the most handy phrases: "Damn how I feel, do what I must."

BIBLIOGRAPHY

Gossop, M., Eiser, J. R., and Ward, E. (1982). The addicts' perceptions of their own drug-taking: implications for the treatment of drug dependence. *Addictive Behaviors* 7: 189–194.

Narcotics Anonymous (1983). *Narcotics Anonymous.* Van Nuys, CA: World Service Office.

Smith, D. E., Milkman, H. B., and Sunderwith, S. G. (1983). Addictive diseases: concept and controversy. In *The Addictions,* eds, H. B. Milkman and H. J. Shaffer, pp. 157–158. Lexington, MA: Lexington Books.

Index